The Deadlock of Democracy in Brazil

Interests, Identities, and Institutions in Comparative Politics

Series Editor:
Mark I. Lichbach, University of California, Riverside

Editorial Advisory Board:
Barbara Geddes, University of California, Los Angeles
James C. Scott, Yale University
Sven Steinmo, University of Colorado
Kathleen Thelen, Northwestern University
Alan Zuckerman, Brown University

The post–Cold War world faces a series of defining global challenges: virulent forms of conflict, the resurgence of the market as the basis for economic organization, and the construction of democratic institutions.

The books in this series take advantage of the rich development of different approaches to comparative politics in order to offer new perspectives on these problems. The books explore the emerging theoretical and methodological synergisms and controversies about social conflict, political economy, and institutional development.

Democracy without Associations: Transformation of the Party System and Social Cleavages in India, by Pradeep K. Chhibber

Gendering Politics: Women in Israel, by Hanna Herzog

Origins of Liberal Dominance: State, Church, and Party in Nineteenth-Century Europe, by Andrew C. Gould

The Deadlock of Democracy in Brazil, by Barry Ames

Political Science as Puzzle Solving, edited by Bernard Grofman

Institutions and Innovation: Voters, Parties, and Interest Groups in the Consolidation of Democracy—France and Germany, 1870–1939, by Marcus Kreuzer

Altering Party Systems: Strategic Behavior and the Emergence of New Political Parties in Western Democracies, by Simon Hug

Managing "Modernity": Work, Community, and Authority in Late-Industrializing Japan and Russia, by Rudra Sil

Re-Forming the State: The Politics of Privatization in Latin America and Europe, by Hector E. Schamis

The Deadlock of
Democracy in Brazil

———

Barry Ames

Ann Arbor

THE UNIVERSITY OF MICHIGAN PRESS

First paperback edition 2002
Copyright © by the University of Michigan 2001
All rights reserved
Published in the United States of America by
The University of Michigan Press
Manufactured in the United States of America
⊗ Printed on acid-free paper

2005   2004   2003   2002   5   4   3   2

A CIP catalog record for this book is available from the British Library.

Library of Congress Cataloging-in-Publication Data

Ames, Barry.
    The deadlock of democracy in Brazil / Barry Ames.
      p.   cm. — (Interests, identities, and institutions in comparative politics)
    Includes bibliographical references and index.
    ISBN 0-472-11160-4 (cloth : alk. paper)
    1. Elections—Brazil.   2. Brazil. Congresso Nacional.   3. Brazil—Politics
and government—1985–   I. Title.   II. Series.
    JL2492 .A44   2000
    328.81—dc21   00-064773

ISBN 0-472-08904-8 (pbk. : alk. paper)

For Olivia

Contents

Acknowledgments

One day in 1989, I heard that the municipal-level votes received by candidates for Brazilian congressional seats had been recorded on a computer tape. Though the tape included only the votes of winning candidates and covered just two elections in a handful of states, I thought the data might help me understand the workings of Brazil's unusual electoral system. One step led to another. The number of elections grew from two to five, coverage expanded to nearly the whole nation, and the behavior of the elected congressional candidates in subsequent legislatures became an integral part of the research program. The project ultimately took over a decade; fortunately, I already had tenure. Not surprisingly I accumulated a great many debts for the support, both personal and institutional, I received over this long period. I am too disorganized to remember them all, but here is a start.

For help on the most diverse aspects of electoral and legislative processes, both in Brazil and outside, I am grateful to Tim Power, David Fleischer, Shaun Bowler, David Samuels, Bolivar Lamounier, Amaury de Souza, Maria Antonia Alonso de Andrade, Glaucio Soares, Richard Foster, Maria Emilia Freire, Teresa Haguette, João Gilberto Lucas Coelho, Gilberto Dimenstein, Luiz Pedone, George Avelino Filho, Peter Kingstone, Maria D'Alva Kinzo, Robert Kaufman, Pedro Celso Cavalcanti, Valentina Rocha Lima, and Simone Rodrigues. The first two on this list, Tim and David, responded to hundreds of inquiries over the years of the project's duration.

In the early stages of electoral data gathering, I received help from Benedito dos Santos Gonçalves, of SINDJUS. Jalles Marques helped me with data from Prodasen, the Senate's data processing office. As the years went by, the Tribunal Superior Eleitoral became the central repository of electoral data. I am especially grateful to Carlos Alberto Dornelles, Roberto Siqueira, Sérgio, Flávio and Conceição.

The electoral mapping was done with Voyager, a geographic information systems program developed by Rudy Husar at the School of Engineering, Washington University, St. Louis. Rudy and Todd Oberman taught me how the program works.

My investigations into legislative behavior were aided by Orlando de Assis Baptista Neto, Geraldo Alckmin Filho, Eduardo Suplicy, Edwiges, Virgínia Mesquita, Murillo de Aragão, Marcondes Sampaio, Rosinethe Monteiro Soares, Feichas Martins, Scott Desposato, and many deputies and aides.

Tim Power, David Samuels, Fabrice Lehoucq, and Scott Morgenstern read all or major parts of the entire manuscript and provided extremely useful comments. Bill Keech read everything and made detailed, line-by-line comments. The manuscript is enormously better for his effort. I am also grateful to the anonymous reviewers for the Press and for various journals who commented on the whole manuscript and on individual chapters. Even though I clearly have not met all their objections, they have made a huge contribution to the quality of the book.

In the study of individual policy areas, I benefited from conversations with Edélcio de Oliveira (INESC), Antonio Carlos Pojo do Rego, Lúcio Reiner, Kurt Weyland, Paulo Kramer, Antonio Octávio Cintra and the permanent staff of the Chamber of Deputies, Eleutério Rodriguez Neto, and Wendy Hunter.

Carmen Pérez aided in the acquisition of critical documents in Brasília and helped me enjoy my long stay in the city. Michelle King spent many hours making sense of dusty documents in the Library of Congress. In Pittsburgh, Lúcio Renno and Luciana Cozman provided able research assistance.

For counsel on the politics of individual states, I am grateful to Consuelo Novais Sampaio, Celina Souza, Samuel Celestino, and Gei Espinhara (Bahia); Paulo Freire Vieira and Moacyr Pereira (Santa Catarina); Antonio Lavareda and José Adalberto Pereira (Pernambuco); Antonio Carlos de Medeiros and Geert Banck (Espírito Santo); Agerson Tabosa Pinto, Aldenor Nunes Freire, Paulo Benavides, and Judith Tendler (Ceará); Marcelo Baquero (Rio Grande do Sul); Clovis Borges and Denise Levy (Paraná); Jardelino de Lucena Filho (Rio Grande do Norte); Maria Antonieta Parahyba Leopoldi (Rio de Janeiro); José de Ribamar Chaves Caldeira (Maranhão); and Francisco Itamí Campos (Goiás). For help in linking micro- and macrophenomena, I often turned to two masters of the problem, Wallace and Gromit.

Without the enormous quantity of institutional support I received, the project could not have gone very far. In 1990 the National Science Foundation (award #8921805) supported my initial field research in Brazil. The IRIS Project at the University of Maryland (directed by Mancur Olson and Christopher Clague) and the North-South Center of the University of Miami supported the congressional phase of the research. In addition to my own interviews, Mauro Porto and Fátima Guimarães (Department of Political Science, University of Brasília) and Clécio Dias (then of the University of Illinois, Urbana) conducted interviews. Washington University, St. Louis, and the University of Pittsburgh provided support for summer trips. The American Philosophical Society contributed a travel grant. In 1995–96, I was a fellow of the Woodrow Wilson International Center for Scholars in Washington, D.C. I am grateful to Joseph Tulchin for his support and to the entire staff of the Wilson Center for making that year the most enjoyable of my academic career.

To Michelle King, who produced our daughter Olivia, I owe a debt beyond words. Since "Miss O" is a lot more compelling than this book, it is fortunate that she was born when the book was essentially done.

Glossary of Major Political Parties

PDC   Christian Democratic Party

PDS   Democratic Social Party. Successor to ARENA, the party backing the military regime, joined with the PDC to create the PPR.

PDT   Democratic Labor Party. Moderately left, led by populist politician Leonel Brizola, whose career began in the 1945–64 period.

PFL   Liberal Front Party. An outgrowth of the old PDS. Conservative, strongest in the Northeast. Has an ideologically neoliberal wing and a substantial wing of nonideological "pork and patronage" types.

PMDB   Party of the Brazilian Democratic Movement. Broad-based, center party that grew out of the Brazilian Democratic Movement. Began as the "official" opposition in the military regime. Plagued by frequent desertions but still the largest party in the Congress.

PPB   Brazilian Progressive Party. Conservative, created by merger of PPR and Progressive Party in 1995. The PPR was formed by the merger of the PDS and the Christian Democratic Party.

PPR   Reformist Progressive Party

PPS   Popular Socialist Party. New name for Brazilian Communist Party. Formerly Moscow oriented (unlike the Chinese-oriented Communist Party of Brazil), now mainstream socialist.

PRN   The Party of National Reconstruction. A vehicle for the ambitions of Fernando Collor de Mello, president from 1990 until his impeachment in 1992.

PSB   Brazilian Socialist Party. A small, mainstream socialist party, becoming an alternative for dissidents from the PSDB and other parties.

PSDB   Brazilian Social Democratic Party. A 1988 spinoff of center-left elements of the PMDB. Allied in 1994 with the conservative and northeastern-based PFL to guarantee the election of presidential candidate Fernando Henrique Cardoso.

PT   Workers' Party. Originally based in the progressive São Paulo
            union movement. Has grown steadily and spread geographically
            since its founding in 1979. Its factions range from moderate so-
            cialist to quasi-revolutionary. Presidential candidate Luís Inácio
            Lula da Silva lost in 1989, 1994, and 1998.

PTB   Brazilian Labor Party. In the 1945–64 period a populist, urban
            party. After 1979, the old PTB leaders could not reclaim the label,
            so they formed the PDT. Became a mostly right-wing collection of
            deputies whose overwhelming interest is pork and patronage.

Introduction

Imagine the following puzzle: A formally democratic nation confronts, over many years, crises of inflation, government waste and corruption, pension system deficits, inadequate social services, violence, and social inequality. Substantial majorities of the population support proposals dealing with these crises. In the legislature, few parliamentarians oppose the proposals because of principles or voter pressure. And yet these proposals rarely emerge unscathed from the legislative process. Many, because they have no chance of passage, never arrive at the Congress's door. Others die in committees. Some proposals ultimately win approval, but long delays and substantive concessions weaken their impact. Rarely can the president avoid paying a high price, in pork and patronage, for legislative support.

This puzzle characterizes the past fifteen years of politics and policy-making in Brazil, Latin America's largest democracy. Brazil is often described as a nation where governability is a permanent problem. *Governability* is the sort of hot topic whose meaning is hard to pin down, but at its core lie two political processes. One involves the efficiency of a nation's executive and legislative branches in the making of programs and policies; the other relates to the government's ability to implement these programs and policies. This book addresses the policy-making aspects of governability in Brazil. More precisely, the book explores the relationship between Brazil's national political institutions, especially the rules and practices of electoral and legislative politics, and the probability that the central government will adopt new programs and policies. Although the empirical analysis centers on the past fifteen years of Brazilian politics along with the last years of military rule, the explanatory ideas and theories come from the broader literature of contemporary political science, and the results of the investigation have implications for developed and developing countries alike.

To comprehend more concretely Brazil's governability crisis, consider just the most recent presidential administration. When Fernando Henrique Cardoso assumed Brazil's presidency in early 1995, his prospects seemed extremely favorable. The new president was credited with authoring the Plano Real, an economic program that had stabilized the economy and lifted millions out of poverty. The five parties backing Cardoso's election (some only in the second round) included more than 400 deputies, easily sufficient to pass regular legislation and even enough to amend the Constitution. Leftist opposition to the administration was in disarray, utterly demoralized and with no credible alternative program. And the president himself was no lightweight; indeed, a distinguished foreign historian claimed that Cardoso would "arguably be the most intellectually sophisticated head of any contemporary state" (Anderson 1994, 3). With such an auspicious—and unusual—beginning, Cardoso's program should sail through the Congress, and Brazil could begin an assault on its central problems: an oppressive and costly state apparatus, economic inefficiency, and widespread poverty.[1]

Has the Cardoso administration, now six years in office, lived up to its heady prospects? Policy successes, mainly in the area of economic reform, surely exist. Liberalization, following the path of Cardoso's predecessor, Fernando Collor de Mello, has proceeded apace, with significant areas of the economy opened to foreign investment, major state enterprises sold, and trade liberalized (Kingstone 1999). In other policy areas, however, progress has been slow and uneven. Congress approved a constitutional amendment allowing reelection for presidents, governors, and mayors. Congressional assent, however, came only after the executive branch doled out pork-barrel inducements and patronage to significant numbers of deputies. In addition, revelations about vote buying suggested that some governors had literally bribed deputies to support reelection in exchange for control over crucial executive appointments in their states (Kramer 1997). By the end of 1998, pension and administrative reform had been approved, but both had languished in the Congress for years, and neither passed without substantial concessions from the administration. Tax reform, long regarded as a centerpiece of economic modernization, had disappeared from the executive agenda. The slow progress of pension and administrative reforms, coupled with the absence of anything resembling a new tax policy, had real consequences. In the massive withdrawals of foreign capital triggered by the Asian crisis in the late summer of 1998, foreign investors and bankers used these policy failures to justify their concerns over Brazil's economic program, and their contribution to the public sector deficit forced the government into an even harsher and more recessionary stabilization program.

---

1. For a summary of Cardoso's career and political ideas, see Resende-Santos 1997.

Cardoso's inability to move his program quickly through the Congress cannot be blamed either on a lack of solid public support or on principled legislative opposition. In all these policy areas (with the possible exception of the reelection amendment), substantial majorities of the population supported the president's reforms. And as political scientist Bolivar Lamounier pointed out, no alternative proposals competed for the Congress's support ("Soltando as Amarras" 1997).

If Cardoso, playing such favorable cards, has had this much trouble advancing his legislative agenda, imagine the situation confronting a "typical" president. Brazilian executives usually lack even nominal congressional majorities but instead depend on deputies mainly interested in their own fortunes, in local pork, or in the defense of narrow interests, and they face publics dramatically dissatisfied with governmental performance at all levels.

The past fifteen years of Brazilian democratic politics, coupled with the pluralist experience of 1946–64, indicate that the nation's political institutions create a permanent crisis of governability, devastating in normal times and debilitating even for presidents like Cardoso, who seem to hold all the cards. I conclude from this experience that Brazil's political institutions simply work badly.

What does it mean to claim that a nation's political institutions work badly? Badly for whom? Do they serve only the rich, the economic elite? The people who design political institutions belong to the elite, and institutions can hardly be faulted for serving their creators. The tragedy of the Brazilian system is not that it benefits elites; the problem is that it primarily benefits itself—that is, the politicians and civil servants who operate within it. All institutions are biased against change, but Brazil's institutional matrix makes it particularly difficult to adopt policies deviating from the status quo. While policymakers have been able to adopt, at least since 1990, macroeconomic programs facilitating the nation's participation in the global economy, they have been unable to push through fiscal reforms that would consolidate stabilization. Policymakers have also been unable to design and implement educational and social programs that could raise the population's productivity and capacity or ameliorate the effects of global competition, and leaders have made little progress in reducing the cost of government itself.

The argument that a state apparatus can benefit mainly those occupying places within it does not imply—contrary to the rhetoric of antigovernment conservatives—that politicians are intrinsically thieves. To the contrary, many Brazilian politicians and civil servants work long hours and sacrifice private gain to serve the public good. Rather, the argument begins with the idea that political institutions generate incentives for politicians. These incentives motivate actions that either facilitate or hinder the adoption of public policies likely to improve life for the average citizen. In the Brazilian case, the nation's political institutions generate incentives that encourage politicians to maximize their own personal gain and to concentrate on delivering pork-barrel programs to narrow groups of constituents or political benefactors. Some politicians, resisting these incentives, struggle to legislate on national issues, but they face an uphill and usually unsuccessful battle.

It is necessary to put some substance in the claim that Brazil's political institutions function poorly. In terms of formal powers, the country's presidents rank among Latin America's most powerful. What they need most, however, is support from a political party commanding a congressional majority, and only rarely do Brazil's chief executives enjoy such support. Instead, presidential authority—even, at times, presidential survival itself—depends on the distribution of construction projects and political jobs to crucial governors, mayors, deputies, and senators. Presidents begin their terms with high-minded pieties about avoiding the *troca de favores* (exchange of favors) that their predecessors so scandalously pursued. But political necessity soon rears its ugly head. Unfortunately, even after liberally spreading the pork, the most presidents can expect from the Congress—and perhaps the most presidents want—is a limited acquiescence rather than active participation in the legislative process.

Because the legislature could not respond nimbly to presidential initiatives, some Brazilian presidents ruled mainly through emergency decrees (*medidas provisórias*). Between 1988 and 2000, more than one thousand emergency decrees arrived at Congress's door. Constitutionally, these decrees took immediate effect, but after thirty days they would lapse unless Congress approved them. Since the presidency had no monopoly on either wisdom or virtue, the light of day quickly revealed serious legal or substantive flaws in many emergency decrees, and they were simply allowed to die. In many other cases, the Congress failed to act, and the president simply reissued the decree. Some emergency decrees did become permanent laws, but rarely did they survive their legislative voyage unscathed. Typically, final versions of these bills included major compromises, sometimes reflecting the pork-barrel demands of particular legislators or parties, sometimes reflecting the power of deputies beholden to economic interests. Overall, emergency decrees were a way of circumventing congressional obstructionism, but they also put up one more roadblock keeping the Congress from meaningful participation in policy-making. A recent constitutional amendment extends the period of decree consideration from 30 to 45 days and prevents voting on other legislation if the 45 days expires without a vote. The effects of these changes remain to be seen.

On its own initiative, the Congress has been too weak, either in the current democratic experiment (post-1985) or in its earlier incarnation (1947–64), to legislate on issues of national concern.[2] The legislature's weakness was especially painful in 1988, when the Senate and the Chamber of Deputies joined together as the Constituent Assembly. The assembly produced a 160–page constitution that included such bizarre items as a grant of life tenure to bureaucrats and a ceiling on interest rates, but it left major issues in health care and education for resolution by future legislatures. These subsequent legislatures, to no one's surprise, resolved nothing, doing little more than react to the many emergency decrees of Presidents Collor de Mello, Franco, and Cardoso. In truth, though Brazil's social services are arguably the worst of any large Latin American country, the Congress has passed, on its own initiative, almost nothing affecting education, health, or housing since the new constitution went into effect in 1988.

Without question, macroeconomic stabilization has been the dominant economic problem in Latin America during the early 1990s. Brazil was the last Latin nation to adopt and stick to a workable stabilization program. It was long understood that inflation discouraged productive enterprise and foreign investment, but even when it became clear that inflation hurt the poor most (Cacciamali 1997, "Um Choque na Desigualdade" 1996), Brazilian politicians found it impossible to reach an accord. Conservative and moderate legislators ultimately accepted Cardoso's program in 1994, but they refused to acquiesce until the only alternative was a victory by a truly leftist candidate, Luís Inácio Lula da Silva (Dimenstein and De Souza 1994). Even then, rural politicians in the Chamber of Deputies extracted major concessions in exchange for their votes. These concessions, worth billions of dollars, represented not policy compromises but personal financial payoffs.[3]

Why are Brazil's political institutions so ineffectual? Consider the party system and the legislature. Major, electorally successful parties fall all across the ideological spectrum. Some parties embrace distant, hostile points of view;

---

2. A number of analysts attempting to explain the military coup of 1964, notably Wanderley Guilherme dos Santos (1979), have stressed the Congress's legislative immobility at the end of the earlier pluralist period. Research on congressional elections or congressional behavior during the 1947–64 democratic period includes Amorim Neto and Santos 1997; Benevides 1976, 1981; Soares 1973; and M. Souza 1976.

3. Many of these reforms, including tariff reduction and the beginning of privatization, needed no congressional assent. Others required ordinary majorities rather than supermajorities. According to Peter Kingstone, in a personal communication, some northeastern deputies supported economic opening because it meant access to high quality goods previously restricted by *paulistas*. Kingstone also emphasized the large size of the coalition benefiting from reduction as opposed to the small group of losers, as in the highly protected computer industry.

others shelter deputies sharing no ideas at all. Party leaders have little control over their members, and many, perhaps most, deputies spend the bulk of their time arranging jobs and pork-barrel projects for their constituents.[4] Parties in Brazil rarely organize around national-level questions; the Congress, as a result, seldom grapples with serious social and economic issues.

Brazil's presidents benefit little from Congress's programmatic weakness. With only a small chance of stable legislative support, the executive faces politically independent governors, a crowded electoral calendar, municipalities depending on federal largesse for their survival, and a substantial core of deputies caring about their personal incomes first, reelection second, and public policy a distant third.[5] Because inflation has been the overriding problem since the end of military rule, new presidents often take office with elaborate macroeconomic plans but rarely with programs going much further. And because congressional support must be built on a very wide, multiparty base, the cabinet is likely to include ministers whose loyalties are tied more to their own political careers than to the president's program.

An Institutional Perspective

What causes these political failures? How can we understand Brazilian politics? The focus of this book is institutional.[6] Douglass North defines institutions broadly, as simply "the rules of the game in a society or, more formally . . . the humanly devised constraints that shape human interaction" (1990, 3). While op-

---

4. Students of the Brazilian legislative process hotly debate party leaders' degree of control over their backbenchers. Adherents to the "leadership predominance" thesis point to the relatively united behavior of Brazilian parties on roll-call votes (Figueiredo and Limongi 1997b; Limongi and Figueiredo 1995). In chapter 7, however, I will demonstrate that disciplined voting among Brazilian legislators results mainly from constituency pressures, electoral insecurity, and pork-barrel concessions to individual demands.

5. The claim that personal income is relatively more important for Brazilian deputies than for deputies in other systems is based only on my experience and on anecdotal evidence, not on empirical comparison. But the salaries of Brazilian federal and state parliamentarians are roughly equivalent to salaries in the House of Representatives, while per capita incomes in Brazil are a tiny fraction of those in the United States.

6. Examples of institutional analyses of Latin American politics include Michael Coppedge's study of Venezuelan parties (1994), Matthew Shugart and John Carey's cross-national examination of presidential and legislative power (1992), Mark Jones's work on Argentine electoral laws (1995), Barbara Geddes's game-theoretic treatment of presidential coalition building (1994a), Brian Crisp's study of Venezuelan institutional design (1999), studies of coups in Brazil and Chile by Wanderley Guilherme dos Santos (1979) and Youssef Cohen (1994), and Fabiano Guilherme Santos's treatment of the microfoundations of clientelism (1995).

erating within North's definition, I focus on institutions in a narrower sense—
that is, I seek to illuminate the effects of the formal structures of politics on the
behavior of politicians and on the outcomes of the political process. The central institutions of Brazilian national politics include the electoral system, the
presidency, and the legislature.[7] As this book will demonstrate, these institutions are inextricably linked: the electoral system influences—simultaneously—the kinds of candidates who compete in elections, their campaign strategies, and their behavior in office. Electoral rules also affect the number of viable
political parties as well as their coherence and discipline. Deputies' preferences
strongly influence legislative outcomes, of course, and the president must continually struggle to mobilize support within the legislature.

An institutional focus implies that institutions have a life of their own, that
they are more than the intentions of the actors who created them. But institutions cannot arise from nothing; people must create them. If institutions are
works of conscious creation, why not treat them simply as the agents of their
creators? Why, for example, is the capitalist state, to employ Marx's famous remark, not merely the executive committee of the bourgeoisie?

The claim that institutions are more than agents of their creators finds support in a variety of research traditions. Scholars have viewed institutions both
as organizations, with routinized operating procedures, and as arenas of bureaucratic struggle. The old saw "where you stand depends on where you sit"
reflects the tendency of members of bureaucracies, legislatures, and judiciaries
to defend purely organizational interests (Allison 1971). Another research tradition emphasizes the short time horizons of politicians. Elected politicians
concern themselves mainly with the immediate consequences of their acts; failure to do so jeopardizes their future as politicians.[8] New institutional arrangements have consequences that may become apparent only in the long run, even
though such arrangements are the consequences of decisions taken to solve immediate political problems. Complex social processes also generate unanticipated outcomes. The more complex the institution and the larger the number of
actors involved, the more likely it is that politicians simply have no way to predict ultimate outcomes.

Even when institutions produce results that diverge grossly from their
founders' intentions, change is slow. Institutions exhibit path dependence. In
North's terminology (1990, 94), *path dependence* means that "the consequence

---

7. *Federalism,* discussed subsequently as one of the major influences on the functioning of
electoral and legislative politics, could itself be regarded as an institution. I treat federalism as a
historical antecedent simply because its origins lie farther back in Brazilian history.

8. This theme is investigated intensively in Ames 1987.

of small events and chance circumstances can determine solutions that, once they prevail, lead one to a particular path." Institutions may have built-in barriers to reform, barriers deliberately created by political actors who believed they could constrain their opponents only if they constrained themselves (Pierson 1996). Actors who benefited from earlier institutional change are likely to resist efforts at reform. And as institutions become more established, actors make commitments that generate sunk costs. Because actors become locked into ongoing arrangements, exit costs rise.

Given these justifications for treating institutions as distinct from their creators, I will now consider the variety of ways scholars have undertaken institutional analysis. At least four different traditions—here I use Hall and Taylor's (1994) terminology—have marched under the "institutionalist" banner.[9] Organizational theorists, notably March and Olsen (1989), stress institutional roles and routines along with duties and obligations. For March and Olsen, institutions themselves are political actors. Treating institutions as actors, of course, presupposes that institutions are coherent. March and Olsen recognize that institutional coherence varies, but they believe that at times collectivities may be viewed as acting coherently (1989, 18). A second group, including economists such as Ronald Coase (1937), Douglass North (1981), and Oliver Williamson (1983), relates transaction costs to economic efficiency and to the organizational form of the firm. Transaction costs in political or policy-making environments include the costs incurred in such activities as the negotiation of agreements, the monitoring of compliance, the use of middlemen, the punishing of the noncompliant, and the creation of quasi-voluntary compliance (Levi 1988, 23). Rational choice theorists such as Kenneth A. Shepsle (1978) cast institutions as "games in extensive form," games in which rules constrain the behavior of actors. In the fourth tradition, historical sociologists, including Theda Skocpol, Peter B. Evans, and Dietrich Rueschemeyer (1985) and Kathleen Thelen and Sven Steinmo (Steinmo, Thelen, and Longstreth 1992), concentrate on the timing and sequence of institutional developments as they affect major areas of public policy. These scholars sometimes call themselves "new institutionalists" or "historical institutionalists." Though their work is in part a reaction to an earlier tradition emphasizing sociocultural factors and class struggle, these scholars maintain that earlier work's analytic focus on long-term processes of change.

Which approaches are useful in a study of Brazilian institutions? The or-

---

9. For scholars such as Levi (1988), transaction-cost analysis is a subset of a rational choice approach.

ganizational analysts will play no significant role. The organizational approach does not quite fit Brazil: institutions like the Brazilian legislature are too incoherent to be viewed as unitary actors, and an electoral system is an institution in a more abstract sense than March and Olsen intend. While transaction-cost approaches can be effective in explaining the development of a particular policy, such as tax collection (Levi 1988), they are too narrow to serve as the theoretical backbone of my argument. Still, transaction costs clearly play a role in the development of particular institutions, including parties and legislative committees (Weingast and Marshall 1988).

This book adopts the perspective of rational choice (RC) theorists, with a bit of historical institutionalism mixed in. To understand this theoretical union, I will begin with the basics of the RC approach. Borrowing Geddes's (1994b) terminology, RC approaches share four principles. The first is methodological individualism—that is, the principle that all social phenomena should be explained in terms of the actions of individuals trying to maximize their goals under some set of constraints. Second, actors along with their goals and preferences are explicitly identified. Third, institutions and other contextual features determining actors' options are also explicitly identified, along with their costs and benefits. And fourth, hypotheses are generated by a deductive logic—that is, the theories tested are causal, falsifiable, and internally consistent (King, Keohane, and Verba 1994).

RC theorists emphasize the short-term constraints and incentives that structures of politics create for political actors. Without denying the relevance of values, RC theorists suggest that strategic preferences are determined by the formal rules of politics themselves. Most importantly, RC institutionalists contend that behavior changes, regardless of underlying cultural attitudes, when institutions change.[10]

Like any new theoretical approach, RC approaches promise more than they deliver. Assumptions are often capricious and self-serving, and institutions are sometimes described in the sketchiest terms. The oft-heard criticism that RC approaches ignore institutions, however, is wrong. On the contrary, as George Tsebelis (1990, 40) points out, "The rational-choice approach focuses its attention on the *constraints* imposed on rational actors—the institutions of a society. . . . The prevailing institutions (the rules of the game) determine the behavior of the actors, which in turn produces political or social outcomes."

---

10. A good example of this approach is Cox 1987. Focusing on English politics after the first nineteenth-century Reform Act, Cox shows how an institutional change, the adoption of cabinet government, led to the rise of disciplined parties, a dramatic decline in clientelism among British politicians, and a increase in party voting among the populace.

Now I will turn to historical institutionalism. How does it differ from the RC approach? Thelen and Steinmo (Steinmo, Thelen, and Longstreth 1992) outline points of convergence and divergence. RC approaches share with historical institutionalism (HI) a concern with the way institutions shape political strategies and influence political outcomes. But for RC scholars, institutions are important as features of a strategic context, imposing constraints on self-interested behavior. Political and economic institutions define or constrain the strategies that political actors adopt in pursuit of their interests. For partisans of HI, institutions provide "the context in which political actors define their strategies and pursue their interests" (7). Because institutions contribute to the shaping of preferences themselves, institutions' role in politics is much broader in an HI framework than in a narrow RC model. HI's breadth, of course, all too easily becomes theoretically or empirically vague arguments.

A second difference between historical institutionalists and rational choice scholars lies in the area of guiding assumptions. For HI scholars, RC assumptions are too narrow. Most political actors are not all-knowing, rational maximizers. They do not stop at every choice and ask how they maximize their self-interest. Instead, political actors are rule-following "satisficers," obeying societally defined rules even when such rules may not directly maximize their self-interest. But here HI partisans overstate their critique. As Tsebelis makes clear, the use of rationality as a model of behavior does not imply that all people act at all times as utility maximizers. Rather, rationality is an appropriate model when the "actors' identity and goals are established and the rules of the interaction are precise and known to the interacting agents" (1990, 32). Tsebelis offers four arguments in support of the utility-maximizing assumption. Behavior, he suggests, conforms to utility-maximization principles when the stakes are higher and when more information is available. Actors able to learn from trial and error are more likely to move toward optimal behavior. Even if only a small percentage of actors maximizes utility, the social outcome will often resemble the outcome obtained if all actors maximized. And natural selection favors those who maximize, since maximization strategies will be rewarded.[11] In sum, utility maximization still provides a useful guiding hypothesis for the behavior of political actors.

Rational choice and historical institutionalism also disagree on the interpretation of preferences. For RC scholars, preferences are assumed rather than

---

11. Tsebelis (1990, 36) also offers a statistical argument: If a few people maximize while most behave randomly, the outcome will reflect the maximizers' goals. An RC analysis can be quite inaccurate about a specific individual but very accurate regarding the average individual.

explained. Advocates of HI regard preferences, especially those related to definitions of self-interest, as requiring explanation. Thelen and Steinmo make this distinction very clear: historical institutionalists argue that institutional contexts shape actors' goals. Class interests, for example, are more a function of class position, mediated by institutions like parties and unions, than of individual choice. For historical institutionalists, only historically based analyses can indicate what goals rational actors seek to maximize and why they emphasize certain goals over others.

The distinction between the two approaches is not simply the exogeneity or endogeneity of preferences. For historical institutionalists, preferences are affected not just by institutions themselves but by such factors as new ideas (such as Keynesianism) and by leadership.

If historical institutionalists and rational choice theorists need not fight over utility maximization, they do differ over the breadth of what they seek to predict and explain. RC theorists are likely to focus on the behavior of generic politicians or generic political organizations such as legislative committees or parties.[12] As a result, RC arguments tend to be probabilistic rather than deterministic. They might suggest, for example, that parties in plurality systems are more likely to converge programmatically than are parties in proportional systems. HI theorists, by contrast, typically direct their arguments at the broader outcomes that result from the strategic behavior of politicians or parties.

This project falls into the branch of choice theory known as soft rational choice. I present no mathematical derivations, and I seek to explain real rather than imaginary political institutions. Along with most RC scholars, I assume that political actors' central motivations are more likely to emphasize personal goals, including desires for reelection and personal riches, than policy interests. Although in much of my argument the centrality of personal goals is assumed, at various points I offer empirical evidence supporting the assertion and providing a finer distinction between personal and policy goals. Specifically, I demonstrate that while some members of Congress seek to maximize their lifetime income from politics and other members have broad, national policy goals, many are motivated simply to help particular firms, discrete economic groups, or even specialized groups of workers.

In some parts of the book's argument, rational choice reasoning contributes much more than just assumptions. A variety of research traditions motivate the

12. Examples include Baron 1991; Cox 1990b; and Shepsle 1988. Major exceptions include Knight (1992), who concentrates on the redistributive quality of political institutions taken as a whole, and North (1981, 1990).

empirical models. In the chapters on the electoral system, for example, the theoretical discussion begins with the literature on legislative "credit claiming" (Mayhew 1974). The argument also draws on studies of candidate behavior in proportional representation systems (Cox 1990a). In the chapters examining the legislative process, theory begins with the "distributional" versus "informational" controversy in the literature on the U.S. Congress.[13] The role in legislative bargaining of Brazil's parties—parties with neither programs nor close ties to voters—is explored with reference to the rise of parties in early U.S. Congresses (Aldrich 1995).

Although many of my arguments apply to "generic" politicians and parties, I focus on illuminating the actions of political actors in a particular country during a particular time. Broader outcomes—individual electoral campaigns succeeding or failing, legislative coalitions forming or dissolving, the Congress adopting or rejecting proposals—all become an intrinsic part of the explanation, because the political life of a real country is composed not of generic outcomes but of the actual outcomes of the strategies and struggles of real political actors. Likewise, a narrative that simply "assumed" preferences would be too limiting. Ideas, leadership, and chance events affect not only actors' preferences about economic and social policy but also ideas about political institutions themselves. In effect, preferences cannot be taken as given; rather, it is necessary to uncover all possible information about them.

A Perspective on Brazilian Politics: An Excess of Veto Players

In any political system, the adoption of a new policy deviating from the status quo requires the agreement of certain political actors. When the absolute number of such crucial actors, or veto players, is large, policy innovation becomes very difficult. Brazil's institutional structure, I argue, inherently produces a large number of veto players. As a result, its central government has enormous difficulty producing innovative policies.

The idea that the number of veto players significantly affects the chances of adopting new policies is a recent innovation in political science. For its originator, Tsebelis (1995), one of the advantages of the veto-players framework is its ability to subsume a host of typology-centered theories. These alternative theories usually take the form of dichotomies: presidentialism versus parlia-

---

13. The terms *distributional* and *informational* are Krehbiel's (1991), but the real distinction is between a distributional, pork-barrel orientation and an orientation to some conception of the broader, national public good (see Knight 1992).

mentarism, two-party versus multiparty systems, and so on. Some have policy implications: Presidential regimes, for example, are thought to be more prone to military coups than are parliamentary regimes (Shugart and Carey 1992). But the policy implications of these alternative theories can often be seen only after they are combined with other typologies, for example, two-party systems combined with presidentialism. When comparing small numbers of countries, these combinations lead to overdetermination; in other words, the variables outnumber the observations.

The veto-players perspective, with its focus on policy change, offers both a general, overarching framework and a clear set of predictions.[14] Whether a government is presidential or parliamentary, whether it tends to a two-party or a multiparty system, whether the legislature has one or two houses, the veto-players logic yields an unambiguous prediction as to the likelihood—in comparison with some alternative system—of policy change.

The argument, then, is that a larger number of veto players increases the stability of policy. Consider the fundamental reasoning.[15] Whenever a choice must be made over alternative policies, every actor has a preferred policy point. Actors are indifferent to policies that are equal distances from their ideal points, but they prefer policies closer to their ideal points. In the language of spatial modeling, their indifference curves are circular. As figure 1 (taken from Tsebelis 1995) demonstrates, when these indifference curves are drawn to intersect the position of the status quo and decisions are made by simple majority rule, any two actors can defeat the status quo. These areas (shaded in the figure) are the winset of the status quo. The larger this winset, the more likely policy change becomes and the more likely it is that policy change will be substantial rather than incremental. If policy change requires the concurrence of more actors, the winset of the status quo cannot increase—and usually decreases—in size. In figure 1, in fact, a decision requiring the concurrence of all three actors results in no action at all.

With increases in the distance (the spread of the ideal points) between the players required to agree, the winset shrinks and policy stability once again increases. Ideological disagreements represent one form of spatial distance. As

---

14. Whether observers prefer political systems facilitating or hindering policy innovation is irrelevant to the logic of the theory, although I do not hide my view that Brazil's institutional structure prevents the adoption of policies benefiting and preferred by substantial majorities of its citizens.

15. The explanation that follows is taken from Tsebelis 1995. Interested readers should consult this piece for a fuller treatment. Empirical verification of the theory can be found in Bawn 1997; Franzese 1996; Hallerberg and Basinger 1998; Kreppel 1997; Treisman 1998; and Tsebelis 1999.

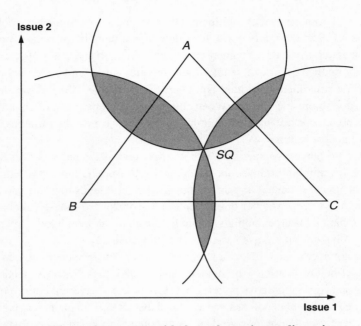

Fig. 1. Winset of status quo with three players in two dimensions

Tsebelis (2000) shows, the winset of the status quo shrinks as the ideological distance between players grows.

Veto players may be individuals, but more often they are parties, factions, or groups. Such collective players typically include individuals with varying ideal points—in other words, the policy positions of collective players are less than perfectly coherent. As the range of positions increases within each of these players—that is, as coherence declines—the winset of the status quo grows. This result is very important, because it means that the chance of adopting a new policy is greater—given a certain number of veto players—when the players are less coherent or united in their policy views.[16]

How are veto players defined and counted? In a broad sense, veto players may include the military, industrial capital, or any other group whose concur-

---

16. If any majority is possible in a legislature, then the legislature is a collective veto player—i.e., no single member is necessary for a majority. If there is a stable majority, or—as is the case in contemporary Brazil—if certain parties are always excluded from the majority, then the players that must be included are veto players. It is more difficult to change the status quo in the presence of a stable majority, since all the players must agree.

rence is required for policy adoption. In this book I limit the concept to actors in formal legislative and executive politics. "Institutional" players include the president, the Senate, and the Chamber of Deputies. "Partisan" players are the organized political parties in the Congress. Though for my purposes an overall, administration-wide count of veto players serves as a useful simplification, the number of veto players may vary by issue. Interest rates, for example, are set by the executive without legislative participation, while ordinary bills must be approved by both chambers. Equally important, especially in the Brazilian case, is the possibility of supermajority requirements. Because constitutional amendments require three-fifths of the total membership of each chamber, while ordinary legislation requires only an absolute or simple majority, the number of parties necessary for approval on constitutional issues may be higher, depending on the size of the parties.[17]

The key to counting veto players is the absorption rule. Suppose the analysis is limited to two policy dimensions, and suppose one veto player is located in the Pareto set of the others—that is, that player is within the polygon produced by connecting the other players' ideal points.[18] Tsebelis (2000, appendix) shows formally that it makes no difference whether this inside player is counted. It follows that if the president comes from a coherent and disciplined party that is part of a stable majority, the president is absorbed as a veto player—that is, the president need not be counted. Likewise, a party can be absorbed in one chamber of a bicameral legislature if it is part of the majority in the other chamber. In a case like that of the United States, where majorities are unstable and where the parties are programmatically incoherent, presidents and parties in each chamber remain distinct veto players.

How does Brazil compare with other Latin American countries in terms of the number of veto players typically present in each presidential administration?[19] For this comparison I eliminate provisional and authoritarian regimes (both civilian and military), and I count only partisan veto players—parties and presidents. The absorption of parties depends on their programmatic coherence and legislative discipline. Given that the existing research on Latin American parties has no accepted criteria for assessing coherence and discipline, it makes

---

17. Supermajorities are particularly important in Brazil, because the nation's extremely detailed constitution imposes a wide range of costly obligations on government.

18. The Pareto set is defined as the area in which one player cannot be made better off without harming another.

19. Focusing on legislative parties, Amorim Neto (2001) presents a variety of data supporting the idea that Brazil's legislature has been extremely fragmented since 1988.

sense to employ a counting method that establishes upper and lower bounds on the number of veto players.[20] The first method, complete absorption, absorbs all presidents and similarly named parties in bicameral legislatures—that is, I count them only once. The second counting method, partial absorption, absorbs parties and presidents only in those cases where most scholars regard the parties as coherent and disciplined: Argentina, Chile, Colombia (between 1958 and 1974 only), Costa Rica, Mexico, Uruguay, and Venezuela.[21]

Since 1900 the average number of veto players for all Latin America is 1.95 using the complete absorption method and 2.79 with partial absorption. With complete absorption, Uruguay has the highest country average at 3.05, followed by Brazil at 2.74 and Chile at 2.65.[22] With partial absorption, Brazil is far and away the leader at 4.43. Given that Brazilian politics became much more competitive after 1945, it is worth repeating the comparison for the postwar period. From 1946 to 1998, the overall regional averages are 2.09 (complete absorption) and 2.93 (partial absorption). By complete absorption, Brazil leads with 3.40 veto players, followed by Ecuador with 2.88 and Chile with 2.75. By partial absorption, Brazil leads with 5.13, followed by Ecuador at 4.50 and Bolivia at 3.88. By either standard, then, Brazil is at the top in terms of the average number of veto players in each administration. Moreover, from 1986 until 1999, Brazil averaged 4.6 veto players by complete absorption and 6.5 by partial absorption.

Brazil's competitors offer some instruction in the consequences of high veto-player scores. Uruguay exceeded three veto players only between 1967 and 1971, when it reached four. Uruguay's democracy began to collapse during this period, finally falling victim to a military coup in 1973. Chile exceeded three veto players only during the presidency of Carlos Ibañez (1952–58), who

---

20. Any counting scheme requires arbitrary choices. Reasonable people will disagree. This scheme characterizes all the parties in a system as either disciplined or not; in reality, Chile's Radical Party was undisciplined in a mostly disciplined system, and Brazil's Workers' Party is disciplined in an undisciplined system. I have tried to avoid counting parties in permanent opposition, like the Workers' Party, but there are undoubtedly some errors. Nothing is assumed about the linearity of the relationship between veto players and innovation. Generally, however, the jump from two to three veto players must be more paralyzing than the jump from four to five. Such powerful figures as committee chairs should not be counted as veto players, because they can usually be overridden by floor majorities.

21. In Uruguay, party factions (*sublemas*) rather than parties were absorbed. I am indebted to Scott Morgenstern for noting that legislative discipline is high among factions but low among parties.

22. Three veto players were counted during the Sarney administration (1986–90), even though the PSDB split off from the PMDB during this legislature.

attempted to govern as an independent with no party backing. Faced with rising inflation, Ibañez tried to implement the recommendations of U.S. consultants, but the Chilean Congress refused to pass tax increases on the wealthy. By the end of the Ibañez administration, as Stallings (1978, 33) puts it, "the initial indecision of the Ibañez government and the later attempts to implement the [consultants'] recommendations apparently convinced Chilean voters that the solution of Chile's problems was not to be found in a leader 'above politics.'"[23] Bolivia is a case in which the number of veto players has varied extensively. Before 1982 Bolivia never had more than two. With the restoration of democracy in 1982, Bolivia has averaged about 2.5 veto players with complete absorption and 5 without. Unless Bolivia's parties act in a programmatic and disciplined way (thus suggesting that the lower veto-players count is more appropriate), the situation seems quite unstable.[24]

In sum, the veto-players framework yields important insights for Latin America in general and Brazil in particular.[25] Excesses of veto players as well as greater ideological distances between veto players both decrease the chances of significant legislation. Supermajority requirements, common for constitutional amendments, also reduce the chances of significant legislation. Finally, control of the agenda matters. In presidential systems, the legislature controls the policy-making agenda. Because the legislature elaborates and modifies legislation, and because the legislature can override presidential vetoes, it maintains agenda control. In Brazil, where the parties cannot control their members and where individuals or groups trade cooperation for particularistic benefits or

---

23. Stallings (1978, 33–34) also points out that the failure of the Ibañez administration led to a union of labor organizations as well as the coming together of the two socialist parties. In other words, the number of veto players, both societal and partisan, declined. The 1973 overthrow of Salvador Allende, the most obvious case of democratic breakdown, occurred when the number of veto players was unexceptional. However, the ideological distance between the parties was extremely large.

24. Ecuador had a large number of veto players between 1948 and 1961, and though a military coup occurred in 1961, the democratic regime survived three presidential administrations. I cannot explain the Ecuadorean case, though it is interesting that Martz (1990, 382) regards this period as an anomaly in Ecuador's normally turbulent politics.

25. Although this discussion of veto players has centered on presidents and parties, the concept clearly has implications for other institutional actors. In systems of many veto players, courts and bureaucracies typically take larger legislative roles. Courts may act as veto players by interpreting the constitution and by providing judicial review of legislation. Bureaucracies adopt the same kind of interpretive role. When the number of veto players is small, the legislature can allow bureaucrats wide discretion, since the legislature can easily restrict them in the future. When the number of veto players is large, however, legislatures whose veto players are close together may try to restrict bureaucracies. If the legislative veto players are far apart, then legislatures are more likely to allow bureaucrats more leeway.

concessions, agenda control means that most legislation includes a pork-barrel component.

It is important to note, however, that the argument that Brazil suffers from an excess of veto players is not equivalent to claiming that Brazil has too many parties. Although Brazil has a great many parties and that number in itself may frustrate the adoption of policy innovations, an overall count of veto players based purely on parties represents a simplification that results from aggregating across issues. On any given issue, veto players may include state governors and their delegations, issue caucuses (such as bankers or rural property owners), or individual legislators. It follows, moreover, that these individual or collective veto players' ideologies or motivations also affect the outcome of policy struggles.

The Origins of Brazil's Institutional Problem

An excess of veto players creates difficulties for democratic regimes, and by any standard Brazil suffers from such an excess. This book argues that the root causes of Brazil's high number of veto players lie in the nation's institutional framework, especially in the electoral system. Still, institutions do not descend from the sky. Political and economic elites create them. Two factors, federalism and the pervasiveness of patronage and pork, have been particularly important in shaping the choice of institutions, and certain historical events have locked Brazil into particular institutional patterns. Over the course of recent Brazilian history, federalism and the extensiveness of patronage and pork vary in form and importance, but they always matter.[26] I will discuss these two factors from a rational choice perspective, but their origins lie so far back in Brazilian history that they can reasonably be taken as givens.

Federalism

States and municipalities, Brazil's subnational units of government, have been important political actors since colonial times. Major governmental activities, including such crucial social services as primary and secondary education, are the responsibility of states and municipalities. These subnational units elect their own officials and possess their own sources of tax revenue. They may is-

---

26. Of course, these background elements potentially raise the same "chicken and egg" causation problem seen earlier. Is their existence a result of institutional or cultural conditions? It seems to me that in the time period analyzed here, the setting can be taken as given.

sue bonds subject only to the approval of the territorially based Senate. Residual powers not enumerated in the constitution fall to the states. Overall, Brazil's federal system meets Riker's (1964) famous criteria: Two levels of government rule the same land and people, each level has a well-defined scope of authority, and each possesses a guarantee of autonomy within its own sphere.

At the national level, federal systems typically represent territories in one legislative chamber and population in another. With three senators per state, Brazil's Senate gives Roraima, with fewer than 250,000 people, representation equal to São Paulo, with more than 30 million. One vote in Roraima thus has 144 times the weight of a vote in São Paulo, and senators representing 13 percent of Brazil's population can block legislation supported by 87 percent.[27] But the disadvantage to more populous regions also occurs in the Chamber of Deputies. No state is allowed fewer than eight or more than seventy deputies. Purely on the basis of population, Roraima's 8 deputies ought to be 1; São Paulo's 70 ought to be 115.

Why did Brazil adopt federalism? Historically, the country had no alternative. Portugal was simply too weak to maintain a bureaucracy capable of controlling the colony. Emperor João III (1521–57) divided the country into hereditary captaincies and handed them over to landowners rich enough to defend and colonize them (José Murilo de Carvalho 1993). Though the Marquis de Pombal ended these captaincies in the eighteenth century, Portugal was really incapable of centralizing. It had to rely on political and administrative decentralization (including tax farmers) and on private power based on big landholdings and on slavery.

The constitutional reform of 1834, a few years after Brazil's break from Portugal, produced a new centralism based on Brazil's emperor. Coffee producers, concentrated in the province of Rio de Janeiro, paid most of the central government's taxes and joined exporters and bureaucrats in support of a strong, monarchical central government.[28] Nineteenth-century centralization was bolstered by the influence of the monarchy in the rural population and by fear of upsetting slave society and fragmenting the country. The proponents of decentralization, by contrast, included liberal professionals and farmers producing for the domestic market.

Though early coffee production had stimulated centralization, the spread

---

27. The worst ratio in the United States is Wyoming to California: One Wyoming vote equals 66 California votes (see Stepan 1999, 35).

28. By 1877 the central government employed 69 percent of all public employees and collected 77 percent of all public income, a figure that fell to 37 percent in 1902 (José Murilo de Carvalho 1993, 65).

of coffee into São Paulo favored decentralization. The *paulistas* thought a centralized system would transfer resources to backward provinces. But resistance to central power also had an oligarchical component: federalism supported private power, inequality, and hierarchy.

When the monarchy ended in 1889, Brazilian states were much stronger than states in federalist Mexico and Argentina. Brazil's states could write their own civil codes, negotiate foreign loans, and sell bonds outside the country (Love 1993, 187). In the 1920s and 1930s, coffee-producing states forced their exchange-rate preferences—favoring devaluation—on the rest of the country. The policy imposed losses on consumers, importers, and the central government itself, which had to repay its foreign loans in a weakened currency. Brazilian states also maintained serious military forces. In 1925–26, for example, São Paulo had a 14,000-man army, its own military academy, and a foreign military mission (Love 1993, 202).

Even in the centralizing years of Getúlio Vargas and the Estado Novo (1937–45), states retained considerable authority. State taxes as a percentage of federal taxes reached 55.9 percent between 1931 and 1937 and 55.7 percent between 1938 and 1945. Comparable figures from the Mexican federation during the same years were 22.7 percent and 17.3 percent, respectively (Love 1993, 218).

Landowning was the traditional base of local power, and though twentieth-century economic development weakened landowners, they never lost their political force, especially in rural areas. With large land areas, sparse populations, and few good roads, states and localities naturally developed independent bases of power. Federalism also grew out of Brazil's strong regionalist tradition. Each region has quite different social, cultural, economic, and political conditions.[29]

Brazil's Northeast contains about 30 percent of its population but produces only 14 percent of the gross domestic product. Sugar production once made the Northeast the center of the Brazilian economy, but sugar has been declining since 1800. Poverty, a recurring cycle of droughts, and the continuing influence of rural bosses all combine to make the Northeast dependent on central government resource transfers. As a result, politics has often revolved around exchanges of political support for pork-barrel benefits from the legislature or the executive. Aid programs have produced countless dams and hydroelectric proj-

---

29. Brazil's regions are defined as follows. The Northeast includes Alagoas, Bahia, Ceará, Maranhão, Paraíba, Piauí, Pernambuco, Rio Grande do Norte, and Sergipe. The North and Center-West include Acre, Amapá, Amazonas, Goiás, Mato Grosso, Mato Grosso do Sul, Rondônia, Roraima, and Tocantins. The Southeast includes Espírito Santo, Minas Gerais, Rio de Janeiro, and São Paulo. The South includes Paraná, Rio Grande do Sul, and Santa Catarina.

ects, mostly benefiting big farmers and local bosses. Business interests from wealthier regions support Northeast aid, even though their taxes finance the projects, because their firms build the dams and roads. The Northeast, in essence, is Brazil's Mezzogiorno.

The North and Center-West are frontier regions, with small but rapidly growing populations. In the absence of traditional landholding families, patronage-based political networks link key political actors. These networks include members of federal and state congressional delegations, state government agencies, and local governments. States in these regions depend on the central government, so the alliances fight to control major local governments and, through these governments, federal and state patronage resources.

The Southeast shelters the bulk of the nation's industry. Coffee profits financed São Paulo's early industrial ventures, and today the state dominates advanced industry. Rio de Janeiro and Minas Gerais are also heavily industrialized. With heavy migration from poor regions (especially from the Northeast), Rio de Janeiro and São Paulo have become megacities, plagued by grossly deficient social services, debilitating pollution, and high levels of crime.

The South is mainly agricultural. With a strong economic base and relatively even income distribution, politics is less likely to be the only lucrative economic activity. As a result, corruption is somewhat lower, bureaucratic competence is higher, and education and health conditions are better.

Given regional income variations and the long tradition of federalism, it is no surprise that government-society relations vary across states. In some, politics has traditionally been a profitable business, monopolized by a small number of families supported by major economic groups such as sugar planters or cattle ranchers. In other states, principally in the South and Southeast, economic interests are more diverse. Ties between citizens and representatives are more direct, and politicians are less a class unto themselves. In Bahia, for example, 40 percent of all deputies in the 1991–94 federal legislature had a close relative holding political office. Among São Paulo deputies, only 5 percent came from such political families.

Brazilian federalism has followed a pendular pattern, with greater centralization under authoritarian rule. During the military regime, from 1964 to 1985, the central government sharply increased its power at the expense of the states. Not unexpectedly, the current democratic constitution strengthened states and municipalities by granting them new tax resources. Though the constitution failed to transfer responsibility for program implementation along with the new money, states have been gradually assuming responsibility for formerly federal programs. Accelerating this uncoordinated and slow shift in responsibilities has been the federal government's policy of holding back transfers to states and municipalities as part of the 1994 Plano Real economic stabilization program.[30]

Though Brazilian federalism meets Riker's narrow definition, the country's federal structure, like most nominally federal systems, is much more a marble cake, with overlapping and interlocking jurisdictions, than a layer cake. And Brazil's federalism is far from the standards that Montinola, Qian, and Weingast (1995) impose for their "market-preserving federalism." Brazil fails this more rigorous test on multiple counts: its subnational governments lack primary economic authority within their jurisdictions, they avoid hard budget constraints by borrowing, they share revenue extensively, and the central government can unilaterally alter allocations of authority and responsibility among the levels of government.

Weingast and his colleagues argue that their version of federalism promotes economic growth through a "Tiebout-like" decentralization mechanism (Tiebout 1956). In a truly decentralized polity, local leaders compete for mobile sources of revenue by avoiding debilitating regulations and the confiscation of private wealth. If leaders fail to implement efficient policies, labor and capital exit. At the national level, the central government must remain weak enough so that it cannot confiscate private wealth but strong enough to enforce contracts and provide public goods.

In practice the political conditions supporting the theory of market-preserving federalism are very hard to realize.[31] Rich but immobile interests exercise de facto mobility, increasing interjurisdictional inequality by walling themselves off in their own municipalities. Cut off from revenue sources, poor and marginalized municipalities see no alternative to welfare and the extraction of pork from the central government. Local leaders, whether operating in democratic or authoritarian environments, often answer to the demands of immobile capital rather than mobile capital or labor. Leaders in democracies respond not only to capital but also to electoral threats, and immobile interests may have greater incentives to organize electorally.

As this brief historical review has demonstrated, Brazil had periods of federalism close to the decentralization of market-preserving federalism, espe-

---

30. Debt financing played a large role in states' assumption of new responsibilities. Between 1990 and 1993 (the last pre-Real year), state debts as a proportion of state internal product (the *produto interno bruto*) climbed from 4.6 percent to 20.6 percent in the North, from 24.5 percent to 47.1 percent in the Northeast, from 10.6 percent to 24.7 percent in the Southeast, from 20 percent to 31 percent in the South, and from 25.7 percent to 45.8 percent in the Center-West (see C. Souza 1998, 584).

31. This section draws on Rodden and Rose-Ackerman 1997. Those authors also note that in the long run local boundaries themselves are flexible.

cially after the fall of the emperor in 1889, as well as periods of central domination. The record of those experiences is not positive. The advantages conferred by money and traditional patron-client ties enormously favored landowners. State-level politicians were able to devalue the currency, aiding immobile coffee producers but penalizing the vast majority of consumers. State leaders arranged debt-forgiveness deals benefiting another immobile group, the northeastern sugar producers. State and local leaders created a pervasive system of pork-barrel projects and political appointments. In sum, because Brazilian federalism grew out of central governments' inability to dominate the national territory, this federalism catered to the power of local interests, especially holders of fixed capital. Federalism provided guarantees to local oligarchs. Rather than facilitating economic progress through the adoption of efficient policies, federalism advanced the interests of the most backward economic groups and increased regional economic inequality.

How does Brazil compare with other federal systems? Federalism always constrains national majorities. In a landmark study, Alfred Stepan (1999) assesses the "majority-constraining" quality of twelve federal democracies along four dimensions: the degree of overrepresentation in the territorial chamber, the "policy scope" of that chamber, the degree to which policy-making is constitutionally allocated to subunits of the federation, and the degree to which the party system is polity-wide in its orientation and incentive systems.[32] After Argentina, Brazil has the greatest overrepresentation of the twelve nations. Its Senate has all the areas of policy-making competence enjoyed by the Chamber of Deputies plus some areas the Chamber lacks. Its constitution is extremely detailed, and in a wide variety of policy areas substantive change necessitates constitutional amendments that require three-fifths of the members of both houses. The electoral system, as part 1 of this book will demonstrate, powerfully hinders the development of polity-wide parties.

The Pervasiveness of Pork and Patronage

Since the early nineteenth century, Brazilian politics has centered on politicians' attempts to fill bureaucratic jobs with their allies and to supply individualized or geographically specific political goods, what Americans call pork bar-

---

32. The twelve systems are Argentina, Australia, Austria, Belgium, Brazil, Canada, Germany, India, Russia, Spain, Switzerland, and the United States. Stepan (1999) uses the terms *demos constraining* and *demos enhancing* rather than *majority constraining* and *enhancing* to avoid implying that a majority always exists or is right.

rel, to supporters.[33] Without question, political support is exchanged for government jobs and public works in every society, but Brazil is unique in the pervasiveness of these exchanges and in their tendency to substitute for broader, more ideologically or programmatically driven policy-making. Pork and patronage particularize policy-making. Politicians sustain themselves not by promoting local prosperity and providing public goods but by supplying pork and services to individuals.

My emphasis on pork and patronage is not just another label for Brazil's political clientelism. For two reasons, I deliberately avoid the term *clientelism.* First, the corrupt, vote-buying behavior of politicians that is commonly labeled clientelistic is more often an outcome of Brazil's institutional structure than a precondition for it. Second, discussions of clientelism frequently drag along intellectual baggage that is wrong or misleading. Anthropological uses of *clientelism* typically refer to individual exchanges of private goods between actors of unequal power, actors called patrons and clients (Greenfield 1977). The origins of such relationships are said to lie in "traditional" rural society, in the ties between landowner and peasant. They are based on reciprocity, trust, and loyalty. Implicitly or explicitly, "modern" society rejects such relationships in favor of ideological or group-based links.

As a recent essay by Geert Banck (1999) makes clear, the anthropologists' concept of clientelism travels poorly to the political realm. Trust and loyalty are not central to contemporary exchanges of patronage and pork precisely because such exchanges are deals (*negócios*) between traders in a political marketplace. Buyers and sellers have to prove the quality and reliability of their goods and their commitments. Loyalty and trust are irrelevant. And since the state, as the source of resources, is intrinsic to the transaction, patronage and pork are as much urban as rural in origin.

As the discussion of federalism illustrated, nineteenth-century property owners wanted a strong, centralized government. Only a strong central government could guarantee order, and in a slave society of grossly unequal wealth, order was the primary concern.[34] At the same time, property owners worked within a formal structure of politics in which elections, though restricted to a

---

33. To any student of developing-country politics, the pervasiveness in the U.S. media of pork-barrel accusations is laughably exaggerated. See Stein and Bickers 1995 for a demonstration of the unimportance of pork in the United States. As to patronage, a prominent U.S. congressman for whom I worked had at most two patronage positions (excluding his personal staff) to which he controlled appointments.

34. The following discussion of nineteenth-century politics owes a great deal to Graham 1990. For criticisms of Graham's use of clientelism, see Bezerra 1999 and José Murilo de Carvalho 1997.

small number of propertied males, were important. The emperor and his cabinet sat at the pinnacle of the system, but the indirectly elected Chamber of Deputies had to ratify the cabinet's decisions. Thus the cabinet needed the support of the deputies.

Both the Conservatives and Liberals, the parties dominating the Chamber of Deputies throughout the nineteenth century, were fundamentally patronage vehicles, exchanging government posts for votes. Both in the Chamber and at the local level, *party* meant simply an affiliation, not a durable commitment to program or policy. Parliamentary parties formed, split, and reformed, taking apparently contradictory positions on major issues right up to the empire's end in 1889. In the electorate, personal ties, not ideological considerations, determined political divisions. As Graham (1990, 148–49) makes clear, the rivalry and violence of local politics often came not from two distinct parties but from two factions both claiming to belong to the party then in power. The cabinet desired electoral support from the local faction most likely to win; from its point of view, party label was irrelevant.

The cabinet controlled deputies by granting patronage to or withholding patronage from local patrons. In Graham's words (1990, 148), "power flowed simultaneously 'downwards' from the Cabinet through the provincial president and 'upward' from local bigwigs to the president and Cabinet." Seekers of bureaucratic positions pursued the preservation or improvement of their place. Job seekers justified their claims, in the rigid hierarchy of Brazilian society, on the basis of social place, deference, and constant loyalty. Graham (1990, 217) shows that deputies and senators, more than other officials, acted as intermediaries in the search for jobs. Legislators' requests went primarily to the prime minister and to the ministers of justice, agriculture and public works, and war.

Over the long run, pervasive patronage affected the quality of public employees, their behavior, and the content of policy itself. Government appointments became political rather than merit-based not merely at the level of minister or secretary-general but also at five, six, or even more levels down.[35] Political parties expected to nominate party faithful to quite technical jobs, and major disputes developed over "fair division" of the spoils (Geddes 1994a). Turnover in technical positions has always been quite high, since each administration replaces its predecessor's appointees. Because holders of high

---

35. For purposes of comparison, in Colombia the secretary of basic education, the third-highest post in the Education Ministry, directs all elementary and secondary schooling. A technical person holds that job. In Brazil under President Collor, the equivalent position was held by an appointee with no experience who was a former teacher of the president's son. All jobs for the next four to five levels down were also political.

bureaucratic positions often expect to run for elected posts, they use their positions to develop personal followings. Politicians are unlikely to devote much effort to making the bureaucracy less oppressive and remote, because they profit from mediating between constituents and the distrusted civil servants.

The fall of the empire in 1889 and its replacement with Republican government had little effect on the centrality of patronage. With the twentieth century's expansion of the scope of the state, however, politicians developed a new resource in the form of public works: dams, roads, infrastructure, and so on. Beginning in the 1930s and accelerating in the 1950s, Brazilian governments adopted a policy of import substitution industrialization (ISI). Characterized by inward-looking growth, ISI included tariffs, import quotas, denial of mineral rights to foreign capital, nationalization of foreign-owned utilities, and overvaluation of the currency (facilitating easy importation of capital goods). Government invested in "strategic" areas: iron and steel, alkali processing, aircraft and truck engines, river valley development.

Patronage-based politics adapts easily to state-led industrialization.[36] Chubb (1981) makes this point effectively in her discussion of Italy's south. In Brazil, faced with the challenge of accommodating the diverse regional and economic interests whose cooperation was critical, the state responded by politicizing its programs and by buying off regional and economic interests through growth and subsidies. In 1950 public administration absorbed 3 percent of the economically active population; by 1990 that percentage had reached 5 percent (Brazil 1990). Regional politicians, big farmers, industrialists—whoever had sufficient clout commanded a subsidy.[37]

Inside the state apparatus, the expansionary drive of the state privileged bureaucrats themselves. State banks offered their employees higher rates of return on the investment opportunities available to the general public. University pro-

---

36. A system characterized by pork-barrel politics and patronage does not require that the government supply large quantities of resources in the form of pork-barrel benefits. If resources are plentiful, in fact, brokers lose their monopoly and hence their control, so patronage can thrive in situations of scarcity and uncertainty.

37. Certain government programs were "privatized" long before neoliberal economics. In the heavy construction sector, for example, a few firms dominate and have become deeply involved in campaign finance. Government reciprocates by shaping major construction projects to benefit the builders. Few observers were surprised by the 1993 revelation that construction companies had been paying legislators hundreds of millions in kickbacks. But construction companies are not alone in shaping public policy to benefit themselves. For years, for example, the central government funded a program providing meals for schoolchildren. Rather than sending money to the schools to buy local products, the central government built warehouses and shipped processed food to the schools. Transportation costs were high, schools ran out of food, and local farmers lost potential markets. The program's logic was political; its real beneficiaries were large food processors.

fessors retired in their forties with generous pensions. Though irrational privileges can doubtless be found in government agencies everywhere, in Brazil the scope and depth of the largesse became exceptional. The combination of state expansionism and patronage yielded not just a bit more in-house corruption or a bit more bias toward the private sector, but a hypertrophied monster.[38]

My stress on patronage and pork does not imply that Brazil lacks politicians devoted to programmatic objectives. The Congress contains a solid contingent of deputies and senators whose interests lie in legislation affecting the whole society. But as this book unfolds, it will become clear that such issue-oriented legislators are a minority. Politicians whose careers center on supplying public works and bureaucratic jobs dominated the conventions that created Brazil's constitutions, and the same politicians have dominated the legislatures those constitutions created. Such politicians have a hard time seeing political benefit in rules that strengthen parties or minimize incentives to distribute pork.

Historical Continuities and Their Consequences

Three historical continuities are important to understanding the linkage between, on the one hand, federalism and pervasive patronage cum pork, and, on the other, the choice of institutions and long-run political outcomes. The first continuity concerns institutional traditions themselves. The framers of Brazil's 1988 Constitution preserved the institutional framework under which they had lived between 1947 and 1964, before the military coup. The second continuity is one of personnel. A substantial number of congressional deputies and senators began their political careers during the pluralist or military periods, and they brought a particular set of preferences to the choice of institutions. The third continuity is one of state-level political organization, a continuity resulting from the legacy of the military regime itself.

In what kind of setting was Brazil's new constitution framed? The Con-

---

38. The private economic exchanges characteristic of patronage-based systems are also inherent in populism, a concept crucial to post-1945 Latin American politics. Unlike its U.S. counterpart, Latin American populism is primarily urban. As cities swelled with the influx of millions of rural immigrants, political entrepreneurs searched for ways to compete for support with socialists and communists, the traditional working-class parties. Populists emphasized social welfare programs and immediate benefits, including government jobs. They bypassed intermediate political organizations such as class-based parties to forge direct links with followers. Economic nationalism helped build coalitions with domestic industrialists. Populist politicians like Vargas and Juan Perón maintained their popularity—and the support of domestic business—as long as their economies enjoyed vigorous growth. For a definitive treatment of the pre-Republican foundations of clientelism, see Graham 1990.

stituent Assembly of 1987–88 was simply a joint meeting, held every morning, of the Senate and the Chamber of Deputies. The deputies had been elected to the Chamber in 1986 under the same open-list proportional representation that Brazil had used since 1947, while senators continued under majoritarian rules. Considerable discussion about alternatives to open-list proportional representation took place, and the delegates extensively debated proposals for a switch from presidentialism to parliamentarism. Not surprisingly, they could not bring themselves to change the electoral rules that had brought them victory.[39]

Perhaps the constitution framers retained the institutional framework of the 1947–64 democracy simply because it had elected them, but that explanation seems simplistic. I will now consider the problem through the optics of the veto-players framework, the role of ideas, and the effects of interests and preferences. The evidence for an excess of veto players is inconclusive but suggestive. The PMDB, the Party of the Brazilian Democratic Movement, had an absolute majority in both chambers at the beginning of this period (in 1986); by the method of complete absorption, the number of veto players is one. But the party was undisciplined and factionalized. During the Constituent Assembly dozens of deputies from the PMDB's left wing deserted to form the Brazilian Social Democratic Party, the PSDB, and even before the split the PMDB had ceased to enjoy any sort of programmatic coherence or legislative discipline. While the number of effective veto players may never have climbed as high as it did in the next administration (reaching seven), it likely did contribute to the absence of significant institutional change. Equally important, however, was the power of pork: President Sarney found many delegates indifferent to institutional issues but not at all indifferent to the friendly persuasion of the pork barrel.

To understand the role of ideas in the Constituent Assembly, a picture of the delegates' perceptions of the 1964 coup is needed. Was there a sense that institutional pathologies played a part in democracy's breakdown?[40] Though

---

39. I do not deny the existence of cases elsewhere in Latin America in which sitting legislators have changed the rules that brought them victory. In these cases researchers might examine party discipline and, in the more disciplined cases, the goals of party leaders as well as the expected career trajectories of individual legislators.

40. Wanderley Guilherme dos Santos (1979) attributes the coup to legislative deadlock. Permanent stalemate, he argues, resulted from presidential inability to command a majority, the conservatism of a legislature elected in malapportioned districts and boss-controlled rural areas, and the weakness of party discipline. Youssef Cohen (1994) argues that moderates on both left and right found themselves in a classic "prisoner's dilemma." Moderates in the major parties could have agreed on reforms, but they had to disavow the extremists in their own camps. Neither group of moderates did so, because each feared the other would retain its links to its own extreme wing. The moderate right thought Goulart was seeking dictatorial powers. Goulart himself believed that the conservative moderates were plotting with right-wing soldiers and businessmen to block reforms

many PMDB leaders strongly supported parliamentarism, my interviews with delegates suggest that only a small fraction of the overall body of constitution writers blamed democracy's failure on institutional factors, at least in a broad sense.[41] The delegates were more likely to focus on short-term triggers: the excesses of populist leaders, reactionary business interests (supported by the United States), the sheer incompetence of civilian President João Goulart, and the downturn in the business cycle.

In the end, the Constituent Assembly nearly adopted parliamentarism, but the weight of the delegates' interests led them to maintain the institutional status quo. A majority of deputies from the more developed states supported a switch to parliamentarism, as did most deputies on the Left, but the issue got caught up in the survival strategies of President José Sarney and other party leaders. As I demonstrate in chapter 5, Sarney's immense pork-barrel power persuaded many deputies to support preserving presidentialism and lengthening his term. Presidential hopefuls Leonel Brizola and Orestes Quércia (former governor and governor of Rio de Janeiro and São Paulo, respectively) also kept their supporters out of the parliamentarist camp. I will return to this issue in chapter 7; suffice it to say here that without the executive's ability to persuade deputies who were otherwise indifferent on the issue, and without the tactics of potential presidential candidates, parliamentarism would have triumphed.

The question of the interests of the constitutional delegates leads to the second continuity, the continuity of personnel. As Francis Hagopian (1996, 246) demonstrates, Brazil's traditional political families—those dominating politics from 1947 to 1964—survived and prospered through the military regime and into the current New Republic. Six governors elected in 1990, for example, had served in the mid-1980s as governors from the promilitary PDS party. The largest party in the Constituent Assembly, the PMDB, had historically opposed the military regime, but by 1986 one-fourth of its delegation were former members of the right-wing, promilitary ARENA party (Fleischer 1987, 2). Overall, more assembly members had begun their careers during the authoritarian regime with the promilitary party than with the opposition.

---

and overthrow his administration. Thus moderates on both sides feared that if they jettisoned their radical allies, they would be overwhelmed by the other side—moderates plus extremists—and the outcome would be unacceptable. It was rational, therefore, for moderates to retain their ties to extremists in their own camps. No one wanted the stalemate and the military coup, but both sides ended up with a worse outcome than if they had cooperated.

41. The constitution writers included one narrow institutional modification: the president and vice president are no longer elected on separate ballots. Thus the situation of 1960, when a center-right president was elected alongside a left-wing vice president from the losing presidential ticket, is no longer possible.

Why stress the durability of the traditional political oligarchy? The military government repressed the Left but made center and right-wing politicians the incumbents in the political marketplace of Brazil's new democracy. In effect, these leaders got a head start, and political competition was waged on their terms. Most of the conservative delegates to the Constituent Assembly of 1987–88 had built personal political machines based on patronage politics; they knew that the electoral system would have a huge impact on their machines' future.[42] But the strategists behind the military regime did more than simply encourage right-wing politicians. As the military withdrew from power, the generals sought to safeguard their legacy by creating conditions maximizing postdeparture support. The regime tried to increase the influence of potential supporters and reduce the weight of likely opponents. Merging two industrial states, for example, eliminated three senators from an opposition stronghold. The formation of new states on the frontier created additional legislators likely to be conservative. Fomenting industrial growth away from Rio and São Paulo could increase jobs in the conservative Northeast. These strategic moves came on top of a long-standing malapportionment that cut São Paulo's proportional representation in the Chamber of Deputies by about 40 percent, or about fifty seats.[43]

The result of all these forces was simple: the entire spectrum of political discourse moved to the right. In the Constituent Assembly and in the legislatures that followed, the delegates increased the length of President Sarney's term and preserved presidentialism. They rejected agrarian reform, a German-style mixed-district electoral system, and party and administrative reform. Obviously, no one can say with certainty what would have happened if right-wing politicians had not been so favored, but (as chapter 1 will demonstrate) the closeness of votes on these issues suggests that many would have turned out differently.

The third continuity is what I have referred to as the continuity of state-level political organizations. The Brazilian military regime (unlike its bureaucratic-authoritarian counterpart in Chile) never implemented an overall bureaucratic reform. Instead, the junta imitated civilian President Juscelino Kubitschek (1956–61), creating, strengthening, and insulating agencies central to its economic project. Agencies delivering social services remained disor-

42. Even presidential elections reflected the effects of local power: in the 1989 contest local political machines played a significant part in an election supposedly dominated by national media messages (Ames 1994b).

43. This figure is about 10 percent of the total Chamber membership (see table 1).

ganized and patronage ridden. Where state-level politicos had good connections with the junta and where they had the luck and skill to achieve momentary dominance, the availability of massive central-government resources enabled the construction of durable political machines that still exist today. These machines wielded a political force out of proportion to their numeric or economic strength, dominating their states' electoral processes and controlling their delegations in Congress. Only a few of these machines have survived until today, but, as chapter 4 will demonstrate, they remain a key part of the story.

The Constitution of 1988 augmented the power of states and municipalities by increasing their share of overall tax revenues.[44] To understand why federal deputies and senators would weaken the central government, it is necessary to remember that career trajectories in Brazil differ from those of U.S. politicians. Turnover in the Chamber of Deputies is around 50 percent per term, but electoral defeat accounts for only about half of this figure. Deputies simply do not seek indefinite congressional careers (Samuels 2001). Legislators may run for state and local offices after a term or two in the federal chamber or return to private business and then seek reelection. Federalism made states and municipalities into political arenas as desirable as the federal capital, and deputies acted to preserve those arenas' prerogatives. At the same time, strengthening the states—in a context of weak parties—reinforced the power of state governors over their delegations in the Congress, especially in the Chamber of Deputies, and augmented their ability to nominate allies and veto enemies for cabinet positions and high bureaucratic posts (Abrucio 1998).

A Note on Methods; or, Why I Did What I Did

Scholarship on Latin American politics, including work by Latin Americans themselves, is certainly the most advanced of all developing regions. So many scholars have undertaken systematic research projects that there is far too much to cite here. Still relatively rare, however, is research that combines theory with empirical analysis and applies this perspective to a broad topic. This book tries to comprehend Brazil's national-level political structure by marrying a consistent theoretical perspective—the perspective of rational choice theory—to

---

44. Between 1985 and 1993, the federal share of all public resources declined from 44.6 percent to 36.5 percent. Federal resources as a share of the gross domestic product (PIB) fell from 6.7 percent to 5.7 percent. State resources grew from 5.6 percent of the PIB to 6.3 percent, while the municipal share grew from 2.7 percent to 3.5 percent (see Rezende 1990, 161).

extensive empirical verification. The book is framed as a series of puzzles. Not every puzzle is solved with equal precision, and the theoretical arguments go further in some cases than others, but every part follows the same pattern: theoretical argument, hypotheses, empirical resolution.

Rational choice arguments applied to political systems in Latin America make no sense unless accompanied by efforts at empirical verification. Otherwise, these arguments cannot be falsified. In a sense, when forced to choose between theoretical elegance and explanatory completeness, I opt for the latter. This commitment to empirical explanation may pose problems for readers unfamiliar with Brazil. The nation has enormous cross-regional variation, and since states are important actors in national-level politics, this variation is often an important factor in determining national political outcomes. In chapter 4, for example, I discuss patterns of political competition in groups of particular states. At times, chance political events, random shocks no general theory would consider relevant, influence long-run outcomes in these states. The danger, of course, is that explanations sacrifice breadth as they gain accuracy. In general, I include explanatory factors if they affect outcomes over the long term; I exclude factors whose effects are brief.[45]

Because my goal is to explain real political outcomes, I use institutional arguments probabilistically rather than deterministically. In other words, I predict propensities rather than certainties. The fact that Brazil's electoral system stimulates deputies to focus on pork does not mean that no deputy will focus on national issues. The fact that hundreds of deputies support macroeconomic stabilization policies only when paid off does not mean that stabilization can never be achieved. In fact, chapter 8 will show that legislators yielded a certain portion of their access to pork when they feared that the alternative was a victory in the upcoming presidential election by the leftist candidate, Lula. A Lula victory, they understood, might lead to a permanent rather than temporary end to business as usual.

Brazil as a Case Study

If all studies focusing on a single country automatically deserve the dreaded label of case study, I obviously plead guilty. More sensitive criticisms are based

---

45. For example, in a cross-national model explaining public expenditures, I once included a dummy variable for an earthquake in Ecuador. Under this criterion, I would include the earthquake dummy if expenditures jumped to a higher level and remained there and exclude the dummy if expenditures soon returned to their pre-earthquake level.

on two criteria. Does the central puzzle interest only traditional country experts? Do the explanatory concepts come from the case itself and remain invariant within it? Hopefully, neither criterion applies here.[46] The functioning of electoral and legislative political institutions interests scholars, politicians, and citizens in all competitive regimes. The core theoretical argument derives mainly from rational choice reasoning combined with historical institutionalism, and there is sufficient internal variation to enable hypothesis testing with standard empirical techniques.

Criticisms of case studies often assume that each variable in a given case is only measured once. In assessing the scientific utility of research, however, the real issue is not the number of cases but the number of observations. As King, Keohane, and Verba (1994, 52) point out, only the number of observations is important in judging "the amount of information a study brings to bear on a theoretical question." Repeating Eckstein's (1975, 85) famous example, "A study of six general elections in Britain may be, but need not be, an $n = 1$ study. It might also be an $n = 6$ study. It can also be an $n = 120,000,000$ study. It depends on whether the subject of study is electoral systems, elections or voters."

The data utilized in this book vary enormously. Here is a partial list: municipal-level electoral returns for thousands of congressional candidates over five elections (between 1978 and 1994) in nineteen different states; 14,000 grants from the central government to individual municipalities; more than 10,000 budgetary amendments submitted by individual deputies to the congressional budget committee; more than 200 interviews with deputies, journalists, and academics; schedules of private meetings between ministers and deputies; and historical materials concerning particular states. In essence, the data provide measures across states, time periods, and levels of government. In other words, this book is about Brazil, but it is not a case study.

Interviews as Data

While the project ultimately employed a wide variety of information, I did not begin with all the data in hand or even in sight. At the start, the only hard data were electoral returns from ten states for the first two elections. More elections were scheduled, of course, but I expected interviews to become the central source of information complementing the electoral results. It turned out differently.

---

46. Ironically, this criticism applies much more strongly to those who make it most often—that is, scholars in American politics. I will return to this topic in the conclusion.

Interviewing congressional deputies is not fun. The first couple of times you make an appointment, the deputy cancels or simply fails to show up. The third time you wait an hour or two until the deputy arrives. When the interview finally begins, the deputy assumes you need a lecture on Brazilian history, so the conversation starts with the 1930 revolution. When you get past the history lesson, lies begin. Interviewing is not fit work even for graduate students.

Interviews really are not that bad. But since they are relatively easy to arrange, too many studies rely on interviews without considering their inherent problems. Interviews with key informants such as politicians almost never constitute samples in the scientific sense, not least because politicians willing to be interviewed tend to be the more high-minded, public-spirited types. And although we all know that information from particular interviewees should be cross-checked with other interviews, verification is often impossible. Few scholars receive any training in interview technique. Interviewing may be a particular problem for men: As countless women have reminded me, men listen poorly and tend to impose their own views on interviewees.

In the course of this project, I interviewed the highly regarded chief economist of the congressional budget committee. We talked about the deputies' pork-barrel proclivities and about his efforts to impose some rationality on the distribution of budget amendments. The discussion was typical of interviews with technical people, who mostly are quite open to academics. Two years later, however, the chief economist was arrested for arranging the murder of his own wife. It turned out that the woman in question was about to denounce her husband's participation in an extortion scheme involving the budget committee. The conspiracy had been going on for years: the staff economist, along with a group of deputies, had received kickbacks from construction companies totaling hundreds of millions of dollars. Most of the accused deputies were well known for their pork proclivities, but among those accused (and convicted) was one of the high-minded types, a favorite interviewee of both local and visiting academics. A number of interviews, one might assume, need reexamination.

The point of this digression is not that scholars should avoid interviewing politicians. Interviews are indispensable, but they should complement, not replace, other sources of information. I hope that the analyses in this book persuade readers that Latin America is rich in data-gathering opportunities. In the course of this research, I discovered bodies of information in Brazil that would never be available in American politics. Political research is more difficult in Latin America than in the United States or Europe, but Latin Americanists should not assume that empirically based scholarship is impossible.

The Plan of the Book

The book is divided into two sections.[47] Part 1 focuses on the electoral system and on the kinds of politicians and parties the system produces. Chapter 1 begins by explaining Brazilian electoral rules and then presents a spatial taxonomy of congressional deputies' voting bases. The taxonomy utilizes a geographic information system capable of graphically displaying deputies' vote bases. The analysis then links these voting bases to political careers, economic and demographic conditions, and chance political events. The chapter concludes by examining the relationships among open-list proportional representation, the spatial structure of competition, and key elements of democratic consolidation. These elements include party building, disproportionality of representation, corruption, and the nature of representation and accountability.

Chapter 2 explores the campaign strategies of legislative candidates under open-list proportional representation. Using concepts derived from rational choice principles, the argument predicts where candidates seek votes. To test the argument, deputies' intentions must be measured without employing, as a dependent variable, the votes they receive, because votes are the outcomes of all candidates' interacting strategies. The analysis solves the problem by utilizing the budgetary amendments submitted by deputies as an indicator of their intent to seek votes in particular municipalities. The chapter concludes by modeling actual electoral results to assess the effectiveness of candidate strategies.

Chapter 3 explains variation, both spatial and temporal, in political competition across Brazilian states. The chapter begins by modeling interstate differences in the average spatial concentration of deputies' vote bases and in their average domination—that is, the degree to which deputies monopolize the votes of municipalities where they pick up important shares of their own total vote.[48] Next, the chapter asks how concentration and domination have changed between 1978 and 1994.[49] The explanation, for both questions, stresses economic and demographic factors.

---

47. This book says nothing about the bureaucracy or the judiciary. On the bureaucracy, Schneider 1991 is definitive. The judiciary, in Brazil and elsewhere in Latin America, remains the great unknown of politics.

48. This distinction may also be made as follows: *spatial concentration* measures the contiguity of a deputy's votes. *Domination* asks what percentage of the total votes cast were received by the deputy in those places where most of the deputy's personal vote was garnered. A group of deputies might each pick up 90 percent of their personal total in the city of São Paulo, but each deputy would get only 3 percent of the city's votes. Their votes are spatially concentrated, but they do not dominate.

49. The choice of the 1978 election as the initial data point simply means that it was the first

Chapter 4 introduces path dependence to the analysis by asking whether chance historical events produce lasting effects on political competition. Brief comparisons of states in different regions illustrate how economic, social, and demographic conditions interact with unique political events to produce durable patterns of political competition. These comparisons include Bahia, Maranhão, and Ceará in the Northeast and Santa Catarina and Paraná in the South.

Part 2 investigates the legislative arena. Chapter 5 asks what motivates members of the Chamber of Deputies. By analyzing voting in two periods, in the constitution-making period of 1987–88 and on a set of emergency measures during the Collor administration, I estimate the effects of variations in the spatial nature of deputies' constituencies, their ideologies, party affiliations, and receptivity to pork-barrel programs.

Chapter 6 focuses on presidential efforts to maintain stable support in the Congress. The chapter begins by identifying and explaining the executive's objectives. What kinds of allies, in terms of region, party, and faction, do leaders recruit? How does the president's approach conflict with the strategies of cabinet ministers seeking to advance their own political careers? Is this coalition building inefficient—that is, does it force government spending to rise? Considering Presidents Sarney, Collor de Mello, Franco, and, briefly, Cardoso, the chapter analyzes presidential strategies by modeling the distribution of *convênios,* the grants made by central government ministries to local municipalities.

Chapter 7 assesses the results of the presidential tactics just identified. In other words, do presidential efforts actually yield greater legislative support? To answer this question, a measure of legislative party discipline and unity is needed. Though roll calls (the recorded *yeas* and *nays* on the floor) have been used as the central indicator of party discipline and unity in many legislatures, they are really quite ambiguous measures. This chapter begins by discussing the problems of roll calls. Roll calls illuminate only the final stage of the bargaining process that culminates in legislation. Some proposals never get to the Congress; others never get out of committee. Even if a proposal culminates in legislation, it may ultimately embody innumerable individual deals as well as compromises with intraparty caucuses. In Brazil very few legislative proposals have emerged from the congress unscathed since 1988. Still, if roll calls do not measure real agreement with the leadership's position, they do measure individual satisfaction with either the private or interest-group bargains that have been struck in the course of the legislative process. In the last sections of this

---

election results I could find. Since electoral laws changed in 1979, the 1978 contest is not a particularly good benchmark. I try to make clear in the text where the electoral dynamic changes for exogenous reasons.

chapter, I analyze individual deputies' tendency to defect from their parties' majorities. Focusing on five major parties, I analyze about 600 votes taken between 1991 and 1998.

Chapter 8 examines the Chamber of Deputies' internal policy-making process. How does policy get made (1) when most deputies care little about national questions, (2) where parties are numerous, lack any sort of programs, and rely on personal inducements to discipline their members, and (3) where the rules discourage the development of expertise? The chapter begins with a review of the theoretical and empirical literatures on legislatures. Two polar explanations characterize this literature: the distribution-centered models of Shepsle and Weingast (1987) and their followers, and the information-centered models of Krehbiel (1991). The chapter first attempts to position the Brazilian legislature between these two poles by modeling the approval of budgetary amendments in the Budget Committee and comparing Budget Committee membership to other committees. The chapter then turns to a problem that is particularly difficult in a multiparty environment, that of legislative coordination. Focusing on a leadership structure known as the college of leaders, the analysis consists of brief case studies of five pieces of legislation, each selected to maximize variance on the conditions affecting bargaining and interparty negotiation. The five cases include macroeconomic stabilization in the government of Itamar Franco, the Bidding Reform Act of 1993, the Law of Directives and Bases in Education, ministerial reorganization in the Franco government, and the Agrarian Reform Law of 1992.

The conclusion begins with a brief summary of the book's findings and then turns to the implications of these results. Can Brazil escape its institutional difficulties? Have reforms in institutional structures helped other nations overcome poverty and inequality? What can Brazil's experience teach other nations undergoing a transition to competitive politics? And last, what are this book's implications for the study of Latin American politics, in terms of the use of rational choice theories, of the meaning of case studies in comparative politics, and of future research possibilities?

PART 1

The Electoral System:
Rules, Politicians, and Parties

Chapter 1

Elections and the Politics of Geography

"Voters are irritating. One hundred percent ask for a job, money or a scholarship. It wears you down."
Deputy Gastone Righi (*Veja,* April 22, 1992, 25)

"All politics is local."
Thomas P. 'Tip' O'Neill

This chapter explains the workings of Brazil's electoral system, focusing, in a broad sense, on accountability—that is, on the link between representatives and voters. Brazil's electoral system is extremely permissive. It gives congressional deputies extremely wide latitude in the kinds of winning electoral coalitions they construct. At the same time, however, the electoral rules allow enormous ambiguity in the postelection reconstruction of these coalitions. Voters cast ballots for individual deputies, but formally these deputies represent their whole states as part of multimember delegations. Subsequent legislative votes usually have little relation to the issues that once defined the electoral coalition; many pit elements of the coalition in conflict. Not surprisingly, deputies easily evade their constituents' monitoring.

After a brief description of the rules, the chapter offers a typology of the multiple kinds of constituencies, or voting bases, deputies develop. The chapter then considers the implications of this electoral system in terms of commonly discussed problems of democratic consolidation, including malapportionment, corruption, the nature of representation and accountability, and party building.

Brazil conducts legislative elections under a set of rules called proportional representation (PR). Such systems allocate legislative seats to parties in proportion to the percentage of the total votes the parties receive. Unlike Anglo-American plurality ("first past the post") systems, PR rules ensure that a party getting 30 percent of the votes will end up with roughly 30 percent of the seats, depending on the precise allocation formula used. PR systems differ, however, in the way they determine the holders of these seats—that is, in the way the systems decide which candidates fill seats.

41

Most PR systems choose candidates through a closed list. Under closed-list rules, voters cast a single ballot for the party of their choice. That party has already selected and ranked its candidates. In parliamentary systems, for example, parties typically ensure a parliamentary seat for their choice as prime minister by placing that person's name at the top of the ballot. Other well-known party leaders might come next, with party newcomers bringing up the rear. The central fact of closed-list systems is that voters determine how many seats each party gets, but parties determine who gets those seats.

Instead of closed-list rules, Brazil uses an open list to determine who occupies each party's legislative seats. Voters face a choice: they may vote for the party label, but they may also cast their ballots directly for individual candidates. Most people—about 90 percent—vote for an individual. After the election, the votes won by all the candidates of each party (plus the votes for the party label) are added together. A formula determines how many seats each party gets, and each party's candidates are ranked according to their individual vote totals.[1] A party entitled to ten seats then elects its ten top vote getters.

All open-list systems thus shift power from party leaders to individual candidates. The Brazilian system magnifies this tendency. Ballots, for example, do not include the candidates' names, so the party cannot list them in a preferred order. Instead, voters entering the polling area must know their candidate's name or code number. The rules allow unlimited reelection, and parties are obligated to renominate incumbents desiring reelection, no matter how they voted in the previous legislative session. Together, these details mean that party leaders lose an important means of disciplining deputies.

Other nations, including Finland and pre-1973 Chile, adopted open-list proportional representation, but Brazil's version differs significantly. In elections for the national Chamber of Deputies, each Brazilian state is a single, at-large, multimember district. The number of seats per state ranges from eight to seventy. Lightly populated states, mostly in the North and Center-West, are overrepresented; heavily populated states, principally São Paulo, have too few seats.[2] State parties, not national parties, select legislative candidates, and the voting district (the state) is an important political arena in its own right. In pre-1973 Chile, by contrast, voting districts cut across provincial lines, so district delegations and local political machines did not match up.[3] In addition, national

---

1. Brazil uses the D'Hondt formula for seat allocation.
2. Until 1994, parties faced no minimum threshold for attaining seats in the legislature. In 1993 Congress approved a 3 percent threshold, but a loophole minimizes the law's effects.
3. The Brazilian system introduces the possibility of what Tsebelis (1990) calls "nested games."

party leaders chose legislative candidates for the whole nation. With this power, they could make adherence to the party's program a criterion for selection.[4] In some Brazilian states, conversely, powerful governors control nominations and dominate campaigns. In other states local leaders deliver blocs of votes to deal-making candidates; in still others neither governors nor local bosses have much influence over individual voters.

Brazilian campaign regulations are both restrictive and permissive. Candidates may not, for example, buy advertisements on radio or television, but free TV time is allotted to parties (not individual candidates). Parties dole out TV time in proportion to the importance of the race, so the hundreds of congressional candidates get only a few seconds each week. Practically everyone advertises in newspapers, but print ads have little impact (Straubhaar, Olsen, and Nunes 1993). Candidates erect billboards and paint signs on walls, but these activities are usually in conjunction with other campaign efforts such as participation in rallies or delivery of public works to local leaders.

Permissive spending laws allow aspirants for the federal legislature to finance state assembly candidates' campaigns.[5] Because state assembly districts are also whole states, with all candidates elected at large, politicians engage in *dobradinhas,* or double-ups, in which federal legislative candidates pay for the campaign literature of assembly candidates whose bases of support lie far away. The assembly candidates reciprocate by instructing supporters to vote for their benefactor for the national legislature. Such deals add little, of course, to linkages between representatives and their constituents.

A Taxonomy of Spatial Patterns

Legally, candidates may seek votes anywhere in their states, but in reality most candidates geographically limit their campaigns.[6] The state-level spatial pat-

---

4. On the Chilean system, see Valenzuela 1977. He notes that party leaders chose candidates who were attractive to local voters, but loyalty to the parties' positions on national issues appears to have been a necessary condition for selection.

5. A good discussion of campaign corruption can be found in Geddes and Neto 1999.

6. Political geography as a political science methodology is more common in Europe than in the United States, but the indispensable starting point is still Key 1949. Although Key drew his maps by hand and utilized no formal statistical methods, his insights are still rewarding, even for those whose interests lie far from the American South. Spatial analysis will probably be most fruitful in multiple-member districts, but of course single-member systems like the United States may include multiple-competitor primaries. Spatial analyses also mesh nicely with aggregate data, since surveys rarely have enough people in the smallest political units to allow the analysis of contextual phenomena.

terns that result have two dimensions, each based on municipal performance. Suppose, for every candidate in each municipality, V_{ix}, candidate i's share of all the votes cast in municipality x, is calculated. Each candidate's municipal dominance is defined as the candidate's share of the total votes cast for members of all parties. These shares represent the candidates' dominance at the municipal level.[7] Now suppose V_{ix} is used to calculate D_i, the average dominance for each candidate across all the state's municipalities, weighted by the percentage of the candidate's total vote each municipality contributes. Candidates with higher weighted averages tend to dominate their key municipalities; those with lower weighted averages share their key municipalities with other candidates. Thus dominance-sharedness is the first dimension of spatial support.

The second dimension also begins with V_{ix}, candidate i's share of the total vote cast in each municipality, but this dimension utilizes a statistical measure called Moran's I to assess the spatial distribution of those municipalities where the candidate does well.[8] These municipalities can be concentrated, as close or contiguous neighbors, or they can be scattered. Combining the two dimensions yields the four spatial patterns shown in the accompanying box:

State-Level Spatial Patterns			
		Share of Total Vote in Key Municipalities	
		Low	High
Spatial Distribution of Key Municipalities	Scattered	Scattered-Shared	Scattered-Dominant
	Contiguous	Concentrated-Shared	Concentrated-Dominant

Concentrated-Dominant Municipalities

This is the classic Brazilian *reduto* (literally, electoral fortress), in which a deputy dominates a group of contiguous municipalities. Domination can stem from a variety of sources. Candidates' families may have long enjoyed economic or political preeminence in a particular region; they might have climbed the ladder of politics from local jobs; they may have struck deals with local bosses. Figure 2, mapping the 1990 vote of Deputy Laire Rosado Maia, illus-

---

7. Note that municipal dominance has nothing to do with winning seats. Whole states, not municipalities, are electoral districts. As an alternative formulation, dominance could be measured solely in terms of votes for candidates of each candidate's own party.

8. For a discussion of Moran's I and other aspects of spatial statistics, see Cliff et al. 1975.

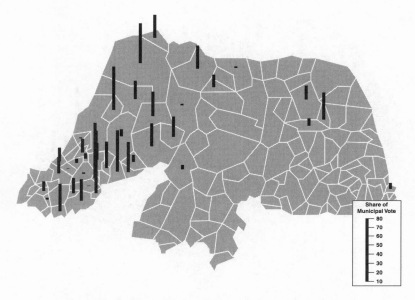

Share of
Municipal Vote
— 80
— 70
— 60
— 50
— 40
— 30
— 20
— 10

Fig. 2. Concentrated-dominant vote distribution
Municipal Vote Share of Laire Rosado Meia, PMDB-RN

trates extreme concentration.[9] Rosado Maia received nearly all his votes in the "elephant's trunk," the western section of Rio Grande do Norte. Maias have long controlled this area—one county even carries the family name. Where Rosado Maia received votes, he averaged at least 50 percent of all votes cast. So not only does Rosado Maia get all his votes in this region, but other candidates rarely dare to compete in his impermeable *reduto*.

Concentrated-dominant distributions often reflect traditional patronage and pork-based relationships between voters and politicians. Such distributions can also develop when skilled local leaders climb through the ranks to mayor or state deputy from posts on municipal councils. Geraldo Alckmin Filho is a doctor who first won election to the municipal council of Pindamonhangaba in 1972, becoming mayor in 1976. After a term in the State Assembly (1983–86), he ran for the Chamber of Deputies on the PMDB slate. With 125,000 votes, he finished seventh (out of sixty successful candidates) on the overall São Paulo list and fourth on the PMDB list.[10] As Figure 3 shows, his vote was highly con-

9. Appendix A discusses the construction of the maps as well as other data problems.
10. São Paulo had sixty Chamber seats through 1990 but seventy seats thereafter. Although winning a seat depends solely on the candidate's place on the party list, candidates envisioning re-

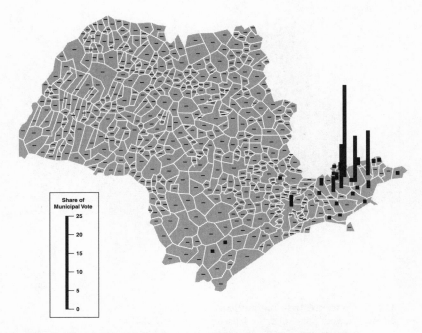

Fig. 3. Concentrated-dominant candidate in modern São Paulo
Geraldo Alckmin Filho, PMDB-SP, 1986

centrated around Pindamonhangaba, where he won 91 percent of the 1986 vote. In the neighboring cities of Guaretinguetá and Taubaté, he took 40 percent and 29 percent of the vote, respectively.

Alckmin's career took a risky turn when he defected, along with eight other PMDB members, to the newly formed PSDB, the Party of Brazilian Social Democracy. Orestes Quércia, then governor of São Paulo, dominated the *paulista* PMDB, and Quércia was not a politician to take defections lightly. Quércia cut off state funds scheduled to flow to Alckmin's key municipalities. When the 1990 election came around, Quércia financed the campaign of a direct competitor, Ary Kara, a businessman and former council member in Taubaté. Kara's likely bailiwick would be in exactly the same region as Alckmin. Could the region support two deputies?

Figure 4 shows the results of this local clash. In two key municipalities Alckmin's vote share declined: in Pindamonhangaba his share of the municipal vote dropped from 91 percent to 60 percent, and in Guaratinguetá he fell from

---

election also evaluate their place on the overall list, and published reports on the election carry the overall order.

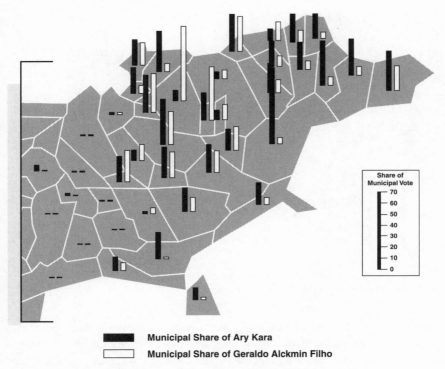

Municipal Share of Ary Kara

Municipal Share of Geraldo Alckmin Filho

Fig. 4. Two candidates compete in a corner of São Paulo
Geraldo Alckmin Filho, PSDB, and Ary Kara, PMDB, 1990

40 percent to 8 percent. But in Kara's home base, Taubaté, Alckmin's share held at 29 percent of the total municipal vote. In the end, Alckmin did well enough to retain his seat for four more years. Kara won as well, so the ultimate result was to convert the region from dominated into highly competitive. In terms of the relationship between Alckmin and his voters, the 1991–94 term saw a sharp increase in his efforts to bring local pork to the district. For the first time, Alckmin submitted budgetary amendments designed to channel federal largesse to Pindamonhangaba and Guaretinguetá. Competition, then, changed the linkage between voters and their representative.[11]

Concentrated-Shared Municipalities

In large metropolitan areas, especially megacities like greater São Paulo, discrete blocs of voters may be so large that their votes alone elect many deputies.

---

11. In 1994 Alckmin won election as vice governor of São Paulo.

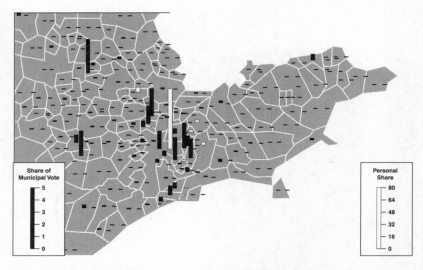

Fig. 5. Vote distribution for a working-class candidate
Eduardo Jorge, PT-São Paulo

In the state of São Paulo, for example, working-class candidates often get three-fourths of their total statewide vote from one municipality, the city of São Paulo. But they may never receive more than 5 percent of the votes cast in the city or in any other single municipality, because they share these municipalities with many other candidates. Figure 5 illustrates this possibility quite clearly: PT member Eduardo Jorge got most of his votes in São Paulo and its industrial suburbs, but he shared these municipalities with dozens of other candidates, including many others from the PT.

Working-class candidates are not the only Brazilian politicians with concentrated-shared vote distributions. Fábio Feldmann, whose 1990 vote map is shown in figure 6, is a PSDB member appealing primarily to environmentalists. He collected nearly 70 percent of his vote in the municipality of São Paulo, but he received only about 4 percent of the capital's vote. In terms of municipal domination, Feldmann's best showing came from Ilhabela (literally, "beautiful island"), an island off the coast of São Paulo where tourism reinforces environmental issues.

Scattered-Shared Municipalities

Some candidates appeal to voter cohorts that are numerically weak in any single municipality. Examples include Japanese-Brazilians and *evangélicos* (Protestants who typically vote for evangelical candidates). These cohorts are cohesive

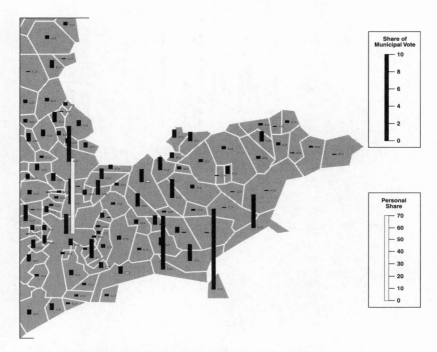

Fig. 6. Shared-concentrated vote of an environmentalist
Personal and Municipal Shares of Fábio Feldmann, PSDB-São Paulo

and loyal, but they are not very large, so candidates relying on them construct coalitions composed of small slices of many municipalities. Figure 7 displays the vote distribution of Antonio Ueno, a Japanese-Brazilian whose career has been rooted in the areas of Japanese migration in northern Paraná. Ueno actively sponsors sports clubs in the region and directs his vote appeals to club members, especially baseball players. Figure 8 displays the vote of Matheus Iensen, a Protestant minister in Paraná. The scattered-shared category also includes candidates occupying ideological niches. Cunha Bueno, a *paulista* conservative, was notorious for his campaign to restore the monarchy. In a nationwide plebiscite, voters rejected his proposal better than seven to one, but he found enough support across the state of São Paulo to win a Chamber seat.

Scattered-Dominant Municipalities

This pattern fits two kinds of candidates: those who make deals with local leaders—a theme examined later in this chapter—and those who once held such state-level bureaucratic posts as secretary of education, a job with substantial

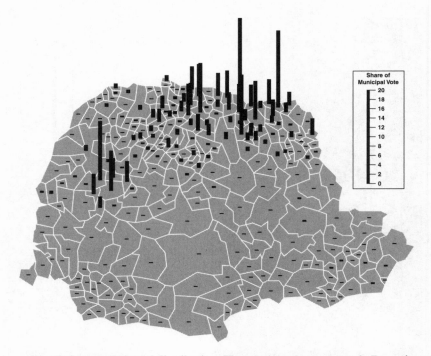

Fig. 7. Scattered-shared distribution: The ethnic and sports vote in Paraná
Municipal Vote Share of Antonio Ueno, PFL-Paraná, 1986

pork-barrel potential. Figure 9 displays the 1990 vote of Jonival Lucas, a conservative politician from Bahia. Linked politically to an ex-governor of the
state, Lucas had been president of the Intermunicipal Road Consortium, a group
with substantial clout in the location of state roads. Lucas also owned a radio
station, a common source of political influence (and revenue) among Brazilian
politicians. Before coming to the Chamber in 1987, Lucas's only elected office
was a single term as state deputy (1983–87). In his first run for the Chamber,
on the PFL ticket, he managed a second-place finish among Bahia's thirty-nine
deputies. He also did quite well in 1990, though he had switched to the small
Christian Democratic Party (PDC). But Lucas's vote bases shifted substantially
between 1986 and 1990. Six municipalities that had contributed, jointly, about
25 percent of his 1986 vote fell to less than 1 percent in 1990. Conversely, five
municipalities contributing only 1 percent in 1986 climbed to 26 percent in
1990. According to Bahian politicians and journalists, Lucas lost support where
other candidates had undercut his arrangements with local bosses. He gained
support where he managed to make new deals with other local leaders. In those

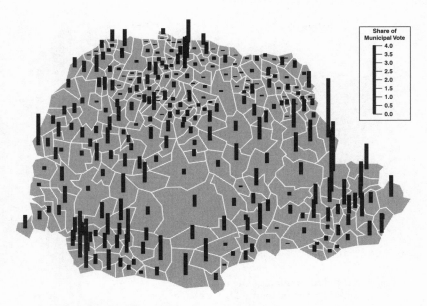

Fig. 8. Scattered-shared vote of an evangelical
Municipal Vote Share of Matheus Iensen, PTB-Paraná

areas where he had been active in his road-building career or where his radio station reached listeners, he managed to preserve his 1986 bailiwicks.

Brazilian deputies thus have enormous flexibility in constructing coalitions of voters large enough to elect them to office. In a sense, the system is extremely democratic. It makes no presuppositions about the kinds of societal cleavages that ought to be the basis of election. Unlike the single-member district, which favors locality as the dominant cleavage, or closed-list PR, which favors class, open-list PR with districts of high magnitude allows the campaign itself to determine which cohorts of voters achieve representation.[12]

Brazil's system may be highly democratic, but openness and flexibility come at the cost of weak parties and personalized politics, and they in turn lead to corruption and policy immobility. The following section examines some of the implications of deputies' widely varying vote bases, highlighting examples

12. Closed-list PR in Brazil would undoubtedly benefit class as the dominant cleavage, but in other societies race or gender might be advantaged—i.e., closed-list PR favors cleavages in which the contenders have relatively constant shares in each district across the entire nation. For a historical discussion of the development of electoral cleavages in Europe, see Bartolini and Mair 1990 and Lipset and Rokkan 1967.

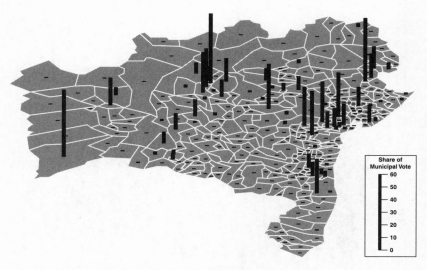

Fig. 9. Scattered-dominant vote distribution
Municipal Vote Share of Jonival Lucas, PDC-Bahia

and cases related to problems of democratic consolidation, including malapportionment, corruption, the nature of representation and accountability, and party building.[13] The strength of the relationship between these aspects of democratic consolidation and the electoral system varies greatly; indeed, malapportionment turns out to have more complex effects than generally expected.

Malapportionment and Its Consequences

Like the U.S. Congress, Brazil's legislature is bicameral, but Brazil's seat allocation rules favor small states in both chambers. In the Senate—where three senators represent each state—a senator from Roraima represents around 24,000 voters, while a senator from São Paulo represents more than 6 million.[14] As a result, senators representing 15 percent of the population can block legislation. In the Chamber of Deputies, seats are allocated by population, but since no state can have fewer than eight or more than seventy seats, the number of voters per deputy (see table 1) varies enormously. The big loser, obviously, is

---

13. For useful discussions of democratic consolidation, see Higley and Gunther 1992; Mainwaring 1999; Mainwaring and Scully 1995; and Shugart and Carey 1992.

14. These estimates are based on the 1989 electorate (see Nicolau 1992).

TABLE 1.   State Representation in the Chamber of Deputies (corrected according to the Sainte-Lague Formula)

State	Electorate[a]	Current Seats	"Corrected" Seats	Difference
Roraima	73,001	8	0	−8
Amapá	118,144	8	1	−7
Acre	182,797	8	1	−7
Tocantins	485,048	8	3	−5
Rondônia	557,781	8	3	−5
Sergipe	776,071	8	5	−3
Amazonas	842,083	8	5	−3
Distrito Federal	857,330	8	5	−3
Mato Grosso do Sul	1,002,232	8	6	−2
Mato Grosso	1,027,972	8	6	−2
Alagoas	1,210,797	9	7	−2
Rio Grande do Norte	1,298,088	8	8	0
Piauí	1,334,282	10	8	−2
Espírito Santo	1,407,759	10	9	−1
Paraíba	1,756,417	12	11	−1
Maranhão	2,144,352	18	13	−5
Goiás	2,178,977	17	13	−4
Pará	2,186,852	17	13	−4
Santa Catarina	2,729,916	16	17	+1
Ceará	3,351,606	22	21	−1
Pernambuco	3,764,143	25	23	−2
Paraná	5,045,626	30	31	+1
Rio Grande do Sul	5,700,461	31	35	+4
Bahia	5,893,861	39	36	−3
Rio de Janeiro	8,166,547	46	51	+5
Minas Gerais	9,432,524	53	58	+5
São Paulo	18,500,980	60	114	+54
Total	82,025,647	503	503	0

[a] Electorate of 1989.

São Paulo; the big winners are the lightly populated frontier states of the North and Center-West.[15]

Does malapportionment matter? Most observers believe that malapportionment weakens progressive forces and strengthens patronage-dependent forces (Mainwaring 1999). With more seats, São Paulo would elect more deputies representing the working class. The frontier states, which not only have few industrial workers but suffer invasions from free-spending political entrepreneurs, would elect fewer deputies. Without question, Brazilian politi-

---

15. For convenience, table 1 utilizes the Sainte-Lague Formula rather than D'Hondt. With the latter, the results would not vary significantly.

cians have acted as if they believed malapportionment favored the Right. In the Constitutional Convention of 1946, conservative delegates from São Paulo supported allocation rules penalizing their own state (Fausto 1970). The military regime followed the same reasoning: it added one senator to each state (from the original two), divided certain states to increase their representation, and joined two states (Rio and Guanabara) to minimize opposition from the former capital.[16] Like the *paulista* conservatives, the military strategists based their tactics on an estimate of the inclinations of São Paulo and frontier delegates.

Is it possible to estimate malapportionment's legislative effects? After any election, we can determine which individual candidates, from which parties, would win or lose seats if a state's allocation were smaller or larger. It is not possible to know, of course, how the newly included deputies would vote. But suppose these deputies—hypothetically added to a delegation by new proportionality rules—vote according to the mean of their parties' current votes. If the *paulista* PMDB delegation expands 25 percent, then each current PMDB vote is weighted by 1.25. If the PFL delegation expands 10 percent, then each current PFL vote is weighted by 1.10. In other words, the *paulista* delegation is assumed to continue to cast its votes in the same proportions, by party, except that the delegation will cast fifty-four more votes. I call this technique the party ratio method. The key to this method is that we know which deputies, from which parties, will be added to the delegation.

This reallocation method assumed that preelection slates (all the people on the ballot) would not change if a state's politicians knew they had 1 seat rather than 8, or 114 rather than 60. This assumption is frequently wrong: party leaders fill out their slates with candidates bringing in a few votes but with no chance of winning a seat. So, as an alternative modeling of proportionality rules, assume nothing about the identity of the new winners or losers. Instead, assume that each delegation preserves its current party breakdown. For example, if a state's delegation shrinks from eight deputies to one, each deputy on a delegation currently including three PTB and five PFL deputies will now cast the same legislative vote, but it will have one-eighth the original weight. *Paulista* deputies will cast the same votes they currently cast, but each vote will be weighted by the ratio 114/60. This is the state ratio method. In this method it is not possible to know which parties will gain or lose deputies under new allocation rules, so current party ratios are assumed to hold.

Now these reallocation rules are applied to some important votes in the Constitutional Assembly of 1987–88. Two of its most important—and most

---

16. I discuss these *casuismos,* or sophisms, in Ames 1987.

conflictual—issues were the vote over parliamentarism (known as the Humberto Lucena amendment) and the decision to grant the incumbent president a five-year term rather than a four-year term. President Sarney lobbied strenuously on both issues. After vigorous debate, presidentialism won, 344–212, and Sarney got his five-year term, 304–223.

How would the two models affect voting on these two issues? Using the state ratio model—that is, simply weighting each vote to reflect the fraction of the delegation added or subtracted—presidentialism still wins, but a five-year presidential term is defeated by the four-year alternative. Using the party ratio model, thus eliminating those deputies who would not have been elected in states losing members and assuming that new members (in states gaining deputies) would vote with their party brethren, the results are the same: presidentialism still wins, but the four-year term vanquishes the five-year term. Taking a broader sample of crucial votes in the constitutional assembly, the results are similarly mixed: about one in five changes.[17]

Why are the effects of correct proportionality in seat allocation not more dramatic? Remember that party discipline in the Brazilian Congress is low. Only the PT votes as a unified bloc, and it has never been more than the fourth or fifth largest party in the Chamber (with even less support in the Senate). If São Paulo increases its seat share dramatically, center and center-left parties can expect a substantial share of the additions. But these parties rarely cast a unified vote, so the additional progressive vote will be much smaller.

As an alternative model of allocation changes, imagine parties voting as blocs. Suppose it is assumed that all the party's delegation voted with the majority's position. Delegates from the states losing seats are eliminated, and delegates are added (according to their rank in the substitute list) for those states gaining seats. In this case, parliamentarism defeats presidentialism, but Sarney gets a five-year term. Why the change? The majority of the PMDB voted for parliamentarism but supported PMDB President Sarney on his quest for a longer term. On the broad range of crucial issues in the constitutional assembly, many other outcomes change from what actually occurred.

In the end, reallocating seats according to population makes a difference, sometimes an important difference, even though the absence of party discipline diminishes the effects of misallocation. However, this experiment treats the Chamber of Deputies in isolation, ignoring the malapportionment of the Senate. Given the Senate's extreme disproportionality, projects prejudicial to

---

17. There is no consistent pattern explaining why some change and others do not. The broader sample utilizes Kinzo's (1989) indexes of crucial votes in the assembly.

lightly populated states have even less chance in that body. As a result, such proposals are not even subject to bargaining or to logrolling with other issues. Proposals that would be dead on arrival tend not to be introduced at all.[18] The inclusion of such nondecisions would greatly magnify the true effects of malappportionment.

Corruption and Patterns of Vote Distribution

In the introduction, I mentioned a 1993 violent crime that led to the unmasking of an extortion ring involving members of the Budget Committee and many big construction companies. The racket's basis was simple: deputies submitted, and the Budget Committee approved, amendments to the general budget law mandating the construction of certain public works. Only particular companies could build these public works, either because a company had already initiated the project or because the bidding would be rigged. Because these colluding firms stood to make substantial profits, they could afford handsome kickbacks to the deputies, often 20 percent or more of the project's value. The deputies laundered their kickbacks through the national lottery: they would go to the lottery office, buy someone's winning ticket for a small premium, and receive "clean" money from the lottery itself.

The ringleaders of the scheme, a group of Budget Committee deputies known as the seven dwarfs (because of their small stature), were investigated by a special parliamentary committee of inquiry. Most either resigned or were kicked out of the Chamber.[19] One rapid resignation was that of the former chair of the Budget Committee, João Alves, a senior deputy from Bahia. Alves had come to the Congress in 1966 with no money; by the early 1990s he had millions of dollars in real estate and a $6 million airplane.

Figure 10 displays Alves's 1990 vote distribution. His votes come from widely scattered municipalities, but where he gets votes, he gets lots of votes. In many of these pockets of support he collects 70 percent or more of the mu-

---

18. In interviews conducted in 1996 with central government officials, including the ministers of finance and state administration, the president, and the former planning minister, Stepan (1999, 43) found a high degree of awareness of the blocking potential of small minorities in the Congress. Their veto power led to the withdrawal from the agenda of potential policy initiatives backed by majorities in Congress and in public opinion.

19. The dwarfs included José Carlos Vasconcelos (PRN-PE), Genebaldo Correia (PMDB-BA), Cid Carvalho (PMDB-MA), José Geraldo Ribeiro (PMDB-MG), Ubiratan Aguiar (PMDB-CE), Manoel Moreira (PMDB-SP), and João Alves (PPR-BA). A secondary group included Ricardo Fiuza (PFL-PE), Ibsen Pinheiro (PMDB-RS), Carlos Benevides (PMDB-CE), Fábio Raunheitti (PTB-RJ), Daniel Silva (PPR-MA), Paulo Portugal (PDT-RJ), and Paes Landim (PFL-PI).

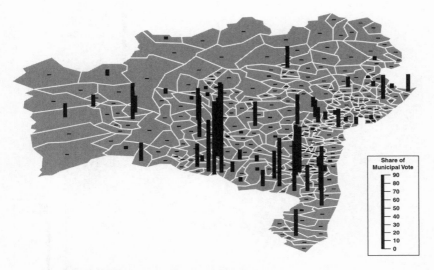

Fig. 10. Vote distributions of the "budget mafia"
Municipal Vote Share of João Alves, PFL-BA

nicipality's total vote. In the municipality right next door he might get nothing. What causes this spatial variation? If he had the kind of support enjoyed by a local mayor or council member, a leader with a strong local reputation, Alves would have a single dominant cluster of votes with a gradual tapering off as his local fame grew faint. It is possible, of course, for a locally based politician to have more than one cluster of votes. For example, a deputy with family in one region might build a political career in another. Alves, however, has too many separate clusters to fit that pattern. It is also possible for candidates appealing to some special bloc of voters to receive scattered support. But in any given municipality such candidates receive only small shares of the total vote. Alves, by contrast, dominates his bailiwicks.

What about the other dwarfs? Figure 11 displays the vote distribution of Pernambucan José Carlos Vasconcelos. Like Alves, Vasconcelos's votes fall into the scattered-dominant category. In fact, with the exception of one *paulista* deputy, all the accused deputies have this type of distribution, and most of the accused deputies who were outside the core group are similar.[20] Is the tie

---

20. The one glaring exception was a deputy from Rio Grande do Sul who had been considered one of the outstanding members of the Chamber and had been very active on national issues. In his case, greed seems to have been stimulated by personal problems.

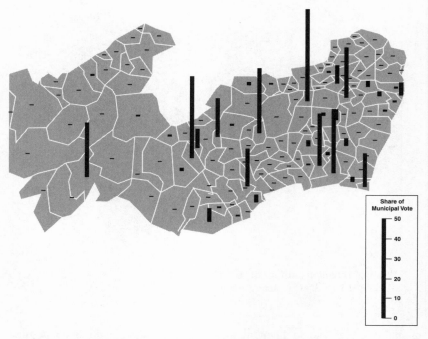

Fig. 11. Vote distributions for the "budget mafia"
Municipal Vote Share of José Carlos Vasconcelos, PRN-PE

between this kind of vote base and corruption mere chance, or does it reflect a
systematic vulnerability of the Brazilian electoral system?

The pork-barrel plus kickbacks scandal depended first on the existence of
a highly concentrated construction industry. Fewer than a dozen huge companies dominate construction. Without government contracts they could not survive. Politicians and bureaucrats have traditionally had great leeway in allocating such contracts. Although a bidding reform (approved in 1993) cleaned up
the process a bit, collusive bid rigging has long been a way of life in the construction industry. Whether a particular corrupt project involves local officials,
the existence of local bosses who can deliver voters en masse is critical to the
survival of this kind of corruption. Deputies get rich on the bribes of the *empreiteiras* (construction giants) but must use part of the money to pay off the local bosses. Although no empirical data are available to support my intuition, I
suspect that the amount of money that goes back to the district in the form of
personal loans and grants, petty favors, and walking-around money accounts

TABLE 2. Political and Economic Factors in the Dominance of a Corrupt Deputy (ordinary least squares estimates)

Parameter	Estimate	T for HO: Para. = 0	PR > I T I
Intercept	25.407	3.90	.0001
Liberal Front Party (PFL)	18.146	2.46	.0146
Intraparty fragmentation	−71.845	−3.12	.0020
Interparty fragmentation squared	62.937	2.95	.0034
PFL × Intraparty fragmentation	−20.890	−1.64	.1030
Municipal employment	651.932	1.54	.1255
Electorate	.0000074	0.48	.6323
Income per capita	−.0039	−2.15	.0323
Migratory population	.0419	.79	.4297
Share of population earning < 1/4 minimum salary	.0766	1.41	.1595

$R^2 = .124$ F = 5.11   Pr > F = .0001 $N = 334$

for a substantial part of the bribes deputies receive.[21] Thus a key part of corruption must be the existence, on the one hand, of politicians willing to sell blocs of voters and, on the other, of politicians with the money to buy such support. To probe more deeply into the basis of scattered-dominant distributions, table 2 presents a statistical model of Alves's vote.

The idea behind this regression model is to search for the determinants of Alves's vote among political and economic variables. The political variables include a dummy variable indicating whether the mayor came from Alves's party (the PFL), a measure of intraparty fragmentation, and a measure of the importance of government employment in the municipality. Alves should gain votes in PFL-dominated municipalities, he should do better when there is less intraparty fragmentation, he should do especially well in less fragmented PFL municipalities, and he should do better where high proportions of the workforce are in the municipality's employ. His dominance is likely to be greater in municipalities that are sparsely populated, poorer overall, more stable (fewer migrants), and where more people live in absolute poverty.

The model's results suggest that the political characteristics of municipalities are much more important than their economic and demographic charac-

---

21. During a congressional recess, one deputy's chief aide told me that the deputy had not returned to his district, as he had no money to respond to the hundreds of requests for small financial favors that he would inevitably receive.

teristics. Alves was more successful, in terms of his share of total municipal votes, where the municipality's mayor represented the PFL and where the fragmentation of PFL candidates was low.[22] In addition to these direct causal relationships, he also did slightly better in counties that were both PFL-controlled and low on fragmentation. And finally, he gained a small increment of votes in municipalities where a higher share of the workforce was employed in municipal government.[23] In such municipalities politics is often the only thriving business, and municipal employees understand the importance of remaining in the local boss's good graces.

In general, demographic and economic factors explain little of Alves's vote. When the level of absolute poverty is higher, Alves does a bit better, but the relationship is weak.[24] Neither population size nor the percentage of migrants in the municipality matters at all. Given the strong negative relationship between income per capita and municipal vote share, poverty seems to be a necessary but not sufficient condition for the existence of dominant vote bases. Only amidst poverty is dominance possible, but it also requires a set of favorable political conditions. The particular kind of dominance enjoyed by deputies accused of corruption results from the interaction of poverty with stable, machine-based politics. When deputies dominate a concentrated set of municipalities, they usually represent some family with a long history of political influence. When the dominated municipalities are scattered, arrangements exist with local leaders, bosses seeking the best deals available.

Could electoral reform end this kind of corruption? Brazilian politicians and social scientists have extensively discussed one reform, the German "mixed" electoral system. The German system divides the legislature into two halves: one half elected in single-member districts, the other half elected by closed-list proportional representation. In theory, the German system strengthens parties through its reliance on closed-list PR for half the seats but maximizes local accountability through single-member districts. The German system would also reduce campaign spending, because candidates would only campaign as individuals on the district side and the districts would be relatively small. Whether these gains would really be achieved is unclear, but it does seem

---

22. Alves's vote was subtracted from the municipal total before calculating the fragmentation of PFL candidates. In effect, the variable measures the fragmentation of all PFL candidates except Alves. Interparty fragmentation was also squared, because Alves's connections in Salvador might bring him a slightly bigger share in the capital.

23. Population size and percent employed in municipal administration are unrelated, so Wagner's Law is not in effect here.

24. Absolute poverty is measured by the share of the population earning less than one-fourth the monthly minimum wage—about sixty dollars at the time.

certain that the German system would eliminate exactly the corrupt deputies considered here, simply because scattered-dominant distributions would be extremely difficult to maintain. Deputies such as Alves could not be elected on the district side, because they could not compete, in any given district, with popular local leaders. On the closed-list side such candidates would have difficulty getting nominated, and, if they did get nominated, business interests and local bosses would have little incentive to make deals with these deputies. So, regardless of other benefits, the adoption of a mixed German-type system would kill off deputies relying on dispersed deal making.

Issue Caucuses and Accountability: Who Represents Whom?

Caucuses of like-minded deputies occur naturally in legislatures. When parties have little control over their members, issue caucuses are likely to cut across party lines. In the U.S. Congress, for example, a single legislator may belong simultaneously to the black caucus, the steel caucus, and the women's caucus. Another legislator may belong to the textile and tobacco caucuses. These issue-specific caucuses usually have regular meetings and permanent staff, and they are an important form of representation in a legislature basically organized around spatial communities— that is, around single-member districts. Through issue caucuses, deputies represent their constituents' economic, ethnic, and social interests.

As mentioned earlier, seats in Brazil's Chamber of Deputies are filled from multimember districts. Because each district elects many members, political scientists characterize Brazil as a country with high district magnitude.[25] Given open-list PR and high district magnitude, communities lose the privileged position they hold in a single-member district system like that of the United States. Any politically mobilized cohort of sufficient size can elect a deputy whose sole function is the representation of that cohort. Figure 12 presents a curious example: Deputy Amaral Netto, from the state of Rio de Janeiro, occupied a unique ideological niche: he ardently defended the death penalty. The resulting pattern of electoral support was remarkably even: with the exception of the lightly populated northeastern end of the state (where he campaigned little), Netto received 3–5 percent of the vote in nearly every municipality. In Rio de Janeiro and its populous suburbs, where crime is a huge problem, his vote was at the high end; in the more bucolic regions, the death penalty was less impor-

---

25. Japanese districts, by contrast, send between three and five representatives to the Diet.

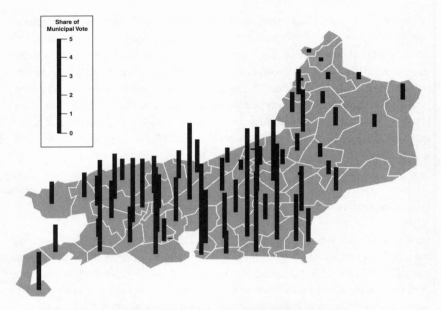

Fig. 12. Support for the death penalty as an ideological niche
Amaral Netto, PDS-RJ

tant. Netto was unsuccessful in promoting the death penalty in Brazil, but no one doubted the authenticity of his ideological base.

Observers of the Brazilian Congress identify at least fifteen caucuses. The largest, with about one hundred deputies each, are the agricultural (or rural) caucus, the construction industry caucus, and the health caucus, followed by Petrobrás (the national oil company), Catholics, bankers, evangelical Protestants, and communications, each with between fifty and eighty members. Caucuses of twenty to thirty members include education, the pension system and its employees, state banks, civil servants, multinational firms, auto dealers, and unions ("Bancada de Interesse" 1994). These estimates, however, are based on guesses: no caucus, even those meeting regularly, has permanent staff or a fixed membership list.

In the issue caucuses of the U.S. Congress, and in cases like the Brazilian deputy advocating the death penalty, the authenticity of a claim to representation is based on the interests of the voters sending that deputy to the legislature. In the House of Representatives, members of the steel caucus come from steel-producing regions. No one would expect a member of the steel caucus to own a steel mill personally; such a tie would be a conflict of interest. In Brazil, however, such ties are often exactly the motivation behind caucus membership. A deputy from Rio Grande do Sul represents the interests of the civil construction industry in the Congress. A map of his vote base reflects no concentration of construction workers or firms. Rather, the construction industry supports his campaigns; he responds by working for their interests. The health caucus includes doctors lobbying for improved public medical facilities as well as doctors owning private hospitals and lobbying for their personal interests.

The Brazilian Congress, then, shelters multiple bases of representation, especially in states with more legislators. Some are direct. The evangelical caucus lobbies for subsidies for Protestant churches and schools, but caucus members get their votes from precisely the interest they represent. Similarly direct ties with voters also characterize the union and civil servant caucuses. But self-representation—that is, representation of an economic group in which a deputy has a personal interest—characterizes many of the members of such caucuses as health, civil construction, and state banks.

To examine self-representation further, consider the rural caucus, usually considered the strongest organized interest in the Congress. The rural caucus is so large and so unified that it can stop any major agrarian reform effort. In 1994 the caucus prevented the government from pushing through its economic stabilization package until the government bargained on completely unrelated agricultural debt issues. Caucus members claim, of course, that they represent farm interests. The question, however, is whether they represent districts where agriculture is central to the economy or whether they represent their own personal interests. Table 3 shows the determinants of two votes central to the interests of the rural caucus during the 1991–94 legislature. One issue concerned a tax benefiting the pension system but calculated in terms of agricultural production; the second concerned a tax increase penalizing nonproductive rural properties. Farm interests opposed both taxes. I combined support for the two rural caucus positions, scoring each deputy as pro–rural caucus or anti–rural caucus. The explanatory variables include measures of personal economic interests, region, the economic base of a deputy's voters, party affiliation, and membership in the evangelical caucus. Biographical directories facilitated identification of deputies with agricultural interests—that is, owners of large estates or significant agricultural enterprises.[26] The indicator "rural base" (the inverse of urbanization) came from the 1980 census. I aggregated the character-

---

26. These sources included Istoé 1991 and Brazil, Câmara dos Deputados 1987. I also consulted the lists prepared by DIAP, the union research office in Brasília. The government agricultural extension agency Embrapa had also prepared its own list of deputies holding substantial rural property.

TABLE 3.   Personal Interest versus Constituency Interest in the Rural Caucus
(logistic estimation of support for rural caucus)

Parameter	Estimate	Wald Chi-square	Pr > Chi-square
Intercept	−1.783	52.09	.0001
Agricultural interest	1.411	27.95	.0001
Northeast region	−.553	1.74	.1867
South region	.719	1.95	.1630
Rural base	.070	3.75	.0529
PFL	1.155	11.56	.0007
PDS	0.434	.93	.3341
PTB	1.040	3.68	.0552
Evangelical	1.419	4.45	.0348

Note: Likelihood ratio significant at .0001 level, $N = 408$.

istics of the municipalities where each deputy received votes, weighted by the percentage of the deputy's total votes the municipality contributed.

Table 3 offers striking results. Deputies' personal agricultural interests were by far the dominant influence in their voting on agrarian issues. Those who owned rural properties essentially made up the rural caucus, and they voted to defend their economic interests. Region turned out not to matter significantly, although deputies from the supposedly traditional and backward Northeast were actually a bit more likely to support agrarian reform than their "modern" southern colleagues.[27] A rural base made deputies more likely to oppose agrarian reform, but the relationship was much weaker than the linkage between support for reform and personal economic holdings.[28]

This test of the bases of the rural caucus supports the contention that the Brazilian electoral system's rules distort representation and accountability. Obviously, not all caucuses are self-representing. Unions, evangelicals, and civil servants trade voting support for real representation. But like the ruralists, caucuses representing civil construction, telecommunications and state banks have a different claim to legitimacy. The ordinary voters electing a particular deputy who clearly and unequivocally represented civil construction did not vote for him to represent their construction interests, because the overwhelming majority of his voters have no ties at all to that industry.

---

27. The South has recently been the site of many violent conflicts between huge, modern agricultural operations and the landless poor.

28. Party mattered. Membership in the PFL or PTB was associated with strong antireform positions. PDS partisans, however, took no clear position, most likely because their delegation was split between urban and rurally based deputies. Evangelicals also opposed agrarian reform, probably because of both their natural conservatism and their willingness to logroll: they traded support to the rural caucus for its support on their bills.

Open-list proportional representation and high-magnitude districts seem to be necessary but probably not sufficient conditions for self-representation. The inevitable vagueness of voter-deputy ties in Brazil makes it easy to hide self-accountability to voters. Self-representation is also encouraged by Brazil's tradition of state corporatism in the executive branch (Schmitter 1971). The corporatist state sanctioned, regulated, and controlled economic interests' participation in policy-making. With government financial support and a guaranteed place at the policy-making table, economic interests found it profitable to penetrate the state, both from inside the state apparatus and from the legislative branch.

Open-List Proportional Representation and Party Building

By this point it should be clear that open-list PR personalizes politics and hinders party building. If, in a given state, the average number of voters per congressional seat is 50,000, and if a candidate has 200,000 voters that will follow the candidate to any party, then that candidate has enormous power. Whichever party attracts the candidate can be assured of another four seats—that is, the candidate plus three others elected by the 150,000 "extra" votes. Party leaders, of course, will be very tolerant of ideological deviations between such heavyweights and the party's official program. To explore party building under such rules, this section examines four systemic ramifications: the growth of blank and null voting, the incentives for inconsistent cross-party alliances, the consequences of party switching by incumbents, and the weakness of links between social groups and parties.

Null and Blank Voting

Voting in Brazil is obligatory for all literate persons over eighteen; it is optional for illiterates and those between sixteen and eighteen.[29] Since obligatory voting forces many unwilling people to the polls, it is not surprising that Brazil has high levels of blank (*em branco*) and invalid (*nulo*) voting (Power and Roberts 1995). In the 1989 presidential election, null and blank votes together reached 5 percent of the electorate. In 1994, in an election characterized by the absence of negative campaigning and by the presence of two serious candidates, null voting alone doubled, to 7.8 percent of the electorate. Blank voting climbed

---

29. Those who abstain without a valid excuse, such as illness, pay a small fine.

even faster, reaching 7.6 percent. Thus, null and blank voting together surpassed 15 percent of the electorate.

Are these levels of null and blank voting an indicator of underlying problems in the electoral system? It is obviously not possible to compare Brazil to polities in which voting is optional. But even on its own terms, the 1994 election was a complex one: simultaneous voting for five levels of office and the recent impeachment of the 1989 presidential victor, Fernando Collor de Mello. Resources available for clientelistic trading of favors had certainly decreased by 1994, so voters may have felt that bosses could no longer hold up their end of the bargain.

In certain races, however, high levels of null and blank votes merit special attention. Null votes in senatorial races surpassed 8 percent of the electorate, and blank votes were greater than 20 percent. In a number of senatorial races, null and blank votes outnumbered the votes of the winning candidate. Null and blank votes in the Chamber of Deputies races were the highest of all, reaching 41 percent (Tribunal Superior Eleitoral 1995).

Most Brazilian observers point to obligatory voting as the essential cause of null and blank ballots. Such observers suggest that invalid votes result from forcing to the polls people who either do not want to vote or do not know how to vote. The strongest partisan criticism of obligatory voting comes from the Left, which remembers that Lula would probably have beaten Collor de Mello for the presidency in 1989 if voting had been optional. The strongest defense comes from the Right: rural oligarchs back obligatory voting because they depend on a manipulated vote. These partisan reactions are predictable, but are there larger issues? Can null and blank votes demonstrate anything more about the functioning of the Brazilian electoral system?

Given the local character of Brazilian electoral politics, an analysis of invalid voting must build on electoral results at the municipal level. Utilizing data from Ceará and Santa Catarina, I tested regression models explaining null and blank voting on the basis of municipal-level aspects of political competition.[30] Political competition affects the information available to the voter—that is, the voter's knowledge of the candidates and the political process. Competition also affects the anger voters feel toward a political process that has produced extraordinary corruption and abysmal public services.

The spatial structure of political competition is quite different in Ceará and Santa Catarina. Ceará's deputies have mostly scattered distributions, with the

---

30. The regressions also include measures of socioeconomic characteristics. Complete results are available on request.

majority falling into the scattered-dominant type, while Santa Catarina's deputies typically have concentrated distributions, mostly in the concentrated-shared camp. How did competition affect blank and null voting? In both states, the higher the mean personal share (the percentage of a candidate's total statewide vote earned in a given municipality), the lower the level of blank voting. When candidates pick up more of their overall votes in a particular municipality, it becomes more important to them. Thus, when the average personal share of all candidates in a given municipality is low, the municipality is important to no one. Little campaign effort will be devoted to the municipality, and few efforts will be made to inform its voters. Because voters have no basis on which to choose, they cast blank votes. In Ceará, the higher the fragmentation of the vote of the state's dominant party (at that time the PSDB), the more blank voting occurred. Santa Catarina saw the same effect: high levels of fragmentation in the dominant PDS were tied to more blank voting. Why? Pulverization of a municipality's vote by many candidates from one party is not simply the sign of even competition. Rather, fragmentation results when no candidate has real ties to the municipality. Faced with a plethora of unappealing candidates, voters increasingly cannot choose at all, so they vote blank.

How does the spatial structure of competition affect the null or "anger" vote? When candidates had a higher stake in a municipality's votes, the level of null voting declined in both Ceará and Santa Catarina, presumably because candidates were attentive to the district during the previous legislative term. In Ceará, fragmentation both within the PFL and PMDB and between the two parties was positively associated with higher levels of null voting. In Santa Catarina, however, neither of the fragmentation measures affected null voting. Perhaps voters in these two states were responding to the presence or absence of dominant politicians. In Ceará more than half the delegation elected in 1986 had scattered-dominant distributions. Such vote patterns occur only when local bosses command voter loyalties and deliver voters in blocs. Null voting should be low in such places, but in the few municipalities that are truly fragmented, mostly big cities, voter anger emerges. In Santa Catarina, more than two-thirds of the deputies had concentrated-shared distributions, which means that most voters faced a choice of candidates with ties to the district. Since this kind of distribution predominated in both urban and rural areas, fragmentation of party competition had no independent effect on levels of null voting.

Overall, then, Brazil's electoral rules combine with the socioeconomic characteristics of each state's communities to generate particular patterns of spatial competition. In turn, the pattern of spatial competition affects the information available to voters and the alternatives they perceive. Frustrated and ill informed, voters in communities where few candidates have strong ties respond by casting ballots expressing anger or by refusing to cast ballots at all.

Multiparty Alliances

Brazil's formula for apportioning legislative seats (the D'Hondt method) hinders small parties' chances of attaining the electoral quotient that would entitle them to a seat. As a result, they often ally with larger parties so that their joint total, which determines whether they reach the quotient, is larger. A candidate with a personal total insufficient to earn a seat—because the total of all the party's candidates is inadequate—may have enough votes as part of a multiparty alliance. These electoral alliances are truly just electoral: they do not imply joint action in the legislature. At the same time, the parties have to agree on a common set of promises—it would be a stretch to call them programs—to offer their electorates during the campaign,

If electoral alliances are inconsistent across the states, delegations from the same parties from different states are less likely to share a common program at the national level. Consider the 1986 election. The PTB allied with the PMDB in Acre and Pará, but the PMDB joined anti-PMDB alliances in Bahia, Goiás, Mato Grosso do Sul, Santa Catarina, and São Paulo. In most states the PFL aligned with the PDS, but in Piauí, Rio de Janeiro, Rio Grande do Sul, and Santa Catarina, the PFL either opposed the PDS or ran a separate slate. The PDC joined the PFL in Bahia but allied with the PMDB—against the PFL—in Ceará.

The apparent capriciousness of state-level alliances results from a conceptual confusion. With the exception of the Workers' Party and, on some issues, the PFL, Brazilian parties really exist only at the state level. At that level, moreover, parties can be surrogates for traditional factional disputes. So politics in Maranhão is either pro-Sarney or anti-Sarney; in Bahia the lineup is pro– or anti–Antônio Carlos Magalhães. In the 1994 presidential election, PSDB candidate Fernando Henrique Cardoso defeated the PT's Luís Inácio Lula da Silva in the first round of the election, but in the second round Cardoso supported the PT candidate for governor in the state of Espírito Santo. The PT and PDT are fierce enemies in most states, but in Rio Grande do Sul and in Rio de Janeiro they cooperate. Leonel Brizola, the PDT's founder, controls the party in Rio Grande do Sul and Rio de Janeiro, but in Paraná he has no influence whatever. An even stranger example is found in São Paulo. Former Governor Orestes Quércia naturally dominated a wing of the *paulista* PMDB, but for a few years he also dominated the *paulista* PFL, which answered to him rather than to national party leaders.

Party Loyalty and Party Switching

I have previously demonstrated how Brazil's version of open-list PR personalizes politics and hinders party development. Party leaders lack the means to discipline deputies seeking the party label, and efforts to rein in individualistic or deviant behavior can be costly to the parties themselves. At the same time, parties do nominate governors, senators, and presidents, and, in spite of their ideological vagueness, many of the major parties (especially the PT, PSDB, PMDB, and PFL) occupy recognized positions on a left-right spectrum. Could partisan affinities develop in spite of the hostile environment of open-list PR, and will these affinities prevent deputies from changing parties?[31]

Public opinion surveys during the past ten years suggest that low percentages of Brazilian voters, compared with voters in other industrial democracies, identify with political parties or consider party when casting a vote. In 1994, for example, respondents to a national survey were asked the following question: "When you choose candidates for various positions, do you make an effort to vote for candidates of the same party, or do you vote taking into consideration only the candidate, regardless of his/her party?" Mainwaring (1999, 112) reports that 24 percent of the respondents chose the party-based response, while 67 percent claimed to ignore party. Open-ended questions on surveys between 1989 and 1994 found that 44–57 percent of the Brazilian electorate identified with a party (Meneguello 1994). In 1994, the last survey year, 48 percent of respondents were party identifiers. While these figures are lower than those of other industrial democracies, they remain significant.[32]

Clues about the strength of party loyalties can also be found in the electoral fates of deputies who change parties.[33] Between the elections of 1986 and 1990, seventy deputies left the parties they originally represented and sought reelection under a different party label, and only sixteen were reelected in 1990. Since the 1990 success rate of all deputies seeking reelection (both switchers and nonswitchers) exceeded 50 percent, party switching may seem a fairly lame tactic. Do the switchers' failures imply that party loyalties really matter, that party switchers lost because they were unable to carry their voters to their new party? Before party loyalty is blamed for the switchers' failure to survive, it is necessary to assess their electoral chances if they had remained in their parties

---

31. For discussion of party switching outside Latin America, see Canon and Sousa 1992.

32. Industrial democracies range from Canada's 90 percent to Denmark's 54 percent (see Mainwaring 1999, 114, using figures from Dalton, Flanagan, and Beck 1984, 300–301, 196),

33. Here I ignore the difference between mass loyalties and the loyalties of political bosses. In Ames 1994b, I distinguish empirically, at the municipal level, between mass partisan tendencies and the effects of the political machine.

of origin. One basis for such an inquiry is the switchers' individual ranks in their states' 1986 deputy lists. High-ranking 1986 deputies had a better chance of winning in 1990, but not by much. Of the thirty-four party-switching deputies who had finished in the lower half of their states' lists in 1986, six won in 1990. Of thirty-six switchers who had finished in the upper half in 1986, ten were re-elected in 1990. So a higher finish in 1986 did help, but only a little, and switchers were almost equally likely to have done well or poorly in 1986. Deputies should not change parties because they think their chances with the original party are poor.

Politicians know that while some of their voters will support them regardless of their party affiliation, others will remain loyal only as long as candidates belong to a given party. Deputies considering a shift to a new party ought to examine the spatial configuration of their vote. If their personal vote is highly correlated with the overall party vote (the vote for all members of that party together), then it will be tougher to move their voters to another party.[34] However, in most states, party switchers were about as likely as nonswitchers to have received their 1986 votes in party bailiwicks. In Bahia and Minas Gerais, switchers were a bit more likely to have done well in party bailiwicks than were nonswitchers, while in São Paulo and Paraná, switchers were less successful in party strongholds.[35] Overall, then, switchers were not loners with essentially personal votes. Their willingness to change parties underscores their belief that party loyalties would not cripple their reelection chances.

Could switchers hold their 1986 voters in 1990? One answer is found in the correlation between the spatial distributions of deputies' personal vote shares in the two elections. In other words, did deputies get their votes in the same places in the two elections? In Bahia, Rio de Janeiro, and Paraná, party switchers held their voters better than nonswitchers, and in other states switchers did about as well as nonswitchers in transferring their bailiwicks. But the fact that party-switching deputies maintained the same bailiwicks could indicate merely that deputies contemplating a change in party did not foresee that party loyalty would be a problem and, as a result, failed to extend their campaigns out from their 1986 bailiwicks.

The best way to test party loyalty is to compare the vote gains and losses between 1986 and 1990 of switchers and nonswitchers from the same party. Deputies leaving the PMDB constitute the biggest group of potential switchers.

---

34. The overall party vote is defined as the sum of all party members' shares of each municipality's total vote minus the share of the deputy in question.

35. São Paulo and Paraná are two traditional strongholds of the PMDB, so here party loyalties may play a real role in voter decisions.

In almost every state, switchers did much worse in 1990 than did nonswitchers. In Bahia, for example, switchers from the PMDB lost an average of 20,550 votes between 1986 and 1990, while nonswitching PMDB candidates gained 9,611 votes. In Paraná, switchers lost almost 50,000 votes apiece, while non-switchers lost only 13,480. In only two states, Rio Grande do Sul and São Paulo, did switchers do better than nonswitchers, and in these states the deputies who did well in 1990 had all been extremely popular vote getters in 1986.

The poor performance of deputies who changed parties between 1986 and 1990 becomes even more dramatic in light of the fact that switchers, overall, had previously performed as well in 1986 as nonswitchers. In other words, the failure of party switchers cannot be dismissed on the grounds that they were merely weak candidates. In addition, few switchers lost their seats in 1990 simply because their new parties could not muster enough votes from all their candidates to guarantee the switchers' seats, even though these candidates personally had about the same totals as in 1986. Only about one-third of losing switchers could plausibly argue that their defeat resulted from the party's failure to accumulate enough total votes rather than from their personal decline.

The surprising strength of party at the mass level is even more dramatic in the context of the PMDB's debacle in 1990. Riding the strength of the Cruzado economic plan in 1986, the party had swept most state assemblies and governorships and was easily the biggest party in the Chamber of Deputies. But by 1990 the Cruzado was a bitter memory, the PMDB's presidential candidate had finished with only a few percent of the national vote, and the party was in disarray. Leaving the PMDB should have provided candidates a boost, and many clearly saw switching as a political lifeboat. They were wrong, as it happened. Loyalty would have paid off.

The discovery that party identification may develop more quickly and resist poor governmental performance more sturdily than commonly believed needs qualification. The results discussed here are mainly based on switches of former PMDB members. As the party associated with resistance to the military dictatorship, the PMDB enjoyed the highest levels of partisan identification in the Brazilian electorate. Other parties, except for the PT, are unlikely to do as well. In addition, the PMDB's recent decline helps explain the overall fall in partisan identification in Brazil. Party switching inevitably reinforces that decline.

Ultimately, the origins of party switching lie in career calculations. Brazilian deputies are less likely to seek long-term legislative careers than their U.S. counterparts. Enticed by committee positions, pork projects, or other benefits proffered by party leaders seeking to expand their delegations, Brazilian deputies often switch parties early in the legislative term. Benefits accrued during the term under the new party label must outweigh the risks in the subsequent election. For some deputies, the immediate objective may not be reelection to the legislative seat at all. Rather, they plan off-year runs for municipal mayoralties. Other deputies may have only a token interest in an immediate reelection campaign. For these deputies, party switching maximizes the short-term gain of a legislative seat.

Society and Party: The Missing Link

Party systems are usually classified as institutionalized when parties have stable shares of the popular vote, when parties and elections clearly determine who governs, when party organizations have stable rules and structures, and when parties have roots in society.[36] As scholars often point out, Brazil's parties fail all four tests. The PMDB, the nation's largest party, had 43 percent of the national legislative vote in 1982, 48 percent in 1986, 19.3 percent in 1990, and 20.3 percent in 1994. In 1989, just three years after the PMDB's sweeping 1986 legislative and gubernatorial victories, the party's presidential candidate received just 4.4 percent of the national popular vote.[37] Parties and elections determine who governs in Brazil, at least in the sense that military coups, in the view of most scholars, are highly unlikely (Hunter 1996). But at the national level, parties—with the exception of the Workers' Party—really do not exist, and the strength of state party organizations varies enormously. Still, these aspects of institutionalization are all fairly obvious. More interesting and more complex is the question of roots—that is, the problem of parties' links to societal groups.

For a political party to offer a coherent national program, it must represent essentially the same social groups in each of the major regions of the country, and it must maintain these ties over time. Because Brazil's party system is still evolving, with new parties appearing, old ones fading, and politicians switching parties, it is not possible simply to chart the correlation between each party's candidates and various socioeconomic indicators.[38]

---

36. For an extended discussion of these themes, see Mainwaring and Scully 1995.

37. For a treatment of the 1989 presidential election, see Ames 1994b.

38. Moreover, the votes of city-based candidates would correlate with such characteristics as urbanization and manufacturing whether their votes come from the working class, the upper middle class, or—as in the case of charismatic candidates—a multiclass coalition. A perfect test of the stability of party-societal ties requires information that is simply unavailable—i.e., longitudinal survey data in different states.

I will now return to the four-category typology of electoral bases: concentrated-dominant, concentrated-shared, scattered-shared, and scattered-dominant. In an open-list proportional system of Brazil's type, would any single category predominate if the system were evolving in the direction of tighter party-society linkages? It is clear that neither the concentrated-dominant nor the scattered-dominant cells reflects society-party linkages. A scattered-shared pattern usually represents groups like evangelicals or ideological niche fillers like the *paulista* candidate favoring the monarchy. Scattered-shared patterns also reflect candidates relying on narrow social groups, such as pensioners, but in this case these candidates represent very specific interests. The remaining pattern, concentrated-shared, seems more promising. Given the large size of Brazil's districts, candidates appealing to broad social forces are likely to do so in individual metropolitan areas (which encompass multiple municipalities), and these areas are usually large enough to elect more than one candidate. In such districts, contact between voters and their representatives is possible. Thus the PT candidates who share the votes of São Paulo's working class have concentrated-shared bases, but middle-class candidates successfully mine the same metropolitan area for votes. Such distributions, in other words, reflect competition along group or class lines.

Over the four elections from 1978 until 1990, how can the number of candidates with concentrated-shared vote distributions be determined? If all four elections are pooled and then each dimension is divided by its median, the result, for the entire universe of deputies serving between 1978 and 1990, is a rough balance between the four distributional types. In 1978 19 percent of the deputies had concentrated-shared distributions. In 1982 this number rose to 27 percent, and by 1990 it reached 33 percent. Some parties deviate from this evolutionary pattern. The PDS (now called the PPB), once the promilitary party and long the largest conservative party, shows no shift at all in its deputies' vote distributions. In 1986 the PDS lost most of its northeastern adherents to the PFL. Those PDS members who remained in the party tended to have secure, noncompetitive vote bases, so the party looks increasingly anachronistic. But the general rise in competitiveness does seem to fit the nation's largest party, the PMDB. It gained many new members in 1986 and then watched many members defect between 1987 and 1989 to the PSDB, the PTB, and other smaller parties. Since the PMDB lost deputies who tended to dominate along with deputies who shared vote bases, this overall change does not merely reflect the defeat of a particular type; rather, it reflects the overall shift of the universe of deputies. New PMDB politicians were more likely to invade old PMDB bailiwicks, and old PMDB deputies adopted the same campaign style as the newcomers.

In sum, the evolution of the party system—a theme to which I shall return in chapter 3—has reduced the number of traditional, municipally dominant deputies, and the result has been an increase in community-based deputies who appeal to broad social strata but face competition. This kind of competition forces deputies to deliver pork-barrel benefits to communities. But to the degree that parties shape the behavior of their deputies (a topic examined in chapter 6), such competition also leaves open the possibility that parties will develop programs responding to their voters' class affiliations.

Conclusion

This chapter began with a discussion of the workings of the Brazilian electoral system. The central theme was simple: open-list PR, as it functions in Brazil, personalizes politics and weakens party control over politicians in both campaign and legislative behavior. The system is extremely democratic in the sense that all potential cleavages receive equal treatment. But openness and flexibility weaken the ties between voters and deputies, and parties have difficulty aggregating interests into anything resembling a coherent program.

Campaigning for legislative seats in Brazil is a competition for space. This space can be ideological (like the "spatial modeling" literature in political science), but more often space really means physical space. Candidates seek municipalities whose voters and/or leaders will give them support. The fight for space produces a four-cell taxonomy combining vertical penetration of municipalities (domination) with horizontal coverage (contiguity). The taxonomy classifies deputies as concentrated-dominant, concentrated-shared, scattered-shared, and scattered-dominant. Deputies with certain kinds of occupational backgrounds and political histories tend to concentrate in each of these categories. Local mayors, for example, have concentrated vote distributions, while businessmen more often have scattered patterns. In traditional regions of the country, deputies get most of the votes of municipalities that contribute a substantial part of their personal vote, while in other regions deputies face much higher levels of interparty and intraparty fragmentation.

To explore the functioning of this unique electoral system, I then explored a series of topics central to contemporary political debate in Brazil: malapportionment, corruption, accountability, and party building. Malapportionment refers to the distribution formula for legislative seats. São Paulo is more than fifty seats short of its proportionate share of the chamber, while states in the Center-West and North have far too many seats. At times, it seems to be expected that granting São Paulo its just share, while cutting the delegations of the frontier states, will move the Brazil's political center of gravity sharply to the left. However, reasonable assumptions about new deputies' voting (given the weakness of party discipline) somewhat temper radical expectations. Some important votes in the National Constituent Assembly would have turned out differently under true proportionality, but many others would have been unchanged. In the permanent legislature, however, the fact that both chambers sharply reduce the influence of populous regions may prevent certain issues from ever becoming the object of political debate and compromise.

The outbreak of an extraordinary corruption scandal in 1993 provided the opportunity to test the practical importance of this vote-distribution taxonomy. Deputies accused of corruption overwhelmingly tended to be scattered-dominant types. Such distributions reflect their efforts to make deals with local political bosses. The chapter also demonstrated that a reform of the German type, combining single-member districts with closed-list PR, would probably retire these corrupt types from the legislature.

Brazil's system gives new meaning to that commonly heard term in American politics, "special interests." The openness of the Brazilian system allows deputies to fill ideological niches—the classic being the *paulista* running on a promonarchy platform—but deputies also reflect Brazil's traditional corporatism, in which narrow economic interests penetrate the bureaucracy and legislature. The so-called rural caucus represents not the interests of the voters who elect these deputies but the personal interests of deputies holding rural property, which is not what accountability normally means.

The chapter then turned to the effects of Brazil's system on the building of political parties. After every election, the Brazilian press is full of stories about the high levels of null and blank voting. Such voting mainly is a consequence of obligatory voting but also says something about the electoral system. The analysis presented here suggests (but cannot measure definitively) that null and blank voting has an information component and an anger component. In constituencies where all candidates get small proportions of their personal vote, deputies' campaign efforts are likely to be minimal, and voters simply lack sufficient information to choose. But anger matters as well: with corruption scandals, a perennially unsatisfactory economy, and an impeached president, voters expressed their feelings about politics not by staying home but by defacing their ballots.

In talking about party building, what is really meant is national parties. Brazil has some parties with considerable organizational strength at the municipal and even state levels, but at the national level one can hardly talk about political parties. One reason parties have difficulty forming coherent programs is that the system encourages multiparty alliances. Right-wing parties ally with center parties in some states and with left-wing parties in others. In the 1994 presidential election, a supposedly center-left party made two strange deals: one with a far-right party that includes a neoliberal wing and a pork-barrel wing, the other with a party that has nothing but pork-barrel types.

Brazil's electorate has less than fifteen years experience with open, democratic politics. In spite of the party-weakening effects of open-list PR, there are some signs that party loyalties matter. Deputies who switched parties between 1986 and 1990 provided a kind of experimental sample. Party switching was costly: switchers had a lower reelection rate than did loyal deputies. Perhaps to the switchers' surprise, they failed to transfer their voters to their new parties. For many switchers, this risk may have been worthwhile, because the gains from switching during the legislative term outweighed the electoral risk. For others, however, their behavior may appear quite irrational.

Does the possible irrationality of some party switchers call into question this book's stress on politicians' "rational" behavior? I think not. Brazilian deputies operate in an environment of great uncertainty. The New Republic's first parliamentary election was really 1986, and most conventional political wisdom downplayed the strength of party identification. For some of these politicians, immediate reelection was probably not the primary objective. Last, a focus on rationality means not that irrational behavior will never occur but that it will not be rewarded. Over time, party switching should prove electorally more successful, because only those truly benefiting will switch.

The chapter concludes by returning to the taxonomy of voting bases presented at the beginning of the chapter. The system's evolution is the subject of chapter 3, but here I note merely that deputies with concentrated-shared distributions are becoming more common. Such deputies appeal to broad social strata in particular communities. These representatives' concentrated vote means that they are likely to identify with their communities, but they also face significant political opposition. The increased number of such deputies may magnify interest in delivering pork-barrel benefits, but at least deputies will have to pay attention to the communities where they get votes, and they will have to compete with other candidates for these votes. It may not be much, but it represents the beginning of accountability.

Chapter 2

Campaign Strategy under Open-List Proportional Representation

"I win elections with a bag of money in one hand and a whip in the other."[1]
Antônio Carlos Magalhães, Senator and former governor of Bahia

"I played by the rules of politics as I found them."
Richard M. Nixon

How do electoral systems influence ultimate political outcomes? Electoral rules and structures encourage certain kinds of people to choose political careers. Electoral rules also motivate people who are already politicians to act in particular ways. To understand how an electoral system affects the composition of a political class as well as its subsequent behavior, it is necessary to analyze the strategies of candidates for legislative office. In majoritarian, "first past the post" electoral systems, office-seeking politicians try to position themselves as close to the median voter as possible. Judged in terms of their issue stances, such candidates often seem very close. In proportional systems, however, optimal campaign strategies are quite different. Because small slices of the electorate can ensure victory in proportional elections, strategic office seekers should not pursue the median voter; rather, they should seek discrete voter cohorts (Cox 1990b, 1997). This chapter seeks to illuminate the ways candidates define these cohorts. I will show that candidates choose targets depending on their size and characteristics and on the total votes needed for election. Strategies also depend on the cost of campaigning as candidates move away from their core supporters, on the existence of local leaders seeking patronage, on the spatial concentration of candidates' earlier political careers, and on the existence of concurrent elections for other offices.

---

1. This was ACM's response when asked how he managed, under very difficult circumstances, to elect an unknown candidate as his successor (C. Souza 1997, 127).

The chapter proceeds in four sections. The first considers the ways candidates choose target groups of potential voters. The second assesses the cost of communicating with these voters. The third presents and tests an empirical model of campaign strategy.[2] This model uses amendments to the national budget as a measure of candidates' strategic intentions. The final section models voting results in the 1990 congressional election to assess the ultimate electoral payoff of campaign activities.

I.   How Candidates Calculate the Costs and Benefits of Appeals to Voters

Every candidate knows roughly how many votes guaranteed a seat in the congressional delegation of the candidate's state in the previous election. This benchmark depends on expected turnout and on the number of votes taken by the most popular candidates in the candidate's party.[3] Given a vote target, candidates imagine a variety of ways to construct winning coalitions. Their strategic calculations center on the costs and benefits of appeals to any potential group. In this section I examine some principles affecting candidate calculations under Brazil's electoral rules. These principles operate nationwide—that is, without reference to differing subnational contexts. I then consider aspects of Brazilian politics that vary across states, such as the strength of state-level politicians.

Voters as Members of Politicized Groups

A rational candidate seeks to expend the least resources for the most support. The ideal target is a self-conscious member of a large group carrying an already-politicized identification or grievance. Japanese-Brazilians, for example, always understand their ethnicity, just as evangelical Protestants know they are not Catholics. Evangelicals, however, are more likely than Japanese-Brazilians to see themselves as aggrieved; hence, the evangelical vote is more unified. In both cases, outsiders see the cleavage less intensely; candidates can thus win the evangelical vote without losing all Catholics.

At the other extreme, in terms of the permanence and politicization of identifications, lie occupational groups. For industrial workers, class consciousness depends on the nature of the production process, wages, and labor

---

2. See appendix B for a discussion of data sources.

3. The votes of leading candidates may far outweigh laggards, but since the number of candidates elected is directly proportional to the party's cumulative share of all votes cast, popular candidates make possible the election of those with far fewer votes.

organization. Workers in small factories, especially in the informal sector, tend to be younger, less skilled, more recently arrived in the city, and more deferential toward owners. Such workers support candidates offering particularistic benefits over candidates promising social reform.[4]

Community identification, especially in small communities, falls closer to the automatic side. Local politicians try to strengthen community identification, because their own influence depends on delivering voters to candidates. The centrality of government jobs facilitates voter mobilization in small communities, and the restriction of civil service protection to low-level positions politicizes public sector posts. Because elections for local executive posts and legislatures occur at different times, local officials know they will be on the job both before and after legislative elections, so they are motivated to make deals with legislative candidates.

The Difficulty of Securing Benefits for the Group

Deputies seek support for their campaign promises in the legislature. Legislators opt for geographically separable goods, for pork-barrel programs, when the demand for public goods is strong, when it is relatively stable and district-specific, and when the decisional system is fragmented rather than integrated (Lowi 1964; Salisbury and Heinz 1970). Brazil is characterized by the existence of powerful states acting in their own interests, selection of congressional candidates at the state level, municipalities independently electing local governments, weak national party leadership, and separation of powers between the president and the federal legislature. In addition, enormous regional inequalities leave some municipalities so poor that government employment and subsidies are crucial sources of income. Thus, Brazilian politics favors the provision of local, geographically separable benefits.

The Costs and Benefits of Barriers to Entry

Deputies seek to insulate voter cohorts from the incursions of competitors, because the deputies know that barriers to entry, by eliminating competition, reduce campaign costs.[5] The difficulty of erecting barriers depends on the nature

---

4. Paulo Maluf, a conservative populist politician, could not carry the state of São Paulo in the 1989 presidential election, but he won the 1992 mayoral contest in São Paulo precisely with the votes of such workers.

5. In an excellent analysis of patronage, George Avelino Filho (1994, 229) makes the same point: "Monopoly permits party cadres to make themselves obligatory intermediaries in any transaction with government." See also Bezerra 1999.

of the group to be shielded. Wage hikes, for example, require broad legislative coalitions, so it is difficult for anyone to claim exclusive credit. Barriers against ethnic outsiders, by contrast, are essentially automatic but are more costly to erect against insiders such as other ethnics.

Is it hard to erect barriers around particular localities? A simple "You're not from around here" shields a small, highly integrated community. Violence, in the form of disruption of campaign rallies or physical threats, is routine in rural areas. More diverse communities develop factional competition, with each side relying on strongly partisan supporters. In complex urban areas, no single faction or leader controls a significant portion of the electorate, and the police are not beholden to individual politicians. Many candidates seek votes, and barriers to outsiders from any party are hard to maintain.

Suppose a broker controls access to a group of voters. This control stems from some combination of coercion and prior delivery of employment or services. Deputies seeking brokers' votes offer cash or a slice of the benefit, such as a road-building contract. If the broker successfully erects rigid barriers against the entry of other brokers, candidates know they will pay more for the broker's votes than the sum of the prices they would pay for each vote individually. If, by contrast, the broker cannot protect his turf, candidates pay a lower total price for these votes than their individual prices. Whatever the price and form of payment, brokers' fees require candidates to secure separable resources.

II. The Cost of Communicating with Potential Voters

Brazilian campaigning is a direct, grassroots activity.[6] Candidates visit small communities, holding meetings and rallies. Is it rational to campaign where one's message reaches few voters? It certainly can be. First, the more concentrated the target group, even if small in number, the lower the cost of constructing a coalition that can guarantee those votes. Second, electoral coalitions that cover small areas are likely to be locational—that is, based purely on community identification. While in theory locational and nonlocational criteria might match perfectly (all southerners are black, all northerners are white), few such cases exist in Brazil. Thus, the physical distance between a candidate and

---

6. Media access remains central to campaigning even though candidates cannot buy radio or TV time. Because radio and newspapers in Brazil are generally quite partisan, media connections provide an effective barrier to competition as well as a means of communicating with voters. Many broadcasters, popular as a result of call-in shows, have become candidates in recent years.

the last voter, the voter whose support assures victory, is nearly always small-est for locational coalitions.[7]

Candidates' career trajectories constrain their campaign strategies and vote patterns. "Local" candidates—former mayors or city council members—should always be plentiful.[8] Except for those whose careers are rooted in large metropolitan areas, local candidates naturally develop concentrated distribu-tions, because their name recognition decreases with the distance from their lo-cal job. What happens when candidates appear who have backgrounds in state bureaucracy or who have no political history? This is not a simple question, be-cause at any given election the mix of careers among candidates respond to two sets of factors. One set (which may be called endogenous) stems from the con-text of the election itself, in the sense that new candidacies respond to the initial distribution of incumbent candidates. For example, where transportation costs are high, where statewide name recognition is low, where concentrations of workers or ethnics are weak, and where voters prefer candidates with mu-nicipal political experience, only local types will offer themselves. But the career mixes of candidates also depend on a second set of factors, exogenous in the sense that new candidacies reflect the opportunities and rewards of leg-islative activity. People with different backgrounds become candidates because they seek the personal rewards legislative activity offers.[9]

My argument is simple: in campaigning, what you did affects what you do. For many local candidates, a run for the federal legislature is their first statewide political activity. Because locals begin with a single peak of name recognition, a concentrated campaign is the obvious choice. But suppose the candidate once headed a government department that distributed roads or schools.[10] A bureau-crat considering a political career surely would locate projects with a view to their political advantage, and such candidates would become well known in the

---

7. The exceptions include winning electoral coalitions based on class voting in the cities of Rio de Janeiro and São Paulo.

8. This phenomenon may begin to change, since mayors can now seek immediate reelec-tion. Federal deputy, however, is not necessarily a step up: in 1992 about one-fifth of all federal deputies went the other way, running for mayor. Local officeholders are abundant as candidates ex-cept in frontier states, which develop so fast that local politics tends to be extremely weak. Fron-tier municipalities depend on state and federal largesse, and politicians often "parachute" in to pick up votes.

9. The typology that follows is incomplete in the sense that candidates selected by disci-plined parties like the PT may represent a key cohort of voters. Thus the PT runs "labor" candidates typically based on concentrated-shared votes.

10. Former bureaucrats running for deputy also reflect the influence of state governors, who always put persons of confidence in key bureaucratic posts. Hence, as Celina Souza has pointed out (personal communication), gubernatorial power influences the shape of bailiwicks.

communities benefiting from their largesse. Such candidates' voting support should therefore be scattered rather than concentrated. Whether they will dominate or share municipalities depends on the target municipalities and on the programs these bureaucrats directed. In rural communities, domination can result, either because a single program affects many people intensely or because the program may be designed to buy the support of influential elites rather than individual voters.[11] Urban communities absorb multiple programs—often directed by competing politicians—and voters are less easily controlled. Finally, suppose the candidate's career is in business. Businesspeople may begin with some central recognition peak around the location of their business, but such peaks are seldom as large as those of local politicians. Business types' advantage, of course, is money. Money buys voters with T-shirts, pressure cookers (bottom half before the election, top half after), and political jobs. Money buys the political bosses who control voters, and money greases the mutual support double-ups (*dobradinhas*) between state assembly and federal Chamber candidates. For business types, then, scattered support results: the strategic business candidate buys support wherever available.

At this point, I will distinguish between challengers and incumbents. Suppose a local politician challenges the incumbent in a concentrated-dominant bailiwick. Superficially, the challenge resembles a contest over an occupied single-member seat in the U.S. House, but the election is actually more difficult. Local bailiwicks are usually sparsely populated. If the challenger picks up only 51 percent of the incumbent's vote, the confrontation typically leads to mutual defeat. Since pork matters more than national policy, replacing a deputy who has delivered a healthy share serves the interest of neither local bosses nor individual voters. Overall, then, local-versus-local contests are so difficult that they should rarely occur.[12] Unless the incumbent neglects the district or angers the local boss, local challengers should await a retirement.

What should be expected from local incumbents? Given the infrequency of direct challenges within their bailiwicks, locals mainly fear a drop in the ag-

---

11. A road, for example, may be intended to enrich a particular contractor or big farmer.

12. In the 1990 election, the governor of São Paulo, Orestes Quércia, supported a challenge to a deputy who had previously been a member of Quércia's PMDB but had defected to the PSDB. Quércia's well-financed challenger won, but so did his target. For a broader test, consider the 1990 election in Paraná. Of the state's thirty congressional seats, nonincumbents won twenty-four, of which twelve won with concentrated, local bailiwicks. Six of the twelve constructed bailiwicks where none had previously existed. Four essentially assumed the districts of incumbents who did not seek reelection. Only two took over the bailiwicks of incumbents who did compete. In one case the challenger constructed a much bigger bailiwick; in the other the challenger benefited from the state's swing to the right, defeating two incumbents who had shared the same area.

gregate party vote. Were that vote to decline sufficiently, the same postelection rank might no longer guarantee a seat. Thus, local incumbents have to fish for new voters either in the bailiwicks of party colleagues or in the bailiwicks of incumbents from other parties. Party identification in Brazil is weak, so deputies fairly easily attract supporters of other parties. Since proportional representation rewards higher party totals with additional seats, party leaders discourage poaching in the bailiwicks of allies in one's own party. In sum, Brazilian candidates should forage for votes in unfriendly territory. And since shared municipalities are more vulnerable than dominated municipalities, domination as well as concentration should decrease for local candidates.

Changes in spatial concentration also occur among nonlocal candidates. The core constituencies of candidates relying on scattered distributions—evangelicals, broadcasters, and state bureaucrats—are relatively stable in size, so such candidates need new followers. Since some of the pork these deputies deliver to their core supporters benefits others in the same municipalities, and since deputies save resources by remaining near their core support, their spatial concentration should increase.

Businessmen buy their initial votes with payoffs to local bosses, but once in the legislature such leaders are likely to seek more popular backing that will fill in weak municipalities between areas of strength. Concentration among successful business candidates rises. Greater concentration, however, may not produce greater electoral success. Business candidates' electoral support is more fickle than the support enjoyed by local types. Better offers sway bosses loyal only to the highest bidder. Thus, businessmen face contradictory incentives. While opportunities are clearly better for candidates unconstrained by local careers, businessmen can lose support as quickly as they gain it. It should be expected, therefore, that business will supply many new candidates, but business incumbents will be more vulnerable to electoral defeat than candidates with other career trajectories.

III.   Testing the Strategic Model in the 1990 Election

How is it possible to construct an empirical test of the broad outlines of my argument?[13] Because actual electoral results reflect the interacting strategies of dozens or even hundreds of candidates, a dependent variable is needed that

---

13. Given the considerable continuity between the last legislative elections of the dictatorship and those of the New Republic, there are no campaigns without incumbents. In addition, the availability of results for only four elections leaves open the stability of the system.

measures each candidate's campaign effort. I begin, therefore, with a model of campaign strategy that uses budgetary amendments as proxies for the overall campaign activities of candidates in particular municipalities in the period leading up to the 1990 election.

Deputies submit budgetary amendments to retain old followers and attract new ones. During the dictatorship, the Congress could not modify the national budget, but once deputies regained that right, after the adoption of the Constitution of 1988, deputies learned quickly. Between 1989 and 1992, the annual number of budgetary amendments climbed from 8,000 to 72,000, with more than 90 percent targeting specific municipalities.

The model assesses, for each municipality, the chance that a deputy running for reelection will submit a budgetary amendment.[14] Concretely, the probability that a deputy running for reelection in 1990 offered an amendment (in 1989 or 1990) targeting municipality X is a function of six factors: (1) the distance of X from the center of the deputy's 1986 vote, (2) the dominance and concentration of the deputy's 1986 vote, (3) the vulnerability of municipality X to candidate invasion, (4) the socioeconomic and demographic similarity of X to the deputy's core constituency, (5) the deputy's electoral insecurity, and (6) the deputy's career trajectory.

Distance from 1986 Vote Center

I measure the 1986 vote center of each incumbent deputy in two ways.[15] Municipal center, C_m, is based on municipal domination, the percentage of each municipality's total vote received by deputy i. Personal center, C_p, is based on personal share, the percentage of deputy i's statewide total received in each municipality. I then calculate the distance from C_m and C_p to every municipality in the state. As municipalities become more distant, name recognition declines and the cost of campaigning increases; distant municipalities are less likely to

---

14. Budgetary amendments are obviously not the only tactic deputies utilize. They visit numerous municipalities, holding rallies and offering support to candidates for other offices. They nominate loyalists to bureaucratic jobs and offer voters material inducements in exchange for their support. Budget amendments are thus a proxy for a range of campaign activities. For this reason, my analysis focuses on amendments offered rather than amendments approved by the budget committee. The Budget Committee's actions represent a legislative decision process, a process treated in chapter 8.

15. The center is the centroid of a plane surface in which a municipality's votes are assumed to be cast at its center. Note that C_m and C_p are not necessarily at the actual physical center of any particular municipality. The socioeconomic centers in the social match section, however, are indeed individual municipalities.

be targets for deputy *i*. At the same time, deputies with personal vote centers in municipalities where they are not also dominant (typically in big cities) are likely to make amendments further from their personal centers, because they share the central municipality with so many other candidates that credit claiming is hopeless.[16]

Dominance and Concentration

Earlier, I defined dominance and concentration as characteristics of individual deputies measured at the level of the state as whole. Dominance, however, is also meaningful at the municipal level. A deputy could dominate minor municipalities, for example, but share large municipalities with others. Only municipal-level dominance should affect amending.[17] The higher the level of dominance in a given municipality, the more the deputy can claim credit for pork-barrel efforts, and, therefore, the more budgetary amendments the deputy will offer. When dominance reaches very high levels, the deputy has a "safe seat" (as in the old one-party American South); hence, amendments should decline.

What should be the consequences of concentration? Candidates with concentrated 1986 voting support should make more amendments because such candidates are vulnerable to the incursions of candidates with bureaucratic or business backgrounds. Concentrated candidates move out from their original bases in roughly concentric circles. These candidates must be less selective than those with scattered votes, because concentrated candidates choose targets not just on the criterion of vulnerability but also on the criterion of nearness to the core. As a result, concentrated candidates "overamend."

Municipal Vulnerability

If a municipality is dominated by a strong incumbent seeking reelection, challengers have little incentive to invade. But conditions change. Municipalities become penetrable. A dominant deputy retires, leaving an electoral void. An influx of migrants signals an electorate free from control by old leaders and old loyalties. Municipal fragmentation, either in the sense that many candidates

---

16. For a treatment of the effect of voter distance from candidates' home media markets, see Bowler, Donovan, and Snipp 1992.

17. If state-level dominance has any effect at the level of the individual municipality, it must be true that deputies whose support comes mostly from municipalities they dominate are likely to make more amendments even in municipalities they only share—that is, dominant deputies' pork-barrel habits make them behave irrationally.

from a single party share votes or in the sense that candidates from many parties enjoy electoral success, encourages invasion.[18]

Social Match

If incumbents regard certain occupational or ethnic groups as key supporters, these legislators should target new municipalities where similar groups reside. Deputies relying on working-class votes should seek industrial municipalities. Deputies appealing to civil servants should carry that appeal to localities where government is large. Thus, deputies pursue new targets similar in socioeconomic composition to their old bailiwicks. I begin by defining, on the basis of personal vote share and municipal dominance, each deputy's core municipality.[19] Then I calculate the difference between every other municipality and the core municipality on three socioeconomic indicators: size of electorate, per capita income, and percentage of workforce employed by government. The first two indicators reflect the possibility of class-based vote seeking, while the third represents the well-organized interest of government employees. Given that appeals to social class are generally weak in Brazil, government employees are the most likely target. For each indicator, it is expected that municipalities more like the deputy's core municipality should receive more amendments.[20]

Electoral Insecurity

Individual votes largely determine deputies' electoral fortunes. Those whose 1986 rank was low, who barely escaped elimination, ought to work harder in the next election. Their overall number of amendments should increase.

Career Trajectory

Because politicians with local backgrounds are more likely than politicians with bureaucratic or business backgrounds to maintain close ties with con-

---

18. *Interparty fragmentation* is defined as 1 minus the sum of the square of each party's share of the total vote. *Intraparty fragmentation* is defined equivalently at the level of the individual candidate—i.e., 1 minus the sum of the squares of each candidate's share of the party total.

19. If a deputy had a single municipality with a personal share clearly above any other, I selected that municipality as the core. If the deputy's personal shares in two municipalities were within a few percentage points, I chose the municipality with a higher municipal share as the core.

20. The socioeconomic indicators come from the 1980 census, except for the size of the voting population, which is drawn from the 1989 electoral rolls.

stituents, local candidates should amend more. Locals should also concentrate their campaigns—including their budgetary amendments—closer to home. Bureaucratic and business candidates scatter campaign activities, buying support where they once initiated projects and where they identify vulnerable municipalities. Candidates from families with long traditions in politics ought to be more pork oriented, making more amendments.[21]

Pooling and Estimation

Estimation began with observations at the level of individual deputies—that is, all deputies who served in 1986 and ran for reelection in 1990. I then pooled the deputies by state, and in two cases—six small northeastern states and three southern states—I pooled deputies in groups of states. This multistate pooling, which increased the number of observations substantially, combines states similar in size, socioeconomic conditions, and political traditions.[22]

Given that the number of amendments in each municipality cannot be less than zero, and given that most deputies make only a few amendments in any particular municipality, ordinary least-squares estimation is inappropriate. I experimented with an "event-count" Poisson model, but the Poisson results revealed some statistical irregularities, so I ultimately collapsed the amendment data into a dichotomous variable, amendments or no amendments, and implemented a logistic regression.[23] Table 4 presents simplified results for six states or state groups: Bahia, the six small northeastern states, Minas Gerais, Rio de Janeiro, São Paulo, and the three southern states.

---

21. Deputies have political family if a relative of the same or older generation was or had been a mayor, state or federal deputy, federal senator, governor, or president. For biographical data, see Brazil 1989; Brazil, Câmara dos Deputados 1981, 1983, 1991; and Istoé 1991. Interviews with journalists supplemented official sources.

22. The six northeastern states included Alagoas, Paraíba, Pernambuco, Piauí, Rio Grande do Norte, and Sergipe. The three southern states included Paraná, Rio Grande do Sul, and Santa Catarina.

23. In certain states or state groups, the diagnostics for both Poisson and negative binomial models showed overdispersion; for others the Poisson worked well. Since the real issue is whether a candidate targeted municipality x, not how many amendments were made in x, the logistic form is perfectly suitable. Substantively, the results are a bit closer to the model's predictions with the original Poisson, but both forms are very close. The full results, including coefficients and standard errors, are available on request. I preferred the amendment count to the actual money appropriated because the latter has an enormously higher "noise" level. The amount appropriated and the amount eventually spent often bear little relation to each other.

TABLE 4. **Will Deputy Submit Budgetary Amendment for Municipality?**

Municipal and Individial Characteristics	Prediction	Signs of Logit Estimation Coefficients					
		Bahia	Northeast	Minas Gerais	Rio de Janeiro	São Paulo	South
Distance from municipal center	–		–	–			+
Municipal distance squared	+		+	+	+	+	–
Distance from personal center	+		+		–	–	–
Personal distance squared	–		–		+		+
Municipal dominance	+	+	+	+	+	+	+
Municipal dominance squared	–	–	–	–	–	–	–
Concentration	+	+	+			–	
Percent of vote to retired deputies	+	+		+	–		
Percent migrants	+	+	+	+			+
Match to core: Income distribution	?		+	–			–
Match to core: Government employees	–	–	–				
Match to core: Population	?	+			–	–	
Interparty fragmentation	+	+	+	–	+	–	+
Intraparty fragmentation	+		+	+			
Rank in party list in 1986	+	+	+	+		+	+
Local career	+	–			+	+	+
Local career × Municipal distance	–	+	–	+		+	–
Local career × Personal distance	–	–	+	–	+		+
Political family	+		–		+		–
$N =$		6,666	3,841	9,106	1,536	7,410	6,841

Note:

+ means a positive coefficient, significant at the .10 level.

– means a negative coefficient, significant at the .10 level.

All likelihood ratios are significant at the .0001 level.

Interpretation

The empirical results support the overall theory well.[24] In each state or state group, the model achieved a high level of statistical significance. In terms of the theory's specific elements, I will first consider the arguments confirmed in all or nearly all of the six settings, then the hypotheses that failed to receive consistent support.

In all locations, municipal dominance strongly stimulated amendment making. The higher the percentage of a municipality's votes a deputy won in 1986, the more likely that deputy pursued more support in the same place in 1990. The negative slope on the squared term means that deputies at some point regarded a municipality as locked up, meriting no additional effort. In effect, diminishing returns set in, but the actual inflection points (the levels of dominance beyond which deputies lose interest) were beyond nearly all the cases.

The theory argued that vulnerable municipalities—those with high proportions of migrants or with high levels of party fragmentation—would be campaign targets. Municipalities with numerous migrants attracted deputies everywhere except in the states of Rio de Janeiro and São Paulo (where the sign was correct). Rio's deviance and the weakness of São Paulo probably stem from the high proportion of migrants in the cities of Rio and São Paulo themselves. Since so many deputies receive votes in these cities, even a high proportion of migrants cannot make them appealing as amending targets. Deputies who get votes in these megacities should still make campaign efforts, but they might concentrate on holding rallies, mobilizing grassroots support, and placing followers in bureaucratic jobs.

High levels of party fragmentation, both interparty and intraparty, everywhere increase the chances that candidates will target a given municipality. In two states, Minas Gerais and São Paulo, only fragmentation inside individual parties increased candidates' amending activity. In these two states the PMDB had attained a high level of dominance in 1986, the previous election. In 1990 the PMDB would inevitably slip, so survival meant chasing party compatriots' voters.

Deputies who finished low on their parties' 1986 postelection lists certainly had reason to feel vulnerable. Low-ranking deputies (low ranks receive more positive scores) made significantly more amendments than their high-ranking

---

24. Because this is an exploratory study—and to minimize references to insignificant coefficients with phrases such as "signs in the right direction"—I have adopted a .10 level of significance. However, more than 80 percent of the significant coefficients also reach the .05 level.

colleagues in every state except Rio de Janeiro. In Rio the relationship was positive but well below statistical significance. Most likely, the weakness of the relationship between vulnerability and amending in Rio stems from the demographic importance of the capital combined with its unattractiveness as an amendment target.

At first glance, the distance hypotheses seem only weakly supported. Closer inspection, however, reveals that amending behavior does reflect the distance of municipalities from deputies' core support in nearly all cases. Recall the original argument: "amend less with distance from municipal center." In Minas Gerais and the six northeastern states, deputies did in fact reduce their amending as they moved farther from their municipal center.[25] In Rio, São Paulo, and the three southern states, deputies decreased their campaigning as a function of each municipality's distance from the core of their personal support rather than the core of their municipal domination.[26] Why the variation? In Minas and the Northeast the average level of municipal domination is much higher than elsewhere. *Mineiro* and *nordestino* deputies get substantial shares of their personal totals in places where they dominate. These localities remain crucial, and the deputies respond by staying close to home. In Rio, São Paulo, and the South, the average level of domination (the deputy's percentage of the municipality's total votes) is less than half the level attained by *mineiro* and *nordestino* deputies. With low levels of domination, credit claiming is more difficult, so the center of municipal domination should not be the campaign reference point. Instead, deputies focus their campaigns where they receive the largest share of their personal total.

Only in Bahia are budgetary amendments unrelated to the distance of municipalities from the core support of candidates. Why is Bahia exceptional? Chapter 4 elaborates this theme at more length, but I will briefly consider Bahia's political context. Governor Antônio Carlos Magalhães (popularly known as ACM) was powerful enough to command candidates to campaign in particular municipalities.[27] ACM's machine was built on his ties to the old military regime, ties that brought Bahia significant federal largesse. ACM and his allies in the state bureaucracy reaped the political profits, and ACM's lieutenants launched political careers as they inaugurated public works around the state.

---

25. The absence of the predicted sign on the quadratic term simply means that amending behavior showed no diminishing returns.

26. In both Rio and the South, the negative coefficient on the "distance from personal center" variable dominates the coefficient of the "distance from municipal center" variable.

27. ACM's power was most evident in his own party. In other parties he also had a number of allies whose campaigns he influenced, but overall, his leadership polarized Bahia's parties.

Deputies with state-level bureaucratic backgrounds continue to dominate Bahia's congressional delegation. Only one of every eight *baiano* deputies— second lowest of any state—has a career built on local politics, and purely local deputies are weak. Nonlocal Bahian deputies tend to have scattered-dominant vote distributions, so these legislators' amendments are necessarily dispersed. In a sense, the concept of a vote center means little to such deputies; they deal with local bosses wherever one is available.

What about the variables measuring the social match of each municipality to the core constituencies of candidates? If candidates appeal to constituencies resembling those where they have done well, amendments ought to decrease as social distance increases. Government employees are a central constituency for many deputies, and these deputies appear to seek municipalities with numerous civil servants: three states or state groups had significant results in the expected direction; only São Paulo had the wrong sign.[28]

The other social match variables confirm the rarity of ideological appeals in Brazil. The variable measuring similarities in income distribution and population produced weak and inconsistent coefficients.[29] Moreover, if deputies seek targets on ideological bases, social matching ought to be strongest in the most developed regions of the country. Rio, São Paulo, and the South, however, yielded results no more consistent than the Northeast, Bahia, and Minas Gerais. This negative result, of course, is significant, because it shows that most deputies see the social and ideological characteristics of municipalities as minor factors in their decision to use pork-barrel politics as a campaign tool.

Consider now the hypotheses failing to receive consistent support. The original theory predicted, albeit hesitantly, that candidates with backgrounds in local politics would amend more than those with business or bureaucratic careers. The hypothesis received support only in Rio and São Paulo, and in Bahia and the South local candidates made fewer amendments. These differences are not simply functions of the domination of candidates with local origins. In fact, the South and Minas have the highest percentage of locals, while Bahia and Rio have the smallest. Local candidates' tactics, I suggest, depend on historical contexts. Bahia, for example, has few local candidates, and those who venture from their bailiwicks risk ACM's wrath. Rio has even fewer locals, but for demographic rather than historical reasons. Every municipality has a council and mayor. Rio has only sixty-five municipalities to serve as organizational spring-

---

28. São Paulo's deviance probably results from the extreme political unattractiveness of the highly competitive core city, where most bureaucrats live.

29. The failure of candidates to seek municipalities of similar size may have another cause: small communities yield few votes, while big cities are too competitive.

boards for its forty-six deputies, a ratio of 1.41 municipalities per deputy, while Bahia has 8.6 municipalities per deputy. Locals in Rio lack opportunities, but since they confront no coercive machine, they are free to compete with state-wide candidates by overamending. São Paulo has a substantial number of locals, but between 1987 and 1990 many defected from the dominant PMDB. These defectors had to contend with Governor Orestes Quércia's powerful PMDB machine. If a machine cannot limit defection, it is not much of a machine, so Quércia sent competitors into the defectors' bailiwicks. But the machine lacked the power to keep its opponents bottled up; for them, expansion to new areas was the optimal strategy.

Politics in the South and in the Northeast, by contrast, reflect distinct historical contexts. In the South, party labels are meaningful, no governor enjoys the hegemony of an ACM, spatial concentration is intense, and local candidates dominate. Candidates lacking a local base struggle to find support, so wise local politicians stay in their bailiwicks, making fewer amendments. The Northeast and Minas Gerais support intermediate levels of local candidates. Locals neither struggle, as they do in Bahia and Rio, nor dominate, as in the South.

Initially, I expected that local politicians would simply amend less as they moved farther from their bases. In Bahia, the South, and Minas Gerais, local deputies increase their amending activity as they move away from the municipalities where they are most dominant but decrease activity as they move away from the municipalities where they get most of their votes. Capital cities in these cases have little importance as fractions of total state electorates, so few personal centers are cities where the presence of many deputies discourages credit claiming. For most deputies, therefore, it makes sense to stay close to the places contributing most of their votes. In the Northeast and Rio, however, capital cities have much more weight in total state electorates, and more candidates have personal centers in exactly these capitals. But since these capitals are home to many deputies, they discourage credit claiming, and local candidates are forced to flee to pursue new voters.

Retirements (assessed by the percentage of the 1986 vote received by candidates not competing in 1990) stimulated more amendments only in Bahia. In the South amendments actually declined where retirements freed more voters. This finding is a surprise, because in my interviews southern deputies mentioned campaigning in municipalities they thought were vulnerable because of retirements. Perhaps the timing was off: when deputies offered these amendments in 1988 and 1989 (for the 1989 and 1990 budgets), they might not have known who planned to retire.

The original argument suggested that candidates with spatially concentrated support would overamend to compensate for their geographically restricted vote bases. Only in Bahia and the Northeast did the hypothesis prove correct. I suspect that the argument fails because concentration is often related to domination—that is, what really matters is local dominance rather than the spatial contiguity of votes. As a result, the domination variable (which supported the prediction in every case) simply overwhelms concentration. The case of Bahia reflects, once again, the power of the state's political machine. Because the machine discourages candidates from leaving their bases, they overamend to increase local dominance.

Why do deputies from political families fail to distinguish themselves? Political learning, I suspect, is very rapid. Whether or not they hail from political families, deputies quickly learn campaign tactics. Interestingly, members of northeastern political families made significantly fewer amendments than *nordestinos* without family ties. Such ties are much more important in the Northeast than anywhere else: about 30 percent of all deputies in these states have officeholding relatives, compared to fewer than 10 percent in the South. Political family in the Northeast often means old-style deal making, not populism; traditional *nordestino* politicians do less for their constituents—especially in terms of social assistance—and more for local bosses.

Recapitulation

Brazilian deputies' municipal-level campaign strategies respond strongly to local dominance, to the potential targets' vulnerability to invasion, to the legislators' own electoral weakness, and to their previous career patterns. But the absence of campaign efforts in communities sociologically similar to deputies' core constituencies (exemplified by the weakness of the social match variables) confirms the impression that few deputies seek votes along ideological lines. The absence of party programs and the weakness of party control over deputies renders such appeals, except for the Workers' Party, unproductive.

IV.   Does Strategic Behavior Pay Off Electorally?

Do vote-seeking deputies' tactics succeed? Table 5 estimates a model predicting the outcomes of candidates' strategies. This regression resembles the strategy model but has important additions. The outcomes model incorporates 1986 vote as a predictor of 1990 vote. I also added a measure of overall (state-level) dominance (while retaining the measure of municipal-level dominance). This

TABLE 5.   What Determines Electoral Success?

Municipal, Individual, and Electoral Characteristics	Bahia	Northeast	Minas Gerais	Rio de Janeiro	São Paulo	South
Vote in 1986	+	+	+	+	+	+
Amendments by deputy (logged)	+	+	+			+
Amendments × Municipal dominance	+	+	+	+	+	−
Amendment by other deputies	−	−	−		+	−
Distance from municipal center					−	
Distance from personal center						
State-level dominance in 1986		+		+		+
Municipal dominance in 1986	+	−	+	+	+	−
Municipal dominance squared	−	+	−			−
Concentration in 1986			+			
Interparty fragmentation in 1986			+			
Intraparty fragmentation in 1986			−			−
Match to core: Income distribution		+				
Match to core: Government employees	−					
Match to core: Population			−			−
Rank in party list in 1986	−	+	+		+	
Local career						
Allied parties gain from 1986	+	+	+	+	+	+
PFL–PDS candidate	+	+	+		+	+
PMDB or left candidate			+	+		
Political family			+	+		
Political family × Municipal dominance	−	−				
R^2	53%	57%	53%	53%	20%	56%
$N =$	8,040	6,629	13,740	1,536	16,530	8,803

Note:
+ means a positive coefficient, significant at the .05 level.
− means a negative coefficient, significant at the .05 level.
All F tests for the entire model are significant at the .05 level.

new variable should reveal whether overall dominance contributed to candidates' success. Each deputy's amendments, along with the amendments made by other deputies in the same municipality, are now explanatory variables. The model also includes variables measuring the gains made by candidates from allied parties. This variable helps illuminate partisan realignments.[30]

---

30. In the construction of this indicator, PFL and PDS votes measure right-wing gain; PMDB vote measures left-wing gain. The latter measure is clearly imperfect, but in many municipalities the PMDB was the only opposition to the Right. Each deputy was coded, on the basis of party affiliation, in terms of right or center-left orientation. Similar results are obtained by using 1978 and 1982 MDB-PMDB vote totals as a substitute for the 1986 PMDB vote.

The outcomes model works well, explaining more than 50 percent of the variance in candidates' 1990 vote everywhere except São Paulo.[31] The most powerful predictor was vote received in 1986. In most polities this result would be no surprise, but in Brazil it contradicts the conventional wisdom, which holds that deputies' unpopularity makes incumbency a disadvantage.

Campaigning Matters

In Bahia, the Northeast, Minas Gerais, and the South, amendments increased votes.[32] Amendments made a difference in Rio de Janeiro and São Paulo as well, but only for more dominant deputies—that is, amendments in these states became more important as municipal dominance increased. Municipalities in Rio and São Paulo are mostly competitive, with few dominant deputies. Where deputies share votes with many others (as in the state capitals), amendments are futile, but as dominance increases they make more sense.

Amendments by other deputies should lower a candidate's vote, because these amendments mean that opponents have also targeted the same municipality. Except in Rio and São Paulo—where other deputies' amendments had no impact—this is just what happened. The hypothesis failed in Rio and São Paulo for the reason mentioned earlier—the absence of dominated municipalities.[33]

Dominant deputies gained more votes than those with shared distributions, but concentration helped only in Minas Gerais.[34] In an election with more than 50 percent turnover of incumbents, and with substantial losses by center and center-left parties, this result has great importance. Dominance protects

---

31. The poor performance of the model in São Paulo (although it easily attains overall statistical significance), may result from the state's high level of ideological politics, a function of the strength of leftist parties like the PT, which encourages voters to choose the party label instead of individual candidates.

32. The model incorporates logged amendments to reduce the effect of each "additional" amendment. In the South, the negative coefficient on the term representing the interaction between amendments and dominance means that amendments are counterproductive above a certain level of dominance. About 5 percent of southern deputies fall above this inflection point. Such deputies may be engaged in a hopeless struggle to maintain their bases in a region where dominance is increasingly rare.

33. The strategy model demonstrates that deputies make fewer amendments as the distance from their vote centers increases. The outcomes model shows that their 1990 votes were generally unrelated to the distance from the core. However, the model includes the 1986 vote, so the coefficient should only be significant if there is an additional, unexpected concentration of votes. This phenomenon occurs in two cases, Minas and São Paulo, where deputies with more concentrated vote patterns did better in 1990 than in 1986. I cannot currently explain this result.

34. The dominance variable masks any possible effects contributed by the two fragmentation measures. Fragmentation is obviously lower when deputies dominate municipalities.

deputies from partisan swings. The incumbents who lost seats in 1990 mostly shared constituencies. Single-member municipalities, whether contiguous or scattered, are safer. In an environment of weak parties and pork-barrel politics, deal making with local politicos—the classic scattered-dominant pattern— makes sense.

The strategy model demonstrated that deputies rarely seek campaign targets that are similar in a socioeconomic sense to their core municipalities. Not surprisingly, deputies are equally unlikely to gain or lose votes on this basis. Although in big cities deputies make ideological or group appeals, they do not seek or receive support in distant campaign targets on this basis. Given the high cost of poaching on the turf of fellow party members, candidates increase support by appealing to new groups in their base areas, not by pursuing similar but distant groups. Consequently, although changes in the legislature's overall ideological composition may result from electoral realignments, such realignments are not the product of individual campaign appeals.

Partisan shifts play an important role in individual deputies' fortunes. In every state, overall gains by parties nearby on the political spectrum helped candidates. Since this election represented a defeat for the PMDB after its overwhelming success in 1986, right-wing candidates (measured by "PFL-PDS candidate") gained, while PMDB and leftist candidates got a boost only in the Northeast and in Minas Gerais.

Deputies' career paths, at least as measured by previous occupations or by membership in political families, had no consistent effect on electoral outcomes. In the Northeast and Minas Gerais—areas where substantial percentages of deputies come from political families—these deputies had more success. But in Bahia, where political families are most common, such deputies received no help. In addition, local candidates did no better in any states. The 1990 election represented an influx of big money into congressional campaigning. If this trend continues, local candidates, as these results demonstrate, are in serious trouble.

Recapitulation

Congressional deputies' strategies matter. Deputies profit by making their own amendments; they suffer when other deputies target the same municipalities. Deputies with dominant vote distributions are more successful in resisting partisan swings than are those with shared distributions.[35] But most deputies gain

---

35. Deputies can also switch parties to profit from partisan surges.

little from concentrating their vote distributions or from making group or ideological appeals, and career patterns have no broad effect on electoral fortunes.

Conclusion

Most discussions of Brazilian politics stress its traditional, clientelistic roots. The theory developed here, by contrast, is grounded in rational politicians' strategic behavior.[36] Faced with an electoral system whose chief attributes include open-list proportional representation, large multimember districts, candidate selection at the level of politically active subnational units, and the possibility of immediate reelection, most deputies pay little attention to ideological appeals. Instead, deputies seek secure bailiwicks, search for vulnerable municipalities, and strive to overcome their own electoral weakness through wheeling and dealing. Strategic candidates do not behave identically, because their own political backgrounds vary and because Brazilian states' differing demographic and economic contexts reward some tactics and penalize others.

What is the significance of these results? Brazil's electoral system motivates deputies to seek pork. In conjunction with the state-centered quality of Brazilian politics, it is no surprise that the pursuit of pork is endemic in this political environment. Deputies in Brazil's South and in more industrialized states face more competition from candidates of other parties but also have more concentrated vote distributions. Higher levels of education and wealth increase voter interest and involvement in politics, but that interest magnifies incentives for deputies to focus on pork. At the same time, demands for local benefits may contribute to the elevated turnover rates and low seniority levels of congressional delegations from the South, factors that shift the Congress's ideological center to the right.

This chapter has focused on candidate strategy in a single election. How are patterns of competition evolving over time? Is spatial concentration increasing as voters look to pork as the only response they can expect from their representatives? Is domination increasing as deputies learn that it can insulate them from partisan swings, or is it decreasing as levels of political awareness grow? The next chapter turns to these questions.

---

36. Fabiano Guilherme M. Santos (1995) analyzes the 1959–63 legislature in a somewhat parallel framework. Santos focuses on "concentrated transfers of resources"—i.e., laws (similar to pork-barrel amendments) awarding benefits to discrete local groups or interests while dispersing the costs of the proposal over a large population. Santos's assumptions about the electoral system are more abstract than mine, since he makes no specific assumptions about deputies' spatial vote distributions.

Chapter 3

The Evolution of Electoral Support, 1978–94

"He steals, but he gets things done."
(A description first used to describe Adhemar de Barros,
former populist governor of the state of São Paulo)

"One of these days Louisianans are going to get good government . . . and they ain't going to like it!"

Earl Long, 1950s

Brazilian states, as we have seen, play central parts in the drama of national politics. States vary greatly, however, in their ability to influence national politics. Any given state's influence depends in large part on its ability to convert economic strength into national power, a conversion that itself depends on the pattern of political competition within the state. By patterns of political competition, I refer to the tendency of a state to elect deputies via constituencies that are concentrated or scattered, dominant or shared. These patterns of competition—the overall mix of constituency types—are closely linked not just to state-level socioeconomic and demographic conditions but to national-level political developments.

Why are these informal congressional constituencies so important? Consider the power of state governors. Governors from states such as São Paulo are automatically players in national politics, but most governors' political influence depends on their ability to control their congressional delegations. In some states, the context of local and state politics facilitates the construction of a dominant and durable state machine, the kind of machine that enables a marginal governor to exercise national influence. In other states, governors simply cannot amass sufficient resources to affect the careers of lower-level politicians. Consider, too, the problem of corruption. Chapter 1 showed that deputies with certain kinds of vote distributions—especially the scattered-dominant type—

are more likely to be involved in corruption scandals. Voters find it easier to hold deputies with other kinds of voting bases accountable, thus reducing corruption. Last, consider the politicians who run for office. Challengers for legislative seats seek a space, a constituency, in an ongoing distribution of localized electoral support. Are voters free to cast ballots on the basis of candidates' positions on national issues, or are voters embedded in powerful patronage networks organized around the pursuit of local favors? Are constituencies so fragmented that newcomers can compete only by lavish spending, or can careers be built on local reputation? These conditions determine what kinds of citizens become politicians and constrain the choices available to politicians as they pursue their careers.

This chapter focuses on patterns of competition across states and over time. The analysis first investigates differences in concentration and domination between the states. It then asks how concentration and domination change over the course of four elections. In both cases, explanation relies on economic and demographic factors. The inquiry implies an examination of both states and individual deputies, but the ultimate goal is to understand the evolution of the state-level system.

Concentration and Domination across States

Is voting support in some states more spatially concentrated and more dominant than in others? Have spatial concentration and domination changed over the 1978–94 period? Most informed Brazilians regard northeastern bailiwicks as the country's strongest and believe that in recent years bailiwicks have tightened.[1] This conventional wisdom is both right and wrong. On the basis of the five elections between 1978 and 1994, it is clear that (1) northeastern deputies are in fact more likely to dominate the municipalities where they get votes; (2) the most concentrated vote distributions are found not in the Northeast but in the larger, more prosperous states of Paraná, Santa Catarina, Rio Grande do Sul, Minas Gerais, and São Paulo; and (3) concentration of support rose steadily after 1982 but by 1994 nearly leveled off.[2]

---

1. This conclusion was reached by the unscientific method of simply asking social scientists and journalists.

2. Spatial autocorrelation is measured with Moran's I, calculated for each deputy and for each election with an unweighted nearest-neighbor matrix of first-order contiguities. The Z-scores associated with the Moran's I statistic, which are comparable across states, constitute the actual in-

Explaining patterns of support at the state level is a more inductive process than modeling budgetary amendments, and since there are only eighteen cases, the data can be "eyeballed" for testable intuitions. Why are northeastern deputies less likely to concentrate support but more likely to dominate? States in the Northeast are smaller, so deputies easily campaign all over. Northeastern capitals (with their surrounding areas) comprise larger fractions of total state populations than do capitals in the South. Electoral victory in the Northeast more often requires votes in the capital city as a supplement to regional bailiwicks. Northeastern states have fewer municipalities, so deputies easily move around and make deals all over the state.[3] And finally, higher southern educational levels encourage greater political awareness, thus weakening the boss control that facilitates deals with dispersed local leaders. As boss control diminishes, interparty competition grows; while southern deputies may dominate within their own parties, they are rarely able to achieve overall municipal control.

Tables 6 and 7 present the results of models in which average domination and clustering per state are regressed on a series of explanatory variables.[4] Both models attain very high levels of statistical significance (although the high R-squareds result from the small n). Domination is higher where there are more municipalities, lower in states with more urban populations, and a bit higher in the Northeast.[5] The domination regression, in spite of its statistical success, is somewhat unsatisfactory. Because it relies more on the regional dummy, it leaves open the question of exactly which regional characteristics contribute to greater domination. Is it possible to replace the regional dummy with the particular northeastern characteristics affecting domination? Surprisingly, replacing the dummy with measures of socioeconomic conditions (such as per capita income and percentage of the population in agriculture) weakens rather than strengthens the results. The Northeast dummy, in other words, is not merely a proxy for poverty, because levels of domination do not increase in step with increasing poverty. Is there something special about the Northeast that produces more deputies with dominant distributions? Northeastern states are dependent

---

dicator. I am indebted to Art Getis of the National Center for Geographic Information and Analysis for advice on Moran's I. For a discussion of this and other spatial statistics, see Cliff et al. 1975.

3. Overall state-level concentration was regressed on the number of municipalities, the percentage of the population living in the capital city, and state per capita income.

4. To confirm that state-level domination and concentration are unrelated, each model includes the other as a regressor. Domination and concentration are, in fact, uncorrelated.

5. The positive relationship between domination and the number of municipalities probably reflects the importance of Minas Gerais, which has by far the most municipalities and a fairly high level of dominance.

TABLE 6. Explaining Domination at the Level of the State, 1978–94

Dependent Variable: Domination

Parameter	Estimate	T for HO: Parameter = 0	Pr < .05
Intercept	0.4894	9.90	*
Number of municipalities	0.0002	3.74	*
Northeast region	0.0307	1.52	
Percent urban	−.3838	−5.22	*

$R^2 = .807$ $F = 19.48$ $Pr < .0001$ $N = 18$

TABLE 7. Explaining Clustering at the Level of the State, 1978–94

Dependent Variable: Clustering

Parameter	Estimate	T for HO: Parameter = 0	Pr < .05
Intercept	−1.1587	−.44	
Percent in capital	−17.6006	−5.35	*
Percent urban	9.0824	1.52	
Number of municipalities	0.0083	2.77	*
Northeast region	−2.687	−3.44	*
Interparty fragmentation	0.0178	2.09	*

$R^2 = .931$ $F = 32.42$ $Pr < .0001$ $N = 18$

on federal pork. Federal deputies—especially those who build up seniority—play a major role in channeling that pork, and the political families help organize pork distribution. Perhaps over the years this resource has given northeastern deputies more control over their constituencies. To be in the minority when the majority controls all access to critical resources is to starve, hence opposition withers away.[6]

The model explains spatial concentration better than domination. Concentration is much lower when larger fractions of the population live in the metropolitan areas of capital cities, a bit higher when more people live in urban settings, substantially higher in states with more municipalities, lower in the Northeast, and higher when interparty fragmentation is greater. Some states deviate sharply (based on the regression residuals) from this pattern. Bahia, which is both northeastern and large, is much less concentrated than the model pre-

---

6. The states of the South and Southeast also depend on outside resources, but their funds tend to come from sources such as the National Bank for Social and Economic Development (BNDES), which uses more universalistic criteria in its allocations.

dicts. Bahia's low rate of concentration, as chapter 4 will demonstrate, results from the scarcity of locally based deputies and the coordinating skills of the state's boss, Antônio Carlos Magalhães, who instructs candidates where to campaign and who uses federal largesse to prevent the erection of barriers to entry by local bosses.[7]

The Evolution of Concentration and Domination

Do domination and concentration change over the 1978–94 period? While domination is declining almost everywhere, concentration fell at the start of this sequence of elections, from 1978 until 1982, but subsequently began to rise once again. The Brazilian electorate's increasing politicization, furthered by vote-seeking candidates' attempts to venture into new territories, probably caused the fall. The 1978–82 decline in concentration appears to be a result of increases in the number of candidates whose votes naturally scatter, especially broadcasters, evangelicals, and businessmen. By 1990 their numbers, and thus overall concentration, stabilized.

To understand the evolution of concentration and domination, I will compare two explanations: one based on the logic of competition, the other based on changes in the career trajectories of new entrants into congressional races. Do different types of deputies behave differently? The answer is found in tables 8 and 9, which offer models of domination and concentration at the level of individual deputies.[8]

What kinds of deputies maintain dominant distributions?[9] At the level of the individual deputy, domination and concentration are closely related; in other words, most deputies with dominant distributions concentrate their votes spatially as well.[10] Dominant politicians are more likely to have careers in both state and local politics and in state bureaucracies. They are less likely to have

---

7. Bahia is labeled deviant because it had the largest residual of any state.

8. The states represented by dummy variables in these two tables are all large states with many candidates, thus reducing impacts specific to a single candidate.

9. The models include a series of state dummy variables to adjust for overall state differences in domination and concentration and for differences in the number of deputies per state. The dummies are not discussed individually, however, because they have no causal effects—i.e., they are system names rather than variable names.

10. These individual-level results are consistent with the earlier finding that domination and concentration are unrelated at the state level. Few southern deputies have high levels of domination, but those with concentrated distributions are more dominant than their scattered colleagues. In the Northeast, many deputies are dominant, and dominant northeastern deputies tend to con-

TABLE 8.   Domination at the Level of the Individual Deputy, 1978–94

Dependent Variable: Domination

Parameter	Estimate	T for HO: Paramter = 0	Pr < .05
Intercept	20.6816	16.85	*
Concentration	0.0071	12.17	*
Local or state career	0.0351	4.60	*
Bureaucratic-state career	−.0232	−2.00	*
Local career only	0.0003	0.03	
State career only	0.0041	.39	
Bureaucratic career only	0.0309	4.15	*
Year (1978–90)	−.0102	−16.56	*
Political family	0.0126	1.34	
Age of deputy	−.0006	−1.99	*
Terms served in chamber	0.0030	1.10	
Party: PMDB	0.0568	7.35	*
Party: PFL	0.0766	6.87	*
Party: PDS	0.0540	6.02	*
Party: PDT	−.0089	−.66	
Northeast	0.0189	2.14	*
Interparty fragmentation	−.0004	−4.76	*
Rio Grande do Sul	−.0704	−3.77	*
Santa Catarina	−.0291	−1.61	
Paraná	−.0626	−5.11	*
São Paulo	−.0861	−4.54	*
Rio de Janeiro	−.0861	−4.33	*

$R^2 = .46$ F = 75.80   Pr < .0001 $N = 1,871$

business careers or to have careers limited to either state or local politics. Until 1990, dominant deputies had more seniority in the Chamber, but the 1993 budget scandal persuaded many of the old lions that it was time to retire. As a result, after the 1994 election, dominant politicians were a bit younger than their less powerful colleagues, and seniority no longer mattered. Dominant deputies are more likely to be members of the major national parties (PMDB, PFL, or PPB) than of any small party, but political families make no difference. Dominance is higher in the Northeast than in the South, Rio, or São Paulo, and dominance drops when the states are more fragmented. Dominance decreases sharply over the course of the five elections analyzed.

It is clear that differing factors explain concentration and domination. Politicians with purely bureaucratic careers or with state-level careers have

---

centrate their votes. If domination and concentration are plotted on the ordinate and on the abscissa, respectively, northeastern deputies have a higher intercept.

TABLE 9.   Concentration at the Level of the Individual Deputy, 1978–94

Dependent Variable: Concentration

Parameter	Estimate	T for HO: Parameter = 0	Pr < .05
Intercept	−237.72	−4.73	*
Domination	10.412	12.17	*
Local or state career	0.381	1.30	
Bureaucratic-state career	−.048	−0.11	
Local career only	0.443	1.06	
State career only	−1.115	−2.76	*
Bureaucratic career only	−1.208	−4.25	*
Year (1978–90)	0.129	5.13	*
Political family	0.020	0.06	
Age of deputy	−.006	−0.47	*
Terms served in chamber	−.011	−0.10	
Party: PMDB	−0.371	−1.24	
Party: PFL	−.993	−2.30	*
Party: PDS	−.753	−2.17	*
Party: PDT	0.841	1.62	
Northeast	−5.500	−17.53	*
Interparty fragmentation	−.030	−8.33	*
Rio Grande do Sul	6.844	9.78	*
Santa Catarina	6.119	9.03	*
Paraná	1.848	3.94	*
São Paulo	9.571	13.94	*
Rio de Janeiro	1.029	1.35	

$R^2 = .461$ F = 75.46   Pr < .0001   N = 1,871

much less concentrated votes than those with other career mixes. Thus, as politicians move away from local trajectories, they campaign more widely. This result is not tautological. State assembly and federal chamber districts are identical—that is, in both legislatures, whole states are districts. Furthermore, there are more state deputies than federal deputies. State deputies can easily run purely local campaigns, because they can win seats in even smaller bailiwicks than federal deputies. Former state deputies running for the federal chamber campaign more widely, so concentration falls.

Over the 1978–94 period, the typical deputy relied on a pattern of electoral support that was steadily more concentrated. By 1994, the trend toward concentration appears to have slowed in the states that were already quite concentrated. It continues, however, in the states that began with more scattered patterns.

Until 1994, political party affiliations had no effect on concentration. When the 1994 election is included, however, the picture changes: members of both the PFL and the PPR exhibit more scattered vote patterns. This result has important implications for future debates on the electoral system, particularly on the prospects for adopting a mixed system along German lines. By 1994, both region and party divide deputies on issues of redistricting, because incumbent northeastern conservatives will have the hardest time gaining reelection under a district system.

Why does interparty fragmentation—weakly associated at the state level with greater concentration—reduce concentration at the individual level? In theory, deputies in competitive regions may still collect their votes in contiguous municipalities—the concentrated-shared distribution—but such deputies are a minority. Consider a region with high interparty fragmentation but low intraparty fragmentation, a region where a single deputy dominates the party vote but faces opposition from other parties. Such deputies are vulnerable to the kind of party swings occurring in 1986 and 1990, when the PMDB first scored a huge gain and then suffered a massive defeat. Recognizing their vulnerability, concentrated-dominant deputies expand their search for votes. If successful, these efforts reduce concentration. At the state level, however, the South remains more competitive and more concentrated than other parts of the nation.

What do the individual findings reveal about changes in concentration? Individual concentration levels over 1978–90 show (like the analysis at the state level) a trend toward tighter informal districts. Since neither deputies' seniority nor their ages bears any relationship to vote concentration, it appears that the driving force behind the increases in concentration might be changes in the kinds of people who go into politics.

Thus I turn to the final piece of the evolution puzzle—that is, the occupational mix of new entrants. Consider first those candidates who have business backgrounds but lack any experience in state or local politics. Such "pure business" candidates constituted only 5.8 percent of seat winners in 1978, but that number rose to 15 percent by 1990, with a slight decline in 1994. Candidates whose political experience was limited to local politics declined steadily through 1990, falling from 9.3 percent in 1978 to 3.9 percent in 1990, then jumped sharply, to 10.7 percent in 1994. Deputies with backgrounds in any kind of bureaucracy climbed from 33.1 percent in 1978 to 44 percent in 1990, then fell almost by half in 1994. Deputies with experience in state politics fell until 1994: 40 percent in 1978, 35.7 percent in 1986, 32 percent in 1990, 40.6 percent in 1994.

If occupational background is the central determinant of campaign tactics, these changes, largely a reflection of the increased importance of money in campaigning, ought to lead to lower levels of both concentration and domination, because the ascendant career types are more likely to receive scattered and shared support. Domination has indeed fallen, and its decline is matched by gains in business and bureaucratic deputies in each individual region.[11] Concentration, by contrast, shows no trend, even though the same occupational types reducing domination tend to campaign in wider areas. Why the difference? Some new seat winners inherit old bailiwicks and stick with them. Others simply find it profitable to adapt to their state's modal pattern. And still others decide to begin their legislative careers by mounting a concentrated campaign, while anticipating that over time they will diversify. Overall, then, the logic of Brazil's electoral system yields to new entrants' vote-sharing tendencies but overcomes their propensity for vote scattering.

Conclusion

Chapter 2's models demonstrated that domination and concentration, the two central dimensions of vote distributions, influence Brazilian deputies' campaign strategies. This chapter asked why domination and concentration vary across states and individuals. Domination is higher in the Northeast. Because economic measures of poverty and underdevelopment fail to explain domination nearly as well as the simple regional dummy variable, the Northeast seems truly to be a unique area. Its uniqueness may result from two interacting traditions: the high level of families with political traditions and the prevalence of pork-barrel politics. Concentration, by contrast, proved to be lower in the Northeast, lower where large fractions of state populations live in the capital city, and higher where the number of municipalities is greater. In other words, demographic factors were more successful in explaining the spatial concentration of deputies' vote distributions.

To facilitate interpretation of these state-level findings, the analysis then moved to the level of the individual deputy. Dominant politicians stay in the legislature longer, more often begin their careers in state and local politics, and more frequently live in the Northeast. Politicians with concentrated vote patterns are more likely to have local backgrounds rather than careers in state politics, bureaucracy, or business.

Domination is falling everywhere, while concentration seems stable. At the same time, the occupational mix of new congressional contestants is also changing. There are more deputies with business and bureaucratic backgrounds

---

11. Domination should also decline as the number of candidates rise in each municipality.

but fewer local and state politicians. This changing occupational mix, itself a consequence of the rising importance of campaign money, contributes to the decline of electoral domination. Because concentrated electoral distributions are advantageous to deputies, new contestants gradually adopt veterans' campaign tactics.

Chapter 4

History Matters: The Interaction of Social Structure and Political Events

"The corrupt politician of the Northeast manipulates little expenditures, but the corrupt politician of the South is more institutional, manipulating laws and privileges."

Deputy Humberto Souto (*Folha de São Paulo*, November 15, 1993)

"There is only one law in American political science: sometimes it's this way, sometimes it's that way. Except in the South."

Graduate student lore in the 1960s

In the introduction I suggested that in Latin America rational choice models will need broadening before they can explain real political outcomes.[1] One promising direction is Douglass North's (1990, 94) conception of path dependence: "The consequence of small events and chance circumstances can determine solutions that, once they prevail, lead one to a particular path." Actors benefiting from earlier institutional change are likely to resist efforts at reform, and, as institutions become established, actors make commitments that generate sunk costs. A second direction follows historical institutionalists' emphasis on subnational politics. Richard Locke and Kathleen Thelen (1993, 6), for example, see "national political economies not as coherent systems but as rather incoherent composites of diverse sub-national patterns which co-exist (often uneasily) within the same national territory." Both extensions of rational choice methods resonate strongly in the Brazilian case. Contemporary politics exhibits an impressive continuity with the dictatorship's politicians and political practices. States and localities have long played central roles on the national political stage.

This chapter explores the relation between political competition and two sets of causal factors. The first set includes socioeconomic and demographic

---

1. For a good example of a marriage between rational choice and historical narrative, see Ferejohn 1991.

Fig. 13. Brazil: Three northeastern states and two southern states

variables such as measures of wealth, migratory flows, and economic conditions. The second set focuses on certain chance historical events that turned out to have lasting political consequences. The discussion centers on two sets of comparisons.[2] The first comparison includes Paraná and Santa Catarina, two states that are quite similar in economic conditions, at least relative to the whole range of Brazilian states. Over a long period of time, however, their internal pol-

---

2. These cases were selected for multiple reasons. Their politics seemed to vary much more than their economic levels. Local social scientists had conducted extensive research, so background materials and knowledgeable informants were available. In addition, I had begun investigating these states during research for my earlier book (Ames 1987), which contains chapters on Brazilian politics between 1947 and 1964. An excellent example of intensive analysis of elites in a single state is found in Hagopian 1996.

itics, especially the nature of competition for legislative posts, has remained quite distinct. The key appears to be demography: population movements in Paraná created traditions of substate loyalties and extremely localist political orientations that Santa Catarina never experienced. The second comparison includes Maranhão, Ceará, and Bahia, three poor states in the Northeast. Here, too, although their divergence is more recent, political styles differ greatly. Demographic differences, however, seem slight. Instead, chance political events turn out to be fundamental in establishing initial conditions that have influenced political competition over long periods of time.[3]

Paraná and Santa Catarina

At first glance, Paraná and Santa Catarina might be expected to exhibit similar styles of politics. Neighbors in Brazil's prosperous South, the two states are reasonably close on such economic and social indicators as per capita income, education, and urbanization. Observers often classify both, in fact, as part of the "other Brazil," the Brazil that works. Closer inspection, however, reveals significant differences between Paraná and Santa Catarina. Most striking is the enduring strength, in Santa Catarina, of traditional right-wing parties.[4] As figure 14 shows, ARENA and its successors, the PDS, PFL, and PTB, have been stronger in Santa Catarina in every election since 1978. Even discounting the huge gap in 1990 as an anomaly, the difference remains impressive, with PDS, PFL, and PTB deputies holding 45–50 percent of Santa Catarina's congressional delegation but only around 30 percent in Paraná. Partisan differences, however, tell only part of the story. With the exception of the 1986 election, Santa Catarina's deputies have individually been much more dominant. In their key municipalities they tend to get higher proportions of the total municipal vote. *Catarinense* deputies more often get their votes in geographically contiguous municipalities, and they rarely compete with each other for votes.

How can these radically different patterns of political competition be explained? Is Paraná's electorate simply more leftist? Apparently not, for in the

---

3. If the conception of scientific inquiry begins with a deductive model and proceeds to rigorous empirical testing, this chapter falls short. Though it begins with well-established and intuitively plausible concepts, no criteria exist for determining in advance which "chance" events will have long-term political impact. An inductive style is inescapable; with luck it will generate data and ideas for a more rigorous analyses.

4. I define the traditional Right as the sum of the PFL, PDS, and PTB. In 1994 the PDS became the PPR, then renamed itself the PPB.

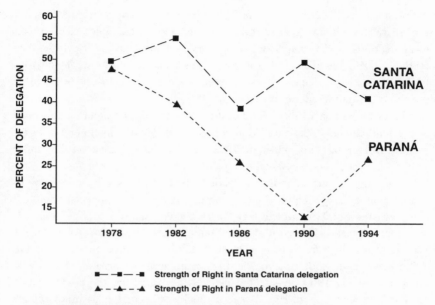

Fig. 14. Strength of Right in congressional delegation

three presidential elections from 1989 through 1998 Santa Catarina gave much bigger shares of its votes to Lula than to his opponents, Fernando Collor de Mello and Fernando Henrique Cardoso.[5] Clearly, then, what separates the two states is not a powerful grassroots cleavage. What does distinguish them, however, is the strength of traditional oligarchies. Santa Catarina's oligarchy has maintained power; Paraná has hardly any oligarchy at all.

In Brazilian politics, Santa Catarina represents continuity. In the 1945–64 democratic period, two conservative parties, the Social Democratic Party (PSD) and the National Democratic Union (UDN), dominated Santa Catarina. Three great families monopolized power: the Ramos clan in the PSD, and the Konders and Bornhausens in the UDN.[6] The Brazilian Labor Party (PTB) provided Left-populist opposition to the PSD and UDN but never really had much influence. The PTB failed to elect a single federal deputy until 1958, and it never had more than two (of fourteen) deputies. The *catarinense* oligarchy easily accepted the 1964 military coup, and the traditional families became the basis of

---

5. In 1998, for example, Lula received 36.6 percent in Santa Catarina but only 27.8 percent in Paraná.

6. This section relies on Viola 1986.

the promilitary ARENA party. The PTB turned into the opposition MDB, but even in this form it remained pitifully weak. In 1976, for example, ARENA won local elections in 154 municipalities; the MDB claimed just 32. By 1988—after the PMDB's Plano Cruzado success—the PMDB and parties to its left controlled 40 percent of Santa Catarina's municipalities; in Paraná the left held 56 percent of all municipalities (Grohmann 1997).

Paraná's political history contrasts strikingly with that of Santa Catarina. Before the military coup, the old PTB almost succeeded in dominating *paranaense* politics. But for the coup, in fact, the PTB would probably have controlled a majority of the state's congressional delegation after the 1964 elections.[7]

Until the ascendance in the 1990s of Jaime Lerner, Curitiba's internationally recognized mayor and two-term governor, Paraná's last important political leader was former Army officer Ney Braga. Descendant of a traditional political family, Braga had been nominated police secretary by the governor, his brother-in-law. In 1956 Braga was elected mayor of Curitiba, the state capital. An effective and popular mayor, he organized Paraná's Christian Democratic Party, and in the 1960 presidential election he supported the coalition that elected Jânio Quadros. In 1962 Braga got lucky, winning the governorship after the sudden death of his PTB opponent.

Braga became the sponsor of a group of politicians who would go on to became powerful leaders in their own right. Many still wield influence in *paranaense* politics. When Braga became minister of agriculture in the first military government, he supported protégé Paulo Pimentel as governor. Pimentel later broke with Braga and developed an independent political base.[8] Braga was also patron of Jayme Canet, the next governor, but Canet eventually followed Pimentel's route, breaking with Braga and becoming an independent politico. José Richa, a third Braga creation, split with his patron even before attaining real power. Richa left ARENA for the MDB, then helped form the PMDB and the PSDB.

Braga, then, was a powerful leader who could not construct a durable political machine. In part, his failure can be attributed to personal style. Observers report that he was very controlling, never allowing his disciples independent authority. In part, however, his leadership style seems based on an understanding of *paranaense* politics. Consider, for example, the origins of the Braga group. Ney himself came from a local family. José Richa, however, hailed from

---

7. The PTB was so strong that it almost elected a substitute candidate to the Senate in 1961 after its candidate died.

8. Between Pimentel and Canet another governor intervened, but the military cashiered him for corruption.

Rio de Janeiro. Leite Chaves, a key PTB leader, was from Paraíba. Canet, Álvaro Dias, and Pimentel were all born in São Paulo. In other words, none of the post-Braga generation of Paraná leaders were actually born there. In terms of occupational backgrounds, Braga and his group were mostly administrators, either in the public or private sector. The previous generation of conservative leaders—those from the PSD in the 1950s and 1960s—came from the landed elite of *mate* growers, a totally distinct social stratum.[9] And finally, politics as a career, as a vocation, lacks prestige in Paraná. The state legislature is extremely localistic and quite weak organizationally. Turnover among deputies, at both federal and state levels, is very high.[10] In a sense, the characteristics of Paraná's leaders, coupled with the low prestige of politics as a career, suggest something unique about Paraná society.

Relative to Santa Catarina, Paraná is somewhat more urban, a bit poorer, and less educated. The income distribution is slightly worse.[11] Paraná's population is more agricultural and substantially less industrial than that of Santa Catarina. But in relation to Brazil as a whole, these two states are really quite close—except for one demographic indicator, migration. Paraná has a much higher percentage of migrants from other states and other countries. Figures 15 and 16 reveal that in a high percentage of Paraná's municipalities more than 70 percent of the population was born in another state or country. In 1980 the total number of out-of-state migrants reached 527 per 1,000 inhabitants in Paraná. For Santa Catarina, the comparable figure was only 343 per 1,000.[12] Paraná's foreign migrants tend to be relatively recent European or Japanese stock. Migrants from Minas Gerais and from Japan are prevalent in parts of the state's northern tier, while *gaúchos* from Rio Grande do Sul dominate the Southwest.

Immigrant groups traditionally keep out of statewide politics. Though quite willing to support politicians with backgrounds in business or bureaucratic activities, immigrants demand that their representatives focus on local issues. And because they are recent arrivals, they rarely belong to traditional patronage net-

---

9. The old *mate* oligarchs faced few challenges after the military regime crushed the PTB, which before 1964 had dominated Paraná's north.

10. In a recent analysis of the "elite" of the national Congress, the lobbying firm Arko Advice (Aragão 1998) compiled a roster of congressional leaders—the movers and shakers—from each state. Paraná, in relation to the size of its delegation, has the fewest prominent members of Congress of any state.

11. The percentage of Paraná residents earning less than one-fourth the minimum salary is twice that of Santa Catarina.

12. These data are from the census of 1980. Underlining the importance of recent migratory flows is Paraná's second largest city, Londrina, which was only founded in 1929 and has more than 400,000 residents.

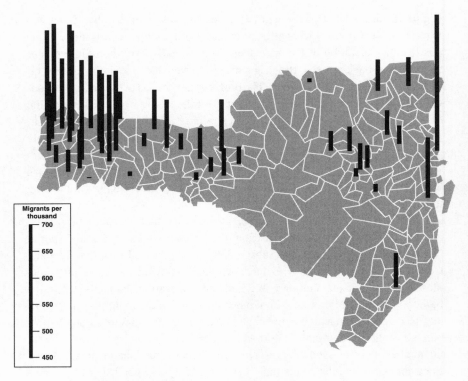

Fig. 15. Santa Catarina: Total migrants

works.[13] As a result, Paraná lacks the kind of well-established economic and social oligarchy characterizing much of Brazil.

Extreme localism gives Paraná's politics an almost apolitical quality. Curitiba, the capital, has one of the weakest federal universities in Brazil. Its social science departments—centers of intellectual debate in most Brazilian universities—are especially poor. The capital's chief newspaper resembles a small-town weekly. On the whole, politics in Paraná is an unpopular business.[14]

Partly as a result of localized migratory flows, Paraná's deputies campaign in contiguous clusters of municipalities. Since party and individual loyalties are

---

13. Rebecca Menes (1997), in a study of U.S. cities, comes to similar conclusions about the difficulties machines face in recruiting migrants.

14. This explanation reflects the perspective of Paraná's active politicians. Every Paraná politician interviewed talked about the intensity of migration both in and out of the state, and all seemed to take for granted that in Paraná, politics really are local.

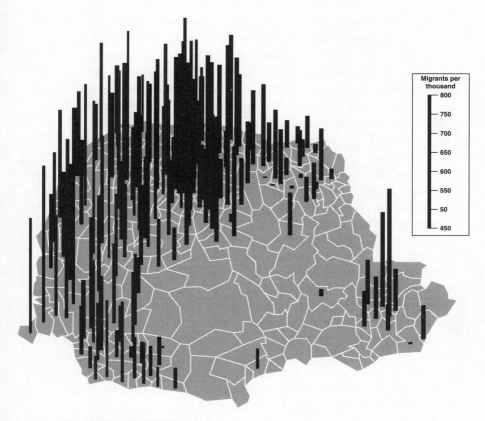

Fig. 16. Paraná: Total migrants

weak, and since deputies seek to expand their vote bases, they invade neighboring bailiwicks. The resulting competition reaches fratricidal levels. Nevertheless, deputies resist governors' efforts to control predatory campaign behavior, preferring instead to maintain independence. Once in office, Paraná's
deputies make more budgetary amendments than representatives from any other
state in the South or Southeast; in fact, they are among the amendment leaders
in all Brazil.[15]

Indicators of other aspects of political competition support this interpretation. Because Paraná's turnover is so high, opportunities for elected office
abound. In the four elections held between 1986 and 1998, an average of 8.0

---

15. Deputy Max Rosenmann, easily the champion in making amendments, targeted well
over one hundred separate municipalities.

candidates ran for each seat in the Legislative Assembly of Paraná, while only 5.4 candidates competed for the same office in Santa Catarina.[16] The Chamber of Deputies saw smaller but similar differences: 6.1 candidates per seat in Paraná, only 4.95 candidates per seat in Santa Catarina. An index of competitiveness taking into account both the number of candidates running for each seat and the size of the delegation shows that over the 1986–98 period, Paraná ranked, on average, just behind the thirteenth most competitive state in Brazil, while Santa Catarina ranked near the bottom, below the twenty-first most competitive state.[17]

Santa Catarina's oligarchic control reduces not only the number of new entrants into politics but also the number of parties competing for office. Between 1982 and 1994 (1998 results were unavailable), the number of effective parties in Santa Catarina's Chamber of Deputies delegation was 3.21; Paraná's delegation formed 4.0 effective parties (Leex 1999).[18]

In the end, even the political fortunes of a leader as well known as Jaime Lerner fail to transcend the essence of Paraná's politics. Lerner had been Curitiba's mayor while a member of the PDT. Though courted heavily by the national leadership of the PSDB, Lerner's entrance into that party was blocked by former governor Álvaro Dias, for whom Lerner would be formidable competition for the party nomination to any high office. Lerner entered the PFL instead, and in 1998 he won reelection over former governor Roberto Requião. Dias picked up a Senate seat for the PSDB. Though these three heavyweights dominate *paranaense* politics, all have strikingly short coattails. In the election for State Assembly, Lerner's PFL led with thirteen victories, but the three major parties together totaled only twenty-six of fifty-four seats . In the Chamber of Deputies, the PFL again led, with six victories, but the three parties jointly won only fifteen of thirty seats.

---

16. Summary tables for these and other common measures of competition can be obtained at the website of the Instituto Universitário de Pesquisas do Rio de Janeiro (www.iuperj.br) (hereafter cited as Leex 1999).

17. The index of competitiveness equals $N/2W - 1$, where N is the number of candidates running for legislative office and W is the size of the corresponding delegation. See also W. Bonfim 1999, 42.

18. In the legislative assemblies the differences were smaller: 4.0 effective parties in Paraná and 3.5 in Santa Catarina. Effective parties were defined according to the Laakso-Taagapera index. In a study of party and electoral fragmentation in eight states (Bahia, Ceará, Goiás, Minas Gerais, Rio de Janeiro, Rio Grande do Sul, Santa Catarina, and São Paulo), Santa Catarina had the second lowest fragmentation (both party and electoral) and volatility, losing only to Ceará (see Lima Junior 1997, 308–10).

Bahia, Maranhão, and Ceará

In casual usage, the notion of a political boss carries a certain ambiguity. Paraná, as demonstrated earlier, no longer has any bosses. But suppose, in a given state, no one becomes a candidate for the Chamber of Deputies without the blessing of a certain leader. Perhaps all campaign financing flows through a single politician, so only approved candidates have any chance of receiving support. One politician may determine where candidates seek votes, directing some to vulnerable municipalities and preventing others from poaching on party colleagues' turf. Or suppose one leader has the strength to control the party delegation's postelection legislative voting. These criteria are not meant to posit an absolute standard for determining when a politician qualifies as a leader or boss. Maranhão and Bahia, however, are distinguished by the distinct power of individual leaders. In Ceará a troika of traditional political bosses ruled until 1986, when a "modernizing" reformist overthrew the machine.[19]

The Sarney family has dominated Maranhão's political life since 1966, when José Sarney became the state's governor.[20] Sarney has always had to contend with opposition from other elite factions, as conservative and promilitary as Sarney himself, when they contested his control of central government largesse. Sarney's predominance did not become truly decisive until he rose to become Tancredo Neves's vice presidential candidate in 1985 and then president after Tancredo's death. Between 1978 and 1994, nearly every federal deputy from Maranhão could be defined as pro- or anti-Sarney, with the "pros" easily outnumbering the "antis." Sarney picked candidates for the Chamber, candidates who might have few local followers. Though a few candidates had family-based or evangelical support, even they needed the machine's imprimatur. The machine could move candidates from one region to another between campaigns, and its representatives told mayors and council members how many votes each would supply.[21] During the Sarney presidency, Maranhão's delegation to the Chamber often voted as a bloc, regardless of party, on key legisla-

---

19. For a comparative study of party and electoral fragmentation in Ceará, see Moraes Filho 1997.

20. This section is based on interviews with journalists, academics, and politicians in Maranhão, a few conducted in 1983 but most in 1990.

21. In the case of Deputy Carlos Magno, for example, the correlation (Pearson R) between the municipal shares of his personal vote total in the elections of 1978 and 1982 is .63. This finding is statistically significant, but it is much lower that the typical cross-election correlation for candidates in other states and is inflated by his substantial vote in the municipalities of Coelho Neto and Chapadinha, where his family is based. Without Coelho Neto and Chapadinha, the correlation is .57.

tion. In 1990 ex-president Sarney got himself elected senator from Amapá.[22] His children, daughter Roseana and son Sarney Filho, both served as federal deputies, as did his former son-in-law. In 1994 Sarney secured Roseana's election to the governorship of Maranhão, and he won the presidency of the Senate. In 1998 Roseana was reelected, Sarney Filho became a minister in Fernando Henrique Cardoso's cabinet, and Sarney himself easily won reelection as senator from Amapá.

In terms of influence within his own state, Bahia's preeminent leader, Antônio Carlos Magalhães (ACM), enjoys a status second only to Sarney. Although Bahia's industrial development and greater urbanization enable leftist opposition, including communist parties, to maintain a significant presence in state politics, ACM has long dominated conservative and moderate elites. ACM is one of the few state leaders in recent Brazilian history who has leveraged regional influence into national predominance before holding a national office. Three times governor of Bahia, he was also Sarney's communications minister, a post with pork-distributing potential throughout the country. ACM's son, Luís Eduardo, a three-time federal deputy, rose to the presidency of the Chamber of Deputies during Cardoso's coalition (PSDB-PFL) administration. Until his sudden death in 1998, Luís Eduardo was probably the chief candidate to succeed Cardoso. ACM himself won a Senate seat in 1994 and held the presidency of the Senate through much of the two Cardoso administrations.

The last of this northeastern trio is Ceará. Until 1986, Ceará was a classic example of the politics of *coronelismo*. Particularly in the Northeast, but also in other parts of the nation, the "colonels" served as intermediaries between the populist state and ordinary citizens. Usually wealthy and prestigious landowners, these colonels delivered the votes of their employees and dependents to any party with the resources to buy them (Roett 1978, 63). In Ceará, three families of *coroneis* (in this case, actual military colonels), the Távoras, the Bezerras, and the Cals, dominated state politics from 1964 until the mid-1980s. Each family had a regional center: the Távoras in Jaguaribana, the Bezerras in Cariri, and the Cals in Ibiapaba. After the 1964 coup, the three colonels found a political home in the progovernment ARENA party, dominating state politics until 1986, when they were swept out of power by Tasso Jereissati, a young reformist business entrepreneur from the PMDB. Jereissati owed his election as governor— like PMDB candidates all over the country—to the enormously successful start of the Plano Cruzado, but both he and Ciro Gomes, the PMDB mayor of Fort-

---

22. Brazilian electoral laws are rather permissive, to say the least, when it comes to establishing a residence.

aleza (the capital) headed extremely popular administrations.[23] While governor, Jereissati founded Ceará's branch of the PSDB. In 1990 Gomes, now a PSDB member, became governor, with Jereissati reclaiming the post in 1994 and winning reelection in 1998 with more than 60 percent of the vote. Ceará's delegation to the Chamber of Deputies had been three-fourths ARENA-PDS between 1966 and 1982, but in 1986 the traditional Right elected only ten of twenty-two deputies. By 1990 the delegation included seven parties. The PSDB led with seven deputies; the PMDB followed with four. The traditional right-wing parties fell to less than one-third of the delegation.

With this sketch of the political scene, I will turn to the nature of political competition. In all three states, dominance follows the broad downward trend characteristic of Brazilian politics. Maranhão, as might be expected of a poor and agricultural state, began with the highest frequency of dominant politicians, but by 1994 the three states were virtually indistinguishable. In all four elections, deputies in Ceará competed more against each other; that is, Maranhão and Bahia had lower levels of interdeputy competition. But the biggest distinction is found in terms of spatial concentration. As figure 17 reveals, Bahian deputies are substantially less likely to get their votes in contiguous municipalities. Since such large states usually exhibit greater clustering, Bahia's position seems even more anomalous.[24]

How does the partisan composition of the three delegations reflect ongoing political changes? As figure 18 shows, Ceará's traditional right-wing parties declined almost out of existence by 1994. In Maranhão, the Sarney machine managed to hold on to 40 percent of the delegation (50 percent if pro-Sarney deputies in other parties are included), while in Bahia these same parties controlled about one-third of the seats.

The occupational backgrounds of deputies from the three states exhibit sharp differences. Since 1978 traditional politicians have dominated Maranhão's delegations: two-thirds of the deputies have prior experience as mayors, council members, or state deputies. Ceará's deputies are somewhat less likely to build on local political careers, and in Bahia state and local politicians are scarce: in 1990 less than half had any local or state experience. The big difference is displayed in figure 19, which plots the bureaucratic backgrounds of the three delegations. The number of deputies with backgrounds in state or (less of-

---

23. The most sophisticated political analysis of Ceará is Washington Bonfim 1999. For an analysis of Jereissati's programs, see Tendler 1997.

24. The degree of clustering is quite stable. In Maranhão spatial clustering rises in 1978, when the PMDB does well, and falls thereafter. Ceará's voting pattern, perhaps as a result of the party fragmentation of the 1990 election, becomes more clustered only in that year.

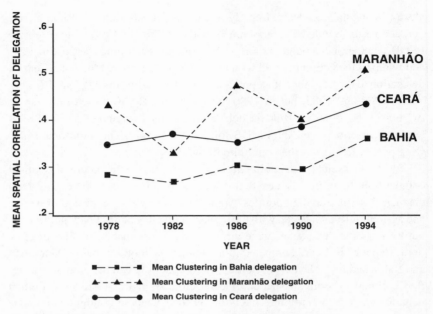

Fig. 17. Average clustering in congressional delegation

ten) federal bureaucratic jobs rose in Bahia to 66 percent by 1990 before falling to 52 percent in 1994. In Ceará less than 30 percent of the deputies had similar histories, and in Maranhão the number fell after 1982, dropping to 34 percent by 1994. Overall, then, Maranhão's deputies are more likely to be state and local politicians, while Bahian deputies are more likely to come from bureaucratic backgrounds.[25]

In sum, then, Bahia has a powerful, nationally significant political figure coordinating the campaigning of the Chamber candidates of center and right-wing parties, and most of these candidates began their careers in the executive branch of state government. Maranhão also hosts a dominant, nationally prominent political figure, but here politicians serve their apprenticeships in state and local politics, and until recently the promilitary, right-wing parties housed both pro- and anti-Sarney factions. In Ceará, traditional families once dominated, but the PMDB onslaught of 1986 decimated them. Because the reformers—now in the PSDB—managed a successful state administration, their victory endured.

---

25. The decline in 1994 of Bahia's cohort of ex-bureaucrats may be a function of the economic crisis of the 1980s and 1990s. As resource declines cut the number of projects available, fewer politicians are able to launch careers based on pork barrel.

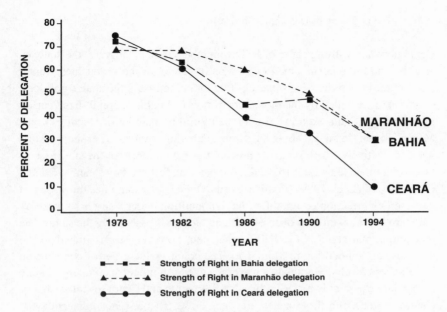

Fig. 18. Strength of Right in congressional delegation

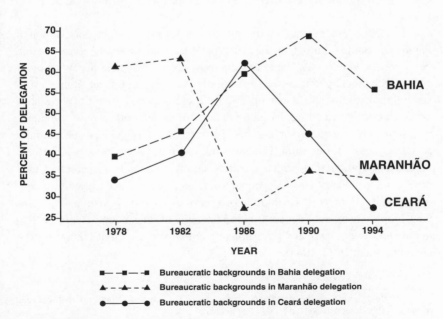

Fig. 19. Politicians with bureaucratic experience in congressional delegation

Ceará now has a strong cadre of PSDB members in the Congress, the state assembly, and the bureaucracy. In Ceará an oligarchy of the probusiness center has replaced the right-wing oligarchs that long dominated the state's politics.

What is revealed by the indicators of political competition utilized earlier in Paraná and Santa Catarina? In competition for Chamber of Deputies seats, Maranhão and Ceará had about the same number of candidates per seat (4.2 and 4.45, respectively), with Bahia a bit behind at 3.9. In races for the state assemblies, Maranhão led with 9.15 candidates per seat, followed by Ceará at 6.4 and Bahia at 5.25 (Leex 1999). In other words, Bahia's oligarchy has the strongest gatekeeping effect on competition, but competition under Ceará's supposedly "modern" administrations of Jereissati and Gomes is essentially the same. The reconciliational style of the Sarney machine, however, seems linked to the openness of competition in Maranhão. The countrywide order of competition echoes these results: Maranhão, on average, is the eighth most competitive state in legislative assembly races, with Bahia fourteenth and Ceará seventeenth. For Chamber seats, the three states are very close, all between nineteenth and twenty-first. Ceará has the lowest number of effective parties in its state legislature, 3.45, followed by Bahia at 3.9 and Maranhão at 4.5. For the Chamber, Ceará again has the fewest effective parties, 3.05, with Maranhão at 3.32 and Bahia at 3.8.[26]

The first attempt to explain this puzzle relies, as it did in the comparison of Paraná and Santa Catarina, on the differences between the states' economic and demographic conditions. Bahia has the most diversified economy. With modern petrochemical plants as well as nonferrous metals and paper, Bahia's substantial industrial sector is responsible for more than 40 percent of the state's gross product. Agriculture, based on exports of cacao, coffee, dairy products, and soybeans, accounts for another 16 percent. Maranhão is substantially poorer and more agricultural. The industrial sector accounts for only 30 percent of the state's production, with agriculture supplying another 22 percent. Ceará has the least industry (just 27 percent of gross product), and agriculture contributes only 15 percent. Ceará relies on services, mainly tourism and government employment. Services contribute 58 percent of state income (far more than in the other two states), and government employment contributes another 10.4 percent (Brazil 1992, 1044).[27]

---

26. Bahia's high number of effective parties in the Chamber of Deputies probably results from the Left's strength in Salvador and other industrial cities.

27. These data are from 1985. Maranhão is second in government's contribution to state product, at 6.7 percent.

Can economic and demographic differences explain the differences in political competition? Bahia is naturally the wealthiest, with per capita income in Ceará and Maranhão standing at 58 percent and 48 percent, respectively, of the Bahian level.[28] In terms of urbanization, Bahia and Ceará are very similar, with Maranhão substantially more rural. Municipalities in Bahia and Ceará have roughly similar levels of migrants; Maranhão has about 30 percent more. Overall, the three states are strikingly different in economic and demographic terms, but the distinctions do not seem closely correlated with their political differences. It is now time to pursue the route of path dependence.[29]

Maranhão

Sarney is actually the second post–World War II politician to dominate Maranhão. In the 1930s, Getúlio Vargas sent Vitorino Freire as part of a team of "interventors." Freire gradually built a powerful machine based on patronage, populism, pork, and violence. Governor in the 1950s and senator until his death in 1977, Freire faced no serious challengers until Sarney himself.

Sarney had been a federal deputy from 1958 to 1965 for the old UDN party. Elected governor in 1965, he presented himself as a conservative modernizer. This position sharply differentiated Sarney from all his predecessors, who made little effort to attract infrastructure programs from the federal government. Maranhão before the 1964 military coup could even be characterized as a state whose elites sought to avoid federal programs—in stark contrast to Ceará's pork-hungry leaders—because such programs implied intervention and change. Only with Sarney's ascendence was a conscious effort made to attract federal largesse.[30] For Sarney, modernization essentially meant development based on modern capitalist agriculture, for the state had virtually no industry even as late as the 1960s (Cleary 1987). The state's chief crops (rice, cotton, and palm nuts) yielded little. The backwardness of infrastructure hindered agricultural development. Paved roads, for example, existed only in São Luís. A dirt road connected the city with the capitals of neighboring states, but no road at all ran to Imperatriz, the state's second largest city. Governor Sarney started an active program of road and bridge building. In addition, his decrees allowed land speculators and large corporations to take over vacant tracts of land and squeeze small landholders off land they had been farming without clear title.

---

28. Santa Catarina and Paraná, by contrast, have approximately three times the per capita incomes of these northeastern states.

29. In addition to North 1990, a useful discussion of path dependence appears in Putnam 1993, 179–81.

30. I discuss this case and that of Ceará in Ames 1987.

As Cleary points out (1987, 18–19), Sarney was hostile to the traditional forms of landholding represented by the agrarian elite. Rather than implementing agrarian reform, the governor bypassed the traditional elite by opening up new lands to agrarian capitalists, especially cattle interests, and directing the state to facilitate these capitalists' endeavors. Those benefiting from cheap land or nearby roads were connected, of course, with the Revolution of 1964, and they rewarded the Sarney machine. The process did not displace traditional elites from their local power bases, because the new capitalists, many from other states, remained out of politics, concentrating instead on their new enterprises.

Sarney's program transformed Maranhão. Rice production soared, beef production expanded, and São Luís became the site of a major aluminum factory. Between 1960 and 1991, São Luís' population grew from 158,000 to 695,000, and the percentage of the state's population living in urban areas more than doubled (Brazil 1992, 208). Not surprisingly, the dislocations that came with these changes, coupled with the total inadequacy of social programs, had disastrous consequences for the poor, but in the heady growth days of the Brazilian "miracle" such effects seemed merely transitory.

In the 1970 election Sarney easily won his own seat in the Senate, and he successfully managed the campaign of his chosen successor as governor. Observers saw this victory as a consecration of Sarney's power, but Freire remained on the scene. The old *caudilho* had been a firm defender of the 1964 coup, and as a federal senator he was well connected in Brasília. From 1970 until his death in 1977, Freire bitterly opposed the Sarney machine.[31] Freire choked off federal funds for Maranhão and in this way contributed to the unpopularity of Sarney's chosen successor.[32] In 1974 Freire maneuvered to ensure the nomination of a distant relative, Osvaldo Nunes Freire, and Sarney had to accept the nomination. When Vitorino died in 1977, Sarney expected to reclaim the governorship and become the sole arbiter of Maranhão politics, but Nunes Freire blocked Sarney's nomination and forced him to accept a supposed ally, Federal Deputy João Castelo (Rolim 1979, 87). In the Chamber of Deputies, Maranhão's ARENA delegation split into a Sarney wing (with six *sarneistas* and two pro-Sarney independents) and a two-deputy wing led by Governor Nunes Freire.

Castelo began as Sarney's ally but immediately broke with the ex-governor and began to build a separate political machine. In part, the Castelo regime was based on precisely the economic development that Sarney had initiated. Its

---

31. This section relies on Cleary 1987.
32. The Santana administration, it must be noted, was incompetent in its own right.

geographic center was Imperatriz, a city strategically located in the southern part of the state, in the heart of the new agricultural development. Castelo allied with the new entrepreneurs of Imperatriz: landowners, builders, mine and timber operators, and so on. His major public project was the construction of a costly and grandiose soccer stadium. Though corruption was rampant, Castelo left office in 1982 with his popularity intact. His election to the Senate provided him with a springboard for the development of his own machine, one capable of posing a constant threat to Sarney. Led by Castelo, the anti-Sarney forces in the PDS delegation peaked in the 1982 election, with eight *sarneistas* and four anti-*sarneistas*.

Sarney then got lucky. The 1985 presidential election was scheduled to be disputed in an electoral college, and Sarney was president of the proregime party, the PDS. The military leaders assumed they had sufficiently rigged the college to ensure their candidate's victory. The leading PDS candidate was Paulo Maluf, ex-governor of São Paulo. Sarney opposed Maluf's nomination on the grounds that Maluf was too unpopular to win. Castelo, however, bet on Maluf. Sarney eventually resigned the PDS presidency and accepted the vice presidential slot on the ticket of the opposition Liberal Alliance. In the end, Tancredo Neves's Liberal Alliance won in the electoral college, Tancredo died, and Sarney became president.

With his archenemy in the presidential palace, Castelo's political death might have been a foregone conclusion. But in late 1985, Castelo engineered his wife's election as mayor of São Luís—over Sarney's candidate—and announced his intention to seek the governorship in 1986. Still, as Cleary (1987, 324) notes, Castelo proceeded to snatch defeat from the jaws of victory. His wife threatened to fire 5,000 city employees hired by the previous administration. A huge demonstration erupted, the city hall went up in flames, and Castelo lost all credibility. A Sarney ally, PMDB member Epitácio Cafeteira, was elected governor over Castelo by more than 1 million votes. The euphoria of the Plano Cruzado helped, of course, and Cafeteira united his urban base with Sarney's rural strength. Cafeteira eventually quarreled with Sarney, but in 1990 the president allied with popular journalist Edison Lobão. With Lobão winning the governorship in 1990 and Sarney's daughter victorious in 1994, the Sarney machine had finally consolidated its domination of Maranhão.

Ceará

Most of Ceará is located in the Northeast's drought region, the dry *sertão*. Because of the economy's extreme fragility, the state has long depended on the federal government. Elite groups rose and fell as their economic fortunes waxed and waned, with each faction struggling to secure a stable share of the available federal relief money. Beginning in the nineteenth century, periodic droughts gave rise to the *indústria da sêca,* a phrase referring to profiteering on pork-barrel projects tied to drought relief. Opposition to the dominant political forces always existed, of course, but the opposition joined with dominant groups in efforts to free more central government funds for the state.[33]

Until the overthrow of civilian government in 1964, conservative forces in Ceará seemed to be losing out to leftist elements. In 1958 the Labor Party (PTB) allied with the PSD to elect a PTB governor. Four years later, groups led by businessman Carlos Jereissati (father of the reformist governor elected in 1986) tried to force the election of a nationalist-populist slate. The UDN responded by joining conservative elements in the PSD and PTB to form the "Union for Ceará," electing Virgílio Távora governor. In 1964, after a brief hesitation due to Távora's friendship with ousted President João Goulart, the UDN accepted the military overthrow. In the end, the coup bequeathed lasting power to the UDN.

As mentioned earlier, three families dominated Ceará's ARENA: the Bezerras, the Távoras, and the Cals. The Bezerras, through their control of a network of banks, had the strongest economic base. In addition, control of state government had enabled them to extend their influence from the Carirí region to the rest of the state. The Távoras (or *virgilistas,* after Virgílio Távora) represented the old UDN. They had benefited from their control of the state government between 1966 and 1970. The Cals group had formed when Cézar Cals de Oliveira, an army colonel who had occupied various federal administrative posts, held the governorship from 1971 and 1974 and then chose to remain in politics. Lacking an independent financial base, the Cals group was the weakest. The rivalry between the Bezerras and the Cals was greater than any other pair, partly because Adauto Bezerra and Virgílio Távora had joint business ventures and partly because a Távora (Vargas's interventor in the state in the 1930s) had persecuted a member of the Cals group.

By 1978 ARENA's domination of state politics was nearly complete. Of the state's 141 municipalities, ARENA controlled all but seven. The administration of outgoing Governor Adauto Bezerra had developed new mechanisms

---

33. I treat the pork ethos of the *cearense* delegation to the 1946–64 legislature in Ames 1987. Another example of the reconciliational nature of party competition comes from the election of 1974, in which Virgílio Távora refused to accept Cézar Cals's nomination of a Távora enemy for the Senate. Távora left the country during the campaign, effectively conceding the seat to the MDB, the party both he and Cals opposed.

to fortify ARENA's control. A Secretariat for Municipal Affairs, headed by Adauto's brother, Humberto, coordinated state activities in each municipality. The Secretariat of Planning, under the control of ally Paulo Lustosa da Costa from the Bank of the Northeast, channeled funds to worthy allies—and later provided the springboard for Lustosa da Costa's own political career (Rolim 1979, 101).

With its domination assured, ARENA's leaders parceled out the available jobs to satisfy its three chiefs. Virgílio Távora would be appointed governor by the military regime in Brasília; Humberto Bezerra (twin brother of Adauto) would be Ceará's appointed "bionic" senator; Cézar Cals would be the elected senator; and Adauto Bezerra would run for federal deputy. Cals, however, feared he would lose a direct election, so he opted for the *biónico* post. Humberto, also fearing a direct election, chose to wait out the election. In the end, a Bezerra ally, José Lins de Albuquerque, accepted the nomination and won easily.

In the elections for the Chamber of Deputies, ARENA won fifteen of Ceará's twenty seats. Fortaleza, with 25 percent of the state's voters, contributed 40 percent of the votes garnered by opposition MDB candidates. In spite of ARENA's decisive victory, it was evident that ARENA's grip was becoming more fragile. Such regional towns as Crato and Juazeiro do Norte, once bastions of the Bezerras, had begun electing opposition deputies.

In 1982 the machine triumphed once again. Now called the Social Democratic Party (PDS), it had the very real help of the military regime. In April, seven months before the election, President Figueiredo came to Ceará to bless the "colonels agreement," a pact splitting up the appointed jobs in Ceará that would be available after the elections. The agreement granted equal shares to the Távoras, the Bezerras, and the Cals. The president's intervention was necessary because both Cézar Cals and Adauto Bezerra wanted the governorship. Virgílio Távora offered his own ally, Aécio de Borba. Figueiredo's compromise made the Távora administration's secretary of planning, Luís Gonzaga Motta, the gubernatorial candidate. Virgílio Távora would return to the Senate. Fearing that the Bezerras would sit on their hands in the election, Virgílio insisted that blood-related Bezerras be on the tickets as vice governor and senatorial substitute.[34] Cézar Cals, though he lost the fight to become governor, was nominated mayor of Fortaleza and received a third of the appointable positions. The PDS candidates for governor and senator won easily, and the party took seven-

---

34. In elections for the Senate, voters can choose any of the candidates a party puts up. The party with the largest total vote gets the Senate seat, and the candidate with the largest individual total becomes the senator, with the others becoming substitutes. On the colonels' agreement, see Barros and da Costa 1985.

teen of the twenty-two Chamber seats. In municipal elections the PDS won 136 mayoral contests against 4 for the PMDB.

The three oligarchic families had created a governing machine based on two fundamental points: unity of the top leaders and division at the bottom, at the level of the bases.[35] As long as the oligarchs got along, the opposition MDB was electorally doomed. But Gonzaga Motta, a governor imposed by the final military president, could not manage the inevitable conflicts between leaders fighting for space in the coming postmilitary era. Though he greatly expanded the number of state secretaries (the state-level equivalent of ministries) to try to accommodate the colonels' demands, the result was unmanageable budget deficits, widespread administrative irregularities, and rapid turnover as cabinet secretaries positioned themselves for electoral office. Motta himself, seeing that he had no future in his own party, switched to the PMDB.

The 1982 election turned out to be the swan song of the old caciques. Three years later, Fortaleza elected its first mayor since the start of the military regime. The Liberal Front Party (PFL), a splinter of the old PDS, nominated Lúcio Alcântara, a federal deputy with a modern image. The PMDB put up a veteran deputy, and the PT nominated a radical sociologist, Maria Luiza Fontenele. With the help of Virgílio Távora (who happened to be a relative of Fontenele) the PT candidate won. Though Maria Luiza's administration was not notably successful, it was clear that the Right, even in a multicandidate election, could no longer pull a significant vote in the state's biggest city.

By 1986 Ceará's political forces had completely realigned. During the Motta administration, the three oligarchic families essentially functioned as veto players under a unanimity rule. Not surprisingly, consistent economic policy could not be implemented in such a political environment. The resulting fiscal chaos was particularly damaging to the state's younger industrialists, and this group took over the state PMDB and gave its support to entrepreneur Tasso Jereissati. With the backing of Motta and the help of the Plano Cruzado, Jereissati defeated the PFL candidate. The PMDB elected both senators and twelve of twenty-two deputies, while the PFL could manage only six deputies.

Though Jereissati could not have won in 1986 without the help of Motta and his PMDB allies, the new governor immediately distanced himself from the Motta group, which constituted the majority of the PMDB in the state assembly. Instead, Jereissati centralized the multiple, patronage-based secretariats into a single government secretary and placed the crucial economic secretariats in the hands of his entrepreneurial allies. With political power centralized,

---

35. In this section I follow the analysis of W. Bonfim 1999.

pork could be distributed much more efficiently—that is, cheaply. The economic secretaries and their policies could be insulated from pork distribution altogether (W. Bonfim 1999, 21). Jereissati successfully substituted a direct, almost populist style of communicating with voters, especially voters on Fortaleza's periphery, as a substitute for the more traditional, mediated style of his predecessors.

Though the PSDB has done poorly in Fortaleza—which contributes almost 30 percent of the total statewide vote—the party's strength in the interior guarantees victories. In 1990 Ciro Gomes succeeded Jereissati as governor, defeating Lustosa, the old Bezerra ally. The PSDB's successes also rearranged party financial coffers. By 1990 the Cals' machine was so short of money that Cézar Cals's son failed in a try for the Chamber of Deputies, and the old bosses could secure seats for just two of their followers, Virgílio's son, Carlos, and Adauto Bezerra's brother, Orlando. With Jereissati's easy reelection in 1998, the PSDB became the state's dominant party, claiming twenty-one of forty-six state assembly seats and twelve of twenty-two seats in the Chamber of Deputies.

While the Jereissati-Gomes administrations have profoundly modernized Ceará's economic management and rationalized (through centralization) the distribution of pork, the oligarchic character of the state's politics has not changed. Before the Jereissati revolution, Ceará, like other northeastern states, ranked low on all the common indexes of party competitiveness, including the number of effective parties, the number of candidates per seat, the fragmentation of the parties, and so on. During and after the revolution, however, Ceará's low degree of competitiveness did not change. In a sense, a more progressive oligarchy replaced the three colonels.

Bahia

For many years, Bahia has been the strongest bailiwick of the Brazilian Right. The National Democratic Union (UDN), Vargas's fiercest opponent, won every gubernatorial contest prior to 1964 except the election of 1950. After the 1964 coup, Bahia's UDN became the heart of the promilitary ARENA, conquering all the state's executive positions until the 1986 gubernatorial election (when Waldir Pires captured the state house).

Unchallenged dominance promotes fragmentation, and by 1978 ARENA had split into three factions: one headed by Antônio Carlos Magalhães (the *carlistas*), another headed by Luis Vianna Filho,[36] and a third headed by

---

36. This group also included Jutahy Magalhães and Lomanto Júnior.

Roberto Santos. ACM's group was usually able to strike a bargain with Vianna, but Santos was unalterably hostile.

Why was Bahia such a stronghold of the Right? The state's only big city, Salvador, has roughly 16 percent of the electorate. Outside Salvador, population density is very low. Centrist and leftist forces are usually successful only in Salvador; elsewhere, traditional oligarchical groups dominate. Before 1978 the MDB had no party organization at all in more than 100 of Bahia's 336 municipalities, and in almost 200 municipalities the MDB won no council seats. In a milieu of such weakness, the more conservative elements of the MDB opted to become *adesistas,* that is, politicians willing to cooperate with ARENA in exchange for a share of state patronage. The MDB's more ideological *auténtico* wing simply lacked the numbers to mount a real opposition.

By 1975, the MDB began to take on a more ideological cast. After the national legislative elections of 1974, in which the MDB enjoyed great success in the states of the South and Southeast, students and workers joined the Bahian MDB in large numbers. When the MDB captured a majority of Salvador's council seats in the 1975 municipal elections, *adesistas* statewide began to leave the party for ARENA. In the 1978 elections, MDB candidates competed fiercely against each other, especially in Salvador and its environs, for the support of ideologically motivated voters. The competition mobilized voters in the capital, but elsewhere the MDB remained almost nonexistent, and the party lost support when it expelled rural mayors who had supported local ARENA candidates. The result was continued ARENA dominance statewide: ARENA's candidate for the Senate received two-thirds of the vote, and ARENA elected twenty-four deputies against just eight for the MDB.

Antônio Carlos Magalhães did not come from a old political family, and the lack of *coronelismo* baggage may have facilitated his reputation for a style of policy-making that was technocratic and modernizing rather than one based on pork and patronage. In the late 1950s, as a state and federal deputy, the young ACM had deviated from the UDN line to defend the developmentalist policies of President Kubitschek. During the early years of the military regime, Governor Luis Vianna Filho nominated ACM as mayor of Salvador, and in 1970 the military made him Bahia's governor. He occupied the statehouse again from 1978 until 1982.

ACM intended to use the 1978–82 gubernatorial term as a springboard to the presidency after the generals completed their withdrawal. Profiting from his strong links to incoming military President João Figueiredo and to ex-president Geisel, ACM was able to attract crucial industrial projects, including a petrochemical complex, and federal transfers to Bahia surpassed those to other states. At their peak, in 1982, such grants amounted to almost 25 percent of the state's total receipts (C. Souza 1997, 47).

Magalhães's political power was never more evident than in the 1982 gubernatorial election. When ACM's candidate, Cleriston Andrade, died unexpectedly just before the election, he was able to marshal sufficient support to elect last-minute candidate João Durval. As governor, Durval followed a course often seen in examining Brazilian state politics: he immediately distanced himself from ACM and began his own political organization. Durval's key appointments, compared to those of ACM, were marked by a much higher level of narrowly political criteria, and his administration became quite unpopular. The smell of corruption, in conjunction with the initial success of the Plano Cruzado, ultimately led to the defeat of conservative forces by the PMDB's Waldir Pires in 1986. Not until 1990 could ACM himself recapture the statehouse, this time by direct election.

ACM's extraordinary influence, both in Bahia and nationally, owes much to his construction of a developmentalist, technocratic image. One crucial component of this technocratic style was administrative. During the military period, Bahia implemented an administrative reorganization paralleling reforms undertaken by the military regime and, much earlier, by Juscelino Kubitschek. ACM's reorganization insulated the bureaucratic agencies dealing with planning, budgeting, and economic programs from patronage but left the social services as reservoirs of partisan criteria and personal favors. Another crucial component of ACM's technocratic style was his appointment policy: he demanded loyalty but also expected competence. Even leftists could be part of his coterie; leftist technocrats, in fact, were so numerous they came to be called the *esquerda carlista,* the Carlist Left. ACM's appointees knew that loyalty had its rewards: in 1993 five deputies in ACM's congressional group were former technocrats.[37]

ACM's influence also owes much to his ability to co-opt or conciliate potential foes and to manipulate the levers of traditional patronage cum pork. At least until 1986, the PMDB still had a substantial complement of *adesistas,* deputies who supported ACM while remaining in the opposition. ACM encouraged them by keeping potential PFL competitors out of their bailiwicks.[38]

---

37. The ACM group totaled eighteen. Five of eighteen may appear a small percentage, but political families are so important in Bahia that this cohort really represents a major innovation. This explanation of the ACM phenomenon owes a considerable debt to C. Souza 1997. See also C. Souza 1999, 256.

38. This protectiveness can be measured by examining the competitive situation of *adesistas* in relation to other PMDB deputies. First it is necessary to count the number of PMDB deputies

They responded, as chapter 7 will demonstrate, by supporting ACM in the legislature.

Social programs, especially education, have also been central tools in the machine's survival strategy. Official studies report that of all teachers in schools financed by the state of Bahia, 40 percent have been appointed by politicians, 21 percent by educational staff, and only 39 percent by competitive exams. Politicians appoint almost three-fourths of all headmasters, and these headmasters are themselves crucial in teacher appointments.[39] Until the 1980s, every state secretary of education in Bahia ran for the legislature after leaving the state bureaucracy.

Under both the generals and their civilian successors, ACM also relied on his powerful ties to the central government. Politicians in disfavor suffered. As chapter 5 will show, Bahian municipalities received few intergovernmental grants (*convênios*) while Pires served as governor (between 1987 and 1989), even though Pires and Sarney were both PMDB members. ACM's support, as a member of the cabinet and commander of a large legislative delegation, was far more important to President Sarney than was the president's partisan ties to Pires. Pires, of course, may have withheld state grants from ACM's local municipalities.

The financing of Bahia's debt provides another example of the importance of ACM's central government connections. In budgetary terms, interest on the state debt falls into the category of "Expenditure on Administration and Planning." In 1990 that expenditure took a big jump, climbing in one year from 23.4 percent to 30.8 percent of all spending. ACM was running for governor and was also serving as a Sarney minister. The administration of incumbent Governor Nilo Coelho was ACM's archenemy: ACM persuaded Sarney to punish Coelho by refusing to negotiate with Bahia over interest payments on the state's debt. Since the governor had to allot more state funds to the debt, he had less cash to spend on the 1990 elections (C. Souza 1997, 140).

---

whose vote bases are significantly related to the vote bases of other PMDB deputies. These deputies, in other words, receive substantial shares of their votes in the strongholds of other deputies. *Adesista* deputies, of course, are a subset of all PMDB deputies. In 1986, the *adesista* faction of the PMDB (identified through interviews with academics and journalists) included Luiz Vianna Neto, Fernando Gomes Oliveira, França Teixeira, Carlos Santana, Jorge Viana Dias da Silva, Genebaldo Correia, and Uldurico Pinto. ACM's friends, the seven *adesistas,* had significant competition with 51 percent of all other deputies. The non-*adesista* PMDB deputies had significant competition with 77 percent of all other deputies. Thus ACM, by keeping PFL candidates out of the bailiwicks of his friends in the opposition party, improved their electoral chances.

39. Waldir Pires told C. Souza (1997, 134) that children could register in state schools only if they had a letter from a local politician or state deputy. The data come from the Department of Education of Bahia (Secretaria da Educação e Cultura 1992, 59, cited by C. Souza 1997).

Even in Cardoso's supposedly postclientelist administration, manipulation of social programs served the short-term political goals of the Bahian machine. The president's wife, anthropologist Ruth Cardoso, directed a new entity (Community Solidarity) located in the president's office. The new agency sought to coordinate federal social programs so that municipal needs and absorptive capacities, not simply political ties, would drive the allocation of funds. Although the program was just getting under way, it seemed to be making some progress in rationalizing the distribution of social funds—except in Bahia. According to informants, the word quickly went out that nothing was to go to Bahian municipalities headed by ACM's opponents.[40]

Media power has also been central to the machine. According to his foes, ACM controls, through either family or protégés, a network of ninety radio and TV channels (C. Souza 1997, 131–32). Although this figure may be exaggerated, the family's properties do include the biggest network in Bahia.[41] In addition, ACM is a main player in the state's highly politicized print media.[42] With such media power, the Bahian electorate is fed a rosy picture of ACM's achievements, while opponents suffer constant, vitriolic attacks.

Conclusion

In this chapter the unit of observation remained the individual state, but the mode of investigation switched from quantitative models to analytic narratives exploring the interactions among economic and demographic factors, extraordinary political events, and political competition. Fortunately, the cases selected exhibit much more variance in their modes of political competition than in economic or social conditions.

Paraná and Santa Catarina are relatively wealthy, but their politics are quite distinct. Paraná seems essentially leaderless, with highly localized competition for elected office, a weak legislature, very high turnover of elected politicians at both state and federal levels, and strong voice for parties on the left. Santa Catarina has maintained a stable political oligarchy since World War II. Though

---

40. Confidential communication from a high-ranking agency staff member.

41. TV Bahia, ACM's network, is linked to Globo, the network of Roberto Marinho. Ex-governor Coelho owns TV Aratú, and Pedro Irujo (erstwhile ally, current opponent of ACM) owned TV Itapoã, which he later sold to TV Record.

42. Major political groups own three of four daily newspapers. ACM's family owns one, ex-federal deputy Joaci Goes owned a second (later sold to its employees), and ex-Salvador mayor Mário Kertész controlled the third (*Jornal da Bahia*) until it closed.

the state is more industrial than is Paraná, Santa Catarina's Left has traditionally been weaker.

Why are Santa Catarina and Paraná so different? The real cause seems to be demography. In Paraná, powerful migratory flows from other states and from other countries created subregions with their own political orientations. Paraná's center—the area around Curitiba—is relatively unimportant both demographically and politically. The economy provides enough opportunities that politics is no longer a highly desirable alternative. As a result, Paraná's leaders lack strong roots in their own state. The delegation to the Chamber of Deputies has too little collective seniority to gain national influence. Moreover, Paraná's population elects deputies with quite local orientations, so pork delivery becomes the litmus test of electability.

Maranhão, Ceará, and Bahia offer quite different styles. No other Brazilian state-level leaders have the clout of Maranhão's José Sarney or Bahia's Antônio Carlos Magalhães. Both have become the elder statesmen of political families: Sarney got his daughter into Maranhão's statehouse and two other family members into the Congress. ACM's son was president of the Chamber of Deputies and a possible candidate for Brazil's presidency, and his brother has been a deputy. The two men's styles, however, are quite different: Sarney is much more given to compromise and tolerance; ACM rules with an iron hand. Ceará was once the classic example of domination by colonels. Now the World Bank and other international lending agencies portray the state as a shining beacon of progressive government. And in truth, although its politicos lack the power and flair of Sarney or ACM, Ceará has gained dramatically in political and administrative management over the past fourteen years. In a sense, though, Ceará simply changed oligarchies. Although the current regime is undoubtedly more efficient and progressive, political competition remains as closed as it was under the colonels. Why have these states developed so differently?

Sarney dominated Maranhão essentially because he was the first state politician to take advantage of Brasília's largesse. At the same time, Sarney never was able—perhaps never cared—to eliminate opposition. He may have been the single most powerful politician, but his protégés usually broke away, and politicians made successful careers in the opposition. In truth, Sarney's margin of preeminence was slight until he became Tancredo Neves's vice presidential running mate and then, after Tancredo's death, president. In the aftermath, Maranhão's share of central government pork became enormous. Sarney took care of his family and even captured a Senate seat from nearby Amapá.

Ceará's cliques of colonels had things too easy. They carved up the state, building political machines through traditional rural control. When the military took over in 1964, the colonels adjusted easily, and the generals happily left such cooperative leaders in place. But the colonels forgot the slogan of a famous populist *paulista* leader: "He steals, but he gets things done."[43] The *cearense* bosses stole (or at least they had a reputation for stealing), but mostly they failed to get anything done. Eventually, urban growth made Fortaleza the dominant factor in Ceará's electorate, and when open politics loomed, the cost of maintaining three families of bosses acting like veto players became unbearable. Reaching agreement on policy, given the unanimity rule the bosses had tacitly adopted, became impossible even with lavish patronage, so the bosses were history. Tasso Jereissati was certainly more progressive than was Sarney, but Jereissati's role—more than twenty years later—was similar. Tasso implemented programs benefiting ordinary people. But when his political management—especially his centralization of patronage—proved as skillful as his policy management, the old bosses suddenly found that they could no longer buy enough votes to stay in power.

Within Bahia, Magalhães commanded a political machine far more powerful than any Ceará *coronel*. ACM, however, was never a traditional political boss. He dispensed favors, made and broke political careers, and grew quite wealthy, but he also modernized Bahia's infrastructure and fostered industrial growth. What made all these developments possible? The military regime gave ACM very strong support, lavishing government spending and favorable industrial policies on Bahia. Salvador, traditionally the Left's stronghold, never was a big part of the Bahian electorate. But these factors cannot explain why ACM thrived even after the generals' withdrawal. What happened, however, illustrates again the importance in politics of timing. ACM used central government resources to create a political machine based on bureaucratic power. When Sarney inaugurated the New Republic in 1986, the Bahian delegation in the Chamber of Deputies was the most united of any large state delegation, and ACM had allies in other northeastern states as well. His support was indispensable to Sarney's political survival. So ACM's regional influence turned into national influence, and he became the most powerful single politician in the Brazilian Congress.

---

43. The Portuguese is better: "Rouba, mas faz."

PART 2

—

The Legislative Arena

Chapter 5

Wheeling, Dealing, and Appealing:
What Motivates Deputies?

"Balanced budgets are the rhetoric of incompetent politicians."
Orestes Quércia, former governor of São Paulo[1]

"I think I can say, and say with pride, that we have some legislatures that bring higher prices than any in the world."
Mark Twain (1875)

At the beginning of this book, I argued that the Brazilian Congress has trouble approving laws on issues of national concern. The legislative branch almost never initiates significant laws. While the Congress does acquiesce in many presidential proposals, final approval of these bills carries a high price in pork, patronage, and substantive concessions to privileged, often minute interests. Why are substantive issues so difficult for this legislature? Why is the Congress so obstructionist? A comparison of Brazil's political institutions to those of other nations might lead to expectations of a very active legislature. David M. Olsen and Michael L. Mezey (1991, 201–14) identify characteristics widely associated with legislative activism, including presidentialism, especially with an open and decentralized executive; a candidate-centered, decentralized electoral system; functionally specialized interest groups; political parties that are numerous, weakly organized, internally fragmented, and autonomous; and legislative committees that parallel the structure of administrative agencies. All these characteristics are found in Brazil, and, indeed, Brazil's Congress is active.[2] Its activism, however, is too often directed at stalling legislation until the executive meets the particularistic demands of small groups of deputies.

---

1. Ciro Gomes, former governor of Ceará, claims that Quércia made this remark. The Portuguese is better: "Equilíbrio financeiro é conversa de político incompetente" (*Veja,* January 29, 1992, 9).

2. Mezey (Olsen and Mezey 1991, 207) notes, however, that in two important cases weak parties led to greater activity but not greater action—i.e., the legislatures ultimately could not resolve issues.

139

The obstructionist tendencies of Brazil's legislature have three possible causes. Perhaps—interpreting the veto-players argument narrowly—the multiplicity of parties is a sufficient cause. A second cause lies internally: the legislature's procedural rules might hinder policy-making, either deliberately or through consequences no one anticipated. Policy weakness could also result from the preferences, or ideologies, of deputies themselves. The deputies' avoidance of serious policy-making may be deliberate, either because their primary interests lie in pork barrel or because they prefer weak, nonprogrammatic parties that are unable to aggregate societal demands.[3] Given that this legislature only dates from 1988, it is not possible to assign definitive weights to the three alternatives; rather, I simply examine the supporting evidence for each. Chapter 8 will discuss the first two causes. The question of motivation, the third cause, is the subject of this chapter.[4]

Congressional deputies are affected by ideology, constituency characteristics, election prospects, and pork-barrel inducements. No perfect methodology for weighing these motivations exists. Deputies could be interviewed, but their responses are likely to be unrealistically honest, above pork barrel, and progressive. Orations on the floor could be dissected, but many deputies rarely speak, and all target their remarks to particular audiences. Voting on regular legislation could be analyzed—such roll calls, in fact, will be the subject of chapter 7—but attempts at party discipline may mask other motivations. An intriguing exception, however, is the National Constituent Assembly (ANC) of 1987–88. During this period Congress, not the president, initiated most of the issues that came to a vote. Parties rarely tried to impose discipline, in part because the president's disinterest in most conflicts reduced the availability of side payments and in part because dissidents freely switched parties. Thus, the ANC's 1,021 votes will be the major set of votes from which to infer deputies' motivations. As a comparison, my models will also be evaluated with a set of votes taken on the emergency economic measures decreed by president Fernando Collor de Mello at the beginning of his term.[5]

---

3. Cox and McCubbins (1993) argue that fragmented bases in the United States do not prevent legislators from delegating to parties. In Brazil, however, parties are more locally oriented, and the ease of party switching reduces deputies' incentives to preserve their parties' national reputations. Thanks to Scott Morgenstern for discussion of this point.

4. This analysis of motives is perfectly compatible with the "excess of veto players" argument. Either as individuals or in small groups, deputies—not just parties—become veto players, so their individual ideologies become relevant.

5. Although roll-call votes are available for the whole post-1987 period, this chapter uti-

The chapter proceeds in three sections. The first offers a general discussion of deputies' motivations. The second presents and evaluates a model of voting in the ANC and on the emergency presidential decrees in 1990. The third discusses the implications of the empirical findings.

I.   What Do Deputies Want?

Most studies of the motivations of parliamentarians, especially studies in the rational choice tradition, assume reelection as legislators' primary goal. This assumption is justified in the U.S. House of Representatives, where reelection probabilities are very high, but rates of return in Brazil's Chamber of Deputies are much lower.[6] These rates are so low, in fact, that it may well be irrational for deputies to focus their energies on reelection. In 1990 only about 40 percent of the incumbent deputies were reelected for the 1991–94 term. Of the 60 percent not returning, about half retired or stood for other offices and about half sought reelection to the Chamber but lost. The turnover rate in 1994 was a bit lower than in 1990, with only 40 percent of the deputies failing to return for the 1995–98 session, but in 1998 48 percent of the deputies were not reelected for the current term.[7] Thus, in each legislative session, about half the deputies are serving their first term. Because turnover rates from both retirement and defeat are highest in the developed states of the South and Southeast, their delegations typically have even lower levels of seniority.

Why such high turnover? Some deputies decline to run because they are sure they will lose. Many deputies opt for executive offices simply because mayors are able to exercise more control over programs and can avoid living in Brasília. Some deputies switch to bureaucratic jobs as a way of fattening their clienteles before returning to elective office. Others tire of their restricted importance in policy-making.[8] But even those running for reelection face a high rate of rejection, a rate that would be even higher but for the retirements of those facing certain defeat. Voters reject deputies for a variety of reasons: the weak-

---

lizes votes only from the Sarney and Collor administrations. In this shorter period, much better information about pork-barrel benefits to individual deputies is available.

6. A classic treatment of the institutionalization of the U.S. House appears in Polsby 1968.

7. The 1998 turnover rate is an estimate based on deputies serving as of August 1, 1999. Since a few reelected deputies might have already resigned by this date, the estimate may be off by a percentage point or two.

8. Based on her interviews with deputies, Celina Souza has made this argument (personal communication). She emphasizes the minimal visibility of congressional committees.

ness of both party and personal ties, corruption scandals, shifts in party alignments, and so on.[9]

These high turnover rates raise a caution against the facile assumption, coming mostly from the traditional stability of the U.S. House of Representatives, that reelection is elected politicians' primary goal. For many Brazilian deputies, especially those from poor regions, politics is a business.[10] These politicians may choose to leave the Chamber, pursue other avenues of mobility, and return later. In the reality of Brazilian politics, it is more reasonable to assume that politicians seek to maximize income over their whole careers.

Faced with such daunting rates of congressional turnover, Brazilian legislators are likely to expect short careers. Does this expectation affect their motivations and behavior? Because deputies know they probably will not be around to profit from efforts to acquire legislative skills, they are less likely to invest in attaining such expertise. They find it better to concentrate on delivering pork to their districts, because pork advances local and state executive or bureaucratic ambitions. Since federal ministries control the distribution of most available pork, deputies cultivate relationships with the executive branch.

Concentration on pork does not automatically preclude broader legislative activity. According to Carlos Alberto Marques Novaes (1994, 109), between 1989 and 1991 deputies introduced 6,601 bills. Only 43 were approved, and the vast majority never got out of committee. Novaes concludes that deputies introduce legislation with no intention of shepherding their bills through to final passage. Deputies submit bills, the Chamber prints them, and these printed versions (*avulsos*) are sent to constituents as proof of "service."

How do deputies view parties? Brazil's electoral rules produce parties with individualistic deputies. Consider deputies with geographically scattered electoral bases. With fragmented bases hindering even minimal accountability to constituents, these deputies should prefer weak parties—that is, parties unable to impose discipline or a common program (Novaes 1994). Even deputies with concentrated vote distributions—with constituencies demanding high levels of local benefits—have little reason to support parties whose leaders will compel the deputies to vote jointly. Only the small minority of deputies focusing pri-

---

9. Chapter 2 demonstrated that deputies with dominant vote bases (electoral bases where they received most of their key municipalities' votes) more easily survived changes in overall party vote shares.

10. In some regions, as demonstrated earlier, politics is a family business. In Bahia 40 percent of the deputies have a relative (of the same generation or older) holding political office. In São Paulo only 5 percent come from political families.

marily on national-level legislation will seek parties with authority to discipline the members and prevent free riders on the party's reputation.[11]

II.　Voting in the Constituent Assembly and on President Collor's Emergency Decrees

In 1987 and 1988, the Chamber of Deputies and the Senate met each morning in joint session as the Constituent Assembly; each afternoon they separated to conduct regular legislative business. Constitution writing is naturally quite different from normal legislative politics. Parties less often define clear-cut positions and seldom attempt to discipline members. Ideological positions are more important in constitutional assemblies than in regular legislation. It would appear, then, that a constitutional assembly more clearly reveals deputies' underlying motivations, but this assumption can be tested by applying the model both to the constitutional assembly and to voting on subsequent legislation in the same legislature.

This analysis of the ANC builds on the pioneering research of Maria D'Alva Gil Kinzo, who fashioned a series of issue scales from key constitutional votes. I selected four scales as indicators of basic dimensions of voting.[12] The

---

11. The broad preference for weak parties does not mean that most deputies prefer no party discipline at all. Along with state delegations and interest-specific caucuses (such as the *bancada rural*, or rural delegation), parties are one way deputies organize themselves to bargain. Deputies join bargaining units because they gain from conceding a certain amount of autonomy. Their acceptance of reduced autonomy contributes to predictability in the group's negotiations with the executive. Predictability is an obvious prerequisite for success in bargaining—i.e., a group leader promising a certain number of votes must be able to deliver. How much unity makes a party credible is difficult to quantify, and most parties allow certain members occasional defections for reasons of constituency pressure or conscience. Chapter 7 elaborates this point. See also Aldrich 1995.

12. Kinzo (1989) leaves unclear whether the groups of votes are true scales or merely indexes. I applied standard scale tests (with the help of David Nixon), retaining only those votes meeting scaling criteria. Logit analyses of individual votes were generally consistent with regressions based on the multivote scales, but these scales are preferable because they minimize the effects of absentee voting and other peculiarities specific to particular votes. I call Kinzo's "Economic Conservatism" scale "Statism-Welfarism," because the items really measure willingness to support government intervention in the economy and defense of issues championed by unions. I renamed her "Support for Democratic Values" scale "Support for Popular Democracy," because a number of its items concern class-action lawsuits and direct democracy, while other items concern military intervention. The Congressional Power scale includes nine items, with a typical item requiring congressional approval for the federal budget. The Support for Executive scale includes five items; a typical item gave future presidents a five-year mandate. The State Economic Intervention–Welfarism scale included six items; a typical item dealt with indemnities paid to workers fired unfairly

four scales include "support for expanded congressional prerogatives," "support for expanded executive authority," "statism-welfarism," and "support for popular democracy."

The second set of votes comes from the same legislature—that is, the deputies voting on constitutional provisions then proceeded to vote on a series of emergency decrees.[13] Brazil's economy teetered at the edge of hyperinflation when Collor assumed power in early 1990. In short order Collor promulgated a series of draconian measures. The most significant and controversial decrees reformed the structure of central government ministries, fixed prices and salaries, established a privatization program, regulated civil servants' conduct, altered business taxes, eliminated fiscal subsidies, and—most dramatically—sequestered private financial assets. Collor's decrees arrived at the legislature as *medidas provisórias* (emergency measures). Though the decrees became law immediately, they would become null if the legislature failed to approve them within a set time period. Given that the president's party had few congressional seats, passage depended on the persuasive power of Collor and legislative allies.

Explanatory Variables

Dominance and Clustering
How should the spatial distribution of electoral support—that is, dominance and clustering—influence deputies' voting? Again, dominance refers to the ability of a deputy to collect high percentages of all votes cast (for any candidate) in those municipalities contributing the bulk of the deputy's individual vote. Dominant deputies are mostly found in less developed, more rural areas. If the wealth of constituencies is held constant, deputies dominating their core municipalities should oppose state economic intervention and short-term welfare measures. Dominance is impossible without the backing of a community's economic elite, and local elites rarely support agrarian reform or expanded workers' rights. Dominant deputies should also uphold executive power. As dominance increases, deputies are better able to claim credit for the pork they deliver, so they work harder at bringing pork home (Shepsle and Weingast

---

by employers. The Support for Popular Democracy Scale included six items; a typical item permitted class-action suits. The index of President Collor's emergency decrees included eight items; the most important allowed the government to confiscate a substantial part of private savings for as long as eighteen months. See appendix C for discussion of the Constituent Assembly. In each case the variable summed across the individual items. Further information about the scales is available on request.

13. For an extensive treatment of emergency measures, see Figueiredo and Limongi 1997a.

1987). Because the executive in Brazil controls most pork-barrel programs, good relations with the president are a must. Moreover, dominant deputies tend to be more senior, so they have time in which to develop good relations. Dominant deputies should also be reluctant to expand congressional authority, because increases would weaken the old guard's monopoly on access.

Clustering means that the municipalities contributing the bulk of the deputy's individual votes are physically close to each other. Clustered votes make deputies more accountable to voters and less responsive to local or regional bosses. Face-to-face contact in clustered constituencies is greater, community organizations participate more in campaigns, and a deputy's career is more likely to be rooted in this core region. Accountability makes deputies more likely to promote a legislative agenda, so they seek expanded congressional power. Greater accountability, however, also encourages deputies to maximize pork, and since the executive plays a central role in pork distribution, clustered deputies might be expected to support expanded executive power. In the South, by contrast, public attitudes were so hostile to President Sarney that deputies were likely to seek reduced executive authority, even though they might individually try to maintain links to the president. Clustered vote bases should produce deputies with a populist bent—deputies who will tend toward economic interventionism and favor organized labor's demands. Last, support for popular democracy is likely to be higher among clustered-vote deputies, because they rarely depend on deals with local elites that enable them to deliver private goods rather than local public goods.

Constituency Attributes[14]

In the political context of the late 1980s, deputies relying on voters in industrial areas should be pro-Congress, antiexecutive, and statist-welfarist on economic issues. At the same time, the control constituencies exert over deputies should depend not merely on the wealth and industrial level of a deputy's voters but also on the constituency's homogeneity. Imagine two constituencies with the same average level of income or industrialization. In one, most municipalities are near the mean on these characteristics; in the other, the communities are more diverse. In the more homogeneous constituency, voters' interests are clearer to their deputy because the municipalities are similar; in a heterogeneous constituency, interests are diverse and conflicting.[15]

---

14. Wealth and industrial development are highly correlated, so only the overall relationship between these indicators and voting is of interest.

15. Per capita income is a reasonable indicator of the economic development of an areal unit, but the concept is more difficult to operationalize when actual voters, rather than a legally fixed dis-

To test the relationship between constituency wealth, the intramunicipal variation of wealth, and the scales measuring voting behavior, I created dummy variables to identify deputies with constituencies of high, medium, and low heterogeneity. I then multiplied these dummies by the measure of wealth. Ultimately, the regression results show the effects of wealth for each range of heterogeneity.

Career Path

Though many career paths lead to the Chamber, most fall into one of three modal trajectories: local, business, and bureaucratic.[16] "Local" deputies are those who served as mayors or on municipal councils as one of their last two jobs prior to joining the Chamber of Deputies. A "business" career implies that the deputy acted primarily in the private sector. "Bureaucratic" deputies held high-level jobs in state or federal agencies. Extensive conversations with Brazilian informants, including journalists, academics, and deputies, persuaded me that business types differed fundamentally from other kinds of deputies. Business types tended to see their activities in the Chamber as an extension of their personal economic interests. When deputies lobby for private hospitals, the construction industry, or poultry processors, they do not merely represent important constituents; in fact, the economic interest may hardly function in their districts. Instead, such "corporativist" deputies represent their own personal interests.[17] Some deputies run lobbying operations out of their offices as a kind of small business, charging fees for representational services.[18] Obviously, not all business deputies embody a corporativist representational style, but they

---

trict, define a constituency. I define the per capita income of a given deputy's voters as the average per capita income of the municipalities in which the deputy received votes, weighted by the percentage of the deputy's total vote received in each municipality. The homogeneity of the constituency is defined as the coefficient of variation across municipalities of these same weighted per capita incomes.

16. This formulation has a weakness: it misclassifies deputies whose expected career path is a combination of two or more discrete careers. In other words, one can be a career politician but leave elective office for a stint in the bureaucracy or business. Knowing that such shifts are probable, the behavior of deputies whose most recent jobs were elected should be closer to the behavior of pure bureaucrats or business types. With the passage of time and the greater institutionalization of Brazil's legislature, a more nuanced career analysis will be possible (see also Samuels 1998, 2001).

17. Henry Jackson was often called the "senator from Boeing," but the label referred to the importance of Boeing to his home state, not to personal business interests.

18. A staff member for one northeastern deputy estimated that she and the deputy divided about $100,000 per year paid by firms for lobbying the executive branch. The staff member did most of the real lobbying; the deputy distributed his share of the money in small payoffs within his constituency.

adopt it more often than do deputies with local or bureaucratic backgrounds. Given the strong regulatory power of the executive and bureaucracy, business deputies should be antilegislature and proexecutive. Their economic attitudes, given their position as private-sector employers, should be antistatist and antiwelfarist. Their support for popular democracy is likely to be low, because many of the scale's items involve antibusiness mobilization.

Another path marks one of the legislature's most notorious factions, the roughly forty Protestant ministers called *evangélicos*. They are widely seen as quite pork oriented, willing to grant the executive practically anything in exchange for public works benefiting their religious ministries.

Seniority and Electoral Insecurity
In a legislature with high turnover, few deputies accrue much seniority. The legislature's internal rules, in addition, barely reward seniority. Committee chairs retain their positions for only two years, senior deputies have no additional staff allowance, and the dominance of party proportionality as a criterion for committee appointment (coupled with the large number of parties) gives senior members little advantage. But senior deputies have time and motivation to establish close ties with ministries supplying constituency-specific goods. In the early legislatures of the new republic, many senior deputies had served during the military period. They were likely to maintain strong ties with executive branch agencies. They are also frequent candidates for ministerial positions, so they are likely to be proexecutive. Because a more powerful legislature would benefit newer deputies, senior members are unlikely to support expanded congressional prerogatives.

In an open-list proportional system, each deputy's electoral fortunes depend partly on the aggregate vote of all candidates from the party. But deputies' chances depend even more on their individual vote totals, and all deputies know how close they were to defeat in the last election. The further from the top of the party's postelection list, the weaker the deputy. Low-ranking deputies—especially deputies whose electoral dominance allows then to claim exclusive credit for the pork they deliver—are particularly vulnerable to executive pressure, because the president controls the pork that a deputy could use to draw a few more votes at the next election.

State Unity and State Interests
A state's deputies will vote as a bloc when they have a common interest or when a state leader demands unity. On economic and social issues some delegations may be predominantly populist or neoliberal, but such positions represent voter

preferences, not geographic interests. States in the North and Northeast, however, hold more congressional seats and receive more pork than their populations merit, so their deputies ought to support expanded congressional prerogatives. Conversely, because these same deputies tend to be quite senior, they profit from close ties to a strong executive. Overall, then, constituency issues are too diffuse to incline state delegations in any particular direction. Still, state politics matters in Brazil, and some state governors lead powerful machines.[19] These caciques may have little to gain or lose on constitutional issues, but they increase their influence by delivering blocs of deputies, including, in some cases, allied deputies from other parties.[20] On the president's emergency measures, delegations' votes depend on state economic interests and, once again, on governors' political interests. Given these multiple constraints, unequivocal predictions as to the strength or effects of state unity are impossible, but the issue can be explored by including dummy variables for the dominant parties of two states, Bahia and Maranhão, both known for their strong state machines.

Party and Ideology

When political parties are stable and disciplined, voting behavior can be confidently predicted on the basis of party affiliations. Brazilian parties are far from stable and disciplined, however, and deputies jump ship with impunity, even in the middle of legislative sessions. Between 1987 and 1990, for example, 40 percent of all deputies changed parties, mostly during the Constituent Assembly. Whether deputies switched for electoral or ideological reasons, the implications are the same: party in the long term is endogenous. Rather than a determinant of issue positions and electoral tactics—at least in the Constituent Assembly—party is a consequence.

If party affiliations are useless as explanatory variables during a time of intense party switching, is it possible to measure ideological position? One possibility is the deputy's party during the military regime. Until 1982 the right-wing military regime allowed only two parties. The National Renovating Alliance (ARENA) supported the government; the Brazilian Democratic Movement (MDB) opposed it. After 1982, ARENA became the Democratic Social Party (PDS), but former ARENA members constitute the most conservative elements in almost every party (Power 1993, 86–93). I expect former ARENA

---

19. On the importance of state politics, see Samuels 1998.
20. Weak governors seek to increase their influence. In the legislative struggle over Cardoso's efforts to promote a constitutional amendment permitting his own reelection, certain small state governors organized their deputies to trade support for the amendment for financial rewards. The governors, it appeared, became brokers to increase their clout in Brasília (see *Folha de São Paulo,* June 25–27, 1997).

members to be proexecutive and anti-Congress, opposed to state intervention and the demands of organized labor, and (given their role in the military regime) less supportive of popular democracy.

By the time the Chamber voted on Collor's emergency decrees, party membership had stabilized. Party can now be more confidently tested as an explanatory variable. The Workers' Party (PT) and the Democratic Workers' Party (PDT) opposed Collor; the PDS and the Liberal Front Party (PFL) supported him; the centrist Brazilian Democratic Movement Party (PMDB) and the patronage and pork-oriented Brazilian Labor Party (PTB) split. In the large majority of votes in the ANC, parties made no recommendations (*encaminhamentos*) to their members, while on the emergency measures such instruction was common, though neither legally nor practically binding.

The Pork Barrel

In single-member systems, all deputies should be equally interested in pork-barrel projects, because they are equally able to claim credit for the projects built in their districts.[21] In multimember constituencies, the ability to claim credit decreases as the number of vote-receiving deputies increases. Brazil's Left-leaning deputies often share working-class constituencies where credit claiming is impossible and where national economic issues take precedence over public works. Thus, in the long run, pork-oriented deputies tend to be anti-labor and proexecutive.[22] In the short run, the executive may offer specific inducements to attract deputies. President Sarney, for example, utilized pork to recruit deputies on key constitutional votes, including both the issue of a five-year term for himself and for future presidents as well as the issue of presidentialism over parliamentarism. Collor claimed to be above such "politics," but the revelations surrounding his impeachment indicate that the Collor administration reached new depths of corruption.

Fortunately, success in attracting pork is measurable. The variable "Pork Payoff to Municipality" is the probability that a deputy could claim credit for an intergovernmental transfer made in 1988 to municipalities where that deputy received votes.[23] "Pork Payoff to Deputy" refers to a 1988 social assistance pro-

---

21. Pork-barrel projects are not necessarily or even largely corrupt. On this distinction see Geddes and Ribeiro Neto 1999.

22. Supporting executive power does not mean weakening congressional prerogatives. Two of the items on the scale involve municipal elections—many deputies may envision a future run for municipal office. It was also unlikely that the vote on lengthening presidential terms was decided on principle; rather, it was decided on pro- or anti-Sarney lines.

23. Municipalities, not deputies, receive intergovernmental transfers. If a deputy wins all the votes in a municipality, then that deputy clearly gets all the credit. Suppose, however, a group of deputies shares a municipality's votes. Do all deputies claim credit equally? Do they divide the

gram of the Ministry of Planning (SEPLAN). Specific deputies sponsored this program in each municipality. "Radio and TV License" calculates the probability that the Ministry of Communications granted a concession during the ANC to a municipality in which the deputy had an electoral base.[24] "Ministerial Request" indicates that in 1990 the deputy met personally with the ministers of infrastructure, agriculture, education, or social action. These meetings were not about the weather.[25]

Results

Table 10 presents the model's results for four basic dimensions of voting in the ANC.[26] Consider first the results for dominance, clustering, and constituency income. Deputies dominating their vote bases were more likely to back the executive and less likely to support congressional prerogatives. Dominance was unrelated, however, to statism-welfarism or support for popular democracy. Dominance does not, therefore, simply predict deputies' Left-Right positions. Rather, it leads to a purely "political" tactic: stay close to the executive and minimize support for a Congress whose structure already affords privileged access to dominant deputies (Novaes 1994).

Clustering of electoral bases produced effects that support and amplify our expectations. Both inside and outside the South, deputies with clustered vote bases supported congressional power and statist-welfarist issues. But clustering led to antiexecutive positions only in the South and to more support for pop-

---

credit in proportion to their vote shares? Does the leading vote getter get all the credit? Does the credit go to deputies from the president's party, or is it divided in terms of party vote shares? Most informants believed that either the leading vote getter of any party or of the president's party would get the pork. I tried various formulations, achieving the best results by assuming that only the leading candidate in a given municipality could claim credit but that leader could be of any party. If a deputy received credit for pork in a municipality contributing only a minute fraction of the deputy's total statewide vote, the credit would do little electorally. In aggregating the individual municipal probabilities, I therefore weighted each municipality's probability by the fraction of the deputy's total vote the municipality contributed. In effect, the indicator measures the probability that someone voting for deputy X benefited from an intergovernmental transfer. The precise period of pork delivery in May–June 1988 corresponds exactly to President Sarney's campaign for a five-year term and for presidentialism. Longer periods produced weaker but similar results.

24. The calculation was analogous to the "Pork Payoff to Municipality" variable. I adjusted the probability where I knew a particular deputy owned the radio or TV station.

25. The parliamentary liaisons of these ministries maintain lists of deputies meeting with ministers. While requesting that individual names remain confidential, they permitted the copying of the lists.

26. To simplify tables 10 and 11, I eliminated the variables measuring the effects of wealth in contexts of high and low variance. Their coefficients were always insignificant.

TABLE 10.   OLS Estimates for Voting in the Constituent Assembly

Independent Variables	Congressional Power	Support for Executive	Statism-Welfarism	Support for Popular Democracy
Constant	−.176**	.136*	.113	.076
Municipal dominance	−.110**	.131**	−.037	.002
Clustering in South	.019**	−.024**	.015*	.008
Clustering outside South	.029**	−.009	.025*	.024*
Wealth × Medium variance	.061	−.115**	.091	.104*
Local career	.033	−.001	.052	−.002
Business career	−.112**	−.146**	−.143**	−.158**
Bureaucratic career	−.059	.044	−.046	−.034
Evangelical	−.204**	.194**	−.095**	−.126
Terms in office	−.037	.045	.007	−.029
Rank in party list	−.005	.113**	.004	.003
Bahia × PFL	−.108**	.087**	−.130**	−.162**
Bahia × PMDB	.103**	−.149**	.116**	.071
Marahão × PFL	−.028	.076**	−.043	−.032
Maranhão × PMDB	−.011	.036	.027	−.003
ARENA	−.304**	.190**	−.342**	−.266**
Pork-barrel indicators				
Pork to municipality	−.104**	.059	−.070	−.119**
Ministerial audience	−.156**	.145**	−.193**	−.182**
Radio-TV license	−.065*	.079**	−.097**	−.141**
Pork to deputy	−.142**	.215**	−.122**	−.095*
R^2	.34	.38	.33	.27
R^2 (without pork variables)	.17	.28	.24	.18
F	9.25	10.89	8.87	6.63
N	403	403	403	403

Note: Entries are standardized regression coefficients.
** $p < .05$, two-tailed test   * $p < .10$, two-tailed test

ular democracy only outside the South. These regional differences come from context: outside the South support for a strong executive is widespread, and even clustered deputies succumb to executive pressure. At the same time, oligarchical rule is still prevalent outside the South, so only when deputies cluster do we find the responsiveness to voters that leads to support for mass, democratic politics.

Wealth and industry had the expected effects—antiexecutive, economically statist-welfarist, supportive of popular democracy—but only in constituencies of moderate heterogeneity. In other words, increasing wealth failed to affect voting precisely where I expected the strongest effects—that is, in the most uniform constituencies. Why? Uniform constituencies, it seems, tend to fall into two groups. One includes deputies picking up nearly all their votes in big cities and industrial suburbs. Such deputies have concentrated-shared constituencies and mostly vote Left: antiexecutive, welfarist, and so on. The other cluster includes deputies constructing constituencies by making deals with local bosses, typically in a scattered-dominant pattern. Such deputies usually vote on the Right, the opposite of their big-city colleagues. These groups tend to cancel each other out: wealthy big cities, especially São Paulo, are more industrial and hence more supportive of PT candidates; wealthy scattered municipalities are likely to be agricultural and more conservative.

The results for the career variables confirmed deputies' and journalists' observations: politicians with business backgrounds supported executive power, opposed congressional influence, and opposed labor's economic demands. Such deputies also opposed—perhaps in defense of their economic interests— popular democracy. Bureaucrats and local politicians manifested no tendencies at all.[27] Evangelicals, as expected, were proexecutive, anti-Congress, antilabor, and antidemocratic.

How important were seniority and electoral insecurity? Many of the most senior deputies had served in the Congress before 1985, during military rule. Their votes were indistinguishable from junior deputies on economic and popular democracy issues and were weakly but positively supportive of executive power. It is striking that the Chamber's most senior deputies opposed increasing congressional influence over policy.

Electoral insecurity influenced only one of the issue scales: weak deputies were proexecutive. That linkage is crucial, however, because the executive controls electoral resources vital to weak deputies. It should be emphasized, however, that the relationship between electoral weakness and support for executive power does not mean a disinterested vote on an issue of principle. Instead, it suggests that even in a constitutional assembly—where long-term perspectives ought to prevail—weak deputies must look to their own political survival. They supported an expansion of executive power because at that moment their short-term future dictated such support.

Strong state leaders matter politically. Some governors polarized their delegations. The single most dominant state-level organization, the Liberal Front Party of Bahia's Antônio Carlos Magalhães, exercised considerable power over its deputies: PFL deputies in Bahia stand out as a coherent bloc. But Bahia's PMDB deputies emerge as a vigorously opposing bloc. Thus, the extra-right-

---

27. The absence of differences for bureaucratic deputies contradicts Power (1993), who found a strong executive orientation.

wing Bahian PFL is matched by an extra-left-wing PMDB. In Maranhão, the Sarney organization, even with its chief in the presidency, unified only on the key issue of executive power. On that issue the PMDB was almost as pro-executive as Sarney's PFL. Thus, Brazil's folk wisdom is on target: ACM polarized politicians; Sarney reconciled them.

Former members of the promilitary ARENA party behaved as predicted: proexecutive, anti-Congress, opposed to labor's economic demands, and low on popular democracy. Fundamentally, the ARENA variable measures long-term ideological predispositions. While many former ARENA members have moved into centrist or even mildly leftist parties—maximizing their electability, one presumes—their positions remain obdurately conservative.

Consider finally the effects of pork. Overall, deputies receiving pork benefits voted to weaken the legislature and strengthen the executive and tended to oppose statism-welfarism and popular democracy. Though a few coefficients are insignificant, the directions are always correct, and the insignificant cases occur on the fuzziest indicator—that is, where the deputy benefiting from a public works project could not easily be identified. Without the pork variables, moreover, the model's percentage of variance explained (R^2) declines by an average of 28 percent. In sum, pork buys—or at least rents—deputies.

In table 11 the model is applied to deputies' support for President Collor's eight emergency measures.[28] Each vote supporting Collor is assigned a 1; each vote opposed receives a 0. The dependent variable is simply the sum of the pro-Collor votes. Though broadly similar to the ANC model, the regression includes a number of important modifications. First, issue positions—the object of explanation in the first model—become explanatory variables. Second, the model categorizes deputies both by their actual parties and by their previous affiliation, if any, with ARENA. By 1990 the party switching of the ANC period had settled down; party now could really mean something. Adding parties also allows the separate measurement of dominance for deputies from the right-wing PFL and PDS and from the centrist PMDB. These two dummies enable examination of the hypothesis that dominance gives deputies autonomy from party leaders.[29]

Both vote distribution and constituency wealth continue to influence voting. Dominant PFL and PDS deputies opposed the president. (The PFL as a

---

28. Two of the emergency decrees dealt with questions of executive-branch organization, four decrees affected economic stabilization and privatization, one established new rules for civil servants, and one concerned the right to strike. See appendix C for details on the emergency decrees.

29. Chapter 7, which focuses on party discipline from 1988 to 1996, revisits this question of autonomy from party leaders.

TABLE 11.   OLS Estimates of Determinants of Support for Collor's Emergency Decrees

Independent Variable	Parameter Estimate
Constant	−.080
Dominance × PFL-PDS	−.073**
Dominance × PMDB	.080**
Clustering in South	−.003
Clustering outside South	.078
Wealth × Medium variance	−.117**
Business career	.048
Bureaucratic career	.014
Evangelical	.080**
Terms in office	−.027
Rank in party list	−.014
Bahia × PFL	.011
Bahia × PMDB	.008
Maranhão × PFL	.008
Maranhão × PMDB	.015
ARENA	.207**
PDT	−.166**
PT	−.235**
PFL	.046
PDS	.120*
PMDB	−.301**
Congressional power	.009
Support for executive	.117**
Statism-welfarism	.127**
Popular democracy	−.023
Pork-barrel indicators	
Pork to municipality	−.021
Ministerial audience	.125**
Radio-TV license	.055
Pork to deputy	.008
$R^2 = .52$ F = 14.62 $N = 379$	

Note: Entries are standardized regression coefficients.
** $p < .05$, two-tailed test   * $p < .10$, two-tailed test

whole neither backed nor opposed President Collor, and the PDS supported him only weakly.) Dominant PMDB deputies also dissented from their party—they backed the president while the party as a whole opposed him. Thus, in both cases, dominance facilitated autonomy. In an open-list system, it is easy to see why dominance frees deputies, but why should autonomous deputies want to oppose their party leaders? The answer, I believe, is that PDS-PFL defectors tend to be located in states where most deputies opposed the president, and

PMDB defectors are mostly in supportive states, so these deputies were moving toward the center of their respective state political contexts.

Constituency wealth affects voting behavior only for deputies whose vote bases are moderately heterogeneous. The mutually canceling effects of the two kinds of low-variance constituencies—scattered rural municipalities and concentrated big city bases—again seem the most likely explanation.

Do powerful governors influence their deputies? Once again paralleling the model of voting in the constitutional assembly, dummy variables for Bahia and Maranhão estimate the influence of ACM and Sarney. In neither case did the deputies from these states stand out in their voting behavior. This result differs from the ANC model, where the Bahian governor polarized his delegation. The difference probably stems from nature of the two kinds of votes. In the Assembly, deputies were more likely to struggle with questions of long-term ideological significance. On the emergency measures, they decided immediate pocketbook issues. Economic interests dominated ideological disputes. ACM remained a mighty force in national-level politics, but the emergency measures did not have a particular effect on Bahia, so the governor's delegation voted along other criteria.

Ideology and party had independent and significant influence. Proexecutive, antilegislature, antilabor deputies supported President Collor. Previous affiliation with ARENA also contributed independently—that is, ARENA's heirs were strongly pro-Collor. Members of the PT and Brizola's PDT opposed the president, while PDS and PFL members supported him. The centrist PMDB and the highly clientelistic PTB fell in the middle. Although this finding might suggest that parties, in spite of their fragmentation and incoherence, play a role in legislative voting, such a conclusion would be premature. Party members vote together because they have common electoral interests, because they have organized themselves into bargaining units to increase individual members' leverage over the executive, or because party leaders impose sanctions. These explanations, which I will attempt to test in chapter 7, affect the view of parties as organizations where leaders dominate followers or where followers choose to delegate certain prerogatives to leaders (Cox and McCubbins 1993).

The only personal characteristic affecting support for the emergency decrees was "Evangelical Background." Former Protestant ministers supported the president more than did deputies with other backgrounds. Seniority and electoral weakness had no effect.

Of the variables measuring affinity for pork-barrel programs, one strongly influenced presidential support. Deputies meeting with ministers voted with the president. Of the four indicators of pork barrel, this variable was the sharpest, since the identity of the deputy receiving the pork was unambiguous. Once again, the evidence supports the idea of a strong linkage between pork-barrel benefits and support for presidentialism.

III.   Discussion and Conclusion

This chapter began with a puzzle. Brazil's legislature is quite active, but the Congress accomplishes little on its own initiative, and its activism often results in obstructing presidential proposals even though a majority of deputies have few objections to the policy innovations themselves. Instead, presidential proposals are subject to intense bargaining over extremely parochial substantive interests and over pork and patronage.

Legislative obstructionism can have three causes: a large number of parties that are far apart ideologically, procedural roadblocks, or an excess of members with little interest in broad legislation. This chapter focused on the third cause—that is, on motivations. What mix of constituency pressures, ideology, electoral needs, and local interests determines voting patterns?

To explore deputies' motivations, the chapter modeled two sets of votes. The first set was linked to a series of broad issue areas in the 1987–88 Constituent Assembly, while the second determined the fate of a group of emergency decrees issued by President Collor in 1990. On the constitutional issues of congressional prerogatives, executive power, statism-welfarism, and popular democracy, the individual consequences of the electoral system made a difference. Deputies with more clustered votes tended to be pro-Congress, antiexecutive, supportive of state intervention and welfare, and supportive of popular democracy. These positions resulted, I suggest, from the greater accountability that vote clustering produces. Dominant deputies, by contrast, backed the executive and opposed a stronger Congress, and dominance gave deputies the autonomy to dissent from their parties' mainstreams.

The social characteristics of constituencies did influence congressional voting, though modestly, in the sense that industrial areas elected more liberal deputies. Overall, however, socioeconomic conditions forged only weak ties between voters and deputies. Brazilian citizens exert pressure for pork-barrel programs but on broader issues have little control over representatives. This finding should not come as a surprise, because no observer of a Brazilian election could feel confident that many voters know anything at all about the positions of their deputies. Ironically, Protestant voters may have the tightest control over their representatives, both in terms of ideological positions and in terms of pork.

Ideology played a large role in legislative voting. Former members of the ARENA party were consistently anti-Congress, proexecutive, antilabor, and lower on support for popular democracy. Deputies with these values clustered in parties that supported President Collor on his emergency economic decrees and constituted his strongest supporters even within the progovernment parties.

Powerful state governors influenced their delegations in identifiable ways. The governor of Bahia cared about constitutional issues, and he polarized his delegation between partisans and opponents. Sarney, a weaker leader, mobilized his home-state supporters only on the issue of executive strength, but his more conciliatory approach brought him support from opponents inside the state as well.

Perhaps the most striking finding was the importance of the deputies' orientations to particularistic benefits and programs as determinants of broader positions. The coefficients of the pork-barrel measures are quite large, and the model's explained variance improves substantially with their inclusion. In the Constituent Assembly, deputies could be bought or at least rented: deputies receiving public works for their bailiwicks were proexecutive, anti-Congress, antilabor, and low on support for popular democracy. At the beginning of the Collor government, pork effects were smaller, partly because the administration was somewhat disorganized and partly because Collor seemed to believe his charisma could mobilize support. Still, pork-oriented deputies consistently backed the executive. The importance of direct benefits to deputies speaks volumes about the absence of links, on issues of national scope, between voters and their representatives and goes far toward explaining the absence of legislative initiative on the part of the Congress.[30]

Nonetheless, a reduction in the availability of particularistic benefits is unlikely to transform the legislature into a paragon of national problem solving. Indeed, if the electoral structure were left unchanged, a shrinkage in pork might prove counterproductive. In the current system, the executive builds coalitions by coupling deputies' disinterest in broad policy with their desire for pork. A reduction in pork would lead to greater turnover and to the gradual replacement of pork-oriented deputies in the legislature. In the absence of programmatic parties, more deputies would rely, by necessity, on ties to "corporativist" organizations—that is, on ties to groups representing narrow economic interests.[31] The resulting legislature might well be more active in the sense that "segmentalist" demands would receive a hearing, but it would also be more conflictual and less responsive to executive guidance.

---

30. See C. Souza 1997 and Martínez-Lara 1996.

31. For a recent work on the importance of "segmental" interests in Brazilian policy-making, see Weyland 1996a.

Chapter 6

Presidential Coalition-Building Strategies

"Give, that you may receive."

Deputy Roberto Cardoso Alves

"Being president is like being a jackass in a hailstorm. There's nothing to do but to stand there and take it."

Lyndon Baines Johnson

In many political systems, including those whose presidents and legislatures are independently elected, chief executives confidently count on the backing of their parliaments in all except the most extreme circumstances. Not so in Brazil, where presidents must continually battle to secure legislative support. This chapter explores the strategies presidents adopt in this struggle. These strategies vary both across and within individual presidencies. Presidents, I will demonstrate, face a dilemma. They need cabinet members to serve as brokers between themselves and deputies. But cabinet members are also politicians, and as such pursue their own political agendas, which may be very different from those of the presidents who appoint them.

The chapter explores the tension between presidential and ministerial strategies by modeling the distribution of grants that municipalities receive from the central government. The grants come from a series of programs across the New Republic: in 1986, the beginning of the Sarney administration; in 1988, while Sarney was seeking support for presidentialism and for his own five-year term; and from 1990 to 1995, including the entire Collor-Franco administration and the beginning of the Cardoso government. A series of models assesses the probability that any given municipality received a grant during a particular period. These periods include the beginning of the Collor administration, Collor's impeachment crisis, and so on. The approach is both empirical and inductive.[1]

---

1. Research using these agreements as indicators of presidential strategy has not previously

By comparing the distribution of grants in different periods and in different programs, I hope to illuminate presidential and ministerial tactics. To what kinds of deputies do presidents target appeals? Do presidents reward their old friends and loyalists? Do they instead pursue wavering deputies? Are appeals targeted to particular parties, regions, or states? Do individual ministers, seeking to further their own political careers, deviate from presidential strategies? Are these deviations costly to the chief executive?

The President's Dilemma

Part 1 of this book demonstrated how Brazil's electoral system produces a legislature with numerous weakly disciplined parties and a surplus of pork-oriented and corporatist deputies. Such legislatures are likely to be much better at distributing pork than at making laws on issues of truly national scope. These difficulties matter less where a president dominates the legislature. But when key proposals in an executive's program require approval by a senate and chamber of deputies, sometimes by a supermajority vote, congressional intransigence becomes a serious problem.

How does Brazil fare in terms of the balance of power between president and Congress? Matthew Soberg Shugart and John M. Carey (1992) rank Latin American presidents according to their prerogatives—that is, their powers. Among presidents' potential legislative powers, Shugart and Carey include the right to veto legislation, to issue decrees, to control the budget, and to propose referenda.[2] Nonlegislative powers include the right to name a cabinet without parliamentary interference, to avoid parliamentary censure, to dismiss cabinet ministers at will, and to dissolve the parliament. Currently, Brazilian presidents possess total and partial vetoes, issue temporary decrees with the force of law, and play central roles in the budget process. Nothing restricts their ability to form cabinets, and the legislature cannot censure ministers. About the only thing presidents cannot do is dissolve the Congress. Overall, Shugart and Carey rank Brazil's presidents among the world's strongest. This dominant presi-

---

been undertaken, and there are no studies of truly parallel situations in other countries. As a result, a purely deductive approach positing optimal strategies in advance of empirical testing is impossible. Amorim Neto 1998, Geddes 1994a, and Schneider 1991 stand out among the few serious attempts to examine presidential appointment strategies outside the United States. Amorim Neto's work is the most directly relevant to the arguments made here.

2. Congress has the power to override presidential vetoes.

dency, moreover, is not just a recent development: Brazilian presidents also ranked among the most powerful in the 1946–64 period.[3]

Still, if Brazil's presidents have so much power, why is governing so hard? The simplest answer is that most new policies, those deviating from the status quo, require legislation. Presidents almost inevitably lack a base of congressional support stable enough to guarantee even simple majorities, and frequently the Constitution requires that legislation be approved by supermajorities of three-fifths of the members of both the Chamber of Deputies and the Senate. As demonstrated earlier, one cause of the executive's difficulties is the electoral system, which causes party support to fragment and small parties to proliferate. Between 1986 and 1990, each of four parties had more than 5 percent of the seats in the Chamber of Deputies. In each of the two post-1991 legislatures, eight parties had more than 5 percent of the seats, but in both cases the largest party held less than 25 percent of the Chamber's seats. As a result, even if every party presented a coherent program, and even if every party was perfectly united, presidents would need party coalitions to govern. Since Brazil's parties are both undisciplined (except for the Workers' Party and, to a lesser degree, the PFL) and generally devoid of serious programs, and since presidential decisions must satisfy regional as well as party interests, presidents are forced to legislate with broad, inclusive coalitions. As Sérgio Henrique Hudson de Abranches (1988) notes, Brazil is unique in combining proportional representation, multipartism, and a strong presidency with an executive branch based on these "grand coalitions."

Appointments to the *ministério,* or cabinet, constitute a central presidential weapon in the search for legislative support. Every chief executive calculates the number of legislative votes cabinet ministers can attract from their parties and states. If each cabinet minister could count on the vote of every party or state colleague, then a rational executive would recruit representatives of the party and state delegations closest to the presidential program until a majority was assured. Unfortunately, putting this tactic into effect is not so simple. Because party discipline is low, and because most state leaders have little control over their delegations, presidents must construct coalitions much larger than bare majorities. In the 1946–64 period, for example, the typical cabinet included parties representing 78 percent of the seats in the Congress.

The tactics of presidents in allocating cabinet posts have varied greatly over the course of the New Republic and between this period and the 1946–64 dem-

---

3. The only Latin American presidency to attain a higher power ranking was Paraguay.

ocratic experiment. Octavio Amorim Neto (2001), in a study of Brazilian cabinet formation in the 1946–64 period, created the "Cabinet Coalescence Rate" to measure the correspondence between party seat shares and cabinet posts. The measure takes values from zero to one, with one indicating a perfect correspondence between the seat shares of the parties in the presidential coalition and their cabinet representation. Cabinet Coalescence Rates reveal that in the earlier period, cabinet allocations corresponded much more closely to legislative seat shares. The nineteen cabinets that formed between 1946 and 1964 had an average coalescence rate of .69, and nine scored above .70. Between 1985 and 1999, by contrast, the average coalescence rate was .49, and no cabinets scored above .66 (Amorim Neto 2001, tables 2 and 3).[4] Amorim Neto implies, in my view correctly, that the key obstacle preventing post-1985 presidents from attaining higher coalescence scores has been the greater number of legislative parties. Between 1946 and 1964, the number of effective legislative parties averaged a bit less than 4; from 1985 until 1999, presidents had to contend with an average of 6.4 legislative parties (Amorim Neto 2001, tables 4 and 5).

If strategic presidents parcel out cabinet positions to maximize legislative support, how successful are these executives? In other words, do presidents gain a lot by allocating according to some "optimal" rule, or are their gains merely marginal? This puzzle turns out to be difficult. Amorim Neto examines the voting discipline of each party as a function of its cabinet posts. He finds that parties favored in the allocation of posts do in fact concede presidents greater support. This method of looking at the results of cabinet allocations, however, does not quite capture what chief executives confront. Presidents know that indulging one party implies punishing another. Strategic presidents are betting, when they favor one party at the expense of another, that they will gain more votes than they lose.

The real test of any allocation strategy, then, is the overall gain or loss, in

---

4. Amorim Neto calculates the Cabinet Coalescence Rate as follows:

$$1 - \frac{1}{2} \sum_{i=1}^{n} \left(|si - Mi| \right)$$

where
   Mi is the percentage of ministries party i receives when the cabinet is formed;
   Si is the percentage of legislative seats party i holds in the total of seats commanded by the parties joining the cabinet when the cabinet is formed.

terms of party support, from its particular distribution of posts. When Amorim Neto implements such a test, he finds that higher coalescence rates have positive and statistically significant effects on party discipline (forthcoming, tables 6 and 7). But this effect is not only small but also depends on the simplifying assumption that each party rewards or punishes the president to the same degree as its share of cabinet posts exceeds or falls below its seat share. This assumption is likely to be wrong. The degree to which a party's members vote together, its "observed party discipline," is really a composite of presidential carrots and sticks combined with party leaders' sanctions, ideological predispositions, pork-barrel proclivities, constituency pressures, and electoral considerations.[5] Since party members vary systematically on these dimensions across parties, each party has a different "baseline" propensity to support the president. If these propensities are graphed, the curves representing the relationship between cabinet positions and presidential support not only have different slopes but may also be nonlinear. Thus, a chief executive may find it expedient to give a particular party "extra" cabinet posts—that is, posts beyond its seat share—because the gain from that party is greater than the loss from the parties whose fair share must be reduced.

Given the inability to estimate the propensities of parties to support the president in the absence of cabinet pressure, I accept Amorim Neto's conclusion that cabinet allocations have statistically significant effects on party discipline. I will turn to a more modest question: How do chief executives use cabinet appointments to satisfy the main determinants of political outcomes—region and party.[6]

Cabinet Construction from Sarney to Cardoso

Do party and regional demands still predominate? Consider the cabinets of Tancredo Neves—who died before taking office—and José Sarney, the first civil-

---

5. In chapter 7 I build a multivariate model with these concepts as a way of measuring individual deputies' willingness to follow their party leaders' voting recommendations.

6. Abranches (1988, 25) claims that in the 1946–64 period, Brazilian presidents regarded certain ministries, including justice, labor, foreign relations, and industry and commerce, as ministries of "political control." The criterion of party strength, mainly favoring the Social Democratic Party (PSD, then the largest party), determined the distribution of these ministries. Regional criteria governed a second group, characterized as "spending" or "clientele" ministries. These ministries, including education, health, and transportation and public works, usually went to politicians from Bahia or Rio de Janeiro. A third group of ministries was both politically and economi-

ian presidents following the military regime. The key economic ministers, from Rio de Janeiro and São Paulo, were appointed to reassure industrialists rather than provide pork. Neves gave the Ministry of Communications, which controls the highly political process of licensing radio and television stations, to Antônio Carlos Magalhães, the powerful Bahian leader. ACM, as demonstrated in chapter 4, had built a dominant state machine by dispensing federal projects to buy loyalties. As communications minister, however, ACM's influence extended to the national plane.

The Ministry of Transportation went first to a politician from Paraná, then to Sarney's fellow *maranhense,* José Reinaldo Tavares. Sarney had built his own career by delivering central government projects to Maranhão, especially roads and bridges, so Tavares's appointment furthered Sarney's postpresidential ambitions. Four different ministers ran the Education Ministry, but for almost the whole period the ministry was a fief for the bosses of Sarney's own Liberal Front Party (PFL). Health remained mainly in the hands of politicians from Bahia, the same state dominating the ministry between 1946 and 1964. This continuity was no accident: by 1986 the Bahian machine had long experience in distributing health-related pork.

At times President Sarney had to swallow painful appointments just to appease powerful state and congressional leaders. His first three ministers of welfare and social assistance, for example, were all political enemies, but the appointments satisfied PMDB congressional leader Ulysses Guimarães. Neves had appointed an economist (supported by the governor of São Paulo) to head the Planning Secretariat, but when this *paulista* departed, Sarney selected a little-known politician from Minas Gerais. Unfortunately, his new appointee seemed bent on converting the Planning Ministry into a conduit for social assistance programs that could help advance his own gubernatorial ambitions in Minas Gerais. After less than a year in office, corruption charges forced the minister to resign. Sarney then appointed a technocratically oriented economist, allowing Newton Cardoso, the governor of Minas Gerais, to make the actual choice. Since Cardoso was part of the historic opposition to Tancredo, the choice confirmed that President Sarney had broken away from his predecessor's base of support.

No single coalitional strategy, no single motivation except the recruitment of personally loyal followers, explains Fernando Collor's cabinet appointments. Consider the traditional spending ministries. Two former members of the Congress, early adherents to Collor's campaign but with little influence in

---

cally strategic. São Paulo PSD members mostly ran treasury, while Pernambucans from the Labor Party (PTB) held agriculture.

the legislature, received the portfolios of education and health. Labor and social welfare went to a pro-Collor labor leader from São Paulo. An unknown from Alagoas (Collor's home state) ran social action, and a respected nonpartisan technocrat headed infrastructure. This mix of politicos and *técnicos* clearly does not reflect a focused attempt to maximize legislative support. Collor—unlike Sarney—preferred ministers with whom he was comfortable politically and personally, and he would have been hindered in any case by his weak party base.

Most of Collor's other ministerial appointments had little political clout. The minister of the economy was an unknown economist but an early Collor adviser. The secretary of science and technology was a former university rector. The environment secretary, who had no party affiliation, had been an environmental activist. Overall, Collor's initial appointments suggest a desire to rule above party. Given his appointments in education, health, social action, and labor, "above party" did not mean "above patronage and pork," because charges of corruption and favoritism plagued all four ministers. The appointments do suggest, however, that Collor was betting on his ability to marshal legislative support not by negotiating with party leaders but instead by dealing directly with individual deputies. Thus, Collor's initial cabinet strategy, reflecting his peculiar mix of populism and arrogance, diverged sharply from his predecessors' strategies.

Cabinet changes during Collor's presidential term seem to show two motivations: a recognition, albeit belated, of the importance of congressional leaders, and a response to the corruption charges leveled against his first cabinet members. Collor replaced the ministers of labor and social action, for example, with experienced congressional leaders from the PFL. When the justice minister's ineptitude—and his romance with the economics minister—became too embarrassing, Collor installed a politically savvy senator. But Collor also appears to have enjoyed the tone of respectability lent by well-known technocrats. He replaced the highly political ministers of education and health, both accused of corruption and favoritism, with a university researcher and a famous surgeon.[7]

Itamar Franco's cabinet appointments seemed to obey three criteria: personal relationship, party representation, and intraparty faction. Of the seventeen nonmilitary ministers, at least ten were the president's personal friends. The ini-

---

7. In Collor's case the corruption was so pervasive that it led ultimately to his impeachment. The extortion scheme masterminded by his confidant, Paulo Cesar Farias, was implemented in part by placing Farias's henchmen in lower-level ministerial positions. These underlings wielded real power; in effect, they made the deals normally arranged by ministers themselves.

tial cabinet represented seven parties: PFL (four members), PMDB (five), PSDB (three), PDT (one), PSB (two), PTB (one), and PT (one). In the case of the larger parties, multiple factions received attention. The two largest elements of the PMDB, for example, the Rio Grande do Sul wing and the Quércia-Fleury (São Paulo) wing, each received one ministry.[8] The PSDB's Ceará wing (Jereissati/Ciro Gomes) garnered the appointment of the Ministry of Social Well-Being, while the São Paulo wing was represented by Fernando Henrique Cardoso (initially foreign relations, then finance).

Cardoso's original cabinet is perhaps best characterized as professional and experienced but not especially political.[9] Eight of his ministers had previously held cabinet-level posts. In terms of technical skills, FHC's first cabinet was probably a new high for Brazil. Of twenty-two ministers, observers typically place thirteen in FHC's "personal" quota—that is, representing neither party nor region—including the leaders of treasury, foreign affairs, education, health, justice, and planning. Cardoso seems to have chosen to reward the loyal. The PSDB picked up six slots (including some in the personal quota) to only three for the PFL and two each for the PTB and PMDB, while nine were regarded as nonparty. The Transportation Ministry, always a prime pork distributor, went to the PMDB's Rio Grande do Sul group, which also received the Justice Ministry. The PTB chose, and FHC accepted, the minister of agriculture. In Minas Gerais, the PSDB and PTB, which had formed a local electoral alliance, nominated a duo: the ministers of labor (PTB) and industry and commerce (PSDB). ACM personally selected the minister of mines and energy, and his PFL also controlled the Social Welfare Ministry. Adding a bit of glitter to the cabinet, Pelé became the minister of sport.[10]

Cabinet selection inevitably creates losers as well as winners. The major loser in Cardoso's first cabinet was the Northeast. With only three ministers (two Pernambucans and one Bahian), and archenemy José Serra holding the Planning Ministry, northeasterners could feel aggrieved. One early winner was ex-president Franco. Although he lacked foreign policy expertise, Franco be-

---

8. In 1993, in the middle of the Franco administration, an effort to secure more PMDB support included a cabinet reshuffle. As part of the deal, directorships in state branches of certain federal agencies were put at the disposal of local and state PMDB leaders. This reshuffle led to the replacement of some state directors of the federal environmental agency, IBAMA. There was no doubt, as I discovered during a private consulting project, that the criteria for replacement were purely political.

9. Cardoso's initial cabinet has a high "coalescence" rate on Amorim Neto's indicator.

10. Ironically, ACM criticized the appointment of the soccer star as premature, arguing that FHC should save it for a low moment in his administration (*Veja,* December 28, 1994, 33).

came ambassador to Portugal. Itamar's adviser, Henrique Hargreaves, a man who knew where the bodies were buried, became the president of the postal service. Another Itamar confidant assumed the presidency of an agency lobbying for small and medium-sized enterprises. Why did Cardoso appoint people who seemed to represent no one and who had no particular policy interests? Noblesse oblige may be part of the answer: the *tucanos* were rewarding Itamar and his group for originally putting Cardoso in the Finance Ministry. Without Itamar's support, Cardoso would not have become president. Itamar's success provides additional support for the thesis of presidential fragility, since the appointments also had the objective of sending the former president into a golden exile. Itamar's group, mostly from the city of Juiz de Fora in Minas Gerais, had considerable influence in the Congress, and the ex-president had dropped hints that he might seek another term in the presidency.

In one sense, the absence of policy interests in Itamar's group gives these appointments the appearance of being cheap payoffs. After all, these appointees draw a salary, and Cardoso avoids further obligations to them. Conversely, the costs of such appointments are not easily limited. Itamar proved embarrassingly reluctant to go to Portugal, while there he behaved inappropriately, and he then demanded and received a post in Washington. In the case of Hargreaves, Cardoso put a trusted ally in the postal vice presidency just to make sure Hargreaves did nothing stupid, but in the end he got caught drawing an enormous "consulting" salary from the private-sector firm of another member of Itamar's group.

Cardoso is the first modern Brazilian president to enjoy a second term in office. Some early observers predicted an easier time for Cardoso in his second term, because most reform proposals will be second-generation measures requiring only 50 percent majorities rather than the three-fifths supermajorities of constitutional reforms. At the same time—and this theme will be taken up at more length in the conclusion—Cardoso will quickly become a lame duck, as all parties maneuver for the 2002 election. His supporting coalition lost ground in the Congress after the 1998 election, and the PSDB lost the governorships of Rio de Janeiro and Minas Gerais along with an allied governor in Rio Grande do Sul.

In this context, FHC's second term began with a more strategic cabinet. The president's personal quota shrank from thirteen to ten ministers.[11] The PFL's share grew from three to four posts. Two went to allies of Antônio

---

11. The count of "personal quota" ministers is inevitably subjective. I rely here on the view of Fleischer 1998.

Carlos Magalhães, now president of the Senate and clearly the second-most powerful politician in Brazil. The third PFL post went to Sarney Filho, son of the former president and representative of the northeastern wing of the party, while the fourth (the Ministry of Sports and Tourism) went to a representative of the PFL's southern wing. PSDB representation shrank from six to four ministries; and at least one (communications) had little clout after the privatization of its major assets. The PMDB had split in 1998 over backing for Cardoso's reelection, but FHC rewarded the supportive wing by maintaining its three ministries, including the pork-rich transportation portfolio. The PPB, which had lost strength in both the Chamber and Senate but had strongly supported Cardoso's reelection amendment and the campaign itself, doubled its cabinet representation. Proportionally, the biggest loser in the new cabinet was the PTB, which lost its only important ministry. Its delegation in the Chamber had dropped sharply after the 1998 election.

Overall, then, Cardoso's second-term cabinet reflects his weaker congressional position.[12] The president reduced his personal choices and paid more deference to the PFL, especially to the Bahian wing under ACM. It is too soon, of course, to gauge the effectiveness of this cabinet in mobilizing congressional support. But the new cabinet, which essentially strengthens the PFL at the expense of the PSDB, signals that the PSDB-PFL alliance may soon be a thing of the past. As both parties launch presidential candidates for 2002, they will increasingly seek policy turf on which to stake claims. The cabinet may soon find itself in a position where none of the available inducements can hold together an already precarious presidential base.

Intergovernmental Grants as Clues to Presidential Strategies

To understand Brazilian presidents' legislative coalition-building strategies, this section examines the distribution of grants from a series of pork-barrel programs that fell under individual ministers' control. The money in these programs flows to individual municipalities through agreements known as *convênios*. In some cases a share of a particular tax is earmarked for local distribution. The responsible ministry then decides which municipalities receive the funds and how much they receive. In other cases the funds are simply line items in the national budget; once again, ministries distribute the funds.

---

12. The Chamber president's August 1999 announcement that he intended to revive the college of leaders also suggests that congressional leaders see the president's weakness.

Typically, ministers and local mayors sign these *convênios*. Accounting mechanisms are almost nonexistent: the central government knows when the money has been moved to the municipality's bank account, but it has no idea whether the money is spent on the project or activity specified in the original agreement. No doubt, a substantial portion of these grants gets diverted to private use, but the dimensions of corruption are unknowable. In any case, the central question is logically prior: What does the distribution of intergovernmental grants to municipalities reveal about the strategies presidents utilize to build legislative support?[13]

It would be comforting if each *convênio* reflected a municipal target chosen specifically by the chief executive for its legislative support-maximizing potential. Unfortunately, Brazilian politics is much more complex. If appeals for legislative support consisted of nothing more than pork-barrel programs, the chief executive could dispense with intermediaries—that is, with cabinet ministers. In actuality, however, the president cannot survive without intermediaries, because appealing for support requires much more than simply distributing pork. By their presence, cabinet ministers reassure leaders of parties, states, and regions that their demands will get a hearing, that they have a channel to the executive.[14] So cabinets must be composed of politicians credible to their party and regional colleagues, politicians with clout. Leaders with clout, however, have their own political objectives and expect their careers to continue after the president's term ends. Powerful politicians accept ministerial appointments to help "their friend the president" but also expect to use the ministry's programs to advance their own careers. Thus, the potential exists for tension between presidential desires and those of individual ministers. A strategy efficient from the point of view of a minister's political goals could be wasteful for the president. And a strategy maximizing the president's short-term legislative support could reward a minister's political enemies.

Need and Capacity

Suppose "politics" plays no part in the distribution of *convênios*. The chances that a particular municipality will receive a grant should then depend on its need

---

13. *Convênios* are obviously not the only arrow in the president's quiver. Appointments to lower-echelon positions are at least as important, but we lack systematic data on appointments. Hopefully, the distribution of jobs and *convênios* follow similar logics.

14. In early 1995, Ciro Gomes, Itamar's last treasury minister, began to voice opposition to the number of *paulistas* in Cardoso's initial cabinet. Ciro's complaints stemmed from two sources: fear that the Northeast's interests would not be heard unless the cabinet included *nordestinos* and

for the funds and on its capacity to absorb them. In political systems where partisan factors operate only at the margins of allocation decisions, need and capacity (usually measured by statistical formulas) explain most of the variation in the distribution of funds among municipalities.[15] Even in Latin America, where political criteria are expected to play a significant role in allocations, measures of need and capacity ought to remain important.[16] The models in this chapter include three "need and capacity" indicators: total population, percentage of population engaged in manufacturing, and per capita income. The inclusion of total population reflects the simple assumption that larger municipalities ought to receive more grants, even though on a per capita basis the amount of money they receive is likely to be less than smaller municipalities. Municipalities with more manufacturing should receive more grants because they have more concentrated populations, increasing their suitability for certain kinds of programs. Wealthier communities have a greater capacity to absorb funds, because they already possess necessary infrastructure.[17] The models tested here will include all three variables, but their inclusion simply accounts for the overall effects of nonpolitical factors on allocation decisions. In other words, whether population matters more than income is unimportant; the objective is simply to control for the general effects of municipal need and capacity.

Indicators of Strategy

In a system of single-member districts like that of the United States, it would be easy to identify the deputies to whom presidents and ministers appeal: if the president was thought to be appealing to southerners, it would be necessary simply to create a dummy variable with a score of 1 for southern districts and 0 for nonsouthern districts. If the hypothesis were correct, the coefficient of the dummy variable (after controlling for all other variables) would be positive and significantly different from 0—that is, southern districts would have received

---

fear that his political future was in jeopardy in a *paulista*-dominated cabinet, especially since he was living at the time in Cambridge, Massachusetts.

15. *Pork barrel* may be an American term, but weight of political criteria in allocation decisions in U.S. politics is enormously less than in Brazil and other Latin American countries. On U.S. pork, see Ferejohn 1974 and Stein and Bickers 1995.

16. I discuss these questions in a comparison of budgetary allocations at the national level in all Latin America in Ames 1987.

17. Above a certain level, wealth may be negatively associated with grants, because community need decreases. I also experimented with a direct measure of poverty, the percentage of the population earning less than one-quarter of a minimum salary. This indicator reached significance in only one regression.

more grants than nonsouthern districts. In Brazil's open-list system, most deputies have districts, but these districts have no legal status, are often shared, and exist within the legal district—that is, the state as a whole. Testing hypotheses based on informal districts is therefore complicated. To measure the president's appeals to deputies from Bahia, the appropriate test is simple: a dummy variable identifies Bahian municipalities. But suppose the president is recruiting PMDB members rather than PFL deputies. How can data on grants to municipalities where various parties share the electorate test a party recruitment strategy?

Grants encourage deputies to support the president either by directly rewarding deputies or by rewarding local political leaders who act as intermediaries, pressuring their deputies to support the president. Thus a president seeking PMDB support should direct grants to municipalities with PMDB mayors, since such mayors are likely to have solid links to PMDB deputies. Or the president can seek out municipalities dominated by a single deputy—that is, municipalities where that deputy gets most of the votes cast and thus clearly gets the credit for pork. In the case of PMDB mayors, dummy variables identifying the mayor's party serve as tests of "pure" party strategies. Interactive variables identify strategies that are simultaneously state and party specific, for example, efforts to recruit in the Bahian PFL as opposed to the Bahian PMDB. In the case of dominant deputies, I rely on an archive constructed by the newspaper *Folha de São Paulo* (1988). This archive lists municipalities that the Planning Ministry thought a single deputy controlled. By separating these dominated municipalities according to the party of the dominant deputy, I test the hypothesis that presidents sought to recruit dominant deputies in any of three major parties: the PMDB, the PFL, or the Party of Social Democracy (PDS).

Thus far, my hypotheses have been linked to two kinds of concepts. One group includes socioeconomic and demographic variables, treated as controls. The other embraces recruitment tactics centering on individual deputies. These strategies focus on individually dominated states, parties, and municipalities or on combinations of all three. But what about municipalities in which multiple candidates—from one or many parties—divide the electorate? Credit claiming is more difficult in multimember constituencies. Are such deputies less likely to pursue pork, and should the president share their perspective? Or, conversely, should executives allocate pork barrel to municipalities where deputies divide the electorate?

Since deputies are entitled to seek votes in all their states' municipalities, the number of deputies getting votes in a particular municipality ranges from one to the total number of candidates for the Chamber from that state. If a particular deputy dominates a municipality, that deputy clearly calls the shots. If a group of deputies divides the municipality's votes about equally, they may have to share credit for whatever federal largesse they attract. Situations between these extremes require some sort of rule. On the basis of conversations with many politicians, I believe that two rules generally prevail. In some cases the deputy with the most votes, regardless of party, gets all the pork. In other cases the winner is the leading deputy from among the parties supporting the president.

Deputies in more fragmented voting contexts are less dependent on pork, so they can charge a higher price for their support. In other words, deputies who have difficulty claiming exclusive credit, whose motivation to seek pork is therefore weaker, ensure their political survival through other tactics. Because pork is marginal, getting them interested requires greater expenditures. As a result, only desperate presidents should recruit deputies in fragmented municipalities. When presidents do compete for such deputies, they ought to target municipalities divided between parties rather than municipalities shared by deputies of the same party.[18] It is easier to deny credit to deputies from opposing parties than to deputies from the same party. And deputies from opposing parties, inherently more antagonistic than deputies from the same party, can be bought at a lower price. Presidential pork, in other words, goes further.[19]

The problem is the operationalization of hypotheses predicting when grant agreements make sense in fragmented political contexts. Suppose I begin with the median levels of interparty and intraparty fragmentation in the PFL and the PMDB. When a dominant deputy from any of the major parties owns a municipality, both intraparty and interparty fragmentation must be low: the dominant deputy dummies cover this case. In municipalities where interparty fragmentation is high, there are three kinds of situations: neither party, one party, or both major parties are highly divided internally. In the first case, a number of parties divide the vote, but a single politician dominates each party.[20] In the second case, party competition is fierce, but in one party many deputies fight over the party vote, while in the other a single deputy dominates. In the third case—of-

18. For a formal, game-theoretic version of this argument, see Santos 1995.

19. Deputies from opposing parties are more antagonistic than those from the same party as a result of open-list proportional representation. For example, take the perspective of Deputy X from Party I. A competitor from Party II takes a vote that otherwise would be available to Deputy X. Not only is Deputy X disadvantaged in Party I's list, but Party II now has a chance to elect more deputies. By contrast, a competitor from Deputy X's own party also takes an available vote, but at least that vote still adds to Party I's total, thereby increasing Deputy X's chances of election.

20. A classic example is Barbacena, a medium-sized town in Minas Gerais dominated since the 1930s by two powerful families, the Andradas and the Bias Fortes (see José Murilo de Carvalho 1966).

ten found in large cities—complete fragmentation is the most common pattern. Many parties compete, and within each party many deputies fight over the party share.

The Sarney Administration

The tables in this chapter report the results of statistical models predicting the probability that any individual municipality received a *convênio* during specific periods.[21] In the case of President Sarney, I compare his strategies at the beginning of his administration to those adopted during a constitution-writing crisis. The agreements his ministers signed between April 1 and November 18, 1986, represent his initial survival strategy.[22] For Sarney, however, the critical phrase of his presidency occurred in 1988. During the late spring, the president faced two key votes in the Constituent Assembly. One threatened to reduce his term from five to four years; the other sought to substitute a parliamentary system for Brazil's presidentialism. Sarney lobbied hard and successfully for five years and presidential rule. Because the decisive period for recruiting legislative support naturally occurred in the months preceding the two votes, the model focuses on the distribution of *convênios* between March 1 and July 1. Table 12 presents results from both Sarney models.

At the start of his term, President Sarney faced a dilemma. As a former governor of Maranhão and as a politician with close ties to the outgoing military regime, he had filled the vice presidential slot on the Liberal Alliance ticket to provide ideological and regional balance. When president-elect Tancredo Neves died before taking office, the new president inherited both a PMDB-dominated cabinet and Tancredo's commitments to that party.[23] Sarney had no other short-run strategy, given the reasoning presented earlier, but to solidify his PMDB base, even faced with the opposition of many PMDB leaders. As table 12 shows, he did just that. Municipalities with PMDB mayors were significantly more likely to receive federal *convênios* than were municipalities with mayors of other parties. Municipalities dominated by a single PMDB deputy enjoyed

---

21. The models are Poisson regressions. Ordinary least squares is inappropriate, because one of its assumptions, that the dependent variable can take on any value, is obviously violated. No municipality can receive fewer than zero *convênios,* and the vast majority receive fewer than three. Poisson models (also known as "count" models) are suitable for this kind of situation.

22. These dates refer to the publication dates of the *convênios* in the *Diário Oficial* (see Brazil 1986–95).

23. The adoption of the Plano Cruzado before the 1986 election is further proof that at least through the 1986 elections, Sarney was content to reinforce his PMDB base even though his ideological predispositions were to the right of the PMDB. On the Plano Cruzado, see Sola 1992.

TABLE 12.   Presidential Strategies: Sarney's Start versus the 1988 Constitutional Crisis (Poisson model predicting intergovernmental grant agreements)

Parameter	Start of Administration (estimate)	Constitutional Crisis (estimate)
Intercept	−1.709**	−1.372*
Party fragmentation variables		
High interparty fragmentation; high PFL, high PMDB fragmentation	−.003	.178*
High interparty fragmentation; low PFL, low PMDB fragmentation	−.028	.201*
High interparty fragmentation; low PFL, high PMDB fragmentation	−.318**	.134
High interparty fragmentation; high PFL, low PMDB fragmentation	.182*	.327**
Electoral dominance variables		
Dominant deputy of PMDB	.206*	.032
Dominant deputy of PFL	.151	.320*
Dominant deputy of PDS	.228	.015
Municipal political condition variables		
PMDB mayor	.155*	−.126*
PFL mayor	−.026	−.191*
PDS mayor	−.089	−.029
Maranhão state	1.336**	1.100**
Bahia × PFL	−.079	.115
Bahia × PMDB	−.499*	−.286
Rio de Janeiro state	.346*	.442**
Rio Grande do Sul × PMDB	−.781**	.562**
Rio Grande do Sul × PDS	−.229	.415**
São Paulo state	−2.112**	−.937**
Need and capacity variables		
Northeast state	.005	.422**
Population	−.000	.000
Percentage in manufacturing	.951	.943
Income per capita	.0003**	.0002**

* = estimate twice standard error   ** = estimate thrice standard error   Obs. = 3,638

more federal largesse than municipalities not so dominated. And the Northeast, a group of states where the PMDB is traditionally weak, failed to profit even though the president was a fellow northeasterner.

Beyond his pursuit of a party strategy, Sarney targeted particular states. São Paulo, as always, registered the largest proportional losses of any state.[24]

---

24. São Paulo has always received a tiny share of central government pork barrel. Most scholars agree that São Paulo's leadership has made a historic trade similar to the deal struck be-

Maranhão, the president's base, received far more than its proportional share of funds. Rio de Janeiro also did well. Maranhão's largesse resulted, presumably, from Sarney's desire to maintain family dominance. Rio, however, is another story: Why reward a state whose political center of gravity was so far to the left? Most likely, Sarney had no intention of rewarding Rio; instead, it was the price he paid for political peace. The social welfare minister, Rafael de Almeida Magalhães, neutralized the opposition of Ulysses Guimarães in the Congress. As Rio's only cabinet member, Rafael was not one to neglect his roots, so Rio came out unexpectedly well.

In two cases, Bahia and Rio Grande do Sul, the factional nature of state politics encourages separation of the states' municipalities into PMDB-governed, on the one hand, and PFL- or PDS-governed, on the other. The results are quite dramatic—that is, PMDB-led municipalities did extremely poorly in both states. In Bahia, the explanation is simple: Sarney needed the backing of his communications minister, ACM. Implacably opposed to PMDB Governor Waldir Pires, ACM fought to eliminate federal funds for PMDB municipalities.[25] In the case of Rio Grande do Sul, the heavy penalty paid by PMDB municipalities remains inexplicable, especially compared with the jump in support they enjoyed later in the Sarney administration. However, the *Rio Grandense* wing of the PMDB was strongly opposed by the *paulista* wing, which was much closer to Sarney.[26]

Finally, what can be learned about the nature of political competition in each municipality? Sarney channeled resources to municipalities where a single PMDB deputy faced many PFL deputies. He withheld resources from municipalities in which a single PFL deputy faced many PMDB deputies. In the first case, Sarney supported PMDB deputies who could unequivocally claim credit for the largesse they attracted. The municipalities where he withheld resources (single PFL, many PMDB), are typically big cities; here Sarney avoided wasting resources on PMDB legislators for whom pork was less important and who could not claim exclusive credit. In this way, Sarney maximized his limited resources' impact.

---

tween Italy's north and south: macroeconomic policy benefiting one region, pork and patronage outputs favoring the other. São Paulo's firms also play a key role in the construction projects that result from the central government's transfers to the Northeast. In terms of constituency pressures, São Paulo has the highest percentage of deputies with shared constituencies—i.e., bases that discourage credit claiming for pork delivery.

25. On the struggle between ACM and Pires, see C. Souza 1997. It may seem surprising that PFL municipalities did not do well under an ACM-influenced government. My guess is that many of these municipalities had coalition governments and thus felt some of ACM's wrath.

26. Jader Barbalho, Sarney's minister of social welfare in 1988, aligned himself with the party's São Paulo wing.

In the 1988 constitutional crisis, President Sarney needed to utilize all his political resources. By 1988 his relations with the PMDB, particularly with Ulysses Guimarães, head of the Chamber of Deputies, had soured. Although Sarney could entice many PMDB deputies to support his positions, the party as a whole had become hostile. Sensing the shift in the political winds, especially after the failure of the Plano Cruzado, Sarney completely abandoned the PMDB-based strategy of his early years. He switched tactics not to a simplistic "support the PFL" but to a more finely tuned approach in which electorally dominant PFL deputies emerged as the big winners. Maranhão, Sarney's home state, still did very well, but its advantage shrank. Bahia's PMDB municipalities continued losing, but the losses were no longer statistically significant.[27] Rio Grande do Sul, however, completely reversed its losses of the earlier period, with municipalities headed by both PMDB and PDS mayors doing extremely well.

In this crisis, how did Sarney deal with the subtleties of political competition? During the earlier period of PMDB support, Sarney favored municipalities where a single PMDB faced many PFL deputies but withheld resources where many PMDB candidates faced a single PFL legislator. In the constitutional crisis, Sarney changed gears. He showered even more resources on lone PMDB members facing multiple PFL deputies. He was generous as well in situations where a single PFL candidate faced a single PMDB deputy. In these situations, where both deputies could claim credit, Sarney favored neither party. Instead, he put resources on any deputy willing to support him. Sarney also favored municipalities with high fragmentation in both the PMDB and the PFL. These are municipalities where only desperate executives should get involved; Sarney must have found some deputies willing to fight over the spoils he sent.

The Collor Administration

Fernando Collor de Mello took office in 1990 as the "Mr. Clean" of Brazilian politics. Scion of a traditional political family and former governor of Alagoas, a very poor northeastern state, the new president portrayed himself as the "hunter of bureaucratic maharajahs." With a legitimate claim as a fresh voice in Brazilian politics, Collor promised to end clientelism and shrink the state. Running on the slate of the Party of National Reconstruction (PRN), which had only a handful of congressional seats, the new president ostentatiously spurned ma-

---

27. By 1988, when the Pires administration had become unpopular, some PMDB mayors struck private deals with ACM.

jor party support. In the end, however, the gap between rhetoric and reality reached epic proportions. Collor soon became implicated in scandals too severe for even the long-tolerant Brazilian Congress to ignore, and the legislature formally impeached the president after only thirty months in office.

In Collor's case, then, there is a president with a penchant for direct, often corrupt, appeals to individual deputies, appeals bypassing traditional party leadership. His initial efforts to construct legislative support were begun without a firm party base. The year 1991 can be regarded as an intermediate period, a period of maturation before the scandals became truly threatening. By 1992 the president was struggling desperately—and ultimately unsuccessfully—to pull together enough support to hold onto his job.

Although commentaries on the 1989 presidential contest often stress the importance of Collor's charismatic television presence, my own research has shown that local party organizations played key roles in the generation of support (Ames 1994b). Most municipalities, especially the poorest, are quite dependent on federal transfers, so local political machines have every incentive to back a candidate with a good chance of taking the presidency. The major competitors understood this motivation and devoted considerable efforts to gaining the active support of mayors around the country. The PFL's candidate, Aureliano Chaves, was so weak that many PFL mayors actively backed Collor even in the first round. In round 2, when Collor faced leftist candidate Luís Inácio Lula da Silva, PFL support for Collor became official. With that support came the backing of hundreds of mayors and other local officials, especially in the Northeast.[28] The PDS candidate, *paulista* Paulo Maluf, was strong enough in the first round to hold most of his local officials, but in the second round the PDS followed the PFL, giving Collor a strong base in the South and Southeast.

Did the support of local machines really help Collor? In municipalities headed by PFL, PDS, or PTB mayors, Collor gained a few percentage points over his PT opponent.[29] His final margin was so large (roughly 53 percent to 47 percent) that he probably would have triumphed even without this backing.

---

28. The analysis centers on the 1989 presidential election, rather than the more recent contests of 1994 or 1998, because better data on transfers are available for that period. The mechanisms of coalition building remain in place. In the 1994 presidential election, the PSDB, a nominally social democratic party, formally allied with the PFL to support Cardoso. Together, they rode the initial success of the Plano Real to an easy victory. The engine of the alliance was obviously not ideology. The PFL wanted to back a winner, the PSDB needed the PFL's local machines in the Northeast, and both feared a Lula victory.

29. I measured the effects of local party endorsements in a multiple regression framework. The model also included demographic and socioeconomic variables along with measures of local partisan tendency. PDS support for Collor in round 2 was easily significant under one assumption,

Still, local machines hardly expected that rewards would be forthcoming only if their help tipped the balance toward Collor. The local machines had done their job—organizing rallies, getting out the faithful, disrupting the opposition—and expected a payoff.

Collor's early strategy, as table 13 shows, seems a straightforward and un-equivocal response to the campaign support he had received only a few months earlier. PDS-led municipalities garnered a substantial share of the fund transfer agreements signed by the ministers of education and social action, and PFL-led municipalities did nearly as well. PMDB-led municipalities suffered. The sin-gle-mindedness of the strategy—at least as compared to Sarney's multifaceted efforts—is apparent given the absence of significant coefficients for the frag-mentation variables and for dominant deputies. Collor's strategy was simple: reward municipalities with right-wing leadership.

Region also proved central to Collor's initial strategy. Municipalities in Alagoas, the new president's home, were easily the biggest beneficiaries of fed-eral largesse, with Bahia, Maranhão, and Rio Grande do Sul (a PDS bailiwick) running just behind. The Northeast as a whole did well, and most states in the Southeast, especially São Paulo and Rio de Janeiro, fared quite poorly. To say the least, the huge payoffs received by Alagoan friends of the president's fam-ily (and his wife's family as well) were politically wasteful.[30] Since the Alagoan delegation was hardly in a position to oppose the president, Collor was simply rewarding allies and family.

In 1991, the intermediate period, Collor's strategy became more subtle, more differentiated. Alagoan municipalities lost about half their advantage, while São Paulo municipalities, once the most penalized, lost less. PDS-led mu-nicipalities still gained, but their advantage declined almost 60 percent. PFL-led municipalities were in a neutral position, neither gaining nor losing, while the losses of PMDB municipalities declined a bit.

The most interesting change in Collor's "mature" strategy was his attempt to aid individual PFL deputies, those facing real electoral challenges, rather than simply to reward the Right regardless of electoral vulnerability. To under-stand this tactic, consider the variables representing various kinds of inter- and

---

but it just missed significance under another. Of the three major right-wing parties, however, the PDS clearly contributed the most support to the Collor candidacy.

    30. Rosane Collor de Mello, Fernando Collor's second wife, is part of one of Alagoas's most traditional political families, the Maltas, centered in the municipality of Canapí. In 1991 the Col-lors were having marital problems, and Fernando began to appear in public without his wedding ring. Rosane's father made clear his perspective on family values: "In our family there are no di-vorced women, only single women and widows." The ring returned, and the Collors remain to-gether.

TABLE 13.   Presidential Strategies: Collor's Start, Maturation, and Impeachment Crisis (Poisson model predicting intergovernmental grant agreements)

Parameter	Start of Administration (estimate)	Maturation (estimate)	Crisis (estimate)
Intercept	−2.026**	−1.444**	−1.798**
Party fragmentation variables			
High interparty fragmentation; high PFL, high PMDB fragmentation	.074	.047	−.029
High interparty fragmentation; low PFL, low PMDB fragmentation	.072	.233**	.009
High interparty fragmentation; low PFL, high PMDB fragmentation	−.065	.195**	.182*
High interparty fragmentation; high PFL, low PMDB fragmentation	.107	−.019	−.037
Electoral dominance variables			
Dominant deputy of PMDB	−.109	−.010	−.078
Dominant deputy of PFL	.083	−.125	.342**
Dominant deputy of PDS	−.108	−.073	−.196
Municipal political condition variables			
PMDB mayor	−.145*	−.132**	−.187**
PFL mayor	.201*	.044	−.167*
PDS mayor	.637**	.232**	.132
Alagoas state	1.052**	.533**	.401**
Maranhão state	.606**	.675**	1.06**
Bahia state	.848**	−.871**	−.331*
Paraná state	.427**	.503**	.341**
Rio de Janeiro state	−.278	−.401*	−1.059**
Rio Grande do Sul state	.861**	.549**	1.077**
São Paulo state	−1.801**	−.946	−2.748**
Need and capacity variables			
Northeast state	1.041**	1.317**	1.085**
Population	.0000	.0000	.0000
Percentage in manufacturing	.973	−.529	.627
Income per capita	.0002**	.0002**	.0002**

* = estimate twice standard error   ** = estimate thrice standard error   Obs. = 3,638

intraparty fragmentation. The two significant coefficients represent situations in which a small number of PFL deputies—usually a single deputy—dominated the PFL vote in a municipality but at the same time faced substantial competition from deputies from other parties. Collor supported the PFL deputy whether the opposition was united (low fragmentation) or divided (high fragmentation). It now becomes apparent why neither the "Dominant Deputy of PFL" variable nor the "PFL Mayor" variable seems to benefit during Collor's mature period.

The president had learned the importance of efficiency, concentrating his resources on deputies who really needed electoral help.

By 1992 the Collor administration was in deep trouble. Collor's brother, Pedro, set off the crisis by denouncing the president's campaign treasurer, Paulo César Farias, for involvement in various extortion rings that had accepted money from big corporations benefiting from government projects. Their "contributions" to Collor's campaign amounted to hundreds of millions of dollars, and the trail seemed to lead directly to the presidency. By mid-1992, as the noose tightened, it appeared quite possible that Collor could not escape a congressional impeachment vote. Could he find a strategy that would allow his survival as president?

In terms of regional politics, the desperate president realigned his tactics in ways that might seem surprising. Alagoas remained a big winner, but the state's gains continued the slide that had begun in Collor's mature period. Maranhão, a state that had always done well, now found itself among the states profiting most. Bahia cut its losses by about 50 percent. Rio de Janeiro did much worse than in 1991, but Rio Grande do Sul was enormously better off. What explains these changes? Alagoas had profited simply because Collor wanted to reward his "homeboys," not because the state's delegates might desert their leader. Under fire, Collor curtailed Alagoas's advantage. Maranhão's gains, along with the improvement in Bahia, probably come from the ideological cleavage that determined most deputies' positions on impeachment. In other words, leftist deputies were strongly anti-Collor from the start, while deputies on the Right defended the president as long as possible. Maranhão's eighteen-member delegation included fourteen members of right-wing parties (the PFL, PRN, PDC, and PSC). In Bahia's delegation, conversely, only nineteen of thirty-nine deputies represented right-wing parties. So, more than three-fourths of Maranhão's delegation was on the right, compared to a bit less than half the Bahians. Likewise, Rio de Janeiro suffered from the precommitments of its deputies. In the highly politicized environment of the former capital, deputies had good reason to fear voter backlash if they supported Collor. Fear made the price of their adherence so high that Collor allocated his resources where cost-benefit ratios were more favorable.[31]

Collor's final efforts included a shift toward dominant PFL deputies and a refinement in his tactics toward deputies in fragmented electoral contexts. Because dominant PFL members were heavily represented in the leadership of the

---

31. The one anomaly in this regional allocation is Rio Grande do Sul. With only about one-third of the deputies belonging to the right-wing PFL or PDS (left and center-left parties held twelve of the state's thirty-one seats), it seems irrational for Collor to have magnified his earlier tilt toward Rio Grande do Sul during this critical period.

Chamber of Deputies, and because the president's survival was impossible without the loyalty of the conservative congressional leadership, these deputies were well placed to seek pork-barrel benefits. Like Rio's leftist deputies, PFL leaders could demand a high price for their support, but, as opposed to the Cariocas, Collor could hardly afford to ignore the PFL bosses. Collor also concentrated on PFL deputies facing fragmented opposition. Such deputies were more vulnerable than those facing a single opponent, so their price was lower and the president could expend fewer resources to recruit them.

The Franco Administration

As has already been demonstrated, Itamar Franco based his cabinet appointments on three criteria: personal relationship, political party, and intraparty faction. The seventeen nonmilitary cabinet members included ten "friends of Itamar," and the cabinet as a whole represented seven different parties. Why construct a cabinet with little political clout but with a high potential for deadlock?[32] Conversations with politicians and close observers of the political scene tend to support one overriding fact: the president assumed office with no program. Itamar had been an honest but obscure senator from Minas Gerais. He was a reluctant vice presidential candidate, placed on the ticket to ensure regional balance. Although the success of the 1994 Plano Real—and, as a result, the public's overwhelming approval of his administration—may have augmented his political ambitions, through most of his abbreviated term Itamar appeared to loathe being president.

The Franco presidency falls naturally into two phases. The distribution of grants during the first four months exposes the strategy of the "uninterested" Itamar.[33] In 1993, however, the scenario changed. Cardoso had shifted from the foreign ministry to treasury. Under his leadership, the Franco government set out to stabilize the economy. Cardoso's team was convinced that any stabilization proposal would require a fiscal shock (euphemistically, a "fiscal adjustment").[34] The government's program included three crucial elements: the provisional tax on financial transactions, which would substantially increase revenues; the social emergency fund (FSE), which would hold back federal transfers to states and municipalities (along with direct programmatic trans-

---

32. The argument that a larger number of parties in the cabinet magnifies the potential for deadlock assumes that cabinet members have a voice in the policies proposed by the president. Most observers would accept this assumption for the Franco government (see Tsebelis 1994).

33. The data set includes only grant agreements signed after Itamar's ministers took office.

34. The best treatment of this period, including the negotiations over the economic program and the development of the 1994 presidential campaign, appears in Dimenstein and De Souza 1994.

fers); and a new indexing device (the unit of real value), which would eventually become a completely new currency, the real. The first two measures required congressional approval.[35] Everyone in the government knew these two measures would be a hard sell in Congress; nobody, after all, wants to vote for a tax increase, and the FSE, in spite of its euphemistic title, was really nothing more than a mechanism to reduce the fiscal deficit by withholding funds owed to states and municipalities.

These measures (especially the FSE) struck at the heart of congressional privileges and appeared to threaten Brazil's distributional politics. Moreover, Finance Minister Cardoso initially engaged in very little of the usual piecemeal bargaining with individual deputies.[36] Although the president could have cut the deficit by refusing to spend money previously approved by Congress, Cardoso insisted that Congress itself participate in the cutting exercise by approving a new budget.

Under normal circumstances, seeking congressional approval for these measures would be like asking condemned prisoners to build their own scaffolds. But circumstances in the spring of 1994 were far from normal. In the approaching presidential election, the clear favorite was the candidate of the Workers' Party, Luís Inácio Lula da Silva. Lula and his party had benefited from popular revulsion to Collor's corruption, and the PT was practically the only party untainted by the congressional budget scandals of 1993. Moreover, Brazil's Right, led by the PFL, had no candidate with the potential to defeat Lula.

The Center-Left, represented by Cardoso's social democratic PSDB, also feared a Lula victory. Lula, and especially the PT's more radical factions, would be an obstacle to the neoliberal ambitions of the PSDB. The economic chaos expected to follow a Lula triumph might trigger another episode of military rule. Although the Center-Left could produce vigorous candidates, it lacked a political base in the countryside, particularly in the Northeast.[37]

The outcome of this political conjuncture was an alliance around the Cardoso candidacy between the PFL and PSDB.[38] PFL leaders knew a successful

---

35. Creation of the new monetary unit required only that Congress not specifically reject the measure.

36. However, as chapter 8 will demonstrate, Cardoso struck a deal with the rural caucus to reduce agricultural debts in exchange for their votes on the FSE. Itamar reneged on the deal, vetoing the relevant item in the resulting legislation. Congress overturned the veto, backing the rural caucus, during the early months of the Cardoso presidency.

37. The importance of local politics in a presidential election is quantitatively assessed in my article on the 1989 Collor election (see Ames 1994b).

38. An alliance between the PSDB and the PMDB, a party closer ideologically to the PSDB than to the PFL, did receive consideration by PSDB leaders. The PMDB, however, was split between its Quércia-Fleury wing and its *auténtico* wing, led by *gaúcho* Antônio Britto.

economic stabilization plan was a prerequisite for a Cardoso victory (Dimen-stein and De Souza 1994). They felt they could deliver the congressional votes crucial to the plan's approval. Thus, the leadership of the traditional Right found itself backing strongly antipork and antipatronage proposals.

Table 14 illuminates both Franco administration's overall approach and the differences between the early months of his administration and the period from January to August 1994, when the Cardoso team was seeking congressional approval for its key stabilization measures.[39] In neither period is there evidence of the kind of fine-grained political strategy apparent in earlier presidencies, especially under Sarney. None of the various combinations of political competition seems to affect grants, and dominant deputies never gain any advantage. In the initial phase, in fact, municipalities with mayors from the PMDB—Itamar's party—do less well than other mayors.

The distribution of grants in the early months demonstrates the importance of ministers themselves. Alagoas, once recipient of Collor's corrupt munificence, now is the biggest loser of all the states. The Northeast in general does well, but this phenomenon may reflect regional poverty more than a deliberate political tactic. More striking are the substantial losses suffered by Itamar's home state, Minas Gerais, and the gains made by relatively wealthy Rio Grande do Sul. What kind of presidential strategy would lead to punishing one's own state and rewarding a state that is polarized between political radicals and conservatives? The answer, I suggest, lies in the nature of the two ministers who controlled the bulk of these grants: Maurílio Hingel (Minas Gerais) in education and Antônio Britto (Rio Grande do Sul) in social well-being. Hingel, an obscure educator from the president's hometown, had no obvious political ambitions. He left office with Franco and has not been visible since. While Hingel was minister, observers of the Education Ministry stressed his apolitical nature and the depoliticization of the ministry's chief grant program, the National Education Development Fund. Britto, by contrast, was a professional politician and former member of Congress. In 1994 he made a successful run for the governorship of Rio Grande do Sul. Since Britto was too good a politician not to have planned his gubernatorial run years in advance, it is likely that he distributed welfare grants with an eye to advancing his political future.

When the identical statistical model is implemented in the period when Congress was debating the stabilization measures of the Plano Real, evidence of a more concerted political strategy appears. The model's explanatory value

---

39. In this table the data on grants to municipalities are mainly limited to two ministries, education and social well-being. In this period, however, these two ministries controlled most of the available grant money.

TABLE 14.   Presidential Strategies: Itamar's Early Months and the Crisis of the Plano Real (Poisson model predicting intergovernmental grant agreements)

Parameter	Start of Administration (estimate)	Plano Real Crisis of 1994 (estimate)
Intercept	−2.456**	−.938**
Party fragmentation variables		
High interparty fragmentation; high PFL, high PMDB fragmentation	.106	.083
High interparty fragmentation; low PFL, low PMDB fragmentation	.156	−.181*
High interparty fragmentation; low PFL, high PMDB fragmentation	.081	−.028
High interparty fragmentation; high PFL, low PMDB fragmentation	−.145	.083
Electoral dominance variables		
Dominant deputy of PMDB	−.098	.037
Dominant deputy of PFL	−.087	.114
Dominant deputy of PDS	−.024	−.027
Municipal political condition variables		
PMDB mayor	−.284**	.081*
PFL mayor	−.338	.054
PPR mayor	−.119	−.143*
Alagoas state	−1.869**	.186
Maranhão state	−.551	.230*
Bahia state	−.214	−1.578**
Minas Gerais state	−.606**	−.975**
Rio de Janeiro state	−.505	−2.306**
Rio Grande do Sul state	.566**	.914**
São Paulo state	−.520**	−1.349**
Need and capacity variables		
Northeast state	.522**	.101
Population	.0003**	.0003**
Percentage in manufacturing	−1.267	−.480
Income per capita	.0003**	.0002**

* = estimate twice standard error   ** = estimate thrice standard error   Obs. = 3,638

is about three times better in the second period.[40] In other words, the initiation of the stabilization program marks the time when the administration finally gets serious.

Consider the three variables measuring the effects of the mayor's party on grant distribution. Municipalities with PMDB mayors do significantly bet-

---

40. In the initial phase, the ratio of regression-weighted sum of squares to residual-weighted sum of squares is 1:6. The same ratio in the Real phase is 1:2.

ter than municipalities led by mayors of other parties, while municipalities led by PPR mayors (the former PDS), do significantly worse. While the gains of Cardoso's coalition partner, the PFL, are positive but not statistically significant, there are striking changes in the fortunes of the PFL from the beginning of the Franco administration. To make sense of these responses to local political conditions, consider the context of the PSDB-PFL alliance and the upcoming election. The PPR had its own candidate, Espiridião Amin. It had to oppose the stabilization program, at least in part, to differentiate its candidate from the administration. In addition, the PPR posed a serious threat to Britto's ambitions in Rio Grande do Sul. The minister would hardly be interested in supporting PPR-led municipalities in his home state. The PMDB, however, did merit support, or at least part of the party merited support. By the time of the Plano Real, the Quércia-Fleury wing of the party, based in São Paulo, had come to oppose the government. Quércia was himself a presidential candidate, although corruption charges stemming from his term as governor crippled his candidacy. The *auténtico* wing of the party, centered on Britto, was much more supportive, and of course Britto was running for office. So the PMDB profited.

Still, why did PFL-led municipalities fail to benefit from Itamar's largesse? After all, the PFL was a big part of the alliance, and its deputies were being asked to sacrifice pork for the party's benefit. The answer is likely twofold. PFL leaders knew their party was tainted by the congressional budget scandal of 1993, which hit many PFL deputies. Moreover, the party leaders were backing the stabilization program and consequently pressured their deputies to support its legislative measures. The PFL is hardly a disciplined party, but leadership influence was sufficient to reduce the need for individual payoffs, especially to marginal deputies.

The gains and losses of Rio Grande do Sul and Minas Gerais illustrate once again the tension between presidential and ministerial strategies. Maurílio Hingel was the perfect minister for Franco: Minas's deputies, according to observers, had a strong propensity to support the fellow *mineiro* in the presidency, and the minister's lack of political ambition enabled the administration to avoid wasting money on deputies who would be supportive anyway. In Britto, however, Itamar was dealing with a minister with a separate agenda. The data show that grants flowed to a number of municipalities whose dominant deputies were strongly anti-PSDB and who opposed the stabilization plan but who were, however, potential allies of the future governor. In the end, of course, the power of the PFL-PSDB alliance, a union based essentially on an "anyone but Lula" rationale, overcame the contradictions in presidential tactics. Still, it is easy to see the inherent inefficiency and costliness of the coalition-building strategies Brazil's presidents are forced to adopt.

Conclusion

This chapter centered on a challenge every Brazilian president faces. That challenge, posed simply, is the maintenance of a consistent base of support for the president in the Congress. This question is simple to pose, perhaps, but is difficult to surmount, because Brazil's political structure fills the legislature with a plethora of weak and undisciplined parties as well as hundreds of deputies who care far more about their personal constituencies and private interests than about national-level issues.

In some countries, executives build legislative support by asking citizens to pressure parties and deputies to support presidential programs. Such tactics generate little response in Brazil, because ties among voters, deputies, and parties are extremely weak.[41] Instead, presidents use political jobs and pork-barrel programs to corral support and make tactical shifts in these inducements over the course of their administrations. The most important political jobs are those in the cabinet itself. Not only do cabinet members control the distribution of lower-level jobs and municipal-level programs, but they also channel party and regional interests.[42] Cabinet appointments, in other words, reassure politicians that their concerns will reach the president's ear.

To an outside observer, cabinet construction may sometimes seem less than optimal. Collor, for example, installed a curious mix of friends, technocrats, and weak politicians. Franco's cabinet had a large component of personal friends who often served the president poorly. In fact, Itamar's great success, the Plano Real, came only after he was effectively marginalized by the economic team assembled by Cardoso and supported by the PFL leadership. Only Sarney, it seems, came close to maximizing the value of every appointment. This finding comes as no surprise, perhaps, when one considers Sarney's long political experience and his commitment to the survival of his dynasty in Maranhão.

---

41. The administrative head of the office of an important senator told me that his office receives only two or three letters a day from constituents, most of them from other states. The senator does not even receive a daily or weekly mail count from the staff.

42. Ministers' control over their ministries' lower-level jobs is far from absolute. In many cases the president or even a particular legislator forces lower officials on the minister, either as a way of ensuring that a certain region receive a larger share of programs or as a way of influencing the overall distribution.

Presidents' lives would be simpler if they could distribute pork personally, dispensing with ministers altogether. But since intermediaries are necessary, presidents continually deal with ministers with their own political agendas. None of the presidents in this chapter was immune to the problem of ministers whose personal survival strategies contradicted those of the chief executive. Collor had to deal with an education minister with political ambitions in Rio Grande do Sul. Franco, ironically, had conflicts with a minister of social well-being from the same state. Stories of second-echelon personnel whose policies depart from the interests of their superiors—the so-called principal-agent problem—are commonplace in every bureaucracy, of course. But the result in Brazil is to decrease the efficiency of the distributional policies executives use as the currency of coalitions. Because distributional policies are less efficient, more money must be spent. The system is thus even more likely to produce pork at the expense of national-level policies.

Chapter 7

Party Discipline in the
Chamber of Deputies

"Our party is so disorganized we can't even throw a party."
A leader of the PSDB

"I am not a member of any organized party. I am a Democrat."
Will Rogers

The previous chapter explored the strategies Brazilian presidents adopt as they strive to construct bases of legislative support. To understand the president's efforts at legislative coalition building, this chapter moves to the Congress itself, seeking to comprehend the role of legislative parties in the context of Brazil's institutional structure. Though political parties play key parts in all legislatures, their role varies enormously. In Great Britain and Argentina, for example, parties are the main actors, and the legislative game can be understood with few references to individual deputies. No one would argue that legislative parties in Brazil have the strength of Argentina's Peronists or Britain's Labour Party. Nonetheless, leaders of Brazil's congressional parties organize the legislative calendar, participate in legislative negotiations, and mediate between individual deputies and ministers.

The chapter takes the first steps toward adapting theories of legislative parties to the Brazilian case. The first section demonstrates that Brazilian presidents are hardly dominant actors. From the administration of José Sarney through the first government of Fernando Henrique Cardoso, most executive proposals come out of the legislature highly modified or fail to come out at all. Why do presidential proposals so seldom emerge unscathed from the Congress? Do party leaders, especially leaders of parties that are nominally part of presidential coalitions, really oppose these proposals? If, instead, party leaders are simply unable to marshal their troops to support these bills, why are backbench deputies so reluctant?

The answers lie in the nature of Brazil's legislative parties. The second section reviews the theoretical literature on legislative parties, a literature based mainly on the U.S. experience. This discussion demonstrates that Brazil ought to be a case of "conditional party government." Given Brazil's electoral rules and its federal structure, influence should flow from the bottom up, from party members to leaders, not from the top down. Arguments about the flow of influence in legislative parties depend, in the final analysis, on leaders' ability to compel backbenchers to follow their lead. The third section utilizes roll-call votes to test a multivariate model of the probability that individual deputies co-operate with their parties. A key indicator of party strength is the party leaders' ability to compel their members to follow the leadership's vote recommendations. A second, less direct indicator comes from the success of individual deputies in garnering pork. The higher the price leaders have to pay to buy support, the weaker the party. These indicators of party strength are embedded in a model that also includes measures of individual electoral security, ideology, seniority, constituency characteristics, and career background. The empirical analysis, presented in the fourth section, demonstrates that party recommendations (and the punishments and rewards that accompany them) rarely matter very much in determining cooperation or defection. The president's problem, in the end, is less party leaders' recalcitrance than their inability, even with lavish pork-barrel spending, to persuade deputies to support presidential proposals.

I.   Do Presidents Dominate?

Presidential success is commonly measured by assessing the approval rates of presidential initiatives on roll-call votes.[1] In any legislative setting, this technique is problematic. First, to the degree that roll calls reflect only those issues actually coming to a vote, they exemplify the classic problem of nondecisions. If congressional opposition is too strong, a presidential proposal may never face an up or down vote. A presidential trial balloon can generate such fierce opposition in the legislature that the president gives up, never sending a formal proposal to the Congress.[2]

Roll-call measures of party unity also fail to reflect the costs of gaining party backing. Presidents and party leaders pay these costs in combinations of

---

1. For a recent analysis of roll calls as a measure of party discipline, see Amorim Neto, forthcoming.

2. Two well-known Brazilian examples include Collor's proposal for administrative reform and Sarney's attempt to impose tuition at federal universities. Both quietly disappeared, never to arrive at Congress's door.

pork and substantive policy concessions. Roll calls, in other words, really represent the end point of negotiations among presidents, party leaders, and rank-and-file deputies. What is needed, and what is usually lacking, are head counts—executive-branch leaders' estimates of the direction in which individual deputies are leaning, estimates made during the process of negotiation.[3]

A third limitation stems from the possibility of fundamental differences between the political processes generating roll calls and those generating other types of congressional decisions.[4] Without question, committees and voice votes on the floor make many key decisions in the Brazilian Congress.[5] Furthermore, roll calls are notoriously subject to "bandwagon" effects. In most congressional votes, 80 percent of the deputies support the winning side.[6] An eight-to-two ratio implies neither that four-fifths of the deputies supported the original proposal nor even that four-fifths support the final bill. In fact, overwhelming victories occur even when only bare majorities are really supportive. Such bandwagons develop when indifferent deputies trade support as part of cross-issue logrolls, or when they join the winning side in the hopes of gaining advantage on future votes. If a proposal has undergone, between its original form and final passage, significant concessions to congressional opposition, and if the proposal then passes with 80 percent approval, either enormous bandwagon effects are operating or the proposal's authors badly overestimated the concessions needed to obtain majority support.

In an important new research development, Brazilian scholars have begun using legislative roll calls to assess presidential success and party strength. In recent essays, Argelina Figueiredo and Fernando Limongi (Limongi and Figueiredo 1995, 1996; Figueiredo and Limongi 1997b) analyze roll calls taken from 1988 (the end of the Constituent Assembly) through 1994.[7] To approximate the concept of the party agenda, these authors concentrate on votes where party leaders made explicit recommendations (*encaminhamentos*) to their members.

---

3. Sullivan 1987 has analyzed head-count data for some issues during the Eisenhower years.

4. In the U.S. Congress, it is clear that leaders exert influence in varying ways in these differing settings. Interest-group representatives, moreover, have varying degrees of access. After intensive research, VanDoren (1990, 311) concluded that "the processes that determine committee and voice-vote decisions are different from those that determine roll-call decisions."

5. Moreover, the Brazilian Congress has adopted rules deliberately hindering the use of roll calls.

6. In addition, few roll calls occur when ideological blocs oppose each other. When the PSDB and PMDB are grouped together in one bloc and the PFL-PTB-PDS are placed in another, majorities of these two blocs opposed each other on only 35 of 473 regular Chamber votes (1988–96) and on only 5 of 77 emergency-measure votes (1988–92).

7. Figueiredo and Limongi's findings have gained considerable attention in Brazil, even in the popular press (see Barros e Silva 1995).

Adopting the Rice index of party discipline, in which the minority percentage is subtracted from the majority percentage for each party on each vote, Figueiredo and Limongi find that even in the weakest parties an average of 85 percent of the members vote the same way. Most parties have even higher discipline scores.[8] The authors conclude that Brazilian parties are truly legislative actors and that parties consistently take predictable, coherent ideological positions. Figueiredo and Limongi admit that Brazil's electoral system fosters individualism on the part of legislators and hinders "accountability" between party and voter (Limongi and Figueiredo 1995, 498).[9] In spite of the electoral system, they argue, the legislature's internal rules allow "party leaders [to] control the work agenda and limit the area open to the individualistic strategies of deputies and senators" (500). Party leaders, as a result, dominate party followers. Arguments linking the electoral system to party weakness stop, in this view, at the Chamber door.

Figueiredo and Limongi's findings are controversial among students of Brazilian politics. As the only truly empirical research, their work must be taken as the conventional (if somewhat beleaguered) wisdom, but questions remain. What level of party unity, in comparative terms, makes a party disciplined? True, Brazil's parties have discipline scores (Rice indexes) in the 80s. Are these high numbers? Cross-country comparisons, as I will subsequently demonstrate, are risky, but even direct comparison leaves Brazil's parties well below those of some neighboring countries. Argentine party unity has traditionally been over 98 percent, and Argentine party leaders achieve these high levels of party voting with neither the pork-barrel wooing of deputies nor the substantive legislative concessions that occur in Brazil.[10] Venezuela, at least until recently, is another case of parties vastly more disciplined than those of Brazil.

Implicit in any judgment about the comparative discipline of Brazil's parties is an assumption of ceteris paribus. Scholars begin with certain questions of primary interest (typically hypotheses linking such concepts as presidentialism versus parliamentarism, single-member versus multimember electoral districts, or open-list versus closed-list proportional representation). Then, in order to make cross-national comparisons of party strength, they assume that institutional contexts are equivalent. Suppose we seek to test the hypothesis that closed-list proportional representation yields higher levels of party unity than open-list proportional representation. The rules of causal inference naturally require the

---

8. Figueiredo and Limongi follow the common convention of calling this indicator "cohesion." Following Tsebelis (1995), I refer to deputies voting together as "discipline" or "unity." Parties are "cohesive" when deputies agree on substantive policy questions.

9. Similar arguments about party weakness have been made by Lamounier (1994), Lima Junior (1993), and Mainwaring (1993, 1999).

10. Mark Jones, personal communication. Chilean discipline seems equally high.

assumption that other institutional rules are constant across the different party systems. Is this assumption reasonable? When deputies easily switch parties, for example, what looks like party discipline may be illusory. If party leaders attempt to punish dissenters, deputies jump to another party. Discipline for the party losing members then rises. Given a sufficient number of alternative parties for the defectors to join, unity for the receiving parties need not fall (Mainwaring and Pérez-Liñán 1997). During the Sarney administration, the PMDB lost members to the PSDB on its left and to the PFL on its right. In the short run, overall discipline rose. In sum, where members easily switch, party itself is a moving target.

In Brazil these caveats represent real problems, not merely theoretical objections. Consider the problem of nondecisions. Any judgment of the strength of presidents presupposes knowledge, as a starting point, of the president's agenda. How is it possible to know what proposals presidents would send to the Congress if they thought passage was remotely possible? Though certain ideas may go unmentioned because they have no chance of passage, most reasonable proposals are at least aired in the media. Tables 15–17 attempt to define and trace the universe of presidential proposals in Brazil from 1990 to 1998. Sources include the *Latin America Weekly Report: Brazil,* the *Economist Country Report,* and the Brazilian financial newspaper *Gazeta Mercantil.* The tables, which include every presidential proposal mentioned in those publications, record what the president proposed, when it was proposed, what the legislature did with the proposal, and when that action occurred.[11]

Though these tables are not amenable to quantitative measures, they are quite revealing nonetheless. Many important proposals, though aired in the media, never arrive at Congress's door. Faced with powerful congressional opposition, President Fernando Collor de Mello gave up his attempts to eliminate

---

11. This tracking makes the strong assumption that initial presidential proposals are sincere rather than strategic. In other words, presidential proposals are assumed to be what presidents really desire. Mark Peterson (1990a), in research on the United States, developed deductive models asking whether presidents get more of what they want by requesting either less or more than they really desire, and his models predict that presidents succeed by asking for less. However, Peterson found no empirical support for either strategy. Peterson's conclusions supported his earlier, interview-based study (1990b) and led him to conclude that U.S. presidents do in fact reveal their preferences sincerely—i.e., what they ask for is what they want. Patrick Fett (1992) came to the same conclusion for the first years of the Carter and Reagan presidencies. Both worked hard for the legislation they really wanted, neither ducking controversial issues nor backing easy winners.

Perhaps a president, knowing the legislature will reject a proposal, uses that rejection to appeal to voters for personal support in a reelection campaign or to campaign for the election of more supportive deputies. Until 1998 Brazilian presidents had no possibility of reelection, and legislative elections have so little programmatic content that it is hard to imagine voters responding to "line in the sand" strategies. There is no evidence that recent presidents have tried such tactics.

TABLE 15. Congressional Response to Presidential Proposals (Collor administration)

Date of Initial Proposal	Substance of Presidential Proposal	Date of Action by Congress	Substance of Action by Congress
March 16, 1990	Collor submits 26 emergency measures. Key measures: [1] blocks access to savings [2] one-month freeze on prices [3] closure of several ministries, agencies, and public companies and privatization scheme [4] 50,000 employees lose jobs immediately, 300,000 on reduced pay [5] fiscal reform, including increased taxes on financial transactions and new taxes on capital gains, wealth, and agricultural incomes [6] elimination of subsidies and incentives and liberalization of imports	June 7, 1990	Four emergency measures are withdrawn, including two granting government police powers over certain kinds of economic behavior. The other two would raise taxes on financial operations and cut wages of public employees. Constitution prohibits increase in taxation and lowering of wages without prior approval of corresponding laws by Congress.
June 25, 1990	Emergency measure 193 (later 211 and 292), which established a new index for calculating "wage losses" and other adjustments	May 25, 1990 and later	None ratified. All end "sem eficácia," i.e., without legal force.
June 25, 1990	Reduction of import barriers. All barriers removed except tariffs, which would drop from a maximum of 105 percent to a maximum of 40 percent	??	Approved.
Late July 1990	Collor vetoes Congress bill linking wage adjustments to rate of inflation	??	Chamber overrides, but no quorum in Senate.

February 14, 1991	*Emendão* (officially "National Reconstruction Project"): [1] eliminates state monopoly on oil, other restrictions on foreign capital [2] eliminates mandated levels of pensions, autonomous pay regime of judiciary [3] eliminates 12 percent of ceiling on real interest rates [4] eliminates free university education [5] eliminates job security for government employees		All of *emendão* dies.
March 21, 1991	[1] Proposes minimum wage of $66 [2] minimum wage adjustments would occur in July and January [3] curbs on speculation and a short-term price freeze	March 1991	[1] Left in Congress wanted $149. Agreement at $77. [2] Timetable for adjustments varies. [3] Curb on speculation and price freeze accepted.
August 1991	Emergency measure granting pay increase to public servants and military	August 15, 1991	Rejected 239 to 11. PFL joined opposition.
September 19, 1991	Collor offers governors rollover of $57 billion owed by states to central government in exchange for their help in persuading party leaders to support *emendão*		Nothing passes.
October 24, 1991	Collor drops *emendão* provisions for job stability, central government control over state and municipal finances, and higher education reform		Congress had passed none of these.

(continued)

TABLE 15.—*Continued*

Date of Initial Proposal	Substance of Presidential Proposal	Date of Action by Congress	Substance of Action by Congress
January 9, 1992	Tax increase proposal to raise income tax ceiling to 35 percent	January 1992	Congress rejects 35 percent ceiling at insistence of PMDB, and Collor is forced to agree to rollover $70 billion in state and municipal debt owed to the central government and foreign banks. Central government guarantees state debts. Deal favors badly managed states like São Paulo.
January 30, 1992	Government offers pensioners adjustment of 54 percent	January 30, 1992	Congress rejects government offer. Regular procedure gives pensioners 147 percent. Fifteen parties, representing 79 percent of Câmara, oppose government. Ministries are then reshuffled: Magri replaced by Stephanes, Procópio by Fiuza. Born-hausen into Casa Civil.
May 1992	Doubling of expected pay raises for military	May 1992	Passed quickly.
June–October 1992	Port legislation	??	Agrarian-reform law proposed by Left passed as part of logroll with Right on port legislation.
June–October 1992	Intellectual property law	??	Passed, terms unclear.

the state oil monopoly, control state and municipal finances, end free university education, and eliminate lifetime tenure for government employees. Itamar Franco never sent Congress his fiscal-reform program or his plan for a wealth tax. Fernando Henrique Cardoso abandoned his drive to install a mixed public-private pension system. Although his economic team regarded tax reform as crucial to its stabilization program, the president sent no tax-reform proposals to the Congress during his first term. He also made no effort to push through the political-institutional reforms he had long advocated. Among the proposals that do arrive at the Congress, many never reach a vote. Collor's proposals for new wage-adjustment indexes failed without ever coming to a vote. Franco's November 1993 package of emergency tax increases met a similar fate. Long delays are common. Pension- and administrative-reform proposals arrived in the Congress at the beginning of Cardoso's first term and received final approval only at the beginning of his second term, four years later. Little gets through the Congress without substantive concessions to individuals, to narrow economic interests, or to states.[12] Collor was forced to roll over $70 billion in debt owed by states to the central government before the Congress would approve an increase in the personal income tax ceiling. Franco had to agree to an accord pegging monthly wage rates to inflation before the governors of eleven states would resume repayments on billions of dollars they owed to the central government. Approval of Franco's plan to cut government expenditures, a key part of his stabilization program, necessitated government concessions on the rural caucus's debts. And during Cardoso's first administration, the government's critically needed social-security reform approached final passage only after a four-year struggle that required a substantial weakening of the original proposal as well as significant outlays in pork-barrel spending.[13]

---

12. In early April 1997 the Chamber passed, by one vote, the president's proposal on administrative reform. The one-vote majority was achieved by doubling the ceiling on the maximum retirement benefit receivable, just for retired parliamentarians. On April 13 the president disavowed the agreement, putting the proposal itself in doubt. The proposal was finally approved in late 1998, but its effects were substantially delayed because Brazilian law prohibits the hiring or firing of government employees six months before or after an election. Since the next election occurred in October 1998, no one could be fired until after April 1999.

13. This pessimistic interpretation notwithstanding, some proposals do survive congressional scrutiny unscathed. Economy-opening measures, including tariff reduction and deregulation, have a high success rate, with especially strong support from the PFL's neoliberal wing and from northeastern deputies, who benefited less from state intervention in the economy. The drive to privatize state-owned enterprises has moved equally smoothly. Here state governors, needing the revenue generated by enterprise sales to cover their deficits or to reduce the fiscal pressure on the central government, joined neoliberals and northeasterners.

TABLE 16. Congressional Response to Presidential Proposals (Franco administration)

Date of Initial Proposal	Substance of Presidential Proposal	Date of Action by Congress	Substance of Action by Congress
October 21, 1992	President calls for "Full and lasting fiscal reform," details unspecified.	October 22, 1992	PMDB leaders in Chamber and Senate tell Franco that only emergency measures can get approval. President agrees.
Late October 1992	Specific presidential proposals: [1] tightening of tax-collection procedures [2] one-year tax on financial transactions [3] selective tax on consumption (alcohol, cigarettes, fuels, etc.) [4] eliminate tax on industrial production from 400 products [5] eliminate a tax collected by state governments and one by municipal government, compensated for by increase in federal tax share [6] banks lift secrecy	January 20, 1993	By 375 to 87, Chamber approves [1] "provisional" .25 percent tax on financial transactions, but government agrees to spend more on specified social programs, [2] new corporate withholding tax on financial gains, [3] rejects new taxes on fuel and corporate assets, [4] tax on financial transactions not officially passed.
August 1992	Official budget of president.	April 1, 1993	In addition to amendments to budget, Congress denies government request for flexibility in administering budget. Congress also includes funds for vacant vice presidency and $320 million for Companhia Siderurgica Nacional. No funds for 147 percent court-ordered increase in pensions or 33 percent pay increase. No funds for Itamar's antihunger drive.
April 1993	Lift 40 percent ceiling on foreign ownership of privatized companies.	??	Approved.

June 1993	FHC's "Program of Immediate Action" [1] slash government spending by $6 billion [2] enforce revenue-raising measures [3] end transfers from federal government to states, municipalities, and agencies [4] force states to start repaying the $40 billion they owe the federal government [5] impose more control over state banks [6] accelerate privatization [7] crackdown on tax evaders	June 22, 1993	Congress approves tax on checks, generating $600 million a month in revenues. Approved after repeated rejections.
		August 1, 1993	Three zeros removed from currency; Congress agrees, bankers support this measure.
June 23, 1993	President vetoes congressional bill calling for monthly wage adjustments pegged to rate of inflation.	Late August 1993	After negotiations with presidents of Senate and Chamber and labor and business leaders, compromise calls for monthly wage adjustments at 10 percent below the monthly rate of inflation; PMDB, PFL, PSDB and PP support compromise.
			After accords, governments of 11 states, including São Paulo, Mato Grosso, Bahia, and Rio de Janeiro, resume repayments of up to $20 billion owed to federal government agencies.
	No executive proposal	October 1–15, 1993	Congress approves a new electoral law, disciplining the financing of political campaigns, television rights, and so forth.
Late October 1993	Cardoso announces a package of anti-inflation measures that would reduce public spending at least $25 billion.		No formal proposal yet. PMDB wants shock treatment, its ministers threaten to resign.

(continued)

TABLE 16.—*Continued*

Date of Initial Proposal	Substance of Presidential Proposal	Date of Action by Congress	Substance of Action by Congress
November 25, 1993	FHC says he wants to speed up privatization and cut government expenditure. He also wants new taxes designed to raise an additional $7 billion in 1994: [1] new tax would be on wealth, applying to those with assets over $2 million [2] higher income tax rates for those earning over $1,500 a month [3] In late October an emergency measure changes rules of privatization and gives Finance Ministry decisive say in program; it also removes ceiling on foreign investors in privatized companies		Congressional budget scandal breaks out, weakening Congress's ability to resist executive initiatives. But Congress cannot debate the constitutional changes FHC wants, so no progress made.
December 29, 1993	"Economic Stabilization Program" Emergency measures with [1] new top tax rate of 35 percent for those earning more than $10,000 a month [2] raise in social contribution from 23 percent to 30 percent [3] owners of farmland would be allowed to pay annual land taxes in six installments		[1] Governors oppose FSE, and in February the idea seems dead [2] PFL and PPR prevent quorum on tax bills on January 28 vote; taxes cannot take effect in 1994, since they cannot take effect in the year they are passed [3] Freeze of transfers at last year's levels, with an expected increase of 15 percent in

December 29, 1993

[4] Emergency Social Fund (FSE) sets aside 15 percent of transfers from central government to state and municipal governments

[5] creation of URV monetary unit.

Set of proposals above.

January 1994

FHC says his cuts in public expenditure include the military. Joint chiefs want $700 million restored.

FHC wants a linear increase of 5 percent in tax rates (to bring $3.7 billion new revenue) and retention of 15 percent of transfers to states and municipalities.

revenues, never gets sent to Congress due to opposition

[4] government agrees to retention of 3 percent, but this is dropped from budget committee's final report

Congress approves

February 8, 1994

[1] new rate of 35 percent for those earning more than $10,000 a month and increase from 25 percent to 25.6 percent for those earning $1,000 to $ 10,000 a month

[2] tax on rural landowners smaller than proposal

[3] shortening of time period to pay taxes like IPI and income tax, but no quorum on vote to institute these in 1994

[4] FSE will be 15 percent of total federal revenues, but excludes the constitutional transfers to states and municipalities, passed on February 8, 1994

[5] to get PFL support on FSE, government agrees to extend to May 31 the deadline for the debate on constitutional reforms,

[6] FHC agrees to raise military pay

Tax increase never sent to Congress, judged politically unfeasible.

TABLE 17. Congressional Response to Presidential Proposals (Cardoso administration)

Date of Initial Proposal	Substance of Presidential Proposal	Date of Action by Congress	Substance of Action by Congress
February 18, 1995	[1] Social welfare minister advocates mixed system of public and private pensions. State retirement pensions could only be 5–10 times minimum wage, with an upper limit of $820 a month. Beyond that, arrangements would be individual. [2] Tax and fiscal reform. [3] Economic opening.	May 4, 1995	[1] Constitution and Justice Committee in Chamber voted to divide up the social-security reform proposals into several separate amendments. Government had wanted them treated as a single package. Eight progovernment deputies vote to separate (one from PFL, 3 from PP, 3 from PMDB, one from PL). Government then puts social-security reform on back burner until after economic reform. [2] Tax and fiscal reform delayed. [3] Economic opening proceeds.
July 13, 1995	Government proposes sale of Vale do Rio Doce company.	July 13, 1995	President promises that Petrobras will remain in public hands. Opposition agrees to sale.
August 1, 1995	Examination of constitutional reform issues resumes. [1] Tax reform proposals, details unknown [2] Social security: government wants to introduce private companies [3] Political reforms: include lengthening presidential term, shortening senatorial term, permitting presidential reelection, abolishing compulsory voting, establishing minimum requirements for minority parties. FHC says he is leaving initiative to Congress [4] Public administration reform: eliminates bureaucratic tenure	August 1, 1995	[1] Governors and mayors attack tax-reform proposals (which had never been formalized). President says he will consult with parties and state governments before submitting detailed proposals to Congress. [2] "Negative reaction" in Congress to introducing private companies in social security. [3] No action on political reform. [4] No action on public administration reform.

August 17, 1995	Bill assigns vetting of all "sensitive" exports (nuclear and missile) to the department of strategic affairs, facilitates space accord with United States.	??	Approved
September 21, 1995	Tax reform details: [1] Income-tax change delayed but will reduce top rate of corporate income tax from 48 percent to 30 percent [2] ICMS and IPI will be merged and rates will be fixed by Senate, not by state assemblies, as in current ICMS [3] Tax on energy will go from state to federal treasury [4] ICMS on exports abolished [5] Banking secrecy will be reduced. Inspectors from tax-collection agency will have access to all confidential information [6] Compulsory savings plans (currently allowed only in wartime, national emergency, or public-interest investment projects) will be allowed to be used to curb consumption or finance projects	September 21, 1995	[6] State governors and city mayors reject the change in compulsory savings plans.
September 21, 1995	Civil service reforms: [1] End tenure [2] Introduce some competitive bidding for services with the private sector	April 9, 1996	Passes Chamber, with concession benefiting parliamentarians. Does not pass Senate.
March 1996	Government tries to get social-security reform to clear the Chamber of Deputies.		Substitute bill approved over government objection.

(continued)

TABLE 17.—*Continued*

Date of Initial Proposal	Substance of Presidential Proposal	Date of Action by Congress	Substance of Action by Congress
March 1996	Financial Stabilization Fund takes place of Social Emergency Fund (retains scheduled transfers to states).		Approved.
April 1996	CPMF tax replaces IPMF tax, earmarked for health spending, government position unclear.		Approved.
November–December 1996	Government submits constitutional amendment allowing reelection for all executive officials, including president. Negotiations had actually begun much earlier.	February 26, 1997 March 21, 1997	Chamber and Senate approve. Evidence of extensive payoffs to individual deputies to secure favorable vote. Certain deputies receive $200,000 for favorable vote.
		June 1997	Congress defeats ceiling of $12,000 per month for salaries of state and municipal employees.
November 11, 1997	Emergency fiscal package of 51 measures, includes 10 percent rise in income tax, tax deductions for individuals limited to 20 percent of overall 1997 tax, price increases on fuels and gas, airport departure tax increase from $18 to $90, tax on car sales rises, federal budget cut, 33,000 civil service employees dismissed, elimination of regional incentives.	December 1997	Increase in income tax dropped because of PFL objection, departure tax increase dropped, regional incentives phased out slowly instead of immediately, cutting savings in half. Other elements approved.

December 2, 1997	Chamber approves end of tenure for civil servants. Government can dismiss employees whenever payrolls are > 60 per-cent of total tax revenues. Ceiling on salaries is $11,300. No one can be fired at state or federal levels until 1999 due to election in 1998. To get vote of PPB, Cardoso promised to release $450 million to city of São Paulo for a public transportation project.
February 1998	Social-security reform approved in Chamber. Main controversial points will be voted in April, and supplementary legislation voted in early 1999.
February 1998	Government released $545 million for local public works projects to get support on administrative reform and social security reforms, more than was spent in all 1997.
May 1998	Social-security reform passes Chamber, but government loses on two important provisions.

The inability of presidents to force their agendas through their legislatures is common in all democracies and, in particular, presidential systems. Still, Brazilian presidents seem particularly crippled. If the supposedly all-powerful president is really far from all powerful, attention should turn to the sources of presidential weakness. Is the problem simply that the multiplicity of parties creates an excess of veto players, thereby hindering any policy representing a movement away from the status quo, or does the problem lie in the propensity of deputies to defect from their party leaders' wishes?

II.   The Concept of the Legislative Party

Why do legislative parties exist?[14] Even where party identification is weak (surely the case in Brazil), enough voters have at least vague conceptions of parties and their records so that party labels affect reelection chances.[15] Legislators need the party label to take advantage of partisan electoral tides.[16] Legislative parties thus exist as solutions to collective action problems. Parties help prevent, in Gary W. Cox and Matthew D. McCubbins's (1993) language, such "electoral inefficiencies" as the overproduction of particularistic legislation and the underproduction of legislation with collective benefits.

The strength of central authority in a party depends in part on the strength of individual motivations to defect. These motivations, in turn, depend on deputies' ties to their constituencies, the homogeneity of those constituencies, their ideological positions, and other factors. As a result, a finding that party membership predicts the voting of individual legislators does not establish the strength of the legislative party. Members may vote together because they share common beliefs about an issue, because their electoral constituencies are similar (Fiorina 1974, 2–3), or because they engage in logrolls or policy alliances.[17]

Cox and McCubbins (1993, 4–5) review three distinct ways in which

---

14. For a comprehensive discussion of the theoretical bases of legislative parties, see Bowler, Farrell, and Katz 1999, esp. chap. 1.

15. In Brazil, however, where turnover between legislative sessions can surpass 50 percent, the goal of reelection is necessarily broader—including election to other offices and possible reelection to legislatures in the more distant future—and is not shared by all deputies.

16. Most observers would regard the PMDB's growth in 1986 and the PSDB-PFL alliance's surge in 1994 as partisan tides.

17. Cox and McCubbins (1993) describe the policy alliance between urban democrats supporting farm subsidies and rural democrats supporting food stamps. When this alliance, which party leaders merely facilitate, breaks down, the decline in average party loyalty is an indicator of the cohesion created by intraparty logrolls (see also Kingdon 1981).

scholars of the U.S. Congress conceptualize the legislative party. As floor voting coalitions, parties are thought to have little systematic influence on prefloor (committee) behavior. Partisans of this view utilize discipline on roll calls as a measure of party strength. As procedural coalitions, parties organize the House, make rules, and establish committees, but seldom do parties assume responsibility for policy. As conditional legislative parties, leaders' actions depend on party members' support on a case-by-case basis. Influence flows from the bottom up, and party leaders take responsibility only when there is widespread policy agreement among the party's members. By contrast, in such countries as Great Britain and Argentina, influence flows from the top down, and the rank and file grants automatic support—within some range of acceptability—to the leadership.

The empirical evidence marshaled by Cox and McCubbins for the U.S. case supports the model of conditional party government. What does this finding mean for the assessment of party strength? In their view, a measure of party strength should combine the size of the party's agenda with the party's discipline in support of its leadership on that agenda. The party agenda is all roll calls where (a) the leadership has a position and (b) where the other party either has no position or is opposed. When both parties have positions, and when these positions are opposed, the roll call is a party leadership vote. Discipline on such votes is the strongest test of party strength.

Scholarly understanding of the U.S. Congress helps provide knowledge about party strength in Brazil. Previous chapters argued that Brazil's electoral system produces a legislature with lots of weakly disciplined parties. Such a legislature is likely to be good at distributing pork but will have trouble making laws on issues of truly national scope. These difficulties matter less where presidents dominate their legislatures. But when key proposals in an executive's program require approval by a bicameral legislature, congressional obstructionism becomes a serious problem.

In retrospect, this argument remains incomplete. Brazil's legislature does, of course, shelter many parties. But while the nation's electoral rules clearly produce individualistic deputies motivated to resist discipline, until recently there has been no evidence from the legislature itself establishing the relative discipline of parties. Moreover, discipline (the propensity of party members to vote together) must be distinguished from coherence (the agreement of members' preferences on policy issues). Greater coherence means that, for any given number of parties, it will be harder to reach a legislative decision departing from the status quo (Tsebelis 1995).

Imagine an electoral structure in which deputies owe their seats and their political futures totally to party leaders.[18] Such deputies have no choice: they must delegate power to party leaders in exchange for access to "party goods." But suppose that sitting deputies have automatic places on party slates, that voters cast votes for individual candidates rather than party labels, and that fundraising is completely centered on candidates. Now deputies can choose. They delegate to party leaders a portion of their freedom to make individual bargains and a portion of their freedom to vote with their constituency's interest. Legislators do so in exchange for a combination of individual and party goods surpassing what they can achieve individually. For some deputies, particularly those who do not dominate their constituencies, who share their electoral base with party colleagues, or who compete with deputies from other parties, the trade-off is an easy one. They need the party. For others, the party is marginal. Such deputies concede autonomy only after adequate compensation.

A finding, therefore, that a party's deputies vote together cannot prove that influence between party leaders and deputies necessarily flows from the top down. Instead, this phenomenon may denote the occurrence of a successful bargaining process in which nearly all deputies are satisfied with their individual payoffs. In a sense, the best predictor of the amount of bargaining likely to occur is the structure of electoral rules, because these rules determine party leaders' control over the ballot as well as deputies' propensities to negotiate with party leaders and with the executive. As should be obvious by this point, Brazil's structure produces a plethora of deputies motivated to drive hard bargains.

In this political context, roll-call analyses can measure legislative parties' strength only within a multivariate model. Figueiredo and Limongi's work, while truly pioneering, is essentially univariate; the only variable is the level of unity of each party in the Chamber of Deputies. To make inferences about the strength of party leaders, it is necessary to assess the importance of other determinants of party voting, including ideology, constituency characteristics, pork-barrel benefits, and seniority.

III.   A Model of Cooperation and Defection from Party Majorities

Motivation to Defect

Deputies desert their parties when they have the motivation and the autonomy. Motivations can be both ideological and electoral. *Ideological* motivation

---

18. Coppedge's (1994) portrait of pre-1991 Venezuela fits this description.

means that on a given issue a deputy's preferences differ from those of the party majority. These preferences may be predictable on the basis of the deputy's political career or personal background, but they are analytically distinct from the interests of the deputy's constituency. In 1995 (before the 1995–98 legislative session), Maria das Graças Rua constructed a six-point left-right ideological scale. This measure, formulated from surveys of deputies and from background information, is reasonably free from contamination by actual votes, but it can be utilized only in the 1995–98 period. For earlier legislatures, deputies' links to ARENA (the right-wing political party created by the military dictatorship) serve as a crude indicator of conservatism.[19]

Electoral motivations, which come from demands made by the constituencies deputies represent, are more complex. Constituencies in Brazil, as chapter 1 showed, include the actual voters who put deputies into office, the interest groups and lobbies financing them, and their states' governors. Given Brazil's combination of open-list proportional representation and regionally specialized vote bases, defining a voting constituency is far from easy. It is possible to say, however, that deputies with more concentrated or clustered votes ought to have closer links to their voters; hence, they will have greater motivation to defect when their constituents' interests diverge from the party position. At the same time, these deputies will need to deliver pork-barrel programs to their constituents to ensure political survival. Local politicians, whose political careers include a stint as mayor or councilperson, are likely to emphasize their independence from party control.

I noted previously the inapplicability to Brazil of the "primacy of reelection" assumption typically made by students of U.S. politics. While some deputies want long parliamentary careers, many others see the Chamber of Deputies as a mere stopover. Their immediate objective is a mayoral post, a run at the governorship, or even a return to private business. For these deputies, and for many who do seek Chamber careers, state governors are figures to reckon with. As chapter 4 illustrated, governors' ability to influence their delegations' voting behavior varies across the states as a function of social, historical, and demographic factors. In general, however, cooperation should be higher when a deputy represents the same party as the state governor.

Motivations are only part of the cooperation-defection story; equally important is the autonomy that allows defection. Deputies who are electorally less vulnerable, who are less subject to partisan tides, are clearly better able to go

---

19. See the work of Tim Power (1997a, 1997b), who contributed the Graça Rua scale. I combined these two indicators by standardizing them.

their own way. One measure of electoral vulnerability is postelection rank in the party list. A deputy ranking first in the list has enormously more freedom of action than a deputy coming in at the bottom. Deputies with a greater share of the votes cast for candidates of their party, or with more seniority, are also more autonomous.[20] Finally, a central determinant of individual autonomy is the degree to which deputies dominate their constituencies. As noted in chapter 1, some deputies get high shares of the total vote cast in the municipalities that are important to them; these deputies dominate. Deputies who dominate their voters fear no competition from other parties or from members of their own party. If they change parties, their voters change with them. These party-transcending ties to voters come from an individual's charisma, family tradition, or reputation as an effective leader as well as from deals the deputy makes with local politicians. In either case, domination allows deputies to thumb their noses at party leaders.

Dominant deputies' behavior is complicated by their greater ability to claim credit for public works they deliver to their electoral bases. Greater dominance leads to more activity in such pork-seeking activities as the submission of budgetary amendments. Deputies who share their constituencies with other deputies have much less incentive to attract public projects to their bases, because such legislators cannot claim exclusive credit. This relationship, however, is curvilinear. At some level of dominance, deputies have such control that their seats are safe, and their incentives to fight for voters decline. In sum, the relationship between dominance and defection is linear in terms of autonomy from party control, but it is U-shaped in terms of the relationship between dominance and the deputy's need for pork barrel.

This formulation is implicitly interactive. Three autonomy measures—domination, seniority, and rank—work in concert with vote concentration, the electoral indicator of the potential desire to defect. More defections should be expected among deputies with concentrated votes when (1) they dominate their constituencies, (2) they rank high in postelection vote outcomes, and (3) they attain greater seniority.

No one who follows Brazilian politics doubts that pork-barrel programs and control over appointive jobs are the mother's milk of legislative majorities. Every crucial piece of legislation seems accompanied by the "liberation" of grants and a spate of appointments of party loyalists. Pork-barrel programs strongly affected voting in the 1987–88 Constituent Assembly. Between 1988

---

20. However, seniority is also correlated with leadership positions, which may make defection much more difficult.

and 1993, the Chamber's internal rules allowed deputies to propose unlimited budget amendments, but a major scandal (involving millions of dollars in kick-backs from construction companies) led the Congress to reform the amendment process. Current rules allow each deputy amendments up to a fixed amount, roughly $1.2 million. These amendments are essentially under the deputy's control. The new rules might seem to weaken presidential autonomy, since the money cannot be increased or decreased, but in fact the system simply changed. The executive branch still has to transfer the funds, to sign the checks. In practice, the executive has proved willing to accelerate or hold back on disbursements for individual deputies. Whether the executive seeks the cooperation of deputies from parties supporting the government or the defection of deputies from parties in opposition, speedy disbursements are an appropriate tactic. Utilizing data from SIAFI, the national online accounting system, I calculated, for each year, the ratio of each deputy's actually disbursed funds to the average disbursed funds for all members of the Chamber. The resulting variable measures the pork-barrel favoritism enjoyed by each deputy.

It might be expected that if pork leads to party cooperation (limiting the discussion, for simplicity, to progovernment parties), a positive sign should be found on the pork variable—that is, more pork leads to more cooperation. In a dynamic sense this hypothesis is certainly correct, but cross-sectionally it might be wrong. Suppose the government concentrates its pork on deputies tending to vote no. Some gratefully change their votes to yes, while others remain obstinate. Compared to those who are so progovernment that they need no bribes, the opportunistic deputies are still less likely to cooperate, even though they are more cooperative than they would have been without the pork. Hence the sign on the coefficient of the pork variable could be negative even though it induces deputies to increase their party cooperation. In terms of the overall hypothesis regarding party strength, however, the size of the pork coefficient is crucial. The greater the importance of pork as a determinant of cooperation, the weaker the party's control over individual deputies.

Party Strength and Encaminhamentos

It is now possible to categorize the sources of party voting consensus. Party discipline can be a consequence, on the one hand, of pork inducements, constituency demands, and common policy preferences, or, on the other, of the influence of party leaders. The key to party strength as a determinant of cooperation and defection is the importance of the recommendation, or *encaminhamento,* of party leaders. On most votes, party leaders recommend a vote to their members. Just before votes are cast, the Chamber president calls on each party leader for this recommendation. Leaders respond with "Yes," "No," or "The vote is left open."[21]

Parties frequently recommend votes in situations where the outcome, given the fact that normally opposed parties are on the same side, is a foregone conclusion.[22] In fact, a majority of all recommendations occurs on votes that are essentially uncontested. In such cases, dissent has few consequences for the leadership (or for party followers), since the vote cannot be lost. On contested recommendations, the chances of losing are much greater. A party's membership might live with a few dissenters, but as defections increase, tolerance for free riders drops. If defections are very numerous, of course, it becomes unclear whether the leadership recommendation has much impact on the members.

The central tests of party strength, then, are the coefficients of the variables measuring party leaders' recommendations on contested and uncontested votes. If neither is significant, party unity has nothing to do with leadership sanctions. If both variables are significant, deputies accept party leadership as long as it remains noncoercive—that is, party leaders avoid unpopular recommendations on contested votes, because they know members will reject such recommendations. If the coefficient on contested votes is significantly greater than the coefficient on uncontested votes, then we will conclude that party discipline matters: deputies respond to a leadership recommendation when it is crucial to the ultimate outcome of the vote.

Are All Votes Created Equal?

On many Chamber votes, individual cooperation and defection have little importance in terms of overall results, either because the vote is purely procedural or because the outcome is overwhelmingly one-sided. As a result, I weighted

---

21. *Encaminhamentos* are not intended to force members to cast a particular vote; such compulsion is very rare and normally follows a party membership vote to close the question. Leaders sometimes respond to the Chamber president's questions with "the vote is left open, but the leader votes . . ." I code such recommendations as open.

22. The analysis excludes votes where more than 90 percent of the deputies cast the same vote—i.e., votes classed as uncontested have at least 10 percent dissent from the majority position. For the PMDB, PFL, and PSDB, I defined a recommendation as uncontested if each party made the same recommendation as the other two. For the PDT, a recommendation equal to that of the PFL was uncontested. For the PPB (formerly called the PDS or PPR), uncontested recommendations were identical to those of the PDT and PFL. Inclusion of variables for both contested and uncontested recommendations does not imply a full set of dummies, because the null case ("o") is the condition of no recommendation at all.

the votes by the number of deputies voting and by the closeness of the vote. For ordinary simple-majority votes, the weight was calculated as:

(Total Voting / Chamber Total) × (1 − ((2 × Yes − Total Voting) / Total Voting))

On constitutional issues, those requiring three-fifths of each chamber, the formula was:

(Total Voting / Chamber Total) × (1 − 2 × abs ((308 − Yes) / Chamber Total))

In other words, the closer the vote and the more deputies voting, the more weight given to that roll call in the overall regression.

Absentee Deputies

Most roll-call analyses simply delete deputies who fail to vote, counting them neither for nor against. In Brazil, at least, it is quite certain that party leaders hold a different view. On the basis of interviews with leaders of every major party, it is clear that party leaders know who failed to vote and why they failed to vote. Absentees without a good reason (medical leave, critical local political commitment, and so forth) are regarded as defectors, especially on constitutional issues, where 308 votes are needed for passage.

I obtained lists of deputies absent from the Chamber for "legitimate" reasons, including medical leaves or acceptance of executive-branch posts. After removing deputies from the analysis for each day they had official leave, the remaining absentees were coded "present." I then took the most conservative approach possible, reclassifying these "present but not voting" deputies only on the issues where their votes were most crucial. Thus, on constitutional issues, these deputies were switched from "present" to "defect."

IV. Analysis

Why Do Deputies Cooperate or Defect?

For every recorded vote in the Chamber between 1988 and 1996, I created a dichotomous variable called "Cooperate." This variable measures the agreement or disagreement of each deputy with the majority of that deputy's party.[23] The

---

23. A member can be in different parties on different votes. A few members have three or more party affiliations over the course of these votes. There are only a few cases in which a majority of a party voted against leaders' recommendations.

cooperation variable was then regressed, using a logistic specification, on the independent variables discussed earlier. The resulting regressions take the form:

Cooperation = Contested Recommendation + Uncontested Recommendation + Pork Share + Rank in Postelection List + Share of Party Vote + Municipal Dominance + Vote Concentration + Terms Served + (Concentration × Rank) + (Concentration × Term) + (Concentration × Dominance) + Ideology + Local Career + Governor of State from Deputy's Party + Incumbent Seeking Reelection

The model was implemented separately for each of six parties: on the Right, the Liberal Front Party (PFL), the Brazilian Labor Party (PTB), and the Brazilian Progressive Party (PPB); in the center, the Brazilian Democratic Movement (PMDB) and the Brazilian Social Democratic Party (PSDB); on the Left, the Democratic Labor Party (PDT).[24] The unit of observation, then, is each deputy's individual vote. Separate regressions were run for two periods: all post-1991 votes (utilizing a dummy variable for the 1995–98 period) and Cardoso's 1995–98 administration.[25] Regressions were also implemented, in each period and for each party, with absentees counted as missing or as defectors on constitutional supermajority votes.

No single table can include twenty-four separate regressions, and I have spared the reader the burden of examining twenty-four separate tables. Tables 18–23 present one regression—the whole period model with absentees included—for each party. Appendix D contains the results (for each party) with absentees always counted as missing.[26] All the regressions (including those not presented here) attain high levels of significance, and numerous variables reach high levels of statistical significance in each regression. In other words, the basic model tested here, while far from a complete explanation of party cooperation and defection, is persuasive.

---

24. The model was not applied to the Workers' Party (PT) because party unity in the PT is so high that the logistic broke down. Alone in Brazil, the PT truly is a disciplined party.

25. SAS Proc Logistic was utilized for the regressions. SAS provides tests for collinearity and overdispersion as well as various checks on the residuals. Collinearity was occasionally a problem—though never in the case of the leadership vote recommendations—but little can be done about it except to interpret individual coefficients cautiously. Overdispersion, however, was present and was corrected with the deviance criterion, thus increasing the standard errors of the uncorrected regression. Various residual diagnostics, including the C criterion and the hat matrix diagonal, were examined for outliers and extremely influential observations. None had any visible effect on the coefficients.

26. Results from other periods are available from the author.

TABLE 18.   Cooperation and Defection among PFL Deputies, 1991–98

Dependent Variable: Cooperation with Party Majority (absentees included)

Variable	Unstandardized Parameter Estimate and Probability Level	Standard Error	Standardized Estimate	Odds Ratio
Cardoso administration (1995–98)	−0.3873	.2043	−0.0477	.679
Contested party recommendation	.1657	.1499	.0254	1.180
Uncontested party recommendation	−0.3476**	.1386	−0.0587	.706
Share of pork disbursements	−0.3960***	.1065	−0.0776	.673
Rank in postelection list	1.7097***	.3386	.1569	5.527
Share of total party vote	.0953	2.0308	.0011	1.100
Dominance of key municipalities	3.1012***	.7578	.1386	22.224
Concentration of vote	.1574***	.0313	.3825	1.170
Concentration × Rank in list	−0.1123**	.0385	−0.1444	.894
Concentration × Terms served	−0.0004	.0067	−0.0028	1.000
Concentration × Dominance	−0.4057***	.0925	−0.3067	.666
Ideology	.2775**	.1069	.0629	1.320
Terms served	.0528	.0605	.0281	1.054
Local political career	−0.2654*	.1381	−0.0437	.767
Governor from same party	.3204*	.1594	.0586	1.378
Incumbent seeking reelection	.3917**	.1544	.0568	1.479

−2 log likelihood = 2019.4
Model chi-squared = 455.3 $p < .000$ I
Correctly predicted = 63.9%
$N = 13{,}101$
$R^2 = .0342$ Max-rescaled $R^2 = .1984$

*$p < .05$ **$p < .01$ ***$p < .001$

Although tables 18–23 are limited to one regression for each party, the discussion that follows considers models with absentee deputies counted both as missing and as defectors in both periods. The emphasis is on overall, cross-party patterns, with some attention paid to results for each party. In each case, the crucial tests are the significance and direction (sign) of the unstandardized coefficients and the differences, within a given regression, in the sizes of the standardized coefficients.[27]

27. Standardizing causes variables to have the same mean and standard deviation. The coefficients are then comparable, because the coefficient represents a change in the propensity to cooperate that results from a change of one standard deviation in the independent variable.

TABLE 19.   Cooperation and Defection among PMDB Deputies, 1991–98

Dependent Variable: Cooperation with Party Majority (absentees included)

Variable	Unstandardized Parameter Estimate and Probability Level	Standard Error	Standardized Estimate	Odds Ratio
Cardoso administration (1995–98)	−.9400***	.2014	−0.1150	.391
Contested party recommendation	.1937	.1339	.0302	1.214
Uncontested party recommendation	−0.2853*	.1235	−0.0483	.752
Share of pork disbursements	−0.4223***	.0850	−0.9467	.656
Rank in postelection list	.1997	.3564	.0206	1.221
Share of total party vote	2.8314**	1.1202	.0621	16.969
Dominance of key municipalities	3.5046***	.8855	.1388	33.268
Concentration of vote	.1729***	.0297	.4228	1.189
Concentration × Rank in list	.0232	.0337	.0360	1.023
Concentration × Terms served	−1.0101	.0103	−0.0570	.990
Concentration × Dominance	−0.4962***	.0852	−0.3786	.609
Ideology	.3289***	.0986	.1394	1.481
Terms served	.3928***	.0986	.1394	1.481
Local political career	.007230	.1173	.0014	.765
Governor from same party	−0.2677**	.1284	−0.0484	.765
Incumbent seeking reelection	.3776***	.1145	.066391	1.459

−2 log likelihood = 2348.6
Model chi-squared = 337.7 $p < .0001$
Correctly predicted = 68.1%
N = 14,224
R^2 = .0235   Max-rescaled R^2 = .1363

*$p < .05$ **$p < .01$ ***$p < .001$

Do Leadership Recommendations Matter?

In only two cases (the PFL with absentees excluded and the PPB with absentees included) do leadership recommendations on both contested and uncontested votes positively affect party cooperation. In neither case, however, is cooperation stronger on votes that are contested rather than uncontested. Only in the case of the PDT is a positive recommendation on contested votes stronger than the recommendation on uncontested votes. Moreover, recommendations clearly play a minor role, even for these three parties, in the overall determination of deputies' propensities to cooperate or defect. In table 21, for example, the standardized coefficient of the PPB's contested recommendation variable is smaller than nine other variables, and it is one-ninth the size of the indicator of vote concentration. Overall, then, it appears that recommendations do not af-

TABLE 20.   Cooperation and Defection among PSDB Deputies, 1991–98

Dependent Variable: Cooperation with Party Majority (absentees included)

Variable	Unstandardized Parameter Estimate and Probability Level	Standard Error	Standardized Estimate	Odds Ratio
Cardoso administration (1995–98)	−0.7415**	.3008	−0.0633	.476
Contested party recommendation	−0.0308	.1721	−0.0044	.595
Uncontested party recommendation	−0.2999	.1614	−0.0488	.741
Share of pork disbursements	−0.5192***	.1280	−0.1101	.595
Rank in postelection list	2.5151***	.3528	.3066	12.368
Share of total party vote	14.2774***	2.4760	.1999	999.0
Dominance of key municipalities	2.4301*	1.0115	.1040	11.360
Concentration of vote	.1432***	.0317	.4075	1.154
Concentration × Rank in list	−0.2093***	.0342	−0.4889	.811
Concentration × Terms served	−0.0067	.0108	−0.0387	.993
Concentration × Dominance	−0.0381	.0869	−0.0267	.963
Ideology	−0.2411	.1362	−0.0533	.786
Terms served	.1406	.0880	.0523	1.151
Local political career	−0.0622	.1509	−0.0116	.940
Governor from same party	.9257***	.1580	.1800	2.524
Incumbent seeking reelection	−0.3957**	.1599	−0.0668	.673

−2 log likelihood = 1543.5
Model chi-squared = 429.9 $p < .0001$
Correctly predicted = 66.3%
$N = 10,723$
$R^2 = .0393$ Max-rescaled $R^2 = .2338$

*$p < .05$ **$p < .01$ ***$p < .001$

fect cooperation through threats of sanctions or promises of rewards. Party vote recommendations sometimes matter in the sense that they guide deputies who respond to calls for party solidarity and who simply need to know how the party is voting.[28] But even when recommendations do matter, other factors far outweigh them in determining deputies' cooperation or defection.

Can Pork Buy Deputies' Cooperation?

Chapter 6 demonstrated that pork-barrel expenditures buy or at least rent congressional loyalty. In four of the six parties represented in tables 18–23, the

---

28. In the U.S. context, a more elaborate version of this argument appears in Kingdon 1981.

TABLE 21.　Cooperation and Defection among PPB Deputies, 1991–98

Dependent Variable: Cooperation with Party Majority (absentees included)

Variable	Unstandardized Parameter Estimate and Probability Level	Standard Error	Standardized Estimate	Odds Ratio
Cardoso administration (1995–98)	−0.4469*	.2175	−0.0441	.640
Contested party recommendation	.2696*	.1255	.049700	1.309
Uncontested party recommendation	.5673*	.2490	.0576	1.764
Share of pork disbursements	−0.1170	.0991	−0.0272	.890
Rank in postelection list	1.8857***	.3094	.2032	6.591
Share of total party vote	−1.0858	2.3506	−0.0141	.338
Dominance of key municipalities	−2.7803**	1.0167	−0.1226	.062
Concentration of vote	.0973***	.0242	.2379	1.102
Concentration × Rank in list	−0.2721***	.0443	−0.4320	.762
Concentration × Terms served	−0.0281**	.0095	−0.1701	.972
Concentration × Dominance	.3848**	.1206	.1832	1.469
Ideology	.1489	.0898	.0541	1.161
Terms served	.3246***	.0901	.1448	1.383
Local political career	−0.2148	.1325	−0.0405	.807
Governor from same party	.9368	.7068	.0395	2.552
Incumbent seeking reelection	.2626	.1408	.0438	1.300

−2 log likelihood = 1698.6
Model chi-squared = 261.2　　$p < .0001$
Correctly predicted = 66.6%
$N = 9,024$
$R^2 = .0285$　　Max-rescaled $R^2 = .1462$

*$p < .05$　　**$p < .01$　　***$p < .001$

coefficient on the pork variable is negative and significant; for the other two parties the coefficient is weak, but the sign is correct. The same effect appears when votes are restricted to the Cardoso administration (1995–98). The tables in appendix D, however, demonstrate that the exclusion of absentee deputies (counting them as missing) produces a coefficient that is positive in all cases and significantly positive in three. To interpret this difference (absentees included vs. absentees excluded), note that absentee deputies have a propensity to defect. The threat of defection establishes a claim on pork-barrel spending. Government and party leaders reward defectors, expecting greater cooperation on future votes. Overall, the government concentrates pork-barrel spending on those likely to defect. Though their rate of cooperation increases, they remain

TABLE 22.   Cooperation and Defection among PDT Deputies, 1991–98

Dependent Variable: Cooperation with Party Majority (absentees included)

Variable	Unstandardized Parameter Estimate and Probability Level	Standard Error	Standardized Estimate	Odds Ratio
Cardoso administration (1995–98)	.1889	.5957	.0194	1.208
Contested party recommendation	.4611*	.2155	.0888	1.586
Uncontested party recommendation	−0.1112	.2672	−0.0169	.895
Share of pork disbursements	−0.6556**	.2181	−0.1408	.519
Rank in postelection list	.4559	.7348	.0563	1.578
Share of total party vote	12.5580	9.2882	.1078	999.0
Dominance of key municipalities	3.6081	3.1463	.1557	36.898
Concentration of vote	.1649	.1102	.2907	1.179
Concentration × Rank in list	.0225	.0982	.0302	1.023
Concentration × Terms served	−0.0332	.0420	−0.1076	.967
Concentration × Dominance	−0.2491	.3356	−0.1463	.779
Ideology	.167437	.2682	.0443	1.182
Terms served	.2276	.2066	.1033	1.256
Local political career	−1.0725**	.3457	−0.2067	.342
Governor from same party	1.3073	.8239	.1292	3.696
Incumbent seeking reelection	−0.1962	.3160	−0.0334	.822

−2 log likelihood = 540.7
Model chi-squared = 131.7 $p < .0001$
Correctly predicted = 68.9%
$N = 3764$
$R^2 = .0344$ Max-rescaled $R^2 = .2102$

*$p < .05$ **$p < .01$ ***$p < .001$

more likely to defect (producing a negative coefficient) than are deputies who receive less.[29]

Parties in which influence flows from top to bottom, as in Venezuela's Acción Democratica, maintain discipline without individualized bargaining. Not so in Brazil, where pork-barrel spending is necessary to cement coalitions on practically any serious issue. In part, then, pork compensates for the party weakness that the leadership recommendation variables revealed.

29. This interpretation is obviously extremely tentative. A time-series model would offer a better test, but a game-theoretic approach, as Bill Keech has suggested in a personal communication, is really optimal.

TABLE 23.   Cooperation and Defection among PTB Deputies, 1991–98

Dependent Variable: Cooperation with Party Majority (absentees included)

Variable	Unstandardized Parameter Estimate and Probability Level	Standard Error	Standardized Estimate	Odds Ratio
Cardoso administration (1995–98)	−0.6395	.4771	−0.0659	.528
Contested party recommendation	−0.7079***	.2075	−0.1368	.493
Uncontested party recommendation	−0.4101	.2563	−0.0570	.664
Share of pork disbursements	−0.0620	.1838	−0.0152	.940
Rank in postelection list	−2.2549*	1.0933	−0.2059	.105
Share of total party vote	24.6165***	5.7649	.2985	999.0
Dominance of key municipalities	5.9312*	2.6933	.2417	376.6
Concentration of vote	.0224	.0568	.0452	1.023
Concentration × Rank in list	.3548**	.1139	.5247	1.426
Concentration × Terms served	.0462	.0365	.2525	1.047
Concentration × Dominance	−0.7916**	.3117	−0.4671	.453
Ideology	.9967***	.2758	.2805	2.709
Terms served	−0.1850	.2590	−0.0930	.831
Local political career	−0.5821	.3378	−0.0783	.559
Governor from same party	−1.5557**	.5726	−0.1511	.211
Incumbent seeking reelection	.3299	.3415	.059522	1.391

−2 log likelihood = 671.2
Model chi-squared = 186.1 $p < .0001$
Correctly predicted = 69.0%
$N = 3474$
$R^2 = .0522$ Max-rescaled $R^2 = .2385$

*$p < .05$ **$p < .01$ ***$p < .001$

Electoral Strength, Constituency, Ideology, Career Background

In nearly every case, low ranks in parties' postelection lists are associated with higher degrees of cooperation with party majorities.[30] These weak deputies co-operate because doing so facilitates access to jobs and pork. Cooperation gives deputies a platform on which to stand when running for reelection in districts where they think the electorate cares about the party label. For the PSDB and the PFL, rank's effects on cooperation are strikingly larger between 1991 and 1994 than between 1995 and 1998. The PSDB opposed the government during

---

30. The coefficient on the indicator of deputies' shares of aggregate party vote was much less consistent. Due to the weakness of these coefficients and also to the high collinearity of the two variables, it seems reasonable to emphasize rank's effects on cooperation.

most of the 1991–94 period, but after 1994 the party became a key member of the governing coalition. The decline in the importance of rank for PSDB deputies suggests that the party label, not access to pork, motivates cooperation, because access to pork is much greater for the party in the current period. The PFL had an off-again, on-again relationship with the government before 1995 but, like the PSDB, participated in the governing coalition in the Cardoso administration.[31] In the case of parties like the PDT, no common objectives exist between party leaders and the executive. In the Cardoso period, with absentees included, weak PDT deputies are no more likely to cooperate than are strong deputies. On the basis of interviews with legislators, I believe that the executive targets pork to weak PDT deputies to persuade them to avoid voting against the government; that is, in this situation not voting was preferable to the government than a vote with the antigovernment party majority.

What happens when deputies dominate their constituencies? For the PFL, PMDB, PSDB, and PTB, dominance is associated with greater party cooperation. Dominant deputies, as observed in chapter 1, tend to be a traditional type whose political careers are based either on their family's regional predominance or on their own deal making with scattered local (often rural) bosses able to deliver blocs of votes. For these deputies, continued electoral success requires delivering pork-barrel projects to their local intermediaries.

The only exceptions to the dominance-cooperation linkage were the PPB, which was significantly negative, and the PDT, which was positive but insignificant. I have no definitive explanation for these deviant party members. Since their parties took opposing positions on most government-sponsored proposals, the ideological positions of dominant deputies are not the motivating factor. Instead, the explanation might lie in these two parties' supracongressional leadership. In both cases, a powerful presidential hopeful dominated the party, but neither the PPB's Paulo Maluf nor the PDT's Leonel Brizola controlled any pork. For deputies in these two parties, defecting from the party majority could be a tactic of political survival that only dominant deputies had the autonomy to pursue.

A much stronger constituency effect comes from the geographic concentration of the votes of individual deputies. Vote clustering has strong and positive effects on cooperation in nearly every party, time period, and absentee condition.[32] Given the assumption that concentration of votes increases deputies'

---

31. This explanation does not work for the PPB. I have not determined why.

32. The only negative relationship is found in one PDT case, but given the opposition status of the party, this finding is really confirmatory.

accountability to their voters, it might be argued that this observation simply reflects popular support for executive initiatives. To some degree this finding is plausible, but issue-based links must be rare in Brazil, because the ties between voters and deputies are so weak and because deputies have little idea what constituents think. Instead, vote concentration means that deputies are simultaneously more likely to be able to claim credit for public spending directed to their constituencies and under more pressure to deliver.

Seniority produces small and inconsistent effects. The original hypothesis suggested that senior deputies, other things equal, have the autonomy to defect if they so desire. Conversely, senior deputies tend to get along by going along, and they may be thoroughly tied to the leadership. Many senior deputies hold some sort of minor leadership position.

Deputies with local political backgrounds did not cooperate or defect at different rates than did other politicians, and governors did not consistently influence the deputies from their states. But deputies in states with PSDB governors were exceptionally cooperative, probably because three PSDB governors represented industrial states with similar economic problems and with close ties to the origins of the PSDB and to President Cardoso.[33] PFL governors, led by the powerful PFL machine in Bahia, also influenced their deputies in the direction of cooperation. PTB and PMDB deputies in states with governors from these parties seemed more likely to defect, but this finding may simply be a result of particularly fractious intrastate politics.

Incumbents seeking reelection consistently cooperated with their parties. Among the larger parties, only PSDB members cooperated significantly less often if they planned reelection campaigns. If the causal story behind this relationship is the currying of favor by deputies expecting to seek reelection, what explains the PSDB defections? Here, perhaps, are the consequences—on its more left-of-center deputies—of the PSDB's increasing neoliberalism. For those deputies whose constituencies are vulnerable to invasions from the Left, usually from the PT, or who are ideologically uncomfortable with their party's rightward drift, defection may be a rational survival strategy. This argument once again suggests that the decision to seek reelection is causally prior to, and therefore affects, voting decisions.

Ideology is a moderately strong and fairly consistent force, but its effects at first glance seem counterintuitive. With the exception of the PDT, more con-

---

33. The three PSDB governors include Eduardo Azeredo in Minas Gerais, Marcello Alencar in Rio de Janeiro, and Mário Covas in São Paulo.

servative members within each party are more likely to follow party recommendations. If most legislation is aimed at the median legislator, then the conservative members of right-wing parties ought to be most disaffected and hence most prone to defect. Likewise, left-wing members of left-of-center parties ought to be most disaffected and prone to defection. Why do conservative right-wingers cooperate? In part, pork-barrel inducements must overwhelm ideological disagreement. At the same time, ideological conformity with party programs fails to affect deputies' behavior because most Brazilian parties simply lack any sort of coherent programs.

Last, consider the three variables representing the interaction of clustering with electoral rank, seniority, and dominance. Contrary to my earlier prediction (that strong deputies with concentrated votes would defect), weak but concentrated deputies are the defectors. An examination of residuals shows that such deputies tend to share their electoral bases with other deputies.[34] Sharing limits their ability to claim credit for pork, so currying favor with party leaders is pointless. However, their constituencies have higher levels of voter awareness and include cohorts of voters negatively affected by neoliberal economic policies. For weak deputies facing such voters, defection from the party yields a positive electoral payoff.

Clustered PFL and PMDB deputies who dominate their key municipalities defect more from their leaderships, but their counterparts in the PSDB cooperate more with the party. This finding is not surprising: concentrated-dominant PFL and PMDB types are mostly in the Northeast and reflect the strength of traditional political families and deal making.[35] For these deputies, the party label has little importance for their electoral futures. By contrast, concentrated-dominant PSDB deputies usually have strong local backgrounds, often as mayors or state deputies from medium-sized communities. These deputies cooperate because party labels and access to pork matter.[36]

---

34. A typical example of this kind of concentrated and shared electoral base is the municipality of São Paulo. While the whole state constitutes the legal electoral district, this single municipality effectively elects twenty to thirty deputies, or nearly half the state total. No candidate gets more than 10 percent of the municipality's votes, but all get 60–70 percent of their personal vote there.

35. As demonstrated earlier in this book, the party label is quite important in Bahia. Magalhães built his PFL machine on access to central government funds, and former state secretaries of programs such as health and education dominate his congressional delegation. I am indebted to Simone Rodrigues da Silva for help on this question.

36. The combination of senior deputies with concentrated vote bases does not seem to affect cooperation.

Conclusion

Though Brazil's democratic presidents have an impressive range of formal and informal powers, they face constant, crippling difficulties in moving their agendas through the legislature. Many proposals fail to come to a vote. Others cannot get out of committee. Still others never arrive at the Congress at all. Proposals that survive the legislative process emerge disfigured by substantive concessions and saddled by high costs in pork-barrel side payments. This chapter took the first steps in exploring Brazilian executive-legislative relations by searching for the microfoundations of congressional intransigence. I sought to resolve an apparent contradiction raised by two strands of research. One strand points to the electoral system as the culprit: Brazil combines open-list proportional representation, high-magnitude electoral districts, unlimited reelection, and candidate selection at the level of states. This institutional structure should produce a legislature full of individualistic, pork-oriented deputies and weakly disciplined parties. But a second strand of research suggests that the sanctions and rewards wielded by party leaders are strong enough to counteract the fragmenting tendencies of the electoral system and produce legislative parties with very high levels of voting unity.

As in many political systems, votes on the floor of Brazil's legislature represent the culmination of a process of intensive bargaining among presidents, party leaders, interest-based caucuses, and individual deputies. Given the nation's institutional structure, Brazil should be a prime example of conditional legislative parties, where leaders' actions depend on the support of party members on a case-by-case basis and where influence flows from the bottom up.

In this setting, analysis of roll-call votes requires a theory of legislative behavior that is necessarily multivariate. As a first step, this chapter developed a model predicting cooperation or defection from party majorities. If the conditional party influence model is incorrect, if influence flows from the top down, party leaders ought to be able to persuade their members to follow leadership vote recommendations. Leaders too weak to compel cooperation can try to buy support with pork-barrel programs and job appointments directed at individual deputies. But many deputies have the autonomy and motivation to resist party leaders or to extract a high price for support. The freedom to resist depends on electoral security, which in turn is determined by deputies' postelection rank, share of their party's vote, legislative seniority, and municipal-level dominance. The motivation to resist depends on ideology, constituency characteristics, and political background.

Applied to Brazil's six major parties in the 1991–98 period, this model of cooperation and defection fares well. Overall, it provides persuasive evidence that party leaders lack the power to compel cooperation. Leaders make voting recommendations to their members, and these recommendations sometimes positively affect cooperation. But vote recommendations have no more effect on crucial, highly contested votes than on uncontested votes and have much less influence than constituency characteristics and pork-barrel spending.

Deputies cooperate at higher rates when they are weak electorally and when their constituencies are geographically concentrated. Electoral weakness makes deputies reluctant to surrender the benefits of the party label. Legislators may bargain hard for substantive compromises on legislation and may extract high prices in pork or appointments for support, but in the end the party label helps defend deputies against interparty and intraparty competitors. When a deputy's constituents are geographically concentrated, they are more likely to know who their deputy is and more likely to demand results from their deputies. Given the absence of programmatic content in Brazil's parties, results implies pork.

The model's most notable misprediction resulted from the indicator of ideology. Brazil's parties do have broadly distinct ideological centers, even if the distinctions are very broad indeed. In general, however, conservative deputies cooperate more, regardless of the relationship between their party and the median legislator. I expected more defections from conservative members of right-wing parties and leftist members of left-wing parties. Perhaps the error lies in the use of a unidimensional indicator of ideology in a multidimensional voting space. It is also possible that legislators rarely care much about ideological questions, so their ideological predilections are overwhelmed by their need for pork.

Chapter 8

Procedures, Parties, and Negotiations in a Fragmented Legislature

"You leave with the deal made, but at payoff time, the minister won't receive you, and no one wants to talk with you anymore."
A deputy allied with Fernando Henrique Cardoso (Pinheiro 1997, 32)

"I have no trouble with my enemies. I can take care of my enemies in a fight. But my friends, my goddamned friends, they're the ones who keep me walking the floor at nights!"
Warren G. Harding

This chapter focuses on the legislative process. Why, in the study of legislatures, is process important? The previous chapter focused on political parties' role as organizers of deputies with shared electoral and policy interests. If party leaders' recommendations totally determine deputies' legislative choices, policy outcomes would be no more than the sum of ballots, weighted by the size of each party, cast by party leaders. If deputies needed to vote at all, they could do so while remaining in their local districts, totally isolated from each other. That vision, of course, makes little sense in most legislatures and no sense at all in Brazil. Brazil's electoral rules produce individualistic legislators only occasionally constrained by party leadership. The executive, though nominally very powerful, struggles continuously to hold together a legislative coalition large enough to pass its program. But, more importantly, legislatures are organizations. Real legislative outcomes cannot be reduced to the sum of individual, once-and-for-all preferences. All legislatures adopt procedural rules that, either deliberately or through consequences no one anticipated, hinder or facilitate policy-making. Legislators organize themselves into caucuses (as opposed to parties) based on state, region, and group interests. And legislatures make certain members leaders, granting them privileges and influence over some range of issues.

The chapter begins with a brief discussion of the theoretical literature on legislatures. This literature highlights the ways legislatures use rules and institutions to overcome their tendency to cycle when facing broad issues. In the chapter's second section, the inquiry turns to congressional committees. The Budget Committee is examined in depth as a way of exposing the biases a powerful committee can introduce into the distribution of pork. Bargaining and legislative negotiation are the subject of the third section, which offers brief analyses of the fates of five legislative proposals.

I. Preference-Induced Equilibria and Structure-Induced Equilibria

Procedures and rules shape deputies' motivations and weight their influence in bargaining. For theoretical guidance, I will begin with the most rigorous literature on legislatures, the rational choice research examining the U.S. Congress.

In 1951 Kenneth J. Arrow demonstrated that instability of coalitions cannot be eliminated in majority-rule institutions. In voting among three alternatives, for example, it is always possible that three distinct majorities prefer A to B, B to C, and C to A, respectively. This coalition structure results in a cyclicality of majority preferences such that the outcome of a series of paired comparisons includes the Condorcet winner and is determined solely by the order of voting. If A and B are considered first, with the winner paired against C, the outcome will be C. If B and C are considered first, the outcome will be A. If A and C are considered first, the outcome will be B. Arrow's famous "impossibility theorem" (which itself goes back to the eighteenth century and Condorcet) demonstrated that such cyclicality is always possible in simple majority-rule institutions.

Richard D. McKelvey (1976), moving a step beyond Arrow, showed that instability of coalitions is probably the rule rather than the exception. He noted that alternatives are endogenous to the voting body—that is, the power to propose alternatives is shared by each voting member. An endless variety of alternatives is possible, and whenever legislative bills involve several distinct issues or dimensions, members of a minority coalition nearly always have many opportunities to propose alternatives tempting away some of the majority, thus creating a new majority coalition. The new majority may be destroyed through a similar consideration of alternatives. Arrow identified precisely this cyclicality, framed directly in legislative terms. McKelvey's "chaos theorem" demonstrates that almost any majority coalition is subject to disintegrative tendencies. Cyclicality and instability are thus pervasive elements of legislatures.

The notion of instability conflicts with the most basic understanding of normal legislative activity. "If we look at the real world . . . we observe that not only is there no endless cycling, but acts are passed with reasonable dispatch and then remain unchanged for very long periods of time" (Tullock 1981, 190). From a modeling standpoint, instability eliminates all hope of prediction. Yet it is intuitively believed, based on empirical observations, that at least some elements of legislative outcomes are predictable. There seems to be much more stability—that is, predictability—of outcomes in legislative settings than the instability theorems suggest (Niemi 1983; Tullock 1981).

Most formal theory responds to this majority-rule instability problem. The "new institutionalism" literature points out that the instability proofs of Arrow and McKelvey ignore the crucial structural factors guiding and constraining legislative choices. Institutional elements—political parties, constitutional design, committee structure, and agenda procedures—may be responsible for the stability observed in legislatures.

Two perspectives, the distributive and the informational, dominate the formal literature on the U.S. Congress. Formal theory utilizing the distributive approach includes the "structure-induced equilibrium" work of Kenneth A. Shepsle (1978) and of Shepsle and Barry R. Weingast (1987) and the "industrial organization of Congress" approach of Weingast and William Marshall (1988). The distributive perspective emphasizes legislators' desire to maximize their chances of reelection by delivering pork-barrel programs to their districts. Legislators have varying preferences and, most importantly, varying intensities over those preferences. This variation creates opportunities for mutual gains from logrolling. Farm members vote for urban renewal programs; urban representatives reciprocate by backing commodity price supports. In geographically based electoral systems, this kind of exchange redounds to the advantage of all, because bringing home the bacon helps legislators' reelection chances. Still, logrolling agreements are inherently unstable, because members are tempted to defect. The granting of parliamentary rights to committees is a way of stabilizing logrolling arrangements. Such rights guarantee that committees realize their preferences within their specialized "domains."

Keith Krehbiel (1991) has championed an alternative to distributional theories, the informational approach, which emphasizes specialization. For Krehbiel, the problem confronting procedural rule makers is one of inducing members to develop expertise and to share their expertise with the Chamber as a whole. If they do so, the legislature enacts better policy, reduces uncertainty about policy outcomes, and competes better with other branches of government.

Because, in the Arrow/McKelvey theorem, control over the agenda is a crucial element of legislative outcomes, and because committees play a key role in agenda setting, the committee system has been a favorite topic for formal theorists. Legislatures conduct much of their business in specialized committees, and committee members often draft the major alternatives for floor consideration. In effect, abdicating authority to committees may be a way of achieving stability.

Perhaps the committee focus just pushes the problem back a step, because stability is no more likely on a committee than on the floor. But committees are not necessarily governed by majority rule. Chairs have substantial power over agendas, and thus over the outcomes, of committee work. Besides, it has long been argued that committees are more homogeneous than their parent chambers.

Authors working from the distributive perspective emphasize the pathological consequences committees produce for the legislative institution as a whole. Committee privilege results in irresponsible, expansive, and intrusive government. Budget politics is the classic example. Logrolling among high-demand, specialized, authorizing committees yields chronic and severe budget deficits (Shepsle and Weingast 1984).

From the information perspective, the primary purpose of committees is the gathering of specialized information. This phenomenon, too, is intuitively reasonable, meshing well with empirical observation of committees. Krehbiel describes the primary benefit of the committee system as a collective one, but specialization in the information model creates a fundamental tension between collective and individual goals. As students of principal-agent problems are aware, information is a significant bargaining resource. Specialists exploit their expertise to bias legislative outcomes toward their own preferences and away from the Chamber median. The fundamental issue of committee organization is therefore the problem of encouraging specialization, which results in significant benefits to all members, while simultaneously keeping specialists from using their expertise to exploit the majority. Krehbiel views all legislative organization decisions within this framework. Institutional elements such as the prerogatives of committee chairs, the strength of the Speaker, and the number of committees to which bills are referred must all be seen as elements in the resolution of conflict between individual and collective outcomes.

These two legislative perspectives, distributive and informational, make distinct predictions about committees. Distributive theorists expect committees to be essentially self-selecting bodies of members who have extreme positions in an issue area and who make intense demands. Information theorists expect majorities—the legislature as a whole—to monitor carefully the composition of committees and to ensure that committees represent a cross-section of positions in the issue area as well as a variety of demand levels. Committees, in other words, should neither be "preference outliers" nor composed exclusively of "high demanders."

The two perspectives go beyond committee assignments to offer predictions about seniority rules, the openness to floor amendments of bills reported by committees, and the kinds of controls majorities exert over postfloor conference committees. The current state of the empirical debate in the American context is not relevant here; what matters is the guidance these theoretical positions provide for empirical investigations of other legislatures. Whether in committees, in floor debates, or in conferences, internal rules and procedures matter, especially those favoring, on one side, high demanders and outliers or, on the other, specialists and median legislators.

II.   Rules and Outcomes in the Budget Committee:
Does Pork Dominate?

No other piece of legislation takes as much time, effort, and attention as the annual budgetary appropriations bill. Not that the Congress makes major changes in the substance of the president's proposal; rather, Congress struggles to find ways to rank and to finance the thousands of budgetary amendments for projects deputies seek to bestow on their bailiwicks.

Consideration of the budget occurs in a single committee composed of both senators and deputies. The "Mixed Budget Committee" is very large, usually numbering about 10 percent of the Chamber and 20 percent of the Senate. In the 1987–90 legislature, eighteen of the forty-five deputies on the committee were serving their first term. In the 1995–98 legislature, thirty-one of the sixty-one deputies were freshmen. Both proportions are fairly close to the percentage of freshman deputies in the whole Chamber.

After the implementation of the 1988 constitution, the Budget Committee and the legislative budgetary process in general passed through several stages. Between 1988 and 1992, a simple set of procedures governed committee operations. After the arrival of the executive's budget proposal, deputies had a few months to submit amendments. Each amendment was required to name a source of revenue matching the expenditure envisioned. The Committee then established subcommittees corresponding to each broad program. After extensive meetings and negotiations, the Committee issued a report rejecting or accepting (wholly or partly) each amendment and adding its own amendments. Many of these committee amendments subsumed or combined those of other deputies, but thousands were totally new. Over the course of the pre-1992 period, deputies steadily expanded their use of electorally motivated budget amendments. In 1990 deputies made about 12,000 amendments (including those made by the Budget Committee itself), up from 8,000 two years earlier.[1] By 1992 the number of amendments had passed 72,000. The committee came to function, at least in the view of many deputies, as a machine for delivering benefits to the committee's senior members.[2] A clique of ranking deputies called the "budget mafia," led by committee Chair João Alves (PFL-Bahia), dominated. Alves and his followers—nicknamed the seven dwarfs—seemed to have few compunctions about reserving the lion's share of pork for themselves. Their greed became so excessive, however, that in 1992 marginalized deputies revolted, replacing Alves with a chair whose intentions were more egalitarian.

The overthrow of Chairman Alves affected the distribution of amendments between members and nonmembers of the committee, but rapid growth in the number of budget amendments continued unabated until the outbreak, in the fall of 1993, of the budget scandal discussed in chapter 1. That scandal, in which deputies received kickbacks from construction companies profiting from budgetary amendments the deputies introduced, forced the retirement of a number of senior deputies and discredited the Congress as a whole. The corruption also helped persuade leaders of the congressional right wing that the presidential candidate of the leftist Workers' Party, Luís Inácio Lula da Silva, would likely win the 1994 election. For the Right, the only escape was to back the economic stabilization plan (the Plano Real) of Itamar Franco's finance minister, Fernando Henrique Cardoso, and eventually to support his presidential candidacy. Cardoso's stabilization program, however, included a rigorous fiscal austerity package that eliminated most individually submitted budgetary amendments.

With the budget mafia out of the Congress, Cardoso as president, and former deputy José Serra—known to despise pork-barrel politics—as minister of planning, the congressional leadership bowed to the new realities and reorganized its budget procedure. Under the new rules, state delegations submit most amendments collectively. In addition, each deputy and senator may submit up

---

1. Amendments that mentioned no particular municipality as well as those benefiting a municipality in a state other than the deputy's own were eliminated. The latter were often submitted as favors for deputies who did not want to be associated with what was likely a payoff to a local boss or campaign contributor. Fewer than 10 percent of the amendments failed to benefit a particular municipality in a deputy's own state.

2. Interviews held with deputies in 1991 and 1992.

to ten amendments with a total value of $2 million reals (currently about $1.2 million). The total value of these individual amendments equals about 1 percent of the budget.

During the budget mafia's reign, 15–20 percent of all deputies profited enormously from the budget process, but the new system benefits the majority. If the president exercises a line-item veto on these amendments, the game of course changes, but this phenomenon seems not to occur. Instead, the executive simply stalls the "liberation" of the money—the actual transfer of the funds. As of this writing, it is too soon to undertake an empirical analysis of the new arrangements, but fragmentary evidence suggests that parties and states will gain at the expense of individuals. States whose delegates supported the executive on key votes found that the executive branch liberated funds for amendments at a much higher rate than did states dominated by opposition delegates. Acre, for example, had the second highest rate of disbursements; Acre's governor had organized the trade of support for votes on the amendment permitting Cardoso's reelection.[3] Amendments submitted by PT deputies had about one-fourth the chance of getting the money, relative to progovernment parties' amendments.

The empirical analysis that follows is based on the outcomes of 1990 Budget Committee procedures. I seek to distinguish winning legislators from losing legislators. Although the explosive trajectory of the pre-1992 budget process seems to indicate a desire to resolve conflict by expanding the overall pot so that every deputy could realize a gain, the committee in 1990 still faced a ceiling and rejected a majority of the amendments submitted.

Table 24 presents the results of a model of the amendment process that predicts the final total awarded by the committee for each amendment submitted.[4] The socioeconomic and demographic variables determine whether amendments benefiting any particular type of municipality had a greater chance of success.[5] Amendments clearly had more chance in communities with larger populations,

---

3. This linkage was confirmed by Acre Senator Nabor Junior (see *Folha de São Paulo,* July 20, 1997, 1–4).

4. Because the committee awarded nothing to most amendments, the dependent variable has a lower bound of zero. In such cases ordinary least squares is inappropriate, so the models in tables 24 and 25 are estimated with a Tobit regression using SAS Lifereg. Amendments made by Alves have been removed from the data. If his amendments are retained and a dummy variable for the chair included, the dummy receives an extremely high coefficient and the rest of the model is essentially unchanged.

5. Dummy variables for certain states were included to clarify the effect of municipal-level characteristics. Deputies in states such as São Paulo make few amendments, but they have a high success rate. Maranhão's deputies submit many amendments, each with a low success rate. With-

TABLE 24. Explaining Amendment Success: Tobit Model of Total Awarded by Budget Committee and Approved on Floor, by Amendment

Parameter	Estimate	PR>/T/
State dummies		
Maranhão	−23.210	.046
Alagoas	148.408	.000
Bahia	34.511	.000
Minas Gerais	31.271	.001
Rio de Janeiro	52.901	.000
Rio Grande do Sul	87.099	.000
São Paulo	106.590	.000
Socioeconomic and demographic variables		
Voters in municipality	.001	.001
Voters in municipality squared	−1.008 E-11	.001
Government employees	652.885	.011
Agricultural employees	−0.041	.252
Migrants in municipality	0.013	.191
Income per capita	−.001	.150
Manufacturing population	−182.661	.016
Party variables		
Share of own party vote in municipality	5.341	.038
Share of total party vote in municipality	−12.276	.000
PDS	54.660	.000
PTB	33.087	.134
PFL	55.803	.000
PMDB	36.782	.000
PT	29.740	.157
Security and seniority variables		
Terms served in Chamber	−1.147	.621
Rank in party list	1.127	.000
Budget committee member × Terms served	22.877	.000

Log Likelihood for Normal Distribution, −17132.
Left Censored Values 6,534   Noncensored Values 2,330

lower levels of manufacturing, lower levels of agriculture, fewer migrants, and more government employees.[6] Perhaps this portrait looks a bit strange, because the winners appear to be communities lacking either a strong manufacturing base or a strong agricultural base. This combination, however, is common in many poor communities for whom the tertiary sector, especially public em-

---

out these state dummies the coefficient on manufacturing, for example, would be negative, because more northeastern, low-manufacturing municipalities would seem successful. Inclusion of the state dummies justifies the inference that within each state more developed municipalities do better.

6. The squared term shows that success rates declined for the largest communities.

ployment, drives the economy. Politics is the most viable economic activity in precisely these communities. Government employees are a powerful political force, and deputies fight hard to reward them.

What kinds of electoral conditions influenced amendment success? Deputies were more successful when they received higher shares of all votes cast for their own party in their targeted municipalities. They were less successful when they received a higher share of the votes of all parties. The basis of the first result is clear: deputies dominating their party's vote are no threat to party colleagues, so the Budget Committee supports them. Still, why would deputies who do well among voters of all parties enjoy less amendment success? Perhaps the Budget Committee engages in a certain amount of rationing. If you dominate the voters in your municipality, party leaders reason, you really do not need much pork. Scarce resources, instead, should go to those not threatening party colleagues but needing help against invaders of other parties.

A second group of variables looks at the parties of the deputies making amendments. These coefficients measure the probability of success for each amendment, not the overall success of the given party. Table 24 shows that the PT had a high success rate, but in fact its deputies made few amendments. PDS and PFL deputies amended heavily and enjoyed great success. The PMDB and PTB had low success rates, but these deputies made many amendments. Why were PMDB and PTB deputies less successful? Because their vote bases are more urban and hence more fragmented and less controllable, PMDB and PTB deputies who compete in the same bailiwicks are more likely to contest each other's amendments. In fact, urban deputies admitted in interviews that they tried to limit the pork available to their direct competitors.

What kind of deputies were successful in making amendments? Deputies who were more vulnerable electorally (lower in party lists) tended to be more successful, presumably because they worked harder. Seniority by itself did not help, but the highly positive coefficient of the variable measuring the experience of Budget Committee members (membership times number of terms served) confirms the huge advantage committee membership gave to ranking members.

While table 24 considers the budget-amendment process in terms of the probability of success of each amendment, table 25 examines the probability that any given municipality received an amendment. Some municipalities clearly do better than others. Municipalities in the Northeast did well; municipalities in most of the rest of the country come out even; municipalities in São Paulo lose. There is a simple but compelling explanation: São Paulo is about 40 percent underrepresented in terms of the size of its delegation relative to its population. That shortfall translates into a loss of influence in the Budgetary Committee. São Paulo simply lacks the votes. While table 25 confirms the overall regional bias in the distribution of amendments, the table also shows that larger, less industrial, and less agricultural municipalities lost. The winners were state capitals and communities with more government employees.[7]

Table 24 linked the electoral characteristics of the vote bases of individual deputies to the success of their amendments. Similarly, table 25 reveals that municipalities' electoral characteristics create conditions discouraging or impelling deputies to expend political resources pushing pork-barrel amendments. Two hypotheses guided the inquiry. First, deputies should submit amendments for municipalities in which they received a higher proportion of their own total vote. In other words, you fight hard for communities contributing 25 percent of all your votes, less hard for communities contributing 2 percent. Second, you fight harder for communities you dominate. If you won 50 percent of a municipality's votes, you defend it with more vigor than if you only took 5 percent of its votes. Once again: where you dominate, you are able to claim credit.

To test the hypothesis of personal dominance and the link to the expenditure of political resources, I calculated the average, in each municipality, of the personal shares of all deputies collecting votes in the municipality. The results support the speculation: in those municipalities where more deputies got high proportions of their total vote, amendments were more likely to be successful.

To test the second hypothesis—linking municipal dominance to the expenditure of resources—I followed two routes, examining interparty and individual fragmentation in the previous election as well as fragmentation in communities of different sizes.[8] Fragmentation by itself does not seem to matter. In conjunction with population size, however, fragmentation has a substantial impact. Large communities with high partisan fragmentation as well as small communities with low partisan fragmentation tend to be successful in the pork-barrel struggle. At the same time, large communities with high fragmentation among all the candidates as well as small communities with little individual fragmentation tend to be unsuccessful. This rather complicated result requires an explanation, although the explanation can only be tentative.

The description "large communities with vigorously competing parties" fits big cities. With growth either in the number of parties or in the population, more votes are available. The success of this combination demonstrates that members of the Budget Committee try to help their compatriots and that intraparty loyalty

---

7. This gain in state capitals adds to the favoritism of the Northeast, because state capitals in the Northeast are a bigger share of state population than are capitals in the South and Southeast.

8. This route refers to the interaction term in the model.

TABLE 25.   Which Municipalities Get the Most Amendments? (total awarded by budget committee and approved on floor, by municipality)

Parameter	Estimate	PR>/T/
Intercept	−137.800	.001
State and city dummies		
Alagoas	−39.189	.163
Maranhão	58.993	.001
Bahia	130.786	.000
Ceará	91.821	.000
Pernambuco	126.004	.000
Piauí	109.200	.000
Minas Gerais	31.642	.023
Paraná	24.268	.143
Rio de Janeiro	16.651	.508
Rio Grande do Sul	22.007	.240
Santa Catarina	9.035	.629
São Paulo	− 79.276	.000
Capital of state	258.030	.030
Socioeconomic and demographic variables		
Voters in municipality	0.002	.002
Voters in municipality squared	−1.593 E-10	.000
Manufacturing population	−331.270	.004
Government employees	1351.114	.001
Agricultural population	−0.223	.000
Income per capita	0.001	.787
Fragmentation and target variables		
Interparty fragmentation in 1986	−8.661	.746
Individual fragmentation in 1986	45.122	.134
Mean of personal shares in municipality	25.734	.000
Interparty fragmentation in 1986 × Voters	0.001	.000
Individual fragmentation in 1986 × Voters	−0.002	.019
Bailiwick of Budget Committee member	63.743	.019

Log Likelihood for Logistic Distribution, −9450.
Left Censored Values 2,330   Noncensored Values 1,274

and cooperation exist. And the parallel success of small communities with little partisan fragmentation reflects the power of senior Budget Committee deputies from rural municipalities. By contrast, when there are large communities in conjunction with high individual fragmentation, intraparty solidarity drops—creating a kind of prisoner's dilemma—and incentives to make amendments fall.[9] In the fourth and final pairing—small communities and low individual fragmenta-

---

9. Deputies have been known to request that the Budget Committee reject other deputies' amendments.

tion—there are too few voters to attract political entrepreneurs and too little competition to signal that the community is open to new entrants.

The final variable identifies, for each committee member, the municipality providing the largest share of the member's personal vote. Do Budget Committee members take care of their bailiwicks? They truly do, and since the committee is so large, a substantial chunk of amendment largesse goes to these favored municipalities.

Overall, the distributive model fit pre-1994 budgetary politics in the Chamber of Deputies better than the informational model. Given the rapid turnover of members, there was little chance to develop expertise. The committee's large size, along with its limited staff resources, explains why little serious attention was given to amendments' economic bases. Rather, the committee captured the lion's share of available resources for itself and its allies. Budget Committee members were high demanders. When, in 1991, the committee's inner elite took a huge share for itself, backbenchers rebelled. But the purpose of their rebellion was not to guard the treasury but simply to spread the wealth a little wider— distributive politics, it would appear, at its best.

Distributional and informational perspectives relate to many issue areas beyond budgetary questions. Can hypotheses about preference outliers and high demanders apply more broadly? The models of campaign strategy presented in chapter 2 employed, as an indicator of interest in pork, the probability that a deputy requested an audience with a minister. These petitioning deputies were, in effect, high demanders on questions relating to agriculture, infrastructure, and social action. Were they also more likely to sit on the relevant committees than nonpetitioning deputies? Deputies who met with the agriculture minister were about three times as likely as nonpetitioners to land an agriculture committee seat. Petitioners on infrastructure and social-action issues, however, were no more likely than nonpetitioners to obtain seats on their committees. As I will demonstrate later in this chapter, agriculture committee members are mostly owners of substantial rural properties, and their behavior marks them as preference outliers.[10] Education committee members turn out to be high demanders and preference outliers as well, although their ideological positions are on the Left. Thus, all the evidence available suggests that members of these committees—budget, agriculture, and education—were simultaneously preference outliers and high demanders. Members of committees related to infrastructure

---

10. Probably 70 percent of the members of the Agriculture Committee come from the *bancada rural* (rural caucus). Nearly all its members have personal interests in large-scale agriculture or agribusiness.

and social action, however, may be closer to the median legislator in terms of the level of their demands.

III. Parties and Negotiations

I will now turn to legislative negotiation. Why is negotiation important? By this point, the reader understands that getting bills through the Congress, whether these bills originate in the executive branch or in the Congress itself, is rather difficult. The Congress may ultimately approve a proposal, but almost nothing gets through quickly and few bills get through without significant concessions or side payments. Chapter 5 demonstrated that pork-barrel inducements weigh heavily in the typical deputy's voting calculus. Chapter 6 argued that the need to appeal simultaneously to party, region, and faction complicates the coalition-constructing objective of cabinet formation. Chapter 7 revealed that practically nothing on the president's agenda survives its legislative journey unscathed and that party leaders exert little independent control over their followers. And chapter 8 has shown that key congressional committees are overweighted with deputies making intense and extreme demands. Given that the electoral system tends to produce individualistic deputies organized into numerous parties, and given that the traditional tools of party discipline are weak, presidents and their parliamentary supporters must continually reconstruct their majorities. Building majorities is a process that requires more than pork-barrel inducements; it requires negotiation. Legislative negotiations proceed, simultaneously, on three fronts: intraparty, interparty, and executive-legislative.

In the bargaining processes at the core of this section, the central actors are parties and party leaders. To the casual observer of Brazilian politics, their prominence is obvious. Newspaper accounts of particular legislative battles, for example, always emphasize party leaders' coalition-building tactics. However, I have already explored at length the antiparty aspects of Brazilian politics. Is there no conflict here? If parties do not matter, why are parties the main units of negotiation? What do party leaders do?

Party leaders, especially those in center and right-wing parties, spend most of their time facilitating contacts between ordinary deputies and ministers and between mayors and ministers. Party leaders also appoint presidents and members of committees. Since there is no strong tradition of appointing specialists, committee appointments are part of party leaders' political strategies. In this game ordinary deputies retain considerable autonomy. Passed-over members can leave one party for another, deputies can get on committees and make private deals with lobbyists, and renegade members can avoid sanctions simply by leaving their original party before the sanctions become official.

Variations in Party Structure

In the previous chapter, parties were portrayed as one of the institutions helping legislatures escape from the cyclicality and instability that, from the perspective of formal theorists, is their equilibrium state. For parties to fulfill their potential as equilibrium institutions, they need some minimum level of formal structure. The degree of structure in Brazil's legislative parties varies greatly across parties and over time. The leftist PT, well organized outside the legislature, holds weekly meetings and generally votes as a unified bloc. The PDT has no extraparliamentary existence but maintains an active party life and has long been led by a politician outside the Congress. The centrist PMDB rarely holds delegation meetings, because its members are too divided. Instead, the leadership uses questionnaires to discover members' positions. Between 1991 and 1993, the PMDB met to close ranks on a unified position only twice, once on the question of the retirement system, where the party backed pensioners against the government, and again on impeachment of President Fernando Collor de Mello, where the party supported his ouster (Novaes 1994, 127). On the right, recommendations from the leaders of the PPB, PFL, and PL (the Liberal Party) do not compel members to cast particular votes; in fact, these parties practically never close ranks on a position. As the PL's legislative director put it, "When there are three, four or five different opinions, the leader himself wants to leave things open. . . . Deputies ought not to be compelled to violate their principles" (Novaes 1994, 127, 130).

Is ideology an important cause of the differences in parties' behavior in the legislative arena? Carlos Alberto Marques Novaes thinks so. He suggests that leftist parties meet to consider substantive ideas, while center and right-wing parties form preferences around the distribution of individual resources that the leader manages. For these parties a collective forum is of no use; the leader deals with deputies in solitary interactions, and there is reciprocity between leader and follower. When a leader gets the votes of his followers, he receives "not the formal realization of a substantive collective agreement, but reciprocity for the success and/or consideration with which he conducted the interests of each one of his equals" (Novaes 1994, 139). The least popular leaders are those who fail to solve their deputies' day-to-day problems. My legislative interviews confirm Novaes's view of leader-follower interactions—those in the center and on the Right are distribution oriented rather than policy oriented. But it should not be concluded that members share preferences only in leftist parties. The existence of leftist parties (including the very slightly left-of-center PSDB) leaves all other parties with mostly right-wing deputies and thus more ideological coherence. On the right, parties like the PFL harbor nationally oriented neoliberals along with localistic pork-barrelers, but on most issues the two wings find common ground. The fundamental difference is that the leftist parties have a collective practice, while the rightist parties are based on individualistic leader-follower bargains.

Over time, party structure is by no means constant. The PSDB, once a center-left party with considerable ideological coherence, seems to be paying an organizational price for its alliance with the right-wing PFL. The alliance successfully elected Cardoso in 1994, and Cardoso has relied heavily on the PFL to shape and support his legislative program. His reelection strategy centered on shunting possible opponents off to state-level races. Since all possible opponents were outside the PSDB, this strategy naturally produced conflicts with the PSDB politicians who had to face, in state-level races, Cardoso's disappointed presidential aspirants. Coupled with Cardoso's antiparty strategy is his willingness to rely on individual inducements to maintain his legislative base. Some PSDB deputies have turned to jobs and pork barrel as their central legislative activity, but the old leaders, those who founded the party, feel themselves marginalized. As one old activist deputy commented, "The PSDB used to be a party that held meetings to take serious decisions, but now it never meets, not even for parties." Euclides Scalco, former party president, agreed that the party's survivors have lost motivation as a result of "unimaginable alliances and impossible party colleagues" (Carvalho and Pinheiro 1997, 28).

The Need for Negotiators

Even if individual parties were more than merely collections of like-minded deputies—even if, that is, all parties were organized to participate in stable policy coalitions—a leadership structure would be needed to coordinate interparty and executive-legislative bargaining. Until the first Cardoso administration, it appeared that this negotiating structure would be permanently embodied by the college of leaders (*colégio de líderes*), a group composed of congressional party heads. The centrality of the *colégio* turned out to be less than permanent, because the Cardoso administration usurped the *colégio*'s hegemony, moving the locus of negotiating to the presidential palace.[11] Nevertheless, the *colégio* is central to the puzzle of how a legislature with so many parties can do anything at all.

---

11. In August 1999, as President Cardoso's approval ratings hit all-time lows, the president of the Chamber of Deputies announced the resurrection of the *colégio* (see Fleischer 1999).

The *colégio* did not exist until the Constitutional Assembly of 1987–88. As former Deputy Nelson Jobim put it, "As you did not have a majority to vote anything, you had to organize anew for each question. So there developed prior meetings of the leadership to begin to try to organize the voting process . . . to sit at the table to figure out what subjects were consensual and identify the subjects that were not consensual. From this came the college of leaders, which began to dominate the process" (Novaes 1994, 115).

The Chamber's Internal Rules (*Regimento Interno*) create the *colégio*. Headed officially by the Chamber president, the *colégio* includes representatives of all the parties in the body. The *colégio* sets the agenda for floor consideration of proposals that have completed committee hearings. A system of informal voting governs decisions, with each vote weighted by the number of members a leader represents. If all parties agree, they take a "global" vote. When they cannot reach consensus, the issue is left to be resolved on the floor.

Although the official *colégio* plays a role in agenda setting, the real work is done by a smaller *colégio*—absent the *mesa* (presiding board) president—with a different decision-making structure.[12] Led by the leader of the largest party, the group discusses the substantive merits of proposals approved by the first *colégio*. This "substantive" *colégio* holds both public and private "leaders only" meetings. At its public meetings it invites experts, lobbyists, other deputies, even senators. Though the *colégio* considers only bills that already have a place on the Chamber's informal agenda, the *colégio* encourages committees to include items the leadership wants. No voting occurs in these substantive meetings, and unless all the leaders agree, the *colégio* cannot modify legislation. The leaders have no formal authority over their members in subsequent floor votes.

The difference in voting rules between these two versions of the college is crucial. Rather than utilizing weighted voting, as prescribed in the official rules, substantive decisions are made by a "one party, one vote" rule, regardless of the size of the participating party. This rule encourages party proliferation, because small parties have enormous power and the potential for blockage and sabotage is very high. To avoid the cycling endemic to such structures, the habit is to seek consensus. As Deputy Roberto Campos put it, almost restating veto-players theory, "Attempts at conciliation reduce the project to the least common denominator, and the least common denominator is something dangerously close to the status quo" (Novaes 1994, 140). In addition, individual deputies, especially

---

12. The president of the *mesa* is a deputy, of course, but is generally thought to represent the government and abstains on roll-call votes.

those from small parties, are able to force their leaders to put items of interest only to themselves on the agenda. The power of these small delegations comes from the fact that the leaders of the bigger delegations cannot count on the votes of their followers.

Committees seldom play a central role in bargaining and negotiation, and, by default, their absence further increases the influence of the *colégio*. Since committee appointments are made along party lines, why are committees ill-suited for negotiations? Most deputies, it seems, believe that committee members represent their own interests and convictions rather than their parties' positions. In a study of the Social Security and Family Committee, for example, Regina Balieiro Devescovi (1994) found that the *colégio* sometimes interfered with the committee's decision process. Such interference occurred when the committee was likely to produce results at variance with the balance of power between the parties, when the committee could not reach any decision at all, or when the executive branch was pressing for congressional action. Devescovi (1994, 80) concluded that if the arrangements made by the leadership had occurred on the floor of the Chamber, conflictual issues could not have been swiftly concluded.

Not surprisingly, many deputies express dissatisfaction with both the *colégio*'s power and the plethora of pork-barrel legislation that filled the Chamber's agenda. In 1991 the Congress established a Modernization Committee to consider reforms. The committee proposed two measures: eliminating the *colégio* and creating a triage committee to establish priorities over pork-barrel legislative proposals. Both proposals failed: the Chamber's elite killed the first, and backbenchers killed the second.

In spite of the realization that the *colégio* plays a crucial role in the legislative process, little is known about the nature of bargaining within the group or between the group and the executive. Three questions are crucial: Where does substantive bargaining occur? Who is involved in bargaining? What factors affect the probability that negotiation will lead to legislative approval?

I now consider five cases of legislative policy-making that occurred between 1988 and 1994.[13] These cases include bidding reform, 1992–93; the Law of Directives and Bases in Education (LDB), 1989–94; the agrarian reform law of 1992, the ministerial reorganization during the government of Itamar Franco, 1992–93; and macroeconomic stabilization policy in the Franco government,

---

13. The IRIS Project at the University of Maryland and the North-South Center at the University of Miami supported this portion of the research. In addition to my own interviews, Mauro Porto and Fátima Guimarães of the department of political science of the University of Brasília and Clécio Dias of the University of Illinois, Urbana, conducted interviews.

1992–94. The final case, that of macroeconomic stabilization, occurred when Cardoso was finance minister but was really acting informally as prime minister. As I will demonstrate, the bargaining style in this case foreshadows Cardoso's subsequent presidential administration. These five policies did not necessarily affect large numbers of people, and all were not crucial to presidential political survival. Although some of the cases do in fact fit these criteria, they were really selected to maximize variance on the conditions likely to affect the nature of bargaining and interparty negotiation.[14] The central criterion of case selection, in other words, was the ability of a policy conflict to reveal the nature of legislative negotiation.

The locus of policy initiation was the first condition. Bidding reform, ministerial reorganization, and stabilization came from the executive branch; the LDB and agrarian reform came from the Congress. The importance of the policy, in the perception of legislators and journalists, was a second condition. When inflation surpasses 25 percent per month, stabilization is obviously crucial. Bidding reform was certainly important, but life would continue even with the level of corruption Brazilian bidding exhibited. The centrality of ministerial reorganization was more indirect, in the sense that reorganization could give the president more leverage with Congress. The LDB and agrarian reform measures had more long-term than immediate significance. The participation of civil society was a third dimension. Bidding reform seemed likely to involve specialists and construction companies. The LDB would obviously engage a broad range of interests in education. Agrarian reform concerned mostly rural interests, both landowners and landless, but for those interests it would be very serious indeed. Inflation affected broad economic groups, and any solution would create winners and losers. Ministerial reshuffling directly affected party leaders' political machines and indirectly impacted the winners and losers from the president's legislative program.

Since the details of these cases can be a bit daunting, a brief summary of the lessons they ultimately furnish may help guide the reader. As a forum for multiparty negotiations and bargaining, the *colégio* was most active on unidimensional issues where lines of compromise were clear. On more complex, multidimensional issues, major actors must actively have sought compromise before the *colégio* could play a role. Issues involving powerful states had to be

---

14. With any case studies, it is easy to exaggerate the rigor of the selection. I tried, as suggested earlier, to pick cases that differed in interesting and relevant ways. But scholars also pick cases because they are doable. The cases chosen furnished enough documentary evidence and willing interviewees that the legislative process became comprehensible. In no sense are these cases a random sampling of legislative controversies.

resolved by the states and the executive before party leaders got involved. For the *colégio* to play a role, parties must have perceived interests as parties, not merely as ideological or regional cohorts of deputies. The allocation of public works and jobs is an obvious concern to parties and their leaders, but the negotiating process could bypass party leaders unless it involved the medium or long-term distribution of pork, as in the case of cabinet reorganization. In such cases, where the executive was constructing a grand coalition and sought commitments about future support, party leadership became central. Finally, the cases underline the importance, in a milieu of mainly weakly disciplined and nonideological parties, of pork-barrel politics. Pork is the cement that binds together legislative coalitions.

Bidding Reform

Brazilian legislators had to see the corruption scandals of the early 1990s, which ultimately led to the impeachment of a president and the ouster of a group of veteran deputies, as threats to their political careers. The nation's voters regularly reject officeholders in all elections, and angry voters might throw out incumbents in even greater numbers than usual. At the core of all the scandals were the payoffs big construction companies (*empreiteiras*) had made to politicians and bureaucrats. For the top dozen *empreiteiras,* government business amounted to more than 90 percent of their annual income. If the regulations allowed corruption, honest behavior would lead to a competitive disadvantage the big firms could hardly accept. In fact, Brazil's bidding regulations facilitated collusion and overcharging, and governments suffered substantial losses.[15]

In the typical bidding process for government contracts, the offering agency set a "basic price." Firms could bid up to 15 percent above or below that price. In case of tied bids, contracts were let according to a series of "technical grades" awarded by the offering agency. In practice, firms colluded, and all bids came in about 15 percent above the basic price. The technical grades opened up a broad range of possibilities for corrupt behavior on the part of officials.

The obvious alternative to the basic price system was simply to award the contract to the firm offering the best or lowest price. How did political parties come down on this issue? Purely as organizations, parties had no stakes in bidding reform, but some did have ideological interests. Parties like the PL (and parts of the PFL) were concerned in a doctrinal sense with liberalization and the breaking up of state monopolies. They argued, as did the PPR and part of the PMDB, that best price should be the only criterion for victory. A perform-

---

15. Most estimates of the amount typically overcharged ran around 30 percent.

ance bond (financed by insurance companies) could be a guarantee against frivolous or corrupt bids. It was clear, however, that big companies would benefit from the institution of a performance bond, because they could more easily get financing for the bond—in part because the insurance companies themselves were inefficient and corrupt. The consequence, in the end, would be greater concentration in the construction sector. For the Workers' Party, seeking to encourage small companies, best price was therefore undemocratic.

A variety of other interests fought over bidding reform. Small and medium-sized construction companies wanted rules facilitating disaggregated bids, because only the largest firms could bid on very large projects or projects combined into packages.[16] Local politicians wanted rules giving the offering agency a certain amount of discretionary authority, because politicians would then be able to collect tips for their contributions to greasing the wheels. The construction companies, regardless of size, wanted rules hindering the entry of out-of-state firms and foreign companies. Out-of-state firms have weaker social ties in a state than do local firms; this weakness hampers collusion, which depends on strong social ties. Foreign firms, more experienced in high-tech construction, could overwhelm even the biggest national construction companies.[17] Finally, the Council of Engineers and Architects played a key role in the dispute. These professionals, working primarily for the big *empreiteiras,* monopolized the technical certification process. Though working for the companies, council members were really lobbying for themselves, pressuring the Congress to maintain some system of technical grades.

The Chamber of Deputies first considered a proposal by Deputy Luís Roberto Ponte. Although most journalistic descriptions of the conflict refer to Ponte as the point man for construction interests, it is more accurate to say that he represented small and medium interests. His proposal eliminated technical grades but kept the basic price criterion. Ponte's version had no least-cost rule, and it adjudicated tied offers through drawings. The maintenance of a basic-price system, however, meant that firms would continue to collude, with all charging 15 percent more than the basic price and with one firm directed to cut

---

16. One large firm, Andrade Gutierrez, supported the small firms' position on this issue. Losses in Iran had cost Andrade Gutierrez so dearly that the firm was nearly broke.

17. Foreign observers of Brazilian construction projects are usually shocked by the primitiveness of techniques, the poor-quality materials utilized, and the long periods in which projects appear completely stopped. Part of this backwardness comes from the financing system. Firms receive payments up front. They opt for labor-intensive techniques rather than equipment purchases, because equipment has to be paid for immediately while labor is paid gradually. Government payments can then be invested in lucrative short-term speculation. The real bar to the entry of foreign construction firms is the complexity of Brazil's labor laws.

a few reals and get the contract. Small firms were the main beneficiaries of the basic-price system, because it kept more efficient out-of-state firms from entering bidding. Local politicos also liked the proposal, because it gave them maneuvering room to seek tips.

In the Chamber, the *colégio* facilitated bargaining over the bidding-reform proposal, but specialists dominated the actual negotiations. Deputies invited to participate in the discussions were typically former heads of state-level departments, former directors of big companies, former mayors, and so on. The PDT's chief negotiator, for example, was Luíz Salomão, an economist and former secretary of works and environment (1982–86) in Rio de Janeiro. Salomão was known as a nationalist and defender of state firms. The PFL's chief negotiator was José Carlos Aleluia, an ally of Antônio Carlos Magalhães (ACM) who had worked in the Bahian state electric company and in SUDENE, a regional development program. For the PT, the chief negotiator was economist Aloízio Mercadante. The bill's reporting officer (*relator*)[18] was Walter Nory, from the São Paulo PMDB. Nory was a former president of the São Paulo Metro and former secretary of works under Governor Quércia. He had once been the construction companies' "Man of the Year."

Simultaneously, the Senate began considering a bill authored by then-Senator Fernando Henrique Cardoso. This bill was much less favorable to the construction companies than the Chamber's proposal. In Cardoso's version, best price was the criterion for awarding contracts, and his proposal required posting a bond to guarantee project execution. When Cardoso became Franco's foreign minister in October 1992, Senator Pedro Simon became the bill's sponsor, and in the fall of 1993 the Senate approved it.

In March 1993, the Chamber rejected the Senate bill and resuscitated Ponte's original version. The Chamber did adopt, however, the Senate's criterion of least price. At the insistence of the party heads (and against Walter Nory's wishes), the full Chamber also accepted the Senate's criminal penalties for collusion. The majority of deputies were persuaded to support criminal penalties, in the view of a strong consensus of Chamber informants, because the Collor scandals made it imperative to adopt measures with strong symbolic value. The Chamber also accepted the Senate's imposition of a performance bond (equivalent to 15 percent of the project's value). From the left, Deputies Mercadante and Salomão opposed the bond, arguing that it would exclude small firms from bidding. The Chamber leadership compromised by limiting the bond

---

18. A *relator* is not a bill's sponsor but is instead a legislator charged with shepherding the bill through the parliamentary maze.

to very large projects. The bill also set a minimum project size for cities wanting to avoid a bidding process altogether. Prior to the reform, the minimum was a single large number, so small cities (with small projects) could often avoid bidding. The new provision had a sliding population level. Small towns, which would now have to conduct more frequent bidding, lobbied against the provision.

When the proposal finally went to President Franco in June 1993, he vetoed eighteen items, including the performance bond. Congressional reaction to the vetoes was sharp and angry. Leaders on all sides criticized the president for acting without regard to the careful consideration Congress had given the legislation. One month later the president sent Congress an emergency measure (*medida provisória*) exempting the military from the public bidding requirement. Because Congress never voted on this measure—although it was discussed—it lapsed. In September 1993, the government sent another emergency measure modifying the bidding legislation, this time by reducing the weight of the least-price criterion for projects built with foreign resources. Since most big projects in Brazil include foreign investment, this provision effectively gutted the least-price principle. Not surprisingly, Congress rejected the president's somewhat odd modification and restored a smaller version of the performance bond.[19]

The *colégio* played a significant role in the debate on bidding reform. Specialists dominated the details of the negotiations, but party leaders in the *colégio* guided them. The bidding proposal had only one important dimension. The fundamental issue was the degree of favoritism the legislation would concede to large firms. That simple dimension was one on which party leaders could compromise, and in the end all parties supported the legislation.

Still, caution is advisable when considering the political parties' definition of the "fundamental question under negotiation." Parties found it convenient to compromise on this issue. But in the end, the legislation maintained the criterion of technical certification on big projects, a criterion that provides an opening for politicians to extract rents from construction companies.[20] Party leaders knew they needed a symbolic response to public outrage over the cost of government projects but also knew that local politicians benefited from the status quo. The ultimate result was a compromise that satisfied organized interests

---

19. The bond's value was ultimately set at 10 percent of project value.

20. Perhaps the only actor in this drama with no domestic political interest was the World Bank. In interviews conducted on June 6, 1995, my informants from the bank stated that they believed that in the end the legislation was mostly smoke and mirrors, designed to quiet the public outcry without really eliminating corruption.

in the policy area and saved the skins of politicians but neglected the public interest.

The Law of Directives and Bases in Education

Although the 1988 Brazilian constitution is mostly quite detailed, in education the document merely lays out broad guidelines, leaving to subsequent legislatures the task of constructing an organizing framework for implementing its guidelines. This organizing framework, the LDB, was under discussion continuously after 1988, but no LDB was passed by both chambers until 1996. The 1986–90 Chamber moved a version of the law out of the Education Committee, but the bill never came to a floor vote. Discussion began again after 1990, and in 1993 the Chamber finally approved an LDB proposal. Passage by the Senate came during the Cardoso administration. This discussion examines the 1988–94 period.

In comparison with the other cases, what makes the LDB unique? First, a very wide range of societal groups had stakes in the legislation. The major cleavage was between defenders of public education and defenders of private schools, but advocates of religious education, scientific groups, university professors, and student organizations all put forward specific demands. The Ministry of Education and Culture (MEC) might be expected to defend fiercely its bureaucratic interest in controlling its programs, but in fact the ministry's position varied across presidential administrations and from minister to minister. The LDB was also unique because almost all the Chamber's technical staff, supposedly neutral policy analysts, strongly identified with "progressive" positions; many, in fact, had worked for groups lobbying on the issue.[21] Third, although political parties' broad philosophical tendencies had implications for education policy, parties as such seldom took clear, negotiable positions on issues related to education.[22]

The LDB debate was also noteworthy for politicians' fundamental disinterest. Perhaps it is surprising, given the wide range of class and corporativist interests involved, but nearly all the politicians interviewed—politicians actively involved in the negotiations—believed that most deputies and senators

---

21. In a sense, the Brazilian pattern is the reverse of what often happens in the United States. Rather than government officials moving to the private sector, Brazilian interest-group representatives move to government. Rarely is there even a pretense of distance from the interest-group's positions.

22. At times parties have committed firmly to positions opposed by many members. The PT, for example, formally supports free university education, but most of its deputies realize that in Brazil, such a policy is regressive.

cared very little about the LDB. Their disinterest stemmed from the passivity toward the legislation on the part of the mass media and the general public. Politicians' apathy reflects both the class cleavage in Brazilian education and the absence of ties between legislators and the poor. By the 1980s public education had become a dumping ground for the poor and lower-middle class; private schools served upper-middle-class and rich children.

The original draft of the LDB was officially authored by Octávio Elíseo, a deputy from the state of Minas Gerais. A former secretary of education in Minas, Elíseo identified with grassroots social movements and organized labor. The draft's real authors, however, were teachers from Minas, mostly from the federal university. The Chamber leadership appointed Jorge Hage, a PDT deputy from Bahia, as the bill's reporting officer. Hage had been an MEC political appointee and rector of the federal university of Bahia. Like Elíseo, Hage identified with grassroots movements and labor. As reporting officer, his task was to conduct hearings, negotiate with deputies and interest groups, and put together a revised version of the original Elíseo proposal.

Nineteen organizations and three individual deputies submitted distinct versions of the LDB. The ministry sent two proposals. From the beginning, conflict centered on three elements of the legislation. One conflict revolved around the issue of financing for public education. The private sector wanted to avoid any increases in the *salário educação,* a tax traditionally earmarked for education.[23] A second conflict involved the makeup and powers of the National Education Council, the highest normative organ making education policy. In the Elíseo proposal, the council had enormous authority, so much that MEC was essentially subordinate to it. The council was to have thirty appointees, ten nominated by the minister of education, ten nominated by the Chamber of Deputies, and ten nominated by teachers' unions. In the Hage version, the council grew to thirty-two, with five members chosen by the president, four by the Congress, six by state and municipal secretaries of education, one by university rectors, one by owners of private schools, five by teachers' unions, two by secondary and university students, two by scientific organizations, and a scattering of others, including members selected by neighborhood organizations. In all, the executive branch of the central government would nominate less than one-third of the council. The third area of conflict involved the extension of "democratic control"—participation by the community, teachers, staff, and students—to governance in private education. The progressive groups generally supported

---

23. The *salário educação* generates the National Educational Development Fund *convênios* analyzed in chapter 6. As a payroll tax, it is paid by all employers.

democratic control, in part because they expected the balance of ideological forces to favor their interests when "entities of civil society" (staff, students, and professors) had more influence.

The Hage version of the LDB seldom tried to reconcile the conflicts in the proposals it received. Instead, the bill took on a crazy-quilt appearance, with numerous contradictory elements and a multiplicity of unresolved differences. Since the proposal made little pretense of aggregating conflicting interests, legislators felt free to represent their own personal interests or those of narrow segments of society.

By 1990 deputies had offered 978 amendments, and of these the Hage version incorporated 447. These amendments were extraordinarily narrow. In many cases, both on the left and the right, organized groups, such as private secondary schools or the university professors' union, wrote the amendments. It is also clear that on educational issues both Elíseo and Hage were outliers from the mainstream of the Chamber. Overall, with no political party interested in negotiating the diverse points of view, and with the bill's leadership far from the median legislator on every conflictual issue, it is no surprise that the LDB never came to a vote.

In the next legislative session (1991–94), the median legislator was substantially more conservative. Hage, Elíseo, and other education progressives had been defeated. When the leadership of the Education Committee passed to a conservative from the Northeast, the Elíseo-Hage version of the LDB was dead.[24] The bill was returned simultaneously to three committees: constitution and justice, finance, and education. Predictably, jurisdictional squabbles generated enormous confusion. When the confusion threatened to spill over into other issues, the *colégio* intervened and created a special supraparty negotiating panel composed basically of members of the Education Committee. The reporting officer of the panel was Angela Amin, a moderate and influential PDS deputy from Santa Catarina. Amin created a negotiating group with deputies representing all points of view in education. From the PT came sociologist Florestan Fernandes. Roberto Jefferson, a PTB member from Rio de Janeiro, made the case for private schools. Eraldo Tinoco, a Bahian and former minister of education under Collor, expounded the views of PFL conservatives, while Artur da Tavola played the same role for the center-leftist PSDB.[25]

---

24. The rules of the Chamber provided, however, that the bill begin on the floor in the new legislature, because it had already been approved by the Education Committee. Since it clearly could not pass, it returned to committees.

25. Other important participants included Ubiratan Aguiar (PMDB, Ceará) and Renildo Calheiros (PCdoB, Pernambuco).

The supraparty group initially adopted a decision-making routine proposed by an organization called the National Forum to Defend Public Schools, which united most of the organizations on the Left. Under this regimen, the Amin group would negotiate whatever issues could be negotiated. Where the group could reach no compromise, the full Education Committee would vote. The first irreconcilable issue was the article defining the principles of Brazilian education. In the full committee, the progressives won, successfully including democratic governance in public schools. After this defeat, the conservatives lost interest in referring disputes to the full committee, so the Amin group dropped this method of voting and resolved most subsequent issues by sticking to the status quo. For example, on the issue of democratic control of private schools, the private-school owners' vigorous opposition to any form of community control prevailed. On the issue of evaluation of universities, the weaker federal institutions successfully fought off any sort of serious performance appraisal. The National Education Council lost some of its independence from political authority. In the Amin version, the council had twenty-four members, with half chosen by the president. Although the council adopted criteria guaranteeing representation to various regions and types of schools, the president had enough nominees to control its leadership.

As the negotiations proceeded in the new legislative session, it became clear that the Collor government had no interest in any sort of LDB. All three of Collor's ministers of education (Carlos Chiarelli, José Goldemberg, and Eraldo Tinoco), fought vigorously against passage. Only when Itamar Franco took over from Collor did the ministry support passage. Itamar's minister, Maurílio Hingel, had been on the Chamber's legislative staff and on the personal staff of Deputy Ubiratan Aguiar. Hingel made Aguiar the government's representative in LDB negotiations, and the bill's pace in the Chamber accelerated.

The chief negotiator for conservative forces in the 1991–94 session was Tinoco, a Bahian PFL deputy, Collor's last education minister, and a fierce defender of private education. Tinoco's leverage derived from the power of his patron, Antônio Carlos Magalhães. Tinoco had participated in LDB negotiations during the Sarney administration. In that period, however, his influence was much less, because ACM, as Sarney's minister of communications, had a privileged position inside the administration and less need for congressional allies. Moreover, Tinoco's clout under Sarney had been counterbalanced by two other progressive Bahians, Education Minister Carlos Santana and the bill's reporting officer, Hage. In 1990, however, ACM retook the governorship of Bahia, and the Bahian presence in the legislature became more focused. No one doubted that Tinoco spoke for ACM and for much of the PFL.

For the progressives, the chief negotiator was Renildo Calheiros, a young Pernambucan from the Communist Party of Brazil (PCdoB), a small spinoff from the older PCB.[26] Though Calheiros was a freshman, rookies can quickly make their mark in a legislature where turnover averages 50 percent, and Calheiros quickly gained a reputation as an articulate and sensible deputy.

Calheiros and the progressives faced a new and much more difficult bargaining environment. The so-called progressive groups from civil society had been represented by an umbrella lobbying organization, the National Forum for the Defense of Public Education. After 1990 the forum began to disintegrate. The departing groups mostly represented scientific organizations disagreeing with the forum over the accreditation and evaluation of universities.[27] Since the scientific organizations had the greatest legitimacy outside the educational establishment, their defection reduced the forum's bargaining power.

Not only was the LDB's bloc of leftist supporters beginning to fall apart, but the Education Ministry was fighting hard to block the Chamber's LDB proposal. The Collor administration chose the tactic of supporting an LDB bill introduced in the Senate. Senator Darcy Ribeiro, a well-known anthropologist in the leftist PDT, had authored this version.[28] The education establishment strongly opposed Darcy's proposal. But under the Congress's rules, if the Senate passed its version first, that proposal would be voted first by the full Chamber. Moreover, the Senate proposal would pick up some votes from Darcy's fellow PDT deputies in the Chamber.[29] So the Senate proposal increased pressure on the Chamber—mostly on the progressives, since they really wanted the LDB—to compromise.

How did the progressive forces, the real driving force behind the LDB, react to these new strategic problems. The initial strategy adopted in the new legislature was to take polemic points, issues unresolvable by the supraparty negotiators, to the full Education Committee for up or down vote. The committee conservatives jettisoned that strategy when it appeared that the progressives

---

26. The PCB was supposedly Moscow oriented, while the PCdoB was China and Albania oriented. As far as I can tell, nothing in the doctrines of these two parties had anything to do with their putative orientations. With the end of the Soviet Union, the PCB has now changed its name to the PPS.

27. One such group was the Brazilian Society for the Progress of Science.

28. At this time, Collor was courting Darcy's patron, Leonel Brizola, the governor of Rio de Janeiro. A central element of Darcy's proposal was the construction of multipurpose, integrated schools and social service agencies called CIACs. Brizola had started some of these centers in Rio; Collor began to construct them in every state. With his impeachment, the idea quickly died.

29. The PDT's Ribeiro wing included Cariocas José Vicente Brizola, Marcia Cibilis, Luís Mascarenhas, Luís Salamão, and Carlos Luppi.

would regularly defeat them, since on education issues the committee was substantially to the left of the full Chamber. In response, the progressive forces made Calheiros their chief negotiator, one on one against Tinoco. The forum's representatives would wait in the Education Committee hearing room while Calheiros negotiated directly with Tinoco in a room above. When the negotiators would reach a polemic point, Calheiros would descend to confer with the forum representatives.

On the basis of many conversations with deputies and staff involved on all sides of the LDB's negotiation process, I am convinced that the process I have described was genuine. It was not, in other words, merely a symbolic exercise designed to pacify the education pressure groups while the real negotiations went on behind closed doors among powerful congressional leaders. As evidence of this contention, consider one example of substantive accommodation reached in these negotiations. The PCdoB (Calheiros's party) had insisted that the National Council should have a representative elected by students, and the forum defended that position in the negotiations. At the same time, the owners of private universities opposed proposals (coming from the scientific organizations) for establishing minimal levels of qualification of the teaching body as a prerequisite for the founding of a university. These proposals would hinder the opening of universities without qualified teachers. In the negotiations, the private-school owners accepted the inclusion of a student representative on the council. In exchange, the forum agreed to reduce to a very low level the minimum necessary qualification of the teaching staff of a new university. By the time of my interviews, in 1994 and 1995, the staffers—all sympathetic to the forum's positions—had realized that this bargain favored the owners and constituted a serious strategic error.

With the departure of the impeached President Collor, the LDB's prospects improved dramatically. The new minister of education, Hingel, had been a congressional staffer in earlier LDB negotiations. His aides, working with the committee and supplying technical inputs, became strong advocates of the legislation. In the end, the Chamber approved the project, but the session ended before the Senate could vote.

It is worth noting that the LDB went to the *colégio* only when interparty struggles threatened the Chamber's harmony.[30] In other words, the *colégio* only functioned where parties mattered as parties. If this is truly a case where public interest was so low that no proposal offered politicians much electoral gain,

---

30. The *colégio* also made certain final adjustments in the proposal before it was voted on the floor, but they were not substantively important.

and where a plethora of societal interests fought to defend hard-won turf, negotiation would inevitably be very difficult. Most party leaders really preferred no LDB at all. Education is thus a classic example of the consequences of an excess of veto players. Movements away from the status quo become extremely difficult. Unfortunately, in this case, the status quo, the Brazilian educational system, is one of the worst in Latin America.[31]

Agrarian Reform

In 1992 the Congress approved an agrarian reform bill. While the new law hardly allowed the poor to expropriate the estates of the rich, it did represent a small victory for the landless. This modestly progressive agrarian reform proposal passed because an unusual set of circumstances, especially the impeachment of President Collor, created an ethical climate in the Congress favoring the Left.

Consideration of a new agrarian reform proposal began in 1991, when the PT resubmitted a project held over from the previous session. The *mesa* (presiding board) appointed Agriculture Committee member Odelmo Leão as the bill's reporting officer. A first-term deputy representing Minas Gerais and the PRN (Collor's party), Leão was a large-scale landholder active in organizations of rural producers. Though an outlier compared to the median legislator, Leão was typical of the Agriculture Committee, where typically 70 percent of the members have personal interests in large-scale rural enterprises. Given this committee context, it was hardly surprising that the PT proposal never enjoyed the support of more than 30 percent of the committee. Leão held no hearings and refused to allow a committee vote on the proposal.

While the corruption investigation of President Collor was gathering steam, lobbying groups from the agrarian reform movement and the Catholic church began to apply pressure. Conflicts between the organized landless and landowners became more common. President Collor claimed that he could not resolve these agrarian conflicts without some sort of legal framework. In this favorable climate, reform activists believed they had begun to convince rural capitalists that owners of productive lands had no reason, from this proposal, to fear expropriation.[32]

In 1992, Vadão Gomes, a young, first-term *paulista* land- and slaughter-

---

31. The Cardoso administration's educational reforms are beyond the scope of this study, but the Education Ministry has begun to institute, with great controversy, a national field examination in all Brazilian universities.

32. This conclusion results from interviews in the agrarian reform movement, including INESC, the pro–agrarian reform policy center.

house owner, became chair. Leão continued as reporting officer and ultimately introduced a substitute proposal. The rural caucus—that is, the big landowners (see chapter 1), made a number of changes in his proposal, and Leão began discussions with the PT, CONTAG (the Confederation of Agricultural Workers), and the employees of INCRA (the agrarian reform institute).

Although Leão claimed to have eight substitute proposals, he refused to show them to the proreform groups, even in meetings supposedly called to discuss the issue. Frustrated, lobbyists for the agrarian reform movement went to Ibsen Pinheiro, the Chamber president, and asked that the original proposal be moved directly to the full house (the *plenário*) under an urgency rule. The lobbyists also asked for a new reporting officer. Pinheiro responded that he needed two weeks to negotiate with Leão and Gomes. At the end of that stretch, nothing had happened. Leão negotiated with the rural caucus, with the agrarian wing of the PT, and with a banker on the committee but refused to negotiate with party leaders. It became impossible to agree on a substitute proposal.

The Economy Committee, led by Fábio Meirelles of São Paulo, then introduced its own substitute. A committee less dominated by big landowners might seem advantageous, but in fact proreform lobbyists preferred bargaining with the Agriculture Committee, believing that no reform would have sufficient legitimacy to guarantee implementation unless it included key members of the rural caucus. At the precise moment when the Economy Committee began to vote on its substitute, the chief lobbyist of the pro–agrarian reform group happened to be nearby. Hearing that the Economy Committee was about to vote, the lobbyist went to Leão and tried to persuade him that the Economy Committee's actions would encroach on the Agriculture Committee's prerogatives. Properly offended, Leão immediately persuaded the Economy Committee to postpone voting its bill while his proposal was being considered in the Agriculture Committee.

Still, the Agriculture Committee was in no condition to approve anything. Leão wanted to approve a bill by consensus, but the committee was far too divided. Pinheiro finally scheduled a vote for the proposal in the full house. In addition, Pinheiro nearly took away Leão's right to be reporting officer, forcing him to compromise to stay on the bill. Serious negotiations now included CONTAG (representing rural labor) and INESC (a pro–agrarian reform think tank), the main lobbying groups in favor of agrarian reform. At times even the landless movement had representatives in the discussions. In the end, the negotiations reached an accord giving the president and the head of the agrarian reform agency the power to approve expropriations.

The *colégio* accepted this version of the proposal and then began to negotiate a trade between the agrarian reform proposal and a completely distinct proposal, promoted by the Collor administration, to regulate the nation's ports.[33] The leftist parties (PT, PDT, PSDB, PCdoB, PSB, and so forth) agreed to support port reform if the Chamber voted agrarian reform. The Left was a minority on the port proposal, but the government's majority was too small to overcome the Left's obstruction. The dock workers were furious, feeling that they had been betrayed, but the agrarian reform proposal passed.

The project then went to the Senate, which ultimately approved a version even stronger than that of the Chamber. When the proposal returned to the Chamber, Leão called all the interests together to resolve the two versions' differences. Each of the six political parties involved had one representative—in each case a deputy from the rural wing—and each party had one vote, regardless of size. If the vote was four to two or greater, the negotiating committee accepted or rejected the amendment; if the vote was three to three, the amendment went to the floor.[34] Of twenty-two amendments, only two went to the floor.

In the end, the Chamber and the Congress as a whole approved a bill contrary to the interests of its best-organized and largest caucus. While individual members of the rural caucus always thought they could use the courts to obstruct implementation, they certainly preferred the simpler route of defeating the bill. At the same time, for some members the bill might forestall more radical demands in the future.

Ministerial Reshuffling[35]

Soon after assuming the presidency (following Collor's resignation), Itamar Franco sent to the Congress Emergency Measure 309, an ambitious proposal creating a series of new ministries and reshuffling the responsibilities of existing ministries. Economy would be split into three ministries: economy, planning, and commerce and industry. The Secretariats of Science and Technology and of Environment would each become ministries. Two ministries that had previously been folded into others, interior and culture, would regain their independence.[36]

---

33. The *colégio* had not been involved in negotiations over the substance of the port reform proposal.

34. The representatives of the parties, with each party having one vote, were as follows: PMDB: Roberto Rollemberg, Odacir Klein, Dejandir Dalpasquale; PRN: Odelmo Leão; PT: Pedro Tonelli and Adão Pretto; PDT: Amaury Muller; PFL: Jonas Pinheiro and Ronaldo Caiado; PDS: Fábio Meirelles.

35. Because I was unable to undertake as many interviews in this case as in the others, readers should regard the conclusions advanced here as more tentative.

36. I am indebted to an anonymous reader for pointing out that Itamar's reform mostly reversed Collor's ministerial reorganization of March 1990.

This rearrangement, together with the people nominated to hold the new appointments, created many winners. The Senate as a whole would profit, because four members were expected to lead the ministries. The Northeast would pick up five ministers (including, for the first time, the minister of finance). The PSDB would become the most influential party in the president's cabinet even though it held only 10 percent of the seats in the Chamber. Governor Luís Antônio Fleury, former protégé of ex-Governor Quércia of São Paulo, would come out ahead, because Franco granted Fleury the liberty to choose certain ministers, mostly as a way of weakening Quércia. The PT would gain, because the minister of labor would come from that party. Franco's home state of Minas Gerais would benefit from its quota of seven ministers.[37]

Reorganization also created losers. Antônio Carlos Magalhães, who had been a ferocious critic of the president, had no allies in the new cabinet. Leonel Brizola had one representative, Maurício Correa in the justice ministry, but Correa was very independent of Brizola. Quércia was not strong enough to impose his own choice in the Ministry of Finance; the most he could do was to veto archenemy José Serra. Against Quércia's wishes, moreover, the PMDB agreed to participate in the government though it named no ministers. São Paulo state also lost, because Walter Barelli, in the labor ministry, was its only cabinet member. And of course Collor was a big loser; Franco threw out even the former president's second-echelon appointees.[38]

Since Congress had to approve the ministerial restructurings, the whole process was open to negotiation. Among the chief lines of cleavage, party interests were central. State delegations mattered as well, because each state wanted to maximize its ministerial quota. But parties also had doctrinal interests. The PT wanted to expand the number of ministries in the social areas but opposed growth in bureaucratic jobs carrying high salaries. The PPR (later called the PPB) wanted to keep ministries with northeastern pork-barrel programs in the hands of politicians from that region. The PFL had three lines of opposition. One group rejected the reform just to oppose Itamar. A second group (organized around Marco Maciel) wanted the executive branch given more flexibility—that is, left with fewer controls. In Maciel's view, Congress should limit itself to investigating executive-branch programs after implementation. The third group, the neoliberals clustered around Jorge Bornhausen, sought simply to shrink the government.

---

37. Minas's count of seven includes Henrique Hargreaves, the head of the domestic policy staff, the Casa Civil.

38. *Globo* (October 9, 1992, 2) estimated that Itamar had 662 second-echelon positions to fill.

Even though state delegations were the single most important group of actors, the *colégio* played an active role in these bargaining sessions. At an early stage, for example, the *colégio* committed itself to an agreement to ignore all corporativist claims. An amendment benefiting accountants, for example, quickly died.

In the end, the legislators modified the president's proposal to reflect more accurately the true balance of forces in Congress. ACM, for example, ended up with three allies in the government, including the president of the Bank of the Northeast, the head of the post office, and the adjunct secretary of communications. The PMDB's northeastern delegates nominated the head of SUDENE, the regional development autarchy that controlled a huge patronage operation. A PPR confidant became director of the credit agency of the Bank of Brazil, an operation crucial to the PPR's base among large-scale farmers. PTB supporters dominated the dock companies in São Paulo and Rio.

What explains the relatively greater importance of the *colégio?* Unidimensionality, as in the case of bidding reform, seems crucial. Everyone dealt in the same currency, the effort to maximize cabinet presence, and everyone benefited from enlarging the size of the cabinet itself. Party leaders (and Itamar as well) all had interests in maintaining the issue's distributive quality (Lowi 1964).

The Franco Administration's Stabilization Program
By 1992 Brazil's inflation once again threatened to surpass 30 percent per month. Inflation had been a persistent near-crisis since the explosion of the international debt problem in the 1980s. Now, however, a broad intellectual consensus had finally been reached regarding inflation's causes. The consensus stressed pervasive indexing, the enormous burden of the internal public debt, and expectations of future inflation.[39] In essence, the consensus view placed the behavior of the state itself at the heart of the stabilization crisis.

The Franco government set out to stabilize the economy with less than two years remaining until the 1994 presidential election. The policymakers knew that any stabilization proposal would require a fiscal adjustment. The govern-

---

39. Indexing means that contracts affecting prices and wages are set with provisions for automatic adjustments to compensate for inflation. When Brazil first adopted indexing, in the mid-1960s, it was regarded as an innovative way to prevent inflation from crippling growth. The downside of indexing, that it gives inflation a momentum difficult to break, was not recognized until later. Expectations of future inflation lead to more inflation as economic actors increase prices preemptively, fearing that others will increase first and thereby create real losses. On the stabilization program itself, see Oliveira (1996) and Franco (1995, chap. 2).

ment's program had three crucial elements: a provisional tax on financial trans-actions (IPMF), the creation of the Social Emergency Fund (FSE) to restrict federal transfers to states and municipalities, and the creation of a new index-ing device (the unit of real value, or URV), which would ultimately become a new currency, the real. I will now discuss the first two elements of the govern-ment's plan, omitting an examination of the URV because it did not depend on congressional action.

The IPMF
The government's economic team proposed the IPMF as a tax on every finan-cial transaction paid by check. The rate would be .25 percent of the value of each check, deducted from the amount paid to the check's bearer. At that rate the tax would yield about $600 million per month. From these receipts, 18 per-cent would be destined for education programs and 20 percent would go to low-income housing.

Passage of the IPMF faced multiple obstacles. First, the tax arrived at Con-gress's door just when potential candidates began staking out positions for the presidential campaign. On something as unpopular as a new tax, declared can-didates wanted to oppose the government. Second, as a new tax, the proposal required a supermajority in the legislature. Third, the PMDB, as the largest party in the Congress, was pivotal to the IPMF's approval. The PMDB, how-ever, had long sought a larger share of federal pork barrel, especially govern-ment jobs. Fourth, state and municipal interests would be damaged, because their transactions would be subject to the tax. Last, banks opposed the tax. They would have to collect it, and the tax would reduce the flow of financial transac-tions on which they profited so handsomely.

The kinds of narrow corporativist interests that usually influence legisla-tion were largely absent from the IPMF debate. Although banks opposed the tax, most industrialists supported it. Moreover, the tax affected all sectors of in-dustry about equally, so the Congress felt little sectoral pressure. Essentially, two kinds of interests were in play: political interests inside the Congress (that is, groups seeing the proposal as an opportunity to wrest concessions from the executive) and political interests outside the Congress (states and municipali-ties resisting a new tax).

After eight months of negotiations the Congress approved the IPMF. The government won the key legislative vote comfortably, 298–103.[40] A vote so lop-sided suggests that either the government made more concessions than neces-

---

40. This vote sent the bill directly to the floor, bypassing committee consideration.

sary or that it enjoyed an overwhelming base of support. Neither conclusion would be correct. During the eight months of negotiations, in fact, the government restructured the cabinet to regain PMDB support and made numerous concessions to individual deputies, senators, and factional interests.

The government's behavior weakened its ability to resist pork-barrel claims. While negotiating the IPMF, the executive promised $24 million for a water project in Ceará, $26 million for the Brasília metro, and $13 million for the "Red Line" highway in Rio de Janeiro. None of these awards had anything to do with the IPMF, but they implied that the government's till was far from empty. Though the government's individual concessions cannot be quantified, all the congressional aides interviewed believed that these concessions were substantial.

How did the parties in this struggle react? The PMDB's problems were many. Its legislative leaders were increasingly unhappy over President Franco's treatment of PMDB ministers. Itamar had already fired the agriculture minister, and the environment minister was expected to be next.[41] The president's elevation of Fernando Henrique Cardoso to the Finance Ministry meant that the chief political enemy of São Paulo's Governor Fleury now controlled economic policy. Even worse, successful stabilization would make Cardoso a viable presidential candidate. The PMDB was also in a continuous battle with Henrique Hargreaves, the head of the domestic policy staff (the *Casa Civil*). Not only was Hargreaves personally directing the distribution of second- and third-level jobs in key states, but he openly favored the PFL over the PMDB.

In May 1993, the PMDB showed its muscle in the Tax and Finance Committee, and it became clear that the IPMF could not pass without PMDB support. The government gave in: Hargreaves lost his control over nominations, a confidant of Governor Fleury became the minister of planning (the number-two economic job), and the PMDB gained the right to name the replacement for the fired agriculture minister. From that point on, the PMDB's support for the IPMF was solid.

Does the appointment of the PMDB's choice, Alexis Stepanenko, as minister of planning mean that political parties were really bargaining over policy rather than pork? The PMDB may have expected the new minister to protect Fleury's interests, but (in the opinion of all informants in this area) Stepanenko's technical incompetence rendered him totally ineffectual, and the PMDB had no credible means of monitoring his performance. By contrast, the Planning Ministry's new undersecretary (Pernambucan Raul Jungmann), a

---

41. In Brazilian parlance, the about-to-be fired minister was *fritado* (fried).

nomination of Roberto Freire, the government's leader in the Chamber of Deputies, used his considerable technical expertise to become quite influential in both the first and second Cardoso administrations.

Then there is the PFL, a party that nearly always backs whatever government is in power. The PFL ultimately allied with the center-left PSDB in support of Cardoso's presidential candidacy, but that alliance was not consummated until May 1994. At the time of the debate over the IPMF the alliance was far from certain, and the PFL expected to field its own candidate. Still, PFL deputy Francisco Dornelles, a former minister of finance and strong supporter of the interests of the federal treasury, led the government's negotiating team in the Chamber, and in the end 70 percent of the PFL's deputies supported the government—some clearly in exchange for individual concessions.[42] But the PFL wing led by Bahia's Governor Magalhães consistently opposed the tax, and another PFL deputy, ACM's son Luís Eduardo, led the opposition to it.

How much help did individual ministers give the president? On the basis of interviews with deputies and party staff, along with anecdotal evidence, the ministers seem to have done little to pressure their party compatriots.[43] The PSB voted unanimously against the tax even though the ministers of health and culture came from that party. The PT voted against the tax although the Labor Minister was a PT member. Brizola's PDT supported the tax, but PDT minister Correa was more a friend of the president than an ally of Brizola, and it is likely that funds for the Rio metro had something to do with PDT support. A share of the pork, it seems, does not guarantee party support, but without a share the party is sure to oppose.

The IPMF turned out to be clumsy and regressive. Legal actions based on the tax's constitutionality led to the exemption of state governments, the poor, salaried employees making less than $750 per month, and others. Even the Finance Ministry admitted that the tax was regressive, inflationary (since the tax was shifted to prices), and only produced revenue while inflation was high ("Importance of Education Investments" 1994, 4).

The FSE

In May 1993, Cardoso, PSDB senator from São Paulo and internationally known sociologist, moved from the Foreign Relations Ministry to Finance. Car-

---

42. Dornelles is another example of the importance of technical expertise. In the area of tax policy, all bargaining between deputies and the government seems to have passed through Dornelles, because he was the only deputy with real expertise in the area. Not only did no other deputies have Dornelles's understanding of taxes, but no one in the congressional staff did either.

43. See "Parties Ignore . . ." 1992.

doso's economic team put together what would have to be the last attempt by the Franco government to tame inflation. The FSE, a key part of the stabilization program, was a fiscal adjustment of almost 16 billion dollars. Of that amount, $2.1 billion came from new taxes, while $12.9 billion came from delinking various other funds legally earmarked for states and municipalities. These funds would be spent in fixed percentages in health and sanitation (30 percent), education (7.5 percent), welfare (45.5 percent), and so on. The losers would be the states and municipalities, which would find their receipts reduced sharply, along with the programs themselves, which would suffer cuts in investment. Because the FSE involved changes in formulas mandated by the constitution, it had to be passed as a constitutional amendment, with the Chamber and Senate acting jointly during the ongoing constitutional revision.

What interests were in play on the FSE? States and municipalities obviously wanted to minimize their losses, particularly with an election approaching. Even before the first public announcement of the FSE, Cardoso met with a group of important governors and accepted their demand that the fund not be financed using a particular transfer program for states and municipalities. This concession reduced the fund's size by 15 percent and forced the administration's economists to find compensatory funds elsewhere.[44] The politicians' anxiety grew when a public opinion survey demonstrated that mayors investing more in education had done better in electing their successors in 1992 ("Importance of Education Investments" 1994, 3). Federal ministers in charge of social programs also faced grave threats: cuts would amount to $5 billion for the Health Ministry, $1.2 billion for Social Well-Being, and $2 billion for Education.

From party leaders' perspective, the FSE game was all about the upcoming presidential succession. No one wanted to help Cardoso, but some parties were more certain of their strategies than others. The PT had its candidate clearly defined, but PT leaders knew it would be enormously easier for Lula to govern if the pain of taming inflation had been absorbed by the Franco administration. The PDT also had an obvious candidate, Leonel Brizola, while the PPR intended either to support ACM in an alliance with the PFL or present its own candidate (which it did). The PMDB and PFL, however, faced more complex alternatives. The *quércista* wing of the PMDB, dominated by former São Paulo Governor Orestes Quércia, wanted to oppose the government, because Quércia intended to be the PMDB's candidate. The Rio Grande do Sul wing hoped for an alliance with the PSDB in which the candidate would be Antônio

---

44. Interview with member of Cardoso economic team, July 9, 1999.

Britto, PMDB minister of social welfare. For the PFL leadership, the stakes in stabilization were high: if Lula won, the party would probably suffer heavy losses in the Congress, and the PFL's ties to business would be seriously compromised. For the PFL rank and file, conversely, successful stabilization could yield electoral dividends, but these dividends might be less than the votes lost from cuts in patronage programs just before the election. Of course, every party leader remembered the 1986 election, swept by the PMDB in the aftermath of the early success of its ill-fated Plano Cruzado. Everyone wanted to negotiate something, just to look good before the electorate.

The early weeks of the debate were characterized by widespread attacks on the plan by the various presidential candidates. Hopefuls Amin (PPR), Quércia (PMDB), and Sarney (PMDB) all voiced their opposition. On the other side, Pedro Simon, the leader of the government forces in the Senate, blundered into saying that it was necessary to isolate the PFL and PPR, a remark that only hardened opposition (*Jornal do Brasil,* February 4, 1994, 3). PMDB leaders were angry when President Franco suggested that the economic plan would help the candidacy of Fernando Henrique. Cardoso then threatened, if the Congress failed to approve the FSE quickly, to resign from the ministry. But party leaders believed he would not leave until and unless Congress clearly refused to support the plan. If Cardoso left earlier, he would be unable to justify his exit before public opinion. The ideal situation, then, was to stall, leaving everything in a "warm bath" (*banho-maria*) until the fragility of the minister vis-à-vis the Congress became clearer.

By the first week in February, serious bargaining could begin, because the opposition had enough votes to block the emergency fund.[45] Just before a key quorum call on January 28, the government agreed to give up $430 million of the $2.5 billion it had intended to collect with new taxes.[46] The government also conceded on PMDB demands regarding salary adjustments for civil servants. The government had wanted to freeze pay in 1994 and 1995 but now offered a higher base to compensate for losses to inflation (*Folha de São Paulo,* February 3, 1994, 1–10). For the PMDB, the electoral payoff from appearing as a friend of the civil servants was considerable. PFL leaders, having learned from

---

45. Some PMDB leaders threatened to vote against the FSE unless the PMDB was granted more ministries. A rumor circulated that the Ministry of Regional Integration was about to go to a PSDB politician from Ceará. At that time, the PMDB had two ministries, while the PSDB had five. The PMDB suggested Aluízio Alves for the job, but the president's inner circle rejected Alves (*Folha de São Paulo,* February 22, 1994, 3).

46. Of this amount, $170 million represented a reduction in the rural land tax (*imposto territorial rural*) and $260 million came from the corporate income tax.

the Plano Cruzado that all schemes work for a few months and that opponents risk political suicide, grudgingly allowed the PMDB to take credit for the new formula. To get the PDT's acquiescence, Cardoso promised Luiz Salomão and Miro Teixeira, PDT leaders from Rio de Janeiro, that he would liberate $80 million for the conclusion of the Red Line.[47] One of the government's chief negotiators—dealing directly with deputies and senators—was its head economist, Edmar Bacha, who promised to fund the pet projects of Minas Gerais's Governor Hélio Garcia.

The deals remained insufficient. On February 2 a key motion could not be voted because Congress fell fourteen votes short of a quorum. This defeat, truly a serious one for the government, led to tears by its negotiators and more threats of resignation by Cardoso. Now the problem was the PFL, PPR, and PMDB, especially the first two.

Although the PFL is occasionally characterized as a clientelistic party (*fisiologista*, in Brazilian parlance), only in part is this label accurate. The PFL also shelters an ideological wing of neoliberals, and this wing led the whole party in negotiations on the FSE. In exchange for support on the FSE, these neoliberals sought government backing for their positions in the ongoing constitutional revision. The most important of these positions called for ending government monopolies and for more rapidly opening the economy to foreign capital.[48]

In the end, government support for the PFL's positions on constitutional revision had little importance, since the Left had enough votes to block revision and since the government could do little about it. But the government could continue to make concessions. Negotiator Bacha granted that he could live with only half the resources that had been taken out of funds destined for housing, producing an electorally useful gain of $500 million.

The PMDB, with the support of the education minister, won a concession removing from the plan the resources of a tax earmarked for education (the *salário educação*), a gain amounting to $250 million. The government also agreed to make obligatory the application of $300 million on housing and $250–300 million on education. Of course, Bacha knew he would later refuse to appropriate the housing money, and Luís Roberto Ponte, the lobbyist for the

---

47. The government knew it would be impossible to get active support from the PDT but wanted PDT members present for the vote so that a quorum would be reached (interview with member of Cardoso economic team, July 9, 1999).

48. Other planks included an end to progressivity in the income tax, a universal tax rate of 10 percent, a mixed-district voting system, and free higher education only for those unable to pay. The main author of the plan was Jorge Bornhausen (see *Folha de São Paulo,* January 16, 1994, 1–10).

housing industry, knew that Bacha would renege.[49] However, Bacha's concession did put the money in the budget, and if Ponte had enough bargaining power at a later time, he might well obtain the appropriation. The agriculture minister promised credits worth $800 million to the rural caucus, and deputies from the Northeast won promises of fiscal incentives.[50] The government changed its regulations on the granting of radio and TV licenses, chiefly benefiting the evangelical caucus.

Ultimately, the government's accords with the Congress removed $600 million from the fiscal savings. Many informants interviewed in 1996 and 1997 thought the administration's economists had built that much cushion into the plan. Perhaps, but after the devaluation crisis of 1998–99, it became clear that the government's fiscal adjustment was hugely inadequate. In regional terms, the Northeast lost the most money, roughly $90 million, while the Southeast lost $30 million.[51] Most observers agreed that the South and Southeast, usually losers in pork-barrel battles, had done relatively well. The larger financial obligations of southern states, especially the debts of Rio de Janeiro, São Paulo, and Rio Grande do Sul, increased their bargaining power. But the greater success of these regions was likely also a product of the political skill and articulateness of the deputies representing them, especially Serra and Dornelles. From all sides in these negotiations, I repeatedly heard disparaging comments about the northeastern deputies' failure to comprehend the details of the taxing and spending issues involved in the FSE. With no serious professional staffing, the northeastern contingent was easy prey for the administration's sophisticated economists. In addition, the generally weaker ties between northeastern deputies and their electorates meant that immediate payoff—even getting on television with the minister—might be more important than the ultimate details of spending and taxing.

Without question, the Chamber's *colégio* played no role until the states and the Ministry of the Economy had reached an accord. The government negotiated directly with state governors and with their representatives in the Congress.[52] Governors such as Fleury came to Brasília to persuade their deputies to support the FSE. Party leaders relied on the administration's economists to

---

49. Interview with congressional informants, July 1997.

50. President Franco vetoed this part of the agreement when it reached his desk. My informants suggested that the deal had been made by a congressional leader without authorization from the administration. I do not know if members of the rural caucus knew a veto was likely. It may have been another exercise in symbolic politics. Congress overturned the veto in 1995.

51. São Paulo alone lost $3 million.

52. For example, Vivaldo Barbosa was Brizola's man in the Chamber of Deputies.

convince individual deputies to back the government's proposals.[53] Even when the government began to deal with the *colégio,* the government's representatives negotiated primarily with the leaders of strong parties. In other words, party equality—the essential operating principle of the *colégio*—prevented it from serving as a locus of bargaining and negotiation in the case of the stabilization plan.

The Cases Compared

When did the Chamber's own negotiating mechanism, the *colégio de lideres,* play an important role in negotiation and conflict resolution? In the debate over stabilization policy, the *colégio* was inactive until the states and the Ministry of the Economy reached an accord. In bidding reform, party leaders in the *colégio* chose and guided specialists who arrived at an agreement the whole Chamber could sanction, but the agreement was largely symbolic. In education, the *colégio* had essentially no role beyond preserving interparty harmony, although after years of discussion the Chamber ultimately approved a bill. In agrarian reform, the *colégio* arranged a logroll between leftist and rightist partisan forces, assuring the joint passage of both agrarian and port reform. In the ministerial reshuffle, the *colégio* itself was the key negotiator inside the legislature and between the legislature and the executive.

In essence, the *colégio* deals with areas that are polemical, need partisan expertise, and require political adjustment. When state delegations are very powerful, conflicts have to be resolved first at that level. Central bank finance bills, for example, do not go to the *colégio,* because state delegations are too strong.

Unidimensionality helps: ministerial and agrarian reform are relatively simple issues where the lines of compromise are clear. If issues are multidimensional, then actors in at least some of the conflicts must want compromise. In stabilization policy, the *colégio* could not resolve the conflict between the states and the executive, but the states' weakness vis-à-vis the executive led them to seek compromise. In education, most actors preferred to stick with the status quo rather than risk a new educational policy structure, and politicians saw no electoral gain from forcing a compromise.

Parties make up the *colégio de líderes,* and for the *colégio* to function parties need to perceive interests as parties in an issue. Parties clearly have inter-

---

53. Interview with government economists and party adviser, July 14, 1997, and July 9, 1999.

ests in ministerial shuffles, and doctrinal party interests were important in bidding reform. In the LDB, however, the parties mostly wished the issue would go away.

The limitations of the *colégio de líderes* become even more evident when comparing stabilization politics to ministerial reshuffling. In both cases, the pork barrel was central. In economic policy, the executive branch offered pork to overcome resistance. Pork bought support from parties, factions, and individual deputies in two ways: (1) by making vague commitments on other issues—though no one had much confidence in these commitments—and (2) by offering regional incentives and individual benefits. Parties were rarely stable or disciplined enough to engage in cross-issue logrolls, especially if the logrolls involved posterior commitments as well, but if the resources were available, the executive could dole out enough largesse to get a bill through. In ministerial reshuffling, by contrast, the executive was constructing a mechanism for distributing future pork. Here the executive had to deal with all parties. In this milieu of undisciplined parties, seat strength and ideological stance might change during a session. The executive could not afford to ignore small parties and govern with a minimum winning coalition, because the coalition might collapse. So the president dealt with all parties, and the *colégio de líderes,* with its principle of party equality, became the appropriate negotiating partner.[54]

Given the constraining influence of the dimensionality of issues and their importance to the executive, what other factors make agreement more likely? The conventional wisdom in Brazil holds that deputies' search for pork hinders legislative policy-making on all kinds of issues. In the sense that deputies fixated on acquiring disaggregable public goods may care little about broader legislation, the criticism is correct. Only a minority of legislators participates actively in legislating on broad issues. In addition, the generally poor quality of staff—itself a function of the deputies' distrust of independent specialists—surely hinders lawmaking. But if each party were coherent and disciplined, a legislature with many parties would have a much more difficult time passing laws. These cases reinforce a central theorem of the veto-players approach: the broader the distribution of views in a party and the wider the range of policy alternatives acceptable to a majority coalition, the easier it is to reach agreement on policies deviating from the status quo. If each of Brazil's current parties had the discipline and coherence of the PT, the legislative process would truly be chaotic.[55]

---

54. Small parties generally oppose the *colégio*'s prerogatives, preferring to fight in committees.

55. The PT's discipline does not help it negotiate. PT leaders, because they have little authority until a final proposal is accepted, cannot make credible precommitments. At the other ex-

The cases also demonstrate the endogeneity of the legislative bargaining structure. Congressional approval of stabilization proposals under Franco and Cardoso was secured with much pork and many substantive compromises but without significant participation by the *colégio de líderes*. The marginalization of the *colégio* foreshadowed the first Cardoso administration's bargaining style. Intense negotiations occurred, but they were usually conducted directly between the office of the president and the targeted individuals, states, and caucuses. In the second Cardoso administration, with the president a lame duck, his supporting coalition weaker, and most parties looking to distance themselves from the administration before the next presidential election, the locus of negotiations seems likely to return to the Congress itself.

---

treme, the undisciplined PDT and PTB are both regarded as bad negotiators. The PMDB is equally pulverized, but its staff (particularly excellent at communicating with deputies and counting votes) facilitates bargaining.

Conclusion

This conclusion has four tasks. Its starting point is a brief summary of the book's findings. The discussion then moves to the argument's broader ramifications. I begin by considering the price Brazil pays for dysfunctional political institutions, spotlighting the economic crisis triggered by the Asian and Russian debacles of 1997. I suggest that President Cardoso's political tactics—his survival strategy—magnified the effects of the crisis. Cardoso's tactics, however, were not merely his idiosyncratic approach to the presidency. Instead, they reflect a rational, almost inevitable response to Brazil's institutional context. The third section of this conclusion considers the reform of Brazil's political institutions. These institutions, I have pointed out, produce an excess of veto players.[1] This excess is not just a question of the number of parties needed to make a legislative majority. More broadly, Brazil's destructive, majority-constraining federalism, coupled with presidentialism and with the nation's electoral rules, creates the excess. Can stronger parties reduce the number of veto players? If so, can Brazil strengthen its parties? What lessons should be taken from the experience of other Latin American countries that have recently reformed their institutional structures, including Colombia, Venezuela, and Bolivia? The final section considers the implications of this work for the study of comparative politics. I appraise the substantive significance of Brazil's institutional struggle for reform in other settings, assess the methodological limits of the case study, and offer a research agenda for the future.

I. The Story Summarized

This book has made the case that a good part of Brazil's political problems stem from the design of its institutions. Under normal conditions, these institutions produce a very high number of veto players. As a result, they hinder the adop-

---

1. In general, the interaction of high degrees of ethnic heterogeneity (or some other basis of complex social cleavage) with electoral rules "naturally" produces a large number of parties

tion of policies that deviate from the status quo—that is, policies that innovate. Prominent among these malfunctioning institutions are the electoral system, the rules of party formation, the nature of the presidency, and the separation of powers between the central government, the states, and municipalities. The book's substantive argument began with the electoral system. That discussion came to a double conclusion: open-list proportional representation (PR), as it functions in Brazil, is extremely democratic in the sense that all societal cleavages receive equal treatment and that the rules favor neither class nor community. But flexibility and evenhandedness come at a price. Open-list PR personalizes politics, and the system weakens party control over politicians both on the campaign trail and in the legislature. Ties between voters and deputies remain weak, and parties struggle to aggregate societal interests into anything resembling a coherent program.[2]

In open-list PR, electoral strategies reflect a unique kind of competition. At times candidates compete over ideological space, but more often their fight is really over geographical, physical space. Candidates seek municipalities whose voters and leaders will give them support. I expressed the outcomes of the fight for space in a simple taxonomy, one combining vertical penetration of municipalities ("domination") with horizontal coverage ("contiguity"). By means of this taxonomy, I classified deputies as concentrated-dominant, concentrated-shared, scattered-shared, and scattered-dominant. Deputies with certain kinds of occupational backgrounds and with varying political histories tend to concentrate in each of these categories. Local mayors, for example, have concentrated vote distributions, while businessmen more often find their support in scattered patterns. In pork-dependent and patronage-oriented regions of the country, deputies get most of the votes cast in the municipalities contributing a substantial part of their personal vote, while deputies in other regions deal with much higher levels of interparty and intraparty fragmentation.

To deepen our understanding of this unique electoral system, I then considered issues central to contemporary political debate in Brazil: malapportionment, corruption, accountability, and party building. São Paulo is more than fifty seats short of its proportionate share of the Chamber of Deputies, while states in the Center-West and North, mostly frontier regions, have far too many

---

(Ordeshook and Shvetsova 1994). Given Brazil's low degree of ethnic cleavage, its large number of parties must be a purely political phenomenon. Cox (1997), relying on joint work with Amorim Neto, replicated results confirming the ethnic heterogeneity—party fragmentation link, but Amorim Neto, in a personal communication, agreed that the party system does not reflect Brazil's ethnic cleavages.

2. For a general theoretical discussion of this issue, see Shepsle 1988.

seats. At times it is taken for granted that conceding São Paulo its just share will move Brazil's political center of gravity sharply to the Left. It turns out, however, that under reasonable assumptions about the voting behavior of new deputies—given the weakness of party discipline in Brazil—radical expectations should be tempered. Under true proportionality, some important votes in the National Constituent Assembly would have turned out differently, but the majority of outcomes would remain unchanged.

The outbreak in 1993 of an extraordinary corruption scandal offered the chance to test the practical importance of the vote-distribution taxonomy. The deputies accused of corruption overwhelmingly tend to be the scattered-dominant type, reflecting their efforts to make deals with local political bosses. A German-type reform, with half the legislature elected in single-member districts and half under closed-list PR, would almost certainly retire these corrupt types from the legislature.

Brazil's electoral system gives new meaning to the oft-used term *special interests*. Open-list PR facilitates what is really self-representation—that is, the tendency for certain deputies to represent their personal economic interests or the interests of very narrow economic sectors. The so-called rural caucus represents not the interests of the voters who put these deputies into the legislature but the personal interests of deputies holding rural property. To say the least, this representational style is far from the usual meaning of accountability.

Chapter 1 then turned to an examination of the effects of the electoral system on the building of political parties. Brazil's high levels of null and blank voting tell us something about the electoral system. In constituencies where all candidates get small proportions of their personal vote, individual campaign efforts are likely to be minimal. Because no one cares enough to campaign, voters lack sufficient information to choose. But anger matters as well: with corruption scandals, perennially high inflation, and an impeached president, voters express their feelings about politics not by staying home but by defacing their ballots.

Though Brazil has parties with considerable organizational strength at municipal and even state levels, at the national level one can hardly call them political parties. Parties have difficulty forming coherent programs in part because the system encourages multiparty alliances. Right-wing parties ally with center parties in some states and with left-wing parties in others. In the 1994 presidential election, the PSDB, a supposedly center-left party, made two strange but successful deals: one deal linked the PSDB and the PFL, a far right party with a neoliberal wing and a pork-barrel wing; the other united the PSDB and the PTB, a party with only pork-barrel types.

Chapter 1 concluded with another look at the spatial taxonomy of voting bases. One category, deputies with concentrated-shared distributions, seems to be increasing in frequency. Such deputies appeal to broad social strata in particular local communities. Because their vote is concentrated, they are likely to identify with these communities, but these deputies also face significant political opposition. Increases in the number of concentrated-shared deputies may thus presage an upsurge in efforts at pork delivery. But at least such deputies have to pay attention to the communities where they get votes, and at least they have to compete with other candidates for these votes. It may not be much, but it might be the beginning of accountability.

Chapter 2 developed and tested a theory explaining the electoral strategies of candidates for the Chamber of Deputies. In place of the usual discussion of the traditional, clientelistic roots of electoral strategy, I began with the assumption that rational politicians behave strategically. Faced with an electoral system whose chief attributes include open-list PR, large multimember districts, candidate selection at the level of politically active subnational units, and the possibility of immediate reelection, most deputies pay little attention to ideological appeals. Instead, legislators seek to build walls around their bailiwicks so that no other candidates will enter. Candidates search for vulnerable municipalities, especially those free (at least temporarily) of boss control, and strive to overcome electoral weakness by delivering pork to municipal targets. Strategic candidates do not behave identically, because their political backgrounds vary and because the differing demographic and economic contexts of Brazilian states reward some tactics and penalize others.

What is the significance of these results? Consider the principal-agent relationship between voters and deputies. Brazil's electoral system hinders voter control. It forces candidates to seek single-issue niches, to spend lavishly, and to make deals with contenders for other offices, contenders with whom the candidates share nothing. In part because they learn little about the importance of national-level issues, rational voters back candidates based on their pork potential.

The combination of pork-seeking incentives and the state-centeredness of Brazilian politics may mean that the overall pork-seeking propensity of Brazilian legislators is still growing. Deputies in more industrialized, wealthy states face more competition from candidates of other parties but also have more concentrated vote distributions. In such constituencies, higher levels of education and wealth raise voter interest and involvement in politics. Greater awareness in turn magnifies deputies' incentives to seek pork. At the same time, the demand for local benefits contributes to higher turnover rates and thus to lower seniority levels.

Chapter 3 explored differences in domination and concentration, the two main dimensions of individual congressional vote bases, across states and over time. Throughout the 1978–94 period, domination was higher in the Northeast. In that region deputies are more likely to get most of the votes cast in their vote bases not merely as a function of widespread poverty but also as a consequence of the combined effects of a tradition of pork-barrel politics and the presence of so many political families. Spatial concentration, conversely, is essentially a function of demography. Voting support was more scattered in states where winning a seat was difficult without votes in the capital, because deputies from the interior were forced to seek votes in the capital as well.

How have domination and concentration changed over the course of these five elections? The general decline of domination results from three factors: the population's increasing political awareness, the explosive growth of cities (which are simply harder to dominate), and the changing occupational backgrounds of new congressional contestants. The number of candidates with business and bureaucratic backgrounds has risen, while local and state politicians are in decline. This changing occupational mix, itself a consequence of the growing importance of money in campaigning, contributes to the fall in electoral domination. Changes in spatial concentration are less clear. Concentration increased immediately after the 1978 election but seems to have stabilized in more recent contests. Concentrated electoral distributions are advantageous to deputies, so new contestants—though many come from occupational backgrounds linked to more scattered vote distributions—are gradually "socialized" into veterans' campaign tactics.

In chapter 4, the investigation moved from quantitative models to a set of case studies designed to explore the interaction among economic and demographic factors, political competition, and extraordinary political events. The cases included Paraná and Santa Catarina in the more developed South and Maranhão, Ceará, and Bahia in the less developed Northeast. Paraná and Santa Catarina are two relatively wealthy neighbors, but their politics are quite distinct. Paraná—at least until the recent ascendance of Jaime Lerner—has been essentially leaderless, with highly localized competition for elected office, a weak legislature, very high turnover of both state and federal politicians, and strong parties on the political Left. Santa Catarina, by contrast, has a definable political oligarchy that has been stable since World War II. Though the state is more industrial than Paraná, Santa Catarina's Left has traditionally been weaker.

Demography seems to be the key difference between Santa Catarina and Paraná. In Paraná, powerful migratory flows from other states and from other countries created subregions with distinct political orientations. Paraná's center—the area around Curitiba—is relatively unimportant in either demographic or political terms. The state's economy has such vigor that political careers are a less desirable alternative. Paraná's political leaders lack strong roots in their state. The state delegation in the Chamber of Deputies has too little collective seniority to give Paraná national influence. Moreover, Paraná's population elects very localistic deputies, so pork delivery becomes the litmus test of electability.

Maranhão, Ceará, and Bahia display a quite different politics. In all Brazil, no state-level leaders have the clout of Maranhão's José Sarney or Bahia's Antônio Carlos Magalhães. Ceará, conversely, lacks politicos with the power (and flair) of Sarney or ACM, but political competition has changed dramatically over the past ten years with the overthrow of Ceará's "colonels" and their marginalization from politics.

Ceará's three cliques of colonels had it too easy. They divided up the state, building corrupt political machines through traditional modes of rural dominance. Eventually, when urban growth made Fortaleza a dominant weight in Ceará's electorate, the bosses were history. The PMDB leaders who began Ceará's electoral revolution implemented policies benefiting ordinary people, and the old bosses suddenly found they could no longer buy enough votes to stay in power.

Sarney became a dominant figure in Maranhão essentially because he was the first politician to improve infrastructure by taking advantage of central government largesse. At the same time, Sarney was never able—perhaps never cared—to eliminate opposition. Though he was the state's most powerful politician, his protégés usually deserted him, and politicians could prosper in opposition. Sarney's margin of preeminence remained slight until he became Tancredo Neves's vice presidential running mate, and then, on Tancredo's death, president. Maranhão's share of central government pork subsequently rose to extremely high levels. Sarney took care of his family politically and got himself elected senator from a neighboring state.

Bahia's Magalhães was far more than a traditional political boss. He dispensed favors, made and broke political careers, and amassed great wealth, but he also modernized Bahia's infrastructure and encouraged industrial growth. ACM had very strong support from the military regime, but his success continued even after the generals withdrew because he had used central government resources to create a political machine based on bureaucratic power. When José Sarney inaugurated the New Republic in 1986, ACM's support was indispensable to Sarney's political survival. Itamar Franco and Fernando Henrique Cardoso found themselves in the same situation of dependence. So ACM's regional influence became national influence, and he remained the most powerful politician in the Brazilian Congress.

Brazil's electoral system, coupled with federalism and the executive authority's long-standing reliance on patronage and pork, produces a very large number of veto players. Part 2 of this book shifts the inquiry to these veto players' ultimate battleground, the arena of executive-legislative relations. The premise of this section is that an excess of veto players, not merely in partisan terms but also in terms of state, municipal, and corporate interests, leads to legislative obstructionism. This obstructionism can have three causes: an excessive number of parties (partisan fragmentation), procedural roadblocks, and a surplus of members with little interest in broad legislation. Chapter 5 investigated deputies' interests and motivations, searching for the determinants of voting patterns in the mix of constituency pressures, ideology, electoral needs, and local interests.

The chapter explored deputies' motivations by modeling voting in the Constituent Assembly of 1987–88 and on President Collor's emergency decrees of 1990. Deputies with more clustered votes tended to be pro-Congress, antiexecutive, supportive of state intervention and welfare, and supportive of popular democracy. These positions, I believe, result from the greater accountability produced by vote clustering. Dominant deputies, by contrast, backed the executive and opposed a stronger Congress, and dominance gave deputies the autonomy to dissent from their parties' mainstreams. The socioeconomic characteristics of constituencies influenced congressional voting only modestly: industrial areas elected more liberal deputies. Overall, however, socioeconomic conditions forged only weak ties between voters and deputies. Brazilian citizens exert pressure for pork-barrel programs but on broader issues have little control over representatives. Ideology played an important role in legislative voting. Former members of the pro-military ARENA party were consistently anti-Congress, proexecutive, and antilabor, and their votes expressed less support for popular democracy.

The most striking finding, without question, was the importance of pork-barrel orientation as a determinant of broader positions. In the Constituent Assembly, deputies could be bought, or at least rented: deputies receiving public works for their bailiwicks were proexecutive, anti-Congress, antilabor, and reluctant to support popular democracy. The importance of direct benefits to deputies speaks volumes about the weakness of the linkage, on issues of national scope, between voters and their representatives.

Chapter 6 focused on a challenge faced by every Brazilian president. Simply posed: how can a president maintain consistent support in the Congress? In some countries, presidents build legislative support by mobilizing citizens to pressure parties and deputies. Such tactics would generate little response in Brazil, because ties among voters, deputies, and parties are so weak. Instead, presidents corral support with political jobs and pork-barrel programs. The most important political jobs are those in the cabinet itself: not only do cabinet members control the distribution of lower-level jobs and municipal-level programs, but they also provide a channel for the representation of party and regional interests. Cabinet appointments, in other words, reassure politicians that their concerns will reach the president's ear.

My examination of the cabinets of Presidents Sarney, Collor, Franco, and Cardoso demonstrated that presidential strategies vary across and within administrations and that cabinet construction, from an outsider's perspective, is not always strategically optimal. Collor, for example, installed a curious mix of friends, technocrats, and politicians without clout. Franco's cabinet included a large component of personal friends, allies who often served the president poorly. In fact, the great success of Itamar's administration, the Plano Real, came only after the president was effectively marginalized by the economic team assembled by Minister Cardoso. Only Sarney, it seems, came close to maximizing each appointment's value.

Chief executives cannot govern without intermediaries with clout in the legislature, so presidents continually face subordinates with their own political agendas. None of Brazil's presidents was immune from the effects of ministers whose personal survival strategies ran counter to those of the chief executive. Collor had to deal with an education minister with gubernatorial ambitions. Franco quarreled with a minister of social well-being. Stories of second-echelon personnel whose policies depart from the interests of their superiors—the so-called principal-agent problem—are commonplace, of course, in every bureaucracy. But in Brazil these disloyalties reduce the efficiency of the distributional policies executives use as the glue of coalitions. Because distributional policies are less efficient, they must be larger. The system, as a result, is even more likely to generate pork at the expense of national-level policies.

Chapter 7 assessed the success of presidential coalition-building strategies by examining the role of legislative party leaders. As in other legislatures, Brazil's party leaders negotiate over the substance of legislation, mediate between deputies and executives, and help distribute pork and jobs to party faithful. The key question at the heart of current debates about Brazilian politics concerns party leaders' authority over their members. Do leaders have authority only on a case-by-case basis, or is their authority absolute over some medium-

or long-term period? The chapter's answer lay in a model of the conditions leading deputies to defect from their party majorities. Applied to Brazil's six major parties in the years between 1991 and 1998, this model of cooperation and defection provides persuasive evidence that party leaders lack the power to compel cooperation. Leadership voting recommendations sometimes yield greater cooperation. But because these recommendations have no more effect on crucial, highly contested votes than on uncontested votes, and because such recommendations have much less influence than constituency characteristics or pork-barrel spending, party leaders ultimately seem impotent.

Deputies who are weak electorally and whose constituencies are geographically concentrated tend to cooperate at higher rates. Electoral weakness, it seems, makes deputies reluctant to surrender the benefits of the party label, because that label defends them against competitors inside and outside their parties. When a deputy's constituents are geographically concentrated, they are more likely to demand results, typically in pork, from their deputies.

Legislative obstructionism stems not just from deputies' motivations but from partisan fragmentation and procedural rules as well. Chapter 8 began with a foray into budget making. The Chamber's budgetary process turned out to be, in Keith Krehbiel's terminology, essentially distributive rather than informational. Some rules governing the distribution of budgetary largesse were crude: the chief beneficiaries of budgetary amendments, for example, were members of the Budget Committee itself. Its senior members did extremely well in pushing through amendments rewarding their bailiwicks. Other rules were more subtle: the Budget Committee, for example, also operated under a norm of intraparty solidarity, rewarding those who did not threaten other members of their parties.

Chapter 8 mapped the policy process through a brief series of legislative histories. The pivot of the investigation, the *colégio de líderes,* seemed to be the single institution capable of reducing the legislature's inevitable tendency toward chaos. It appears, however, that the *colégio* plays this role only under very special circumstances. Coordination by party leaders occurs mainly when issues are unidimensional (another way of saying that compromise is easy), when parties perceive direct interests as parties, and when failure to resolve an issue poses a threat of real electoral losses. Absent these conditions, deputies extract a high price for their support, and interest groups wield influence far out of proportion to their size.

In addition to the dimensionality and the salience to the executive of an issue, what other factors facilitate legislative agreement? The conventional wisdom in Brazil holds that the widespread search for pork hinders policy-making on all kinds of issues. In the sense that deputies fixed on delivering pork may care little about broader legislation, the criticism is correct, for only a minority of legislators participates actively in legislating on broad issues. In addition, the generally poor quality of staff—a function of the deputies' distrust of independent specialists—surely hinders lawmaking. But when each party is coherent and disciplined, a multiparty legislature will have a much more difficult time passing laws. As George Tsebelis (1995) shows, the broader the distribution of views within a party, the wider the range of policy alternatives it finds acceptable and the easier it is to put together a multiparty agreement on policies deviating from the status quo.[3] If each of Brazil's current parties had the discipline and coherence of the PT, the legislative process would truly be chaotic. However, what if pork becomes less available but the rules continue to discourage programmatic parties? Under this scenario, the number of pork-oriented, community-based deputies would decline, and more deputies would rely, by necessity, on ties to "corporativist" organizations—that is, on ties to groups representing quite narrow economic interests. The resulting legislature might well be less obstructionist in the sense of responding to localistic demands, but it would also be more conflictual and less responsive to executive guidance.[4]

II.   The Cost of Brazil's Deadlocked Political Institutions

In Brazil's post-1994 macroeconomic stabilization program, the Plano Real, an overvalued currency always played a central part. By encouraging imports, the strong real kept downward pressure on domestic prices. It drew in foreign capital, helping finance the nation's substantial merchandise trade deficits. The strong real also minimized the impact of the huge fiscal deficits—especially the pension system deficits—of the states and the central government, which amounted in 1998 to more than 7 percent of gross domestic product.

In the absence of a serious attempt at fiscal reform—Cardoso sent no significant tax-reform bills to the Congress during his first term—the stabiliza-

---

3. Tsebelis (1999) shows that the number of important laws passed in different parliamentary systems is an inverse function of the number of parties in government, the ideological distances among them, and the cohesion of each one of them.

4. More abstractly, one might argue that open-list PR, as it functions in Brazil, encourages the development of undisciplined and nonprogrammatic parties both directly, through laws such as those guaranteeing incumbents an automatic place on the ballot, and indirectly, by facilitating the election of deputies who have little interest in strong parties and great interest in pork.

tion scheme could stay afloat only as long as foreign investors maintained their faith in the real. The plan survived the Asian and Russian economic crises of 1997 because the government spent hard currency reserves, cut expenditures, increased taxes, and raised domestic interest rates from about 20 percent to more than 40 percent.[5] These measures, economists predicted, would cut projected growth in 1999 from a bit under 1 percent to −2 percent.[6] Unemployment surpassed 20 percent in 1999 (*Latin American Regional Report* 1999a, 5).

By early 1999 the strong real proved unsustainable. The trigger was a decision by the newly elected governor of Minas Gerais, Itamar Franco (former president and now enemy of Cardoso), to suspend payments on Minas's debts to the central government. The collapse of confidence in Brazil's economic program on the part of foreign investors and speculators was so complete that $200 million per day was flowing out of the country by the middle of January. On January 15 the government belatedly let the currency float. By February 15 the real had moved from 1.30 to 1.98 per dollar. After weeks of negotiation, the administration and the International Monetary Fund concluded a new rescue plan. The accord projected inflation of 16.8 percent, a 3.5–4 percent fall in the gross domestic product, and annual interest rates of 28.8 percent (*Folha de São Paulo,* March 12, 1999).

Although the administration's retreat from tax reform bears part of the blame for the collapse of the stabilization program, the failure to cut expenditures is even more significant. The Cardoso government initially profited from the Asian crisis, using it to pressure the Congress to approve administrative-reform (which ended lifetime tenure for civil servants) and pension-reform proposals. But the measures ultimately passed were too little and too late. Though both reforms had been centerpieces of Cardoso's campaign platform when he won election in 1994, neither became law until 1998, and neither took effect until 1999.

How costly was the long delay in administrative and pension reforms? In the case of administrative reform it is difficult to estimate, because government savings depend on the number of employees ultimately terminated. However, it is illegal for states to spend more than 60 percent of their budgets on personnel.[7] At the end of 1998, seventeen of twenty-seven states, averaging 72 per-

---

5. Reserves fell from $44.28 billion in 1997 to $34.43 billion at the end of 1998 ("International Financial Statistics," CD-ROM. International Monetary Fund 1999).

6. This prediction was made by the economic research institute at the University of São Paulo (FIPE), cited in *Latin American Regional Report* 1999a, 5.

7. This prohibition, approved by the Congress in 1995, is known as the Lei Camata. States that surpass the legal maximum lose central government transfer payments.

cent of all expenditures, passed that limit (Sabino 1999, 46). If the state could simply cut spending to the legal limit, it would save $5 billion. The pension reform finally approved at the beginning of 1999 will reduce the central government's fiscal deficit by somewhat less than 1 percent of gross domestic product annually (*Latin American Regional Report* 1999b, 5). The first version, sent to the legislature in 1995, would have saved substantially more, though no precise estimates exist.[8] Thus the ultimate reform was weak as well as tardy.

Passage of administrative and pension reform took the entire legislative session because of a tactical decision by the executive. In early 1995 the government decided its first priority was a constitutional amendment permitting the president's reelection. During the long negotiations with the Congress over reelection, the process of building a congressional majority for administrative and pension reform came to a complete halt and resumed only after the January 1997 approval of the reelection amendment. In retrospect, of course, the president's priorities proved costly, but his tactics raise more difficult and interesting questions. Why did negotiations on other issues stall while the president constructed his supermajority reelection coalition? Does the ability to seek reelection give a president a substantial bargaining advantage?

Ultimately, only Cardoso can explain his emphasis on reelection at the expense of other reforms.[9] Negotiating all the reforms simultaneously would be possible only if similar coalitions supported all three. If the coalition backing reelection was unrelated to the pension and administrative reform coalitions, then separate deals would be unavoidable.[10] Such seems to have been the case: pension and administrative reform can be seen as tests of support for the Cardoso administration, but reelection had fundamentally different implications.[11] Since the amendment allowed the twenty-seven serving governors to seek reelection, they inevitably became central players in reelection bargaining. Deputies felt the pressure of their governors' interests, but deputies had their own interests as well. Gubernatorial reelection would block some deputies' po-

---

8. After an exhaustive study of the pension reform process, Maria Antonieta Parahyba Leopoldi reached this conclusion, but there were as many estimates of savings in the early version as there were bureaucratic actors involved. Personal communication, March 13, 2000.

9. Thomas Skidmore, a noted Brazilian historian, criticized Cardoso's decision to seek reelection in the strongest possible terms, arguing that it prevented him from consolidating the stabilization program and pushing through a political reform (see Gramacho 1999).

10. Separate deals could be avoided if all inducements were purely individual, e.g., a sum of money to each dissenter. But deputies organized into ad hoc bargaining units, like the rural caucus, which cut across parties. Simultaneous negotiation of all three issues would effectively reward dissenters.

11. I am indebted to Tim Power for help on the reelection issue.

litical ambitions, while other deputies would benefit from their patrons' retaining power.[12]

Having decided to separate reelection from other reforms, the executive then faced the question of sequencing. The president and his advisers may have expected the reforms to require a short negotiation process. The administration could choose to begin with the issue that would take the longest to negotiate. Reelection would be the most expensive in terms of political capital, but, once the amendment passed, the likelihood of the president's reelection would increase his leverage in negotiations over administrative and pension reform. The latter issues could only decrease presidential capital, since they would have short-run electoral costs. In addition, the president's team may have been so doubtful of the success of pension and administrative reform that retaining the presidency for a second term became a necessity.

The negotiations over reelection further demonstrate parties' weakness as bargaining units. The Cardoso administration used every possible weapon to construct its majority: pork-barrel projects, offers of jobs to deputies' allies or relatives, possibly even bribes. Ministers coordinated bargaining with deputies from their parties, but party leaders acted essentially as facilitators, and no collective party goods were exchanged. Everything in these exchanges was reduced to the level of the individual deputy (Rocha 1997, 32–34) or incumbent governor. By contrast, though individual bargains were crucial to consolidating majorities for administrative and pension reform, parties also bargained over substantive concessions in the legislation.

If differences in the composition of supporting coalitions motivated the executive to begin with the reelection amendment, deputies also had good reason to accept this sequencing. One-shot deals were too risky.[13] If all the issues were voted at once, how could deputies hold Cardoso to his commitments?[14] By sep-

---

12. Although party leaders (in formal conversations) seemed convinced that the coalitions supporting administrative and pension reform really differed from the coalition supporting reelection, the Chamber's key roll calls show only small differences, because heavy trading of votes for individual favors reduced opposition from its initial levels.

13. In a logroll among legislators ("I support your project if you support mine"), issues are voted simultaneously precisely because the vote is the only commitment needed. In the present case, however, the president only needs a legislator's vote once, while they need him to release funds over some extended period of time.

14. While serving as finance minister, Cardoso had made a deal with the rural caucus: the government would roll over some rural debts in exchange for support on the Social Emergency Fund. After the vote, Cardoso reneged, but the subsequent Congress forced him to accept the concession. As the epigraph to chapter 8 indicates, deputies were clearly worried about commitments made over the reelection issue.

arating the issues, deputies could force the president to fulfill his commitments before backing him on subsequent issues.

Was reelection worth the trouble? Although most scholars believe that executives are stronger in their initial terms when the possibility exists of a second term, there is little theoretical or empirical evidence of this advantage (Light 1982, Chappell and Keech 1983). If an administration's economic program succeeds, and if deputies foresee the president's reelection, they will understand that better deals cannot be expected by waiting for a new executive. The reelection amendment in Brazil, however, does not merely benefit the president; it also benefits state governors, and their gains in influence inevitably weaken the president.[15]

In terms of Brazil's excess of veto players, what are the implications of executive reelection? The chances of adopting innovative policies—those deviating from the status quo—will improve in a second term only if the president's party becomes so strong that the number of veto players falls.[16] In Brazil such a fall depends on the president's coattails—that is, on the probability that the president's electoral victory will produce a legislative coalition more supportive of the presidential program. Unfortunately, President Cardoso's 1998 reelection strategy suggests that stronger second-term coalitions—coalitions with fewer veto players—will be the exception rather than the rule.

To understand why reelection is unlikely to produce stronger second-term executives, it is important to remember that party alliances vary from state to state. Bitter enemies in one state are allies in another. This pattern of alliances naturally hinders a president's ability to campaign for party allies on a national basis; Cardoso, in fact, hardly participated at all in state-level campaigns. In addition, presidents have powerful incentives to deflect potential challengers toward state-level contests, even if these adversaries could be running against members of the president's own party. Consider Cardoso's tactics in 1998: in Minas Gerais, he remained neutral in the gubernatorial dispute between the incumbent, the PSDB's Eduardo Azeredo, and his PMDB opponent, former president Franco.[17] In São Paulo, Cardoso avoided attacking Paulo Maluf (PPB),

---

15. In a study of Mexican federalism, Diaz-Cayeros (1997, chap. 7) found evidence that in the distribution of federal resources, the number of years left in a state governor's term was directly correlated with the advantages that state could extract from the central government.

16. As of this writing, seven months into Cardoso's second term, a major ministerial reshuffling is in the offing. Cardoso's PSDB wants some of the cabinet posts currently held by the PMDB. Reducing the PMDB's share will hardly strengthen the president's legislative coalition, but the PSDB is betting that FHC's legislative agenda is so slim that the party's 2002 electoral chances are more important (see *Jornal do Brasil,* July 12, 1999, 1, 7).

17. In the struggle for the reelection amendment, Cardoso seems to have promised active support to Franco if he stayed in Minas Gerais.

who was running against PSDB incumbent governor Mário Covas. And in Rio de Janeiro, Cardoso allied with the PFL's candidate against the PSDB's choice. In the end, PSDB candidates lost in Rio and Minas Gerais and won only in São Paulo. With these and other state-level defeats, Cardoso's legislative coalition was weaker in his second term than in his first. The long-term implication of the president's tactic is clear: the weakness of Brazil's parties—and the short time horizons of politicians facing electoral tests—allows presidents to maximize their own fortunes at the expense of their long-term legislative base.[18]

Cardoso's second-term weakness also results from another, chronic difficulty. Executive reelection will produce a "piling up" of strong politicians.[19] If presidential and gubernatorial elections are held simultaneously and reelection is prohibited, powerful governors and other state-level politicians will compete for the presidency. Losers will find themselves unemployed and out of the spotlight for the next four years. When presidential reelection is allowed, however, important politicians will be forced to become (or to remain) governors, and as governors they are well placed to cause serious problems for the president. Stronger governors, seeking to position themselves for the next presidential test, are more likely to mobilize their state congressional delegations and thus more likely to create new legislative veto players.[20]

In the end, presidential reelection is a good example of an institutional change whose effects depend on the overall political context. In a unitary political system, reelection should substantially strengthen presidents. But in Brazil's strong federalism, with powerful governors and with electoral districts coinciding with state boundaries, executive reelection may give the president no advantage at all.[21]

III.   How Should Brazil Reform Its Political Institutions?

For Brazil, a restructuring of federalism might be one avenue for reducing the excess of veto players. Without question, Brazil's federalism is the strongest in Latin America. Constitutionally, Mexico, Argentina, and Venezuela are all federal systems, but only in Brazil can states act so independently of central au-

---

18. Cardoso's tactics begin to resemble those of neopopulists such as Argentina's Carlos Menem (see Weyland 1996b).

19. I am indebted to Tim Power for pointing out this "piling up" effect.

20. It is also possible that governors will be tempted to cause political problems for first-term presidents just to forestall second terms.

21. As the evolution of these rules becomes clear to politicians, any first-term bargaining advantages for presidents may also disappear, because politicians will realize that if they are patient they will soon be facing a weaker executive.

thority. The first Cardoso administration succeeded in reining in some of the worst excesses of state independence—especially governors' ability to force the central government to absorb the debts of state development banks—but states still have far more fiscal privileges than program responsibilities. In early 1999, Minas Gerais's governor, Franco, unilaterally halted debt payments to the central government: the resulting economic crisis triggered the currency devaluation and a recession.[22]

As Eliza Willis, Christopher Garman, and Stephan Haggard (1999, 18) demonstrate, the key to the way federalism functions is the organization of political parties: "When party leaders are organized at the subnational level and occupy positions in subnational government, then national legislators often act as 'delegates' representing subnational interests." This description, of course, fits Brazil precisely, but the relationship has an even stronger causal quality. The creation of strong parties at the national level seems to increase central authority in formerly decentralized systems. Alberto Diaz-Cayeros (1997) shows that in Mexico the foundation of the Revolutionary Institutional Party (PRI) in the 1930s made it possible for Mexico's central authorities to adopt new tax policies facilitating industrialization. The PRI monopolized all channels to higher office in Mexico. Favored politicians could be certain they would face no challengers. Knowing their personal political survival was guaranteed, state politicians accepted federal tax and industrial hegemony. In effect, they traded their states' parochial interests for personal guarantees.

If Brazil is unlikely to transform the formal constitutional basis of federalism, can federalism change de facto if political parties become stronger at the national level? Both publicly and privately, Brazilian political leaders seem quite aware of the need for stronger parties, but concrete proposals usually reflect short-term political calculations more than long-term considerations. In late 1998, for example, leaders of Cardoso's congressional coalition proposed a new rule of party fidelity. By this proposal, deputies failing to vote with their parties would face expulsion.

The government argued that deputies should vote with their parties because nearly all deputies owed their victories to parties.[23] It claimed, in fact, that only

---

22. Most of the decline in Brazilian reserves occurred before Itamar's moratorium. As Celina Souza pointed out (personal communication), Cardoso used the moratorium as political cover for the inevitable devaluation. And since the federal government was legally obligated to halt certain payments to Minas Gerais after the moratorium, its cash flow with the state improved.

23. The government's interest in party discipline is hardly a new phenomenon. Nineteenth-century cabinets, facing Chambers of Deputies in which parties were really collections of personalistic factions, had the same interest in party discipline (see Graham 1990, 160).

13 of Brazil's 513 deputies elected themselves without help from parties.[24] Deputies themselves disagreed. Between 70 and 80 percent of the deputies from the last two legislatures say their election owes nothing to parties and everything to their own efforts (Power 1997b, 198). The government's reasoning was logically flawed as well. Imagine, in São Paulo state, five candidates who expect to collect their votes from electorates that are distinct regionally, occupationally, or ideologically. The five candidates form an electoral alliance and call the alliance a party. With each deputy getting about 200,000 votes, the alliance as a whole garners 1 million votes. Suppose this aggregate vote elects the top three individual vote getters. They win because the system privileges alliances, but their victories have nothing to do with party, at least not in the sense of a party presenting a program voted up or down by an electorate.[25]

As earlier chapters demonstrated, Brazil's deputies elect themselves by their own efforts. During campaigns, leaders contribute almost nothing to candidates. With mandated party loyalty, the backbenchers' reason for existence disappears—they might as well stay home. Once the leadership determines that it has a majority, the minority loses all influence. Interparty caucuses (such as the rural caucus) will be crippled.

Ironically, a rule enforcing party loyalty might worsen the situation of the government if it loses its majority. President Cardoso currently needs the PMDB, PFL, PSDB, and PPB to gain approval for major legislation. Given complete party loyalty, the government wins, without resorting to bargaining, once a majority of each party supports it. But suppose the PMDB, on a given issue, abandons the coalition. Then the government can no longer bargain with PMDB deputies who disagree with the party's dissenting majority. With no PMDB votes, the government always loses.

Part of the weakness of Brazilian parties stems from the absence of linkages between deputies and party leaders. Parties need to grow stronger over the long term, but greater authority at party centers must be accompanied by greater contributions by leaders to backbenchers' career success.[26] Parties with high degrees of discipline, such as those of Argentina and (formerly) Venezuela, need no rules enforcing party loyalty, because deputies know their futures depend on

---

24. The government reasoned that only thirteen deputies had enough votes to reach the electoral quotient without adding votes from any other candidate.

25. It is also possible to imagine a contest with no parties but also with no effective limit on the number of candidates. Since in São Paulo one thousand candidates compete for seventy seats, the vote is naturally pulverized. Almost no one will reach the current electoral quotient. The top seventy candidates would be elected in this partyless system.

26. Democratic parties obviously can be so strong that they become rigid and unresponsive. Venezuela and Colombia are obvious examples (see Coppedge 1994).

the leadership. If a rule of party loyalty is imposed in the absence of strong parties, the consequences will be perverse. Some deputes will simply change parties. Others, dissenters who can find no new party to join, will leave the Congress. Turnover rates will increase, because local voters want deputies who can bring pork back to their bailiwicks. Voters are unlikely to understand that party loyalty has eliminated pork-barrel bargaining, so they will elect someone who promises to do more for the bailiwick. All these consequences have parallel results: Congress will be a less attractive stop in a political career.

What political reforms have a better chance of strengthening parties to reduce the number of veto players but still preserve meaningful legislative careers? Chapter 1 showed that open-list PR can be compatible with strong parties. In pre-1973 Chile, for example, parties were strong because states were weak units of government and because national party leaders controlled nominations for legislative slates. In Brazil, however, it is hard to imagine state leaders offering to abrogate state authority, and national party leaders seem to be getting weaker rather than stronger. One small but possibly significant reform would be the elimination of two-round presidential elections. As Mark P. Jones (1994) shows, two-round elections preserve small parties. Though small parties finish far back in the first round, they survive by trading second-round support to one of the two leading candidates. Making the election into a one-round plurality affair would cause many small parties to be absorbed by their larger brethren.

Public campaign financing can also contribute to reducing party numbers. If candidates can be prohibited from spending their own funds, and if national parties allocate public funding to backbenchers' campaigns, the latter will actually owe something to the former. The question is whether candidates can be prevented from tapping private sources of campaign finance. Optimism may be warranted here, because in recent years the Brazilian press has developed a significant investigative capacity. Along with nongovernmental organizations, the press can be counted on to police campaign-finance regulations. At the same time, public financing schemes tend to favor already strong parties.

The reform most often considered involves the adoption of a German-style mixed electoral regime, a two-ballot system combining single-member districts (SMDs) with closed-list PR. The list of countries that have recently adopted such systems is impressive: Russia, Hungary, Japan, Italy, New Zealand, Croatia, Georgia, Lithuania, Ukraine, Bolivia, and Venezuela. As Regina Smyth (1998) shows, these German-type systems vary enormously in key features, including the ratio of plurality to PR seats, the linkage mechanism between the two elections, the requirement of party membership, the ability of candidates to run in one or both races, the threshold for party representation, and the average district magnitude. Broadly, the differences among these new systems stem partly from the motivations for their original adoption. New Zealand's political leaders expected the mixed system to increase minority representation (Denemark 1996). Italian politicians sought to decrease party fractionalization and increase governmental stability (Morlino 1996). Japan's goal was fighting corruption (Seligman 1997).

In theory, district elections should tend toward two-party contests, and SMD representatives should be more attentive to local interests. Candidates on the closed-list side will focus on party building, stressing policy rather than pork. However, seemingly minor differences between these systems strongly affect the leaders' ability to constrain followers and followers' willingness to cooperate in party building (Smyth 1998, 5). If the rules allow candidates to compete simultaneously in a district and on a party list, the costs of running shrink, and candidates with little chance will run on the district side. Rather than converging, on the district side, toward a race between two moderates (à la Duverger), multiple candidates will fragment the electorate and focus on discrete groups of voters. Other factors also encourage multiple entry, including two typical of Brazil: high district magnitude and regional (rather than national) lists.[27] In Brazil, in other words, a mixed system might yield district representatives with the same vices as the current open-list PR system.

Mixed systems link the plurality and proportional races. In some cases (including Germany itself), the PR contest determines the overall party distribution of seats. As Smyth (1998, 17) puts it, "Candidates with resources invest in party organization to maximize their goals." Where the two races are not linked, as in Russia and Ukraine, "Resource-rich candidates with career ambitions may chose to specialize in either SMD or PR in order to maintain maximum autonomy in the future."

Although only the German case has existed long enough to offer confidence about its long-run tendencies, mixed systems seem to produce mixed results. Smyth (1998) notes that parties have proliferated, not consolidated, under Italy's mixed system. Japan's Liberal Democratic Party has done well in plurality races but poorly on the list side. Neither Russia nor Ukraine shows much progress in consolidating along programmatic lines.

What can be learned from the adoption of mixed systems in the two Latin American cases, Bolivia and Venezuela?[28] Bolivia's mixed system, which has

27. This section is heavily indebted to the pioneering analysis of Smyth (1998).
28. Even though Mexican voters cast only one ballot, for the single-member district, their

been in effect for only one election, splits the Congress almost evenly between single-member districts and PR seats, with the latter distributed (as in Germany) to compensate for disproportionalities in the SMDs. A national threshold of 3 percent serves as the minimum for PR. Because candidates may run in both SMD and PR elections, the system should not dramatically reduce fragmentation. Voters cast two ballots, but the ballot for president, vice president, and senator is "fused" with the proportional ballot for the lower chamber of the legislature. In principle, the fused ballot should itself reduce party fragmentation, because the coattails of the leading presidential candidates should strengthen their parties' legislative contingents. In practice, however, Bolivia's fused ballot is unlikely to reduce fragmentation: unless one candidate wins an absolute majority of the popular vote, the Congress chooses the president from between the top two vote getters. Small parties have an incentive to enter the race and negotiate their support with the leading candidates before the second round. The 1997 election results confirm this possibility. No party received even one-quarter of all the votes, but five parties pulled in at least 16 percent.

Venezuela adopted its version of the mixed electoral system in 1993 and has now utilized the system for two elections. Half the seats are allocated to single-member districts and half to closed-list proportional slates. Compensation—adjusting the deputies elected on proportional lists for the single-member seats won—is carried out at the state level. Candidates may run on both the SMD and proportional sides. Party leaders at the national level exercise a great deal of influence over nominations for the closed proportional slate (Crisp 1998, 5).[29]

Venezuela's reforms essentially sought to open up the political system rather than strengthen parties. The excessive centralization of Venezuela's traditional parties, Acción Democratica and COPEI, had created what Michael Coppedge (1994) calls a "partidocracia," a system in which party domination led ordinary citizens to feel totally excluded from political life. Uninominal district elections were the key element of electoral reform for Venezuela. These districts, it was hoped, would send deputies to the legislature who would be more independent of party leaders and more responsive to local interests.[30]

Though the Venezuelan system is still evolving, district deputies already seem to have somewhat different orientations from list deputies. Michael Kul-

---

votes affect the national proportional outcome, so Mexico in this sense has a mixed system as well (see Nacif 2000).

29. In Acción Democratica's case, regulations adopted in 1998 gave the party's national executive council the right to name all the candidates for state and national legislative seats. COPEI allows two-thirds of its PR candidates to be nominated by regional and local leaders (Crisp 1998, 5).

30. In Germany, Lancaster and Patterson (1990) found evidence that district representatives were more responsive to local interests than were representatives from the closed-list slate.

isheck (1999a, 25) found district deputies more likely than PR deputies to believe they respond more to state and local issues and interests and less to party leaders. District deputies also think they promote projects benefiting their constituents more often than do PR deputies. But party discipline did not drop among the major parties, Acción Democratica and COPEI, after the advent of the new system. Contrary to reformers' hopes, district deputies tend not to cultivate ties with new state and local interests (such as neighborhood associations or environmental groups). Rather, such deputies build ties with long-standing interests such as business and organized labor. Kulisheck speculates that the electoral insecurity of district deputies, who cannot rely on strong party organizations to guarantee their reelection (especially in the case of representatives from the newer, more decentralized parties), pushes them to rely on established interest organizations (1999b, 21). In the presence of centralized parties with strong linkages to established organizations, mixed systems are likely to have less effect on deputy behavior than they would in a weak party system, and even deputies with incentives to cultivate a personal vote will seek the security of alliances with established interests.

Venezuela's dominant parties suffered sharp losses in their vote and seat shares in the past two elections, but most scholars believe these losses, and the resulting fragmentation, would have occurred even in the absence of a new electoral system. The two established parties were expected to do well in the single-member district elections as a result of their widespread organizational advantages, but Acción Democratica and COPEI lost vote share on both sides of the ballot. The Venezuelan experience—especially in the light of Chavez's overwhelming victory in the elections for the new constitutional assembly—proves that institutional reforms may only marginally affect a party system already in an advanced state of decay.

In March 1999, Brazilian politicians seemed to be getting serious about a mixed electoral system. The main parties of the governing coalition, especially the PSDB, the PMDB, and the PFL, proposed a four-part program of political reform.[31] One element called for rules of party fidelity, but, in a nice watering down, each party could determine how and when to apply the rule. Another element of the reform called for strengthening parties by adopting a mixed electoral system, with half districts and half proportional representation. But in the kind of delicious irony possible only in Brazil, the proportional side—often blamed for personalizing politics—would continue to utilize open lists. Since,

---

31. The original proposal also established a 5 percent threshold of votes in the whole country (distributed in nine states), the end of alliances in proportional elections, and a minimum of three years in a party before running for office under that party's label (see Seabra 1999).

as demonstrated earlier, many current deputies already campaign in de facto districts, and since district seats are expected to strengthen not parties but ties with local communities, I leave it to the reader to judge this proposal's party-strengthening qualities.

IV.   Brazil and the Study of Comparative Politics

Substantive Implications

R. Kent Weaver and Bert A. Rockman's (1993) study of institutions and policy outcomes offers a useful comparison to this examination of Brazil, particularly in view of the oft-debated consequences of such "first-tier" regime characteristics as presidentialism and parliamentarism. Comparing seven countries (the United States, United Kingdom, Canada, Germany, France, Japan, and Sweden) on a variety of policy dimensions, Weaver and Rockman found that individual institutional characteristics rarely are the sole determinants of policy outcomes. Still, regime types do create different levels of risk and opportunity in relation to various government capabilities. Separation-of-powers regimes (the United States and Brazil) are at great risk in terms of a series of government capabilities: policy innovation, loss imposition, priority setting, resource targeting, coordination of conflicting objectives, and policy implementation. Such regimes are likely to be better at other capabilities: representing diffuse interests, managing societal cleavages, and maintaining policy stability (448). Unfortunately for Brazil, however, its social cleavage structure would be simple were it not for the regional disputes that are magnified by Brazilian federalism, and the maintenance of policy stability is likely to be a goal only for privileged groups, including politicians themselves.

Weaver and Rockman find that institutional effects on government capabilities work through governmental decision-making characteristics. Stability of decision-making elites, for example, helps ensure that policies will be carried out. The U.S. Congress is very stable, because campaign-finance laws favor incumbents and because seniority rules enhance prospects for continuity in committee leadership positions. In Brazil, by contrast, the Congress is quite unstable: roughly 50 percent of the members in every session are beginners, and the Congress's internal rules inhibit the development of specialized committee expertise.[32]

---

32. The Congress's internal rules prohibit committee chairs from serving more than two years, and chairs cannot be reelected.

Brazil's electoral system is likely to produce presidents without strong legislative backing. Divided government in the United States at times produces stalemate but at other times produces a politics of "bidding up," as in the case of ever-more-generous tax cuts. Stalemate can occur in the U.S. system when the ideological differences between the executive and legislative branches are high and when money is scarce (Weaver and Rockman 1993, 452; Mayhew 1991). Interbranch ideological differences in Brazil are rarely enormous, and the executive has moved policy along through generous use of pork-barrel programs and political jobs. If the current program of neoliberal state shrinking continues, however, the availability of both pork and jobs will decline. The consequences include a greater likelihood of stalemate.

Governments tend to develop mechanisms counteracting the effects of certain institutional characteristics (Mayer 1995). "Fast track" laws in the United States enable the Congress to limit its congenital tendency to represent multiple veto points in trade legislation. The Brazilian Congress has allowed its presidents to use emergency decrees as ways of getting around legislative obstructions as well, but this "work around" is a poor solution. Emergency decrees may be useful for dealing with economic crises, but they cannot be used to resolve complicated questions such as interministerial budgetary allocations. They short-circuit the conflict-management process that should be occurring in the legislature and create a sense of marginality that over the long run weakens the Congress.

In the end, evaluation of a nation's political institutions depends on one's view of the status quo. Brazil's institutions guarantee a multiplicity of veto players. The result is policy stability. If you like the status quo, stability is a good result. If not, stability is a problem. Policy stability locks the overwhelming majority of Brazilians into poverty.

Methodological Implications

Brazil's political institutions constitute, ultimately, a single case. Can the study of a single case aspire to scientific status within "comparative" politics? In his monograph on the politics of coffee, Robert Bates (1997, 165) recalls that Gary King, Robert O. Keohane, and Sidney Verba, in their text on comparative political methodology, advise scholars to "pick our cases with care, so that we might efficiently extract the information available and do so with a minimum of bias." For a study of Brazilian politics, just as in Bates's treatise on coffee, this advice is not very helpful, because the case itself is the object of interest.

One solution (also adopted by Bates) is the utilization of theory developed in other settings. The chapter on campaign strategies introduced arguments based on the pork-barrel propensities of politicians with varying electoral bases. Ironically, the Brazilian case offered the rare opportunity to test what students of American politics take as a given—that is, the idea that politicians distribute more pork in single-member districts than in multimember districts. In the analysis of legislative voting, theories about conditional party loyalty, once again based on the U.S. Congress, guided the investigation of party discipline. In the end, the model developed to explain Brazilian party discipline broadened extant theory by building in measures of constituency characteristics and electoral security.

A second solution to the single-case problem flowed from our ability to disaggregate across both time and space. Electoral results spanning contests from 1978 to 1994 provide a sound basis for confidence in arguments about the interactive effects of demographic and socioeconomic change in the context of increasingly sophisticated politicians. Focused comparisons of states at similar economic levels—but with very different political traditions—illuminate the effects of chance political events on long-term political trajectories. And combining information about individual deputies, both biographical and electoral, with information about individual parties' legislative voting recommendations enabled the separation of the real power of party leaders from other influences on deputies' behavior.

Ultimately, the reader will decide the scientific value of this study. I believe that comparativists too often suffer from an inferiority complex, feeling compelled to demonstrate the relevance of our work for those with no interest in our cases per se. Students of American politics seem immune from this disease, though their work frequently takes the U.S. case not just as the center of the universe but as the universe itself. On the evidence of this book, perhaps the Americanists are right. Even though what Americanists call *theory* often comes from the study of a single case, that theory can often be applied profitably to Brazil. In the same way, the relevance of Brazilian politics to the interests of other political scientists may be most efficiently grasped by its potential consumers rather than by its producers.

An Agenda for the Future

When I began this project, in the early 1990s, few studies on Latin American politics relied heavily either on statistical methods or on rational choice theory. Critics of "rat choice," moreover, harped on its ideological conservatism. By the close of the decade, rational choice had shed the ideological critique, and both formal theoretical approaches and careful applications of quantitative methods had become quite common. In part these shifts reflect improved training in theory and quantitative methods afforded to graduate students in both the United States and Latin America as well as the broad democratic opening of Latin America in the 1980s and 1990s.

Democracy implies openness. With openness comes greater access to information. All over the region, Latin American governments are making such information as electoral results, budgetary reports, and congressional votes easy to obtain, often via the Internet. With so much information available so easily, scholars everywhere are solving empirical puzzles they could once only imagine.

Democracy also implies formal institutions. In the heyday of bureaucratic authoritarianism, elections and legislatures either existed simply as facades or ceased to exist altogether. By the close of the 1990s, not only were formal institutions of obvious importance, but significant institutional reforms were almost commonplace. Natural experiments, involving before-and-after comparisons, were suddenly available.

Where do we go from here? The institutional analysis undertaken in this book obviously can be extended to other settings. In Mexico, where single-party dominance seems to be reaching its limits, legislative research is likely to burgeon. But legislative studies will soon come up against the fact that most active Latin American parliaments are very young. The extended time series that enable U.S. researchers to evaluate multidecade statistical models of committee behavior are simply not feasible for Latin America in the near future. While electoral and legislative studies will remain profitable areas of scholarly endeavor, it is necessary to explore new kinds of institutional puzzles.

Latin Americanists have traditionally paid little attention to bureaucracies, judicial systems, and state-level politics, but in the era of neoliberal state shrinking, all three are likely to increase in importance. To some degree, institutional scholars have focused on elections and legislatures because they are easy to study. Research on bureaucracies and on judicial systems is much harder.[33] Basic descriptive work is still needed, and much of it will have to be done by Latin American scholars themselves. Research on state politics has been neglected in part because of a certain prejudice, particularly on the part of indigenous scholars, against fieldwork outside the dominant cities. Still, state-level comparisons (mainly relevant in larger countries, of course) offer the advantage of holding

---

33. On bureaucracy, see Schneider 1991; on judicial systems, see Wilson and Handberg 1998.

the national political culture constant. In countries such as Argentina, provincial electoral systems themselves vary, while Brazilian states offer a perfect laboratory for the study of gubernatorial-legislative relations.

The issue of the relationship between institutions and equality still remains open for Latin America as a whole. Such policies as the reform of pension systems or the distribution of government spending across levels of education are ripe for comparative institutional analysis. While no single research question is likely to determine definitively which institutional forms magnify or dampen inequality, investigations into individual policy areas might well be profitable steps in advancing the debate.

The future research agenda should also include explorations of the founding of institutions themselves. Constitutional overhauls in Bolivia, Brazil, Colombia, and Venezuela (twice) provide more than an opportunity for before-and-after comparisons. Such reforms also offer the chance to examine these institutions' founding moments. What kinds of interests were at play? What sorts of consequences were anticipated, what sorts unexpected? Did the experiences of earlier reformers, especially in Latin America, affect those coming later?

For Latin America as a whole, institutional scholars still lack a convincing response to Weaver and Rockman's question, "Do Institutions Matter?" I suspect we will come to agree with Dieter Nohlen (Lamounier and Nohlen 1993, 145): institutions do count, but no monocausal theories are possible. Other variables beyond institutional ones must always be taken into consideration, and cause-effect relationships are not unidirectional but circular. In this book, demographic and economic conditions, along with chance historical events, are part of the story. But in the end, Brazil's political institutions not only matter a great deal but are at the heart of the nation's crisis of governability.

Appendix A

The Map and Moran's I

State road maps, a digitizing table, and Autocad were used to construct the computerized maps. The geographic information systems database also includes, in addition to electoral results, social and economic indicators from the 1980 census, all budgetary amendments offered for the 1989–91 budgets, and the results of the 1989 presidential election. The nearest-neighbor matrices used to calculate Moran's I derived from the map coordinates. Paul Sampson of the University of Washington provided the program creating these matrices. For an introduction to spatial analysis, see Cliff et al. (1975). The Brazilian census agency has now produced publicly available coordinates for all national municipalities.

The tendency for municipalities to subdivide, a tendency frequently influenced by purely political considerations, seriously complicates mapping. Since the census data are based on 1980 borders, municipalities created after that date had to be aggregated into old ones. In some cases, the number of new units was so great that aggregation distorted political events. In other cases, old states were compromised by the creation of new states. As a result, the analysis excludes Goiás, Tocantins, Mato Grosso, Mato Grosso do Sul, Acre, Amapá, Rondônia, and Roraima. Although malapportionment gives these states considerable political force, most have very small populations.

Appendix B

Data Sources and Problems

Budgetary Amendments

Each year the Joint Commission on the Budget publishes the amendments of deputies and senators (Brazil, Congresso Nacional 1988–92). Members used to submit these amendments on small cards, roughly two by six inches, and the published volumes contained photographic images of these cards, many of them handwritten. Each card contained the name and state of the deputy or senator, the program modified, the municipality benefited, the amount of money, and the program debited to finance the amendment. I coded all amendments in 1990 and 1991 but only a sample of the 72,672 amendments made in 1992. This analysis does not utilize the 1992 group, because members of the new 1991–94 Chamber offered these amendments. The analysis also excludes amendments (roughly 1 percent) benefiting no particular municipality. After 1993 the process changed, as the text details. I offer my thanks to Orlando de Assis and Carmen Pérez for help in obtaining the 1991 amendments.

The Electoral Results

For 1978 and 1982, the electoral results came from PRODASEN, the Senate's data-processing arm. I thank Jalles Marquess and William for their help. For 1986 the Tribunal Superior Eleitoral provided some data, but eight states never sent election results to Brasília. I copied results at the regional tribunals in these states. For the 1990 election, the Tribunal, with the assistance of Roberto Siqueira, Sérgio, Flávio Antônio, Conceição, and Nelson, supplied data on diskette for fifteen states. Manuel Caetano in Porto Alegre helped with the results from Rio Grande do Sul. Current election results are readily available, usually through the Internet, from the Tribunal Superior Eleitoral's website.

The Constituent Assembly Voting Database

Constituent Assembly Issue Scales

The National Constituent Assembly (ANC) was inaugurated on February 1, 1987, with the intent of promulgating a new federal constitution no later than December of that year. In the early months of the ANC, legislators worked exclusively in thematic committees charged with drafting the various chapters of the future constitution. These chapters went to the powerful central drafting committee (Comissão de Sistematização, or CS), responsible for putting them together into the first draft. Then, according to the initial plan, the ANC would meet on the floor and vote each article one by one, presenting amendments as necessary, until the draft was hammered into an acceptable constitution.

The CS draft was made public in July 1987. It was popularly referred to as the Projeto Cabral, after Deputy Bernardo Cabral, the reporting officer of the ANC. The CS draft was rejected by large segments of the ANC's centrist and conservative forces, which viewed the draft as excessively left wing and statist. They also resented the concentration of power in the CS, which was dominated by the progressive wing of the PMDB. Upon the release of the CS draft in mid-1987, the Center and Right began to realize how difficult it would be to alter the proposed constitution. The ANC rules (*Regimento Interno*) stipulated that to amend or remove any item of the CS draft, it would be necessary to muster an absolute majority, or 280 votes. The PMDB's progressive wing thought these rules necessary to protect the CS draft's integrity.

In the second half of 1987, the forces opposed to the CS draft organized themselves as the so-called Centrão. The Centrão's initial raison d'être was to alter the ANC rules to make it easier to modify the CS draft. On December 3, 1987, after a protracted struggle, the Centrão won the fight, altering the rules in a way that significantly reduced the power of the progressive minority. Instead of requiring 280 votes to remove an item from the draft, the Centrão instituted a rule by which 280 votes would be needed to maintain a given item in the draft. Thus, the burden of mustering votes was shifted to the partisans of the CS draft, who were clearly in the minority.

The modification of the rules paved the way for the Centrão's most important victory, the approval of its own draft of the future constitution. Thus, the CS draft was supplanted by a more conservative version (published in its entirety in the *Estado de São Paulo,* January 12, 1988, 36–41). The new draft was known euphemistically as the substitute (*substitutivo*). I will refer to it here as the Centrão draft.

The main problem caused by the Centrão's victory was that the members of the ANC had already drafted thousands of amendments to the older CS draft. What would happen to these amendments? To avoid starting again at square one, the leadership patched together an agreement whereby amendments could be presented to either of the competing drafts of the constitution. This agreement was inventive, though dubiously grounded in parliamentary procedure. The victorious Centrão draft continued as the "texto-base," or the official draft-in-progress, but amendments could still be presented to the CS draft provided that they were appropriate and did not contradict other victorious amendments.

The amendments were considered in two rounds of roll-call voting. In each round (*turno*), each successive chapter and title of the draft was considered in order, starting with the preamble and ending with the Transitional Articles (*Ato das Disposições Constitucionais Transitórias*). Upon presentation on the floor, each amendment was read aloud by Ulysses Guimarães (president of the ANC), received a nonbinding opinion from Bernardo Cabral, and was then debated. Party leaders laid out the official party positions in debate. Then, finally, the 559 members voted the amendment. The first round of voting (732 votes) consumed five months, January 28–July 1, 1988. This round transformed Projeto A (the CS draft, modified entirely by the Centrão) into Projeto B.

The voting process was then repeated. After the July recess, Projeto B was subjected to a top-to-bottom review in the second round of voting. The second round (289 votes) extended from July 29 to September 2, 1988, and produced the final constitution. The 1,021 votes across both rounds of voting comprise the data file utilized here.

Congressional Power Scale

Vote 0272: March 16, 1988. Establishes selection procedure for the members of the Tribunal de Contas da União (TCU), which verifies government accounts. The CS had two-thirds of TCU members elected by Congress and the remaining third nominated by the executive branch and subject to Senate approval. In this amendment, Deputy Adhemar de Barros Filho wanted the Congress to choose all of the TCU members, via secret vote. Yes is for Adhemar's strengthening of Congress. Yes 194, no 141, defeated.

Vote 0274: March 17, 1988. Amendment making Congress the only power able to authorize the purchase of rural real estate by foreign corporations. Yes gives this power exclusively to Congress. Yes 266, no 89, defeated.

Vote 0277: March 17, 1988. Transfers Senate oversight powers on foreign economic policy and foreign debt to the Congress as a whole. Yes is for giving these powers to the Congress, no is for keeping them in the domain of the Senate. Yes 138, no 312, defeated.

Vote 0279: March 17, 1988. The CS had provided that normal congressional decisions could be taken by a simple majority of the members present, as long as the simple majority was greater than or equal to one-fifth of the total membership. The Centrão changed this provision, requiring an absolute majority. This amendment sought a return to the CS language. Yes is for the CS scheme, no is for the Centrão scheme. Yes 197, no 238, defeated.

Vote 0290: March 18, 1988. Deputy Francisco Kuster wanted to move up the beginning of the legislative session from February 15 to February 1 and have the Congress meet during the second half of August. The congressional recess each year would therefore be reduced from three months to two months. Yes is for his idea. Yes 133, no 280, defeated.

Vote 0315: March 23, 1988. This amendment, known as the Humberto Lucena amendment, was very important. It removed the CS option for parliamentarism and introduced a presidentialist system of government into the text. This was the only time during the ANC that all 559 delegates voted. Yes is for presidentialism, no is for parliamentarism. Yes 344, no 212, approved.

Vote 0354: April 7, 1988. Nelson Jobim sought to institute new rules for the selection of the highest appeals court. Four would be nominated by the president, four by the Camara, and three by the supreme court itself. The nominees would face public confirmation hearings (like the U.S. Senate) and would need to win two-thirds approval from the senators. Yes is for Jobim's suggested procedure. Yes 196, no 232, defeated.

Vote 0471: April 21, 1988. Changes language concerning the budget authorization law, adding two elements: Congress would require details on outlays of capital, and the executive would be required to submit bimonthly reports on the implementation of the budget. Yes is for increased congressional oversight of the federal budget. Yes 312, no 83, approved.

Vote 0477: April 22, 1988. Would require the Congress to approve the federal budget. If the budget were not approved by the end of the legislative session, the president would be able to implement it by decree. Provides that the legislative session will not end until the budget is approved. Yes is for increased efficiency in producing and implementing the budget. Yes 275, no 96, defeated.

Support for Executive

Vote 0005: January 28, 1988. Rewords the preamble. Centrão's new version removes CS allusions to direct democracy. Yes means adopt the new preamble, no means maintain CS. Yes 248, no 227, defeated.

Vote 0624: June 3, 1988. Provides a five-year term for the incumbent president, José Sarney. Yes 328, no 222, approved.

Vote 0320: March 23, 1988. This amendment gives a five-year mandate to future presidents. While not formally affecting Sarney himself, it was an important victory for his strategy of winning a five-year term for himself. Yes is for five years, no is for four years. Yes 304, no 223, approved.

Vote 0965: August 31, 1988. Addresses the question of whether runoff elections for mayor would take effect for the first time in 1988. Yes means suspend runoffs this year, no means maintain them. Yes 293, no 221, approved.

Vote 0633: June 15, 1988. Deputy Rosa Prata moves to postpone the municipal elections scheduled for 1988. Yes 111, no 347, defeated.

Economic Conservatism

Vote 0048: February 10, 1988. Centrão amendment on the right to property removes language whereby the right to private property is subject to owner's observance of its "social function." Yes supports Centrão's trying to kill this language. Yes 236, no 248, defeated.

Vote 0090: February 24, 1988. Two dozen amendments to the Centrão version of the chapter on social rights. The chapter would now protect workers against arbitrary dismissal by their employers but leaves the details up to further legislation. Yes is for Centrão's compromise accord on the chapter, no is to vote with the leftist parties not in the accord. Yes 373, no 151, approved.

Vote 0785: August 17, 1988. On the right to strike. Suppresses language giving workers competence to decide when they should strike. Yes removes the language, no maintains it. Yes 112, no 287, defeated.

Vote 0485: April 27, 1988. An attempt to approve the Centrão's version of Title VIII, Chap. I, the Economic and Social Order, so that the ANC could move on. An interparty accord to approve the Centrão's draft (chapter by chapter) temporarily failed at this point because of controversy over the definition of *national firm*. Yes is for the Centrão's version, no supports the CS version, which had been criticized as nationalist and xenophobic. Yes 210, no 279: The amendment was neither approved nor rejected. The next day, after a new accord, it was approved.

Vote 0131: March 1, 1988. According to this amendment by Deputy Cid Saboia, if someone fires an employee unjustly and for any reason that employee cannot return to work immediately, then the worker will receive an indemnity from the unfair employer, as provided for by further legislation. Yes is for the indemnity. Yes 147, no 213, defeated.

Vote 0102: February 25, 1988. Amendment by Deputy Antonio Perosa that adapts CS text, retaining a six-hour day for workers in continuous duties but adding the phrase "except as provided for by collective bargaining." Yes is for the amendment, which was supported by the Left. Yes 324, no 125, approved.

Vote 0136: March 2, 1988. Confirms that only one union should represent each sector of workers. Yes is for union monopoly, no is for plurality. Yes 340, no 103, approved.

Vote 0943: August 30, 1988. An amendment by Deputy Nelson Jobim on the legality of expropriating productive land for agrarian reform. Yes says it is possible to expropriate productive land. Yes 186, no 233, defeated.

Democratic Values

Vote 0061: February 11, 1988. Institutes collective writ of mandamus (permits class-action suits). Yes is for writ of mandamus. Yes 326, no 103, approved.

Vote 0149: March 3, 1988. Direct democracy, or "popular sovereignty." Provides for referenda, plebiscites, peoples' initiatives, and peoples' veto. Yes is for these measures of direct democracy. Yes 360, no 89, approved. (The people's veto was later struck down in the second round of voting.)

Vote 0291: March 18, 1988. This amendment tries to put certain elements of the *Regimento Interno* into the constitutional text, including proportionality of party representation on the leadership (known as the *mesa*) and in committees, and the responsibilities of committees. Yes puts these provisions into the text. Yes 334, no 67, approved.

Vote 0402: April 13, 1988. This amendment would prohibit the military from intervening to maintain internal order. Yes is for such a prohibition. Yes 102, no 326, defeated.

Vote 0756: August 10, 1988. Allows death penalty. Yes 93, no 289, defeated.

Vote 0959: August 31, 1988. Whether censorship is disallowed for artistic as well as political and ideological reasons. Amendment made by a deputy who was also an evangelical minister. Yes says censorship is only outlawed for political reasons, no says it is also prohibited on artistic grounds. Yes 98, no 325, defeated.

Collor's Emergency Decrees

150: Reorganizes executive branch of government. Eliminates ministries of science and technology, development, industry and commerce, transportation, mines, and energy. Creates a new superministry of the economy. Moves other programs to new ministries.

151: Reorganizes executive branch. Eliminates a series of autarchic entities.

154: Establishes a new system of adjustments for prices and salaries. Creates three readjustment groups: 1–3 minimum salaries, 3–20 minimum salaries, 20+ minimum salaries. Salaries of 20+ group are subject to free negotiation.

155: Creates the National Privatization Program.

159: Creates a disciplinary code for civil servants.

161: Modifies income tax, eliminates certain regional subsidies and incentives.

168: Confiscates a substantial part of private savings for eighteen months.

185: Regulates the right to strike and government intervention in strike activity.

Appendix D

Cooperation and Defection among Deputies

D1.   Cooperation and Defection among PFL Deputies, 1991–98

Dependent Variable: Cooperation with Party Majority (absentees excluded)

Variable	Unstandardized Parameter Estimate and Probability Level	Standard Error	Standardized Estimate	Odds Ratio
Cardoso administration (1995–98)	.7123***	.1530	.0955	2.039
Contested party recommendation	.3374*	.1424	.0518	1.401
Uncontested party recommendation	.3792***	.1148	.0658	1.461
Share of pork disbursements	.1134	.0908	.2231	1.120
Rank in postelection list	1.0978***	.3265	.0974	2.998
Share of total party vote	−1.7189	2.0150	−0.0188	.179
Dominance of key municipalities	2.4470***	.7104	.1087	11.554
Concentration of vote	−0.0209	.0293	−0.0480	.979
Concentration × Rank in list	−0.0074	.0301	−0.0091	.993
Concentration × Terms served	.0090	.0062	.0568	1.009
Concentration × Dominance	−0.1494	.0826	−0.1080	.861
Ideology	.2195*	.0994	.048983	1.245
Terms served	.0217	.0585	.0113	1.022
Local political career	−0.3829**	.1287	−0.0610	.682
Governor from same party	−0.7149***	.1499	−0.1313	.489
Incumbent seeking reelection	1.17019***	.1458	.1688	3.222

-2 log likelihood = 2864.1
Model chi-squared = 4990.6 $p < .0001$
Correctly predicted = 65.3%
$N = 10{,}626$
$R^2 = .3748$ Max-rescaled $R^2 = .7173$

*$p < .05$ **$p < .01$ ***$p < .001$

D2. Cooperation and Defection among PMDB Deputies, 1991–98

Dependent Variable: Cooperation with Party Majority (absentees excluded)

Variable	Unstandardized Parameter Estimate and Probability Level	Standard Error	Standardized Estimate	Odds Ratio
Cardoso administration (1995–98)	−0.4333*	.1926	−0.0578	.648
Contested party recommendation	.1420	.1462	.0223	1.153
Uncontested party recommendation	.1427	.1263	.0247	1.153
Share of pork disbursements	.5427***	.0867	.1234	1.721
Rank in postelection list	.3045	.3757	.0309	1.356
Share of total party vote	−4.2542***	1.0142	−0.0960	.014
Dominance of key municipalities	2.1994*	.9468	.0860	9.019
Concentration of vote	.1714***	.0322	.4191	1.187
Concentration × Rank in list	−0.0486	.0368	−0.0768	.953
Concentration × Terms served	.004293	.0112	.025358	1.004
Concentration × Dominance	−0.5651***	.0864	−0.4318	.568
Ideology	−0.0979	.1075	−0.0220	.907
Terms served	−0.0208	.1010	−0.0074	.979
Local political career	.0709	.1316	.0131	1.073
Governor from same party	.5212***	.1405	.0910	1.684
Incumbent seeking reelection	.6612***	.1220	.1138	1.937

−2 log likelihood = 2217.0
Model chi-squared = 1419.8 $p < .0001$
Correctly predicted = 65.7%
$N = 11,471$
$R^2 = .1164$ Max-rescaled $R^2 = .4285$

*$p < .05$ **$p < .01$ ***$p < .001$

301

D3. Cooperation and Defection among PSDB Deputies, 1991–98

Dependent Variable: Cooperation with Party Majority (absentees excluded)

Variable	Unstandardized Parameter Estimate and Probability Level	Standard Error	Standardized Estimate	Odds Ratio
Cardoso administration (1995–98)	−0.0455	.2397	−0.0043	.956
Contested party recommendation	.1154	.1732	.0163	1.122
Uncontested party recommendation	.3779**	.1368	.0631	1.459
Share of pork disbursements	.2492*	.1090	.0526	1.283
Rank in postelection list	3.0055***	.3256	.3599	20.197
Share of total party vote	4.9735*	2.1542	.0711	144.5
Dominance of key municipalities	−0.7839	.9498	−0.0334	.457
Concentration of vote	.1909***	.0319	.5603	1.210
Concentration × Rank in list	−0.3665***	.0461	−0.8723	.693
Concentration × Terms served	.0037	.0109	.0219	1.004
Concentration × Dominance	.02427**	.1507	.0609	1.311
Ideology	.2704	.1507	.0609	1.311
Terms served	−0.1422	.0776	−0.0537	.867
Local political career	−0.1405	.1627	−0.0259	.869
Governor from same party	.5043**	.1712	.0962	1.656
Incumbent seeking reelection	.3941**	.1464	.0675	1.483

−2 log likelihood = 2016.9
Model chi-squared = 3780.6 $p < .0001$
Correctly predicted = 63.0%
$N = 8.757$
$R^2 = .3506$ Max-rescaled $R^2 = .7241$

$*p < .05$ $**p < .01$ $***p < .001$

D4. Cooperation and Defection among PPB Deputies, 1991–98

Dependent Variable: Cooperation with Party Majority (absentees excluded)

Variable	Unstandardized Parameter Estimate and Probability Level	Standard Error	Standardized Estimate	Odds Ratio
Cardoso administration (1995–98)	.2225	.1874	.0238	1.249
Contested party recommendation	−0.0500	.1250	−0.0093	.951
Uncontested party recommendation	.3612	.2422	.0380	1.435
Share of pork disbursements	.2222*	.1008	.0509	1.249
Rank in postelection list	2.2678***	.4241	.2353	9.658
Share of total party vote	−4.5867*	2.3663	−0.0576	.010
Dominance of key municipalities	−0.6940	1.0217	−0.0306	.500
Concentration of vote	.0987***	.0259	.2430	1.104
Concentration × Rank in list	−0.3313***	.0461	−0.4970	.718
Concentration × Terms served	.0129	.0099	.0732	1.013
Concentration × Dominance	.1765	.1219	.0838	1.193
Ideology	.4595***	.0960	.1574	1.583
Terms served	−0.2526**	.0889	−0.1099	.777
Local political career	−0.1056	.1392	−0.0194	.900
Governor from same party	1.4454	.9917	.0627	4.243
Incumbent seeking reelection	.6431***	.1357	.1080	1.902

−2 log likelihood = 1721.9
Model chi-squared = 9089.7 $p < .0001$
Correctly predicted = 67.2%
$N = 7,504$
$R^2 = .1140$ Max-rescaled $R^2 = .3857$

*$p < .05$ **$p < .01$ ***$p < .001$

D5. Cooperation and Defection among PDT Deputies, 1991–98

Dependent Variable: Cooperation with Party Majority (absentees excluded)

Variable	Unstandardized Parameter Estimate and Probability Level	Standard Error	Standardized Estimate	Odds Ratio
Cardoso administration (1995–98)	.3901	.4414	.0442	1.477
Contested party recommendation	.4134*	.2114	.0776	1.512
Uncontested party recommendation	−0.1339	.2687	−0.0196	.875
Share of pork disbursements	.2321	.1903	.0498	1.261
Rank in postelection list	.5614	.6423	.0689	1.753
Share of total party vote	−10.8177*	5.4370	−0.0959	0.000
Dominance of key municipalities	5.4832	3.1742	.2444	240.6
Concentration of vote	.2643**	.1007	.4547	1.303
Concentration × Rank in list	−0.1142	.0861	−0.1566	.892
Concentration × Terms served	−0.0222	.0392	−0.0731	.978
Concentration × Dominance	−0.5895	.3280	−0.3511	.555
Ideology	−0.4357*	.2229	−0.1147	.647
Terms served	.3889	.2068	.1659	1.475
Local political career	−0.3144	.3408	−0.0585	.730
Governor from same party	.1723	.5442	.0187	1.188
Incumbent seeking reelection	−0.4927	.3389	−0.0841	.611

−2 log likelihood = 671.6
Model chi-squared = 1137.0 $p < .0001$
Correctly predicted = 64.3%
$N = 2,995$
$R^2 = .3159$ Max-rescaled $R^2 = .6969$

 *$p < .05$ **$p < .01$ ***$p < .001$

D6. Cooperation and Defection among PTB Deputies, 1991–98

Dependent Variable: Cooperation with Party Majority (absentees excluded)

Variable	Unstandardized Parameter Estimate and Probability Level	Standard Error	Standardized Estimate	Odds Ratio
Cardoso administration (1995–98)	.5750*	.2840	.0637	1.777
Contested party recommendation	−0.1489	.1723	−0.0285	.862
Uncontested party recommendation	−0.0257	.2387	−0.0034	.975
Share of pork disbursements	.0252	.1646	.0060	1.026
Rank in postelection list	−0.1765	.7465	−0.0160	.838
Share of total party vote	7.1588*	3.6206	.0882	999.0
Dominance of key municipalities	−0.0495	1.8588	−0.0019	.952
Concentration of vote	.1029*	.0420	.2035	1.108
Concentration × Rank in list	.1162	.0830	.1725	1.123
Concentration × Terms served	−0.0115	.0162	−0.0670	.989
Concentration × Dominance	−0.1819	.2030	−0.1093	.834
Ideology	.0992	.1988	.0272	1.104
Terms served	.1131	.1638	.0550	1.120
Local political career	−0.6169*	.2723	−0.0815	.540
Governor from same party	−0.7486*	.3371	−0.0741	.473
Incumbent seeking reelection	.4837	.2645	.088455	1.622

-2 log likelihood $= 1072.4$
Model chi-squared $= 1225.1$ $p < .0001$
Correctly predicted $= 63.6\%$
$N = 2,917$
$R^2 = .3430$ Max-rescaled $R^2 = .6292$

$*p < .05$ $**p < .01$ $***p < .001$

References

Abranches, Sérgio Henrique Hudson de. 1988. "Presidencialismo de Coalizão: O Dilema Institucional Brasileiro." *Dados* 31 (1): 5–34.

Abrúcio, Fernando Luiz. 1998. *Os Barões da Federação: Os Governadores e a Redemocratização Brasileira.* São Paulo: HUCITEC.

Aldrich, John H. 1995. *Why Parties? The Origin and Transformation of Political Parties in America.* Chicago: University of Chicago Press.

Allison, Graham. 1971. *Essence of Decision: Explaining the Cuban Missile Crisis.* Boston: Little, Brown.

Ames, Barry. 1987. *Political Survival: Politicians and Public Policy in Latin America.* Berkeley: University of California Press.

———. 1994a. "Overcoming Legislative Chaos: Strategies of Party Cooperation in Brazil." Paper presented at the International Political Science Association Convention, Berlin, Germany, August 22.

———. 1994b. "The Reverse Coattails Effect: Local Party Organization in the 1989 Brazilian Presidential Election." *American Political Science Review* 88 (March): 95–111.

———. 1995. "Electoral Strategy under Open-List Proportional Representation." *American Journal of Political Science* 39 (May): 406–33.

Amorim Neto, Octávio. 1998. "Of Presidents, Parties, and Ministers: Cabinet Formation and Legislative Decision-Making under Separation of Powers." Ph.D. diss., University of California, San Diego.

———. 2001. "Presidential Cabinets, Electoral Cycles, and Coalition Discipline in Brazil." In *Legislative Politics in Latin America,* ed. Scott Morgenstern and Benito Nacif. New York: Cambridge University Press.

Amorim Neto, Octávio, and Gary W. Cox. 1997. "Electoral Institutions, Cleavage Structures, and the Number of Parties." *American Journal of Political Science* 41:149–74.

Amorim Neto, Octávio, and Fabiano Santos. 1997. "The Executive Connection: Explaining the Puzzles of Party Cohesion in Brazil." Paper presented at the Latin American Studies Association Meeting, Guadalajara, Mexico.

Anderson, Perry. 1994. "The Dark Side of Brazilian Conviviality." *London Review of Books* 16, no. 2 (November): 3–8.

Aragão, Murilo. 1998. "Elite Parlamentar na Câmara dos Deputados." Brasília: Arko Advice Editorial (March).

Arrow, Kenneth J. 1951. *Social Choice and Individual Values.* New York: Wiley.

Avelino Filho, George. 1994. "Clientelismo e Política no Brasil: Revisitando Velhos Problemas." *Novos Estudos Cebrap* 38:225–40.

"Bancada de Interesse." 1994. *Veja,* May 4, 28–30.

Banck, Geert. 1999. "Clientelism and Brazilian Political Process: Production and Consumption of a Problematic Concept." In *Modernization, Leadership, and Participation: Theoretical Issues in Developmental Sociology,* ed. Peter J. M. Nas and Patricio Silva. Leiden: Leiden University Press.

Baron, David P. 1991. "Majoritarian Incentives, Pork-Barrel Programs, and Procedural Control." *American Journal of Political Science* 35 (1): 57–90.

Barros, Hélio, and Lustosa da Costa. 1985. "As Eleições de 1982 no Ceará." In *Nordeste Eleições,* org. Joaquim Falcão. Recife, PE: Fundação Joaquim Nabuco–Editora Massangana.

Barros e Silva, Fernando. 1995. "Pesquisa Revela Que Há Fidelidade Nos Partidos." *Folha de São Paulo,* July 17, 1–8.

Bartolini, Stefano, and Peter Mair. 1990. *Identity, Competition, and Electoral Availability: The Stabilisation of European Electorates, 1885–1985.* New York: Cambridge University Press.

Bates, Robert H. 1997. *Open-Economy Politics: The Political Economy of the World Coffee Trade.* Princeton: Princeton University Press.

Bawn, Kathleen. 1997. "Money and Majorities in the Federal Republic of Germany: Evidence for a Veto Players Model of Government Spending." Mimeo. University of California, Los Angeles.

Benevides, Maria Victória. 1976. *O Governo Kubitschek: Desenvolvimento Econômico e Estabilidade Política.* Rio de Janeiro: Paz e Terra.

———. 1981. *A UDN e o Udenismo.* Rio de Janeiro: Paz e Terra.

———. 1982. *O Governo Jânio Quadros.* São Paulo: Brasiliense.

Bezerra, Marcos Otávio. 1999. *Em Nome das "Bases."* Rio de Janeiro: Relume Dumará.

Bonelli, Regis, and L. Ramos. 1993. "Distribuição de Renda no Brasil." *Revista de Economia Política* 13 (2): 76–97.

Bonfim, Maria Núbia Barbosa. 1985. *Do Velho ao Novo: Política e Educação no Maranhão.* São Luís, MA: Universidade Federal do Maranhão.

Bonfim, Washington Luís de Sousa. 1999. "Vinte Anos de Política Cearense." Unpublished manuscript.

Bowler, Shaun, Todd Donovan, and Joe Snipp. 1992. "Local Sources of Information and Voter Choice in State Elections: Micro-Level Foundations of the 'Friends and Neighbors' Effect." Unpublished manuscript.

Bowler, Shaun, David Farrell, and Richard S. Katz, eds. 1999. *Party Discipline and Parliamentary Government.* Columbus: Ohio State University Press.

Brazil. 1986–95. *Diário Oficial,* sections 2 and 3.

———. 1989. *Assembléia Nacional Constituinte—1987.* Brasília: Câmara dos Deputados.

———. 1990, 1992. *Anuário Estatístico do Brasil.* Rio de Janeiro: IBGE.

———. Câmara dos Deputados. 1981. *Deputados Brasileiros: 46th legislatura, 1979–1983.* Brasília: Câmara dos Deputados.

———. Câmara dos Deputados. 1983. *Deputados Brasileiros: 47th legislatura, 1983–1987.* Brasília: Câmara dos Deputados.

————. Câmara dos Deputados. 1987. *Assembléia Nacional Constituinte 1987: Repertório Biográfico.*

————. Câmara dos Deputados. 1991. *Deputados Brasileiros: 49th legislatura, 1991–1995.* Brasília: Câmara dos Deputados.

————. Congresso Nacional. 1988–90. *Projeto de Lei: Estima a Receita e Fixa a Despesa da União para o Exercício Financeiro de 1989–1991.* Emendas. Brasília: Congresso Nacional.

————. Instituto Brasileiro de Geografia e Estatística. 1980. *Censo Nacional.* Brasília: IBGE. (Tape of national census.)

————. Tribunal Superior Eleitoral. 1994. *Eleicomp.* Brasília: TSE.

Burki, Shahid Javed, and Guillermo E. Perry. 1998. *Beyond the Washington Consensus: Institutions Matter.* Washington, DC: World Bank.

Cacciamali, Maria Cristina. 1997. "The Growing Inequality in Income Distribution in Brazil." In *The Brazilian Economy: Structure and Performance in Recent Decades,* ed. Maria J. F. Willumsen and Eduardo Gianetti da Fonseca, 215–35. Coral Gables, FL: North-South Press, University of Miami.

Camargo, Aspásia. 1993. "La Federación Sometida: Nacionalismo Desarrollista e Inestabilidad Democrática." In *Federalismos Latinoamericanos: México/Brasil/Argentina,* ed. Marcello Carmagnani. Mexico, DF: Fondo de Cultura Económica.

Canon, David, and David Sousa. 1992. "Party System Change and Political Career Structures in the U.S. Congress." *Legislative Studies Quarterly* 27 (August): 347–64.

Carey, John. 1996. *Term Limits and Legislative Representation.* New York: Cambridge University Press.

Carvalho, Joaquim de, and Daniela Pinheiro. 1997. "O Abraço de Reeleição." *Veja,* June 25, 25–28.

Carvalho, José Murilo de. 1966. "Barbacena: A Família, a Política e Uma Hipótese." *Revista Brasileira de Estudos Políticos* 20:125–93.

————. 1993. "Federalismo y Centralización en el Imperio Brasileño: Historia e Argumento." In *Federalismos Latinoamericanos: México/Brasil/Argentina,* ed. Marcello Carmagnani. Mexico, DF: Fondo de Cultura Económica.

————. 1997. "Mandonismo, Coronelismo, Clientelismo: Uma Discussão Conceitual." *Dados* 40 (2): 229–50.

Chappell, Henry W., and William R. Keech. 1983. "Welfare Consequences of the Six-Year Presidential Term Evaluated in the Context of a Model of the U.S. Economy." *American Political Science Review* 77, no. 1 (March): 75–91.

"Um Choque na Desigualdade." 1996. *Veja,* March 6, 113.

Clark, Terry Nichols. 1994. "Clientelism, U.S.A.: The Dynamics of Change." In *Democracy, Clientelism, and Civil Society,* ed. Luis Roniger and Ayse Gunes-Ayata. Boulder, CO: Lynne Rienner.

Cleary, David. 1987. *Local Boy Makes Good: José Sarney, Maranhão, and the Presidency in Brazil.* Occasional Paper 45. Glasgow, Scotland: University of Glasgow, Institute of Latin American Studies.

Cliff, Andrew, Peter Haggett, J. Keith Ord, Keith A. Bassett, and Richard Davies. 1975. *Elements of Spatial Structure: A Quantitative Approach.* Cambridge: Cambridge University Press.

Coase, Ronald. 1937. "The Nature of the Firm." *Economica* 4 (November): 386–405.

Cohen, Youssef. 1994. *Radicals, Reformers, and Reactionaries: The Prisoner's Dilemma and the Collapse of Democracy in Latin America.* Chicago: University of Chicago Press.

Coppedge, Michael. 1994. *Strong Parties and Lame Ducks: Presidential Partyarchy and Factionalism in Venezuela.* Stanford: Stanford University Press.

Cox, Gary W. 1987. *The Efficient Secret: The Cabinet and the Development of Political Parties in Victorian England.* Cambridge: Cambridge University Press.

———. 1990a. "Centripetal and Centrifugal Incentives in Electoral Systems." *American Journal of Political Science* 34 (November): 903–35.

———. 1990b. "Multicandidate Spatial Competition." In *Advances in the Spatial Theory of Voting,* ed. James M. Enelow and Melvin J. Hinich. Cambridge: Cambridge University Press.

———. 1997. *Making Votes Count: Strategic Coordination in the World's Electoral Systems.* Cambridge: Cambridge University Press.

Cox, Gary W., and Matthew D. McCubbins. 1993. *Legislative Leviathan: Party Government in the House.* Berkeley: University of California Press.

Crisp, Brian. 1998. "Variation in Legislative Entrepreneurship in Venezuela." Paper presented at the Latin American Studies Association International Congress, Chicago, September 24–26.

———. 1999. *Democratic Institutional Design: The Powers and Incentives of Venezuelan Politicians and Interest Groups.* Stanford: Stanford University Press.

Dalton, Russell, Scott C. Flanagan, and Paul Allen Beck, eds. 1984. *Electoral Change in Advanced Industrial Democracies: Realignment or Dealignment?* Princeton: Princeton University Press.

Deheza, Grace Ivana. 1997. "Gobiernos de Coalición en el Sistema Presidencial: America del Sur." Ph.D. diss., European University Institute, Florence.

———. 1998. "Gobiernos de Coalición en el Sistema Presidencial: América del Sur." In *El Presidencialismo Renovado: Instituciones y Cambio Político en América Latina,* ed. Dieter Nohlen and Mario Fernández B. Caracas: Nueva Sociedad.

Denemark, David. 1996. "Thinking Ahead to Mixed-Member Proportional Representation." *Electoral Studies* 14:417–39.

De Souza, Amaury, and Bolívar Lamounier, orgs. 1992. *As Elites Brasileiras e a Modernização do Setor Público: Um Debate.* São Paulo: Editôra Sumaré.

Devescovi, Regina Balieiro. 1994. "A Câmara dos Deputados e o Processo Decisório: Um Estudo de Caso sobre a Comissão de Seguridade Social e Família." São Paulo: CEBRAP.

Diaz-Cayeros, Alberto. 1997. "Political Responses to Regional Inequality, Taxation, and Distribution in Mexico." Ph.D. diss., Duke University.

Dimenstein, Gilberto, and Josias de Souza. 1994. *A História Real: Trama de uma Sucessão.* São Paulo: Editora Ática–Folha de São Paulo.

Diniz, Eli. 1997. *Crise, Reforma do Estado e Governabilidade: Brasil, 1985–95.* Rio de Janeiro: Fundação Getúlio Vargas Editora.

Dos Santos, Wanderley Guilherme. 1979. "The Calculus of Conflict: Impasse in Brazilian Politics and the Crisis of 1964." Ph.D. diss., Stanford University.

———. 1993. *Razões da Desordem.* Rio de Janeiro: Rocco.

Eckstein, Harry. 1975. "Case Study and Theory in Political Science." In *Handbook of*

Political Science, vol. 1, *Political Science: Scope and Theory*, ed. Fred Greenstein and Nelson Polsby. Reading, MA: Addison-Wesley.

"Eis a Lista dos Nomes Que Receberam Verbas da Seplan." 1988. *Folha de São Paulo*, February 3, A-6.

"Equipe a la Carte." 1994. *Veja*, December 28, 32–34.

Fausto, Boris. 1970. *A Revolução de 1930: Historiografia e História*. São Paulo: Brasiliense.

Ferejohn, John A. 1974. *Pork-Barrel Politics: Rivers and Harbors Legislation, 1947–1968*. Stanford: Stanford University Press.

———. 1991. "Rationality and Interpretation: Parliamentary Elections in Early Stuart England." In Kristen Renwick Monroe, ed., *The Economic Approach to Politics*. New York: Harper Collins.

Fett, Patrick J. 1992. "Truth in Advertising: The Revelation of Presidential Legislative Priorities." *Western Political Quarterly* 45 (4): 895–920.

Figueiredo, Argelina Maria Cheibub, and Fernando Limongi. 1994a. "O Processo Legislative no Congresso Pós-Constituinte." *Novos Estudos Cebrap* 38 (March): 24–37.

———. 1994b. *Mudança Constitucional, Desempenho do Legislativo e Consolidação Institucional*. Caxambú, Minas Gerais: XVIII Encontro Anual da Anpocs.

———. 1997a. "O Congresso e as Medidas Provisórias: Abdicação ou Delegação?" *Novos Estudos Cebrap* 47 (March): 127–54.

———. 1997b. "Presidential Power and Party Behavior in the Legislature." Paper presented at the Latin American Studies Association Meeting, Guadalajara, Mexico, April 17–19.

Filho, Expedito, and Monica Bergamo. 1997. "Linha de Chegada." *Veja*, January 13, 26–27.

"Finance Minister Opinion on . . ." 1993. *Jornal do Brasil*, September 12, 4.

Fiorina, Morris P. 1974. *Representatives, Roll Calls, and Constituencies*. Lexington, MA: Lexington Books.

Fleischer, David. 1973. "O Trampolím Político: Mudanças nos Padrões de Recrutamento Político em Minas Gerais." *Revista de Administração Pública* 7:99–116.

———. 1976. "Concentração e Dispersão Eleitoral: Um Estudo da Distribuição Geográfica do Voto em Minas Gerais (1966–1974)." *Revista Brasileira de Estudos Políticos* 43 (July): 333–60.

———. 1977. "A Bancada Federal Mineira." *Revista Brasileira de Estudos Políticos* 45 (July): 7–58.

———. 1987. "O Congresso-Constituinte de 1987: Um Perfil Socio-Econômico e Político." Unpublished manuscript, University of Brasília.

———. 1998. "The Cardoso Second Term Cabinet." *Brazil Focus*, Weekly Report, December 23.

———. 1999. "Governability." *Brazil Focus*, Weekly Report, August 13.

Franco, Gustavo. 1995. *O Plano Real*. Rio de Janeiro: Francisco Alves.

Franzese, Robert John. 1996. "The Political Economy of Over-Commitment: A Comparative Study of Democratic Management of the Keynesian Welfare State." Ph.D. diss., Harvard University.

Geddes, Barbara. 1994a. *Politician's Dilemma: Building State Capacity in Latin America*. Berkeley: University of California Press.

————. 1994b. "Uses and Limitations of Rational Choice in the Study of Latin American Politics." In *Comparative Perspectives on Latin America: Methods and Analysis,* ed. Peter Smith. Boulder, CO: Westview.

Geddes, Barbara, and Artur Ribeiro Neto. 1999. "Institutional Sources of Corruption in Brazil." In *Corruption and Political Reform in Brazil: The Impact of Collor's Impeachment,* ed. Keith S. Rosenn and Richard Downes. Miami: North-South Center Press.

Graham, Richard. 1990. *Patronage and Politics in Nineteenth-Century Brazil.* Stanford: Stanford University Press.

Gramacho, Wladimir. 1999. "FHC Está Perdido." *Istoé* (on-line version), September 1.

Greenfield, Sidney. 1977. "Patronage, Politics, and the Articulation of Local Community and National Society in Pre-1968 Brazil." *Journal of Interamerican Studies and World Affairs* 19 (2): 139–72.

Grohmann, Luís Gustavo Mello. 1997. "Santa Catarina: Formato e Tendências do Sistema Partidário. In *O Sistema Partidário Brasileiro,* ed. Olavo Brasil de Lima Junior. Rio de Janeiro: Fundação Getúlio Vargas Editora.

Hagopian, Francis. 1996. *Traditional Politics and Regime Change in Brazil.* New York: Cambridge University Press.

Hall, Peter A., and Rosemary C. R. Taylor. 1994. "Political Science and the Four New Institutionalisms." Paper presented at the American Political Science Association Annual Meeting, New York.

Hallerberg, Mark, and Scott Basinger. 1998. "Internationalization and Changes in Tax Policy in OECD Countries: The Importance of Domestic Veto Players." *Comparative Political Studies* 31 (3): 321–52.

Higley, John, and Richard Gunther, eds. 1992. *Elites and Democratic Consolidation in Latin America and Southern Europe.* New York: Cambridge University Press.

Hunter, Wendy. 1996. *State and Soldier in Latin America: Redefining the Military's Role in Argentina, Brazil, and Chile.* Washington, DC: U.S. Institute of Peace.

"The Importance of Education Investments for Mayoral Success in 1992." 1994. *Jornal do Brasil,* February 20, 3–4.

"International Financial Statistics." 1999. (CD-ROM). Washington, DC: International Monetary Fund.

Istoé. 1991. *Perfil Parlamentar Brasileiro.* Brasília: Editora Trés.

Jones, Mark P. 1994. "Presidential Election Laws and Multipartism in Latin America." *Political Research Quarterly* 47 (1): 41–57.

————. 1995. *Electoral Laws and the Survival of Presidential Democracies.* Notre Dame, IN: University of Notre Dame Press.

Keck, Margaret E. 1992. *The Workers' Party and Democratization in Brazil.* New Haven: Yale University Press.

Key, V. O. 1949. *Southern Politics in State and Nation.* New York: Knopf.

King, Gary, Robert O. Keohane, and Sidney Verba. 1994. *Designing Social Inquiry: Scientific Inference in Qualitative Research.* Princeton: Princeton University Press.

Kingdon, John W. 1981. *Congressmen's Voting Decisions.* 2d ed. New York: Harper and Row.

Kingstone, Peter R. 1999. *Crafting Coalitions for Reform: Business Preferences, Polit-*

ical Institutions, and Neoliberal Reform in Brazil. University Park: Pennsylvania State University Press.

Kinzo, Maria D'Alva Gil. 1987. "A Bancada Federal Paulista de 1986: Concentração ou Dispersão do Voto?" Paper presented at the Associação Nacional de Pos-Graduação e Pesquisa em Ciências Sociais—Águas de São Pedro Meeting, October 20–23.

———. 1989. "O Quadro Partidário e o Constituinte." *Revista Brasileira de Ciência Política* 1 (1): 91–123.

Knight, Jack. 1992. *Institutions and Social Conflict*. Cambridge: Cambridge University Press.

Kramer, Dora. 1997. "Uma Senhora Cruel Chamada Realidade." *Jornal do Brasil*, July 1.

Krehbiel, Keith. 1991. *Information and Legislative Organization*. Ann Arbor: University of Michigan Press.

Kreppel, Amie. 1997. "The Impact of Parties in Government on Legislative Output in Italy." *European Journal of Political Research* 31:327–50.

Kulisheck, Michael. 1998. "Legislators, Representation, and Democracy: An Institutional Analysis of Deputy Responsiveness in Venezuela." Ph.D. diss., University of Pittsburgh.

———. 1999a. "Placebo or Potent Medicine? Electoral Reform and the Electoral Connection in Venezuela." Unpublished manuscript.

———. 1999b. "Political Calculations and Interest Representation: An Institutional Analysis of the Venezuelan Chamber of Deputies." Unpublished manuscript.

Lamounier, Bolivar. 1994. "A Democracia Brasileira de 1985 à Década de 90: A Síndrome da Paralisia Hiperativa." In *Governabilidade, Sistema Político, e Violência Urbana*, coord. J. P. dos Reis Velloso. Rio de Janeiro: José Olympio Editora.

Lamounier, Bolivar, and Dieter Nohlen, eds. 1993. *Presidencialismo ou Parlamentarismo: Perspectivas sobre a Reorganização Institucional Brasileira*. São Paulo: Loyola.

Lancaster, Thomas, and W. David Patterson. 1990. "Comparative Pork Barrel Politics: Perceptions of the West German Bundestag." *Comparative Political Studies* 22:458–77.

Latin American Regional Report—Brazil. 1999a. February 9. London: Latin American Newsletters.

Latin American Regional Report—Brazil. 1999b. September 15. London: Latin American Newsletters.

Levi, Margaret. 1988. *Of Rule and Revenue*. Berkeley: University of California Press.

Light, Paul C. 1982. *The President's Agenda: Domestic Policy Choice from Kennedy to Carter*. Baltimore: Johns Hopkins University Press.

Lima Junior, Olavo Brasil de, org. 1991. *Sistema Eleitoral Brasileiro: Teoria e Prática*. Rio de Janeiro: IUPERJ.

———. 1993. *Democracia e Instituições Políticas no Brasil dos Anos 80*. São Paulo: Edições Loyola.

———. 1997. "A Reimplantação do Multipartidarismo: Efeitos Institucionais e Contextuais." In *O Sistema Partidário Brasileiro*. Rio de Janeiro: Fundação Getúlio Vargas Editora.

Limongi, Fernando, and Argelina Maria Cheibub Figueiredo. 1995. "Partidos Políticos na Câmara dos Deputados: 1989–1994." *Dados* 38 (3): 497–527.

————. 1996. "Presidencialismo e Apoio Partidário no Congresso." *Monitor Público* 8 (3): 27–33.

Lindblom, Charles. 1977. *Politics and Markets.* New York: Basic Books.

Lipset, Seymour M., and Stein Rokkan. 1967. *Party Systems and Voter Alignments: Cross-National Perspectives.* New York: Free Press.

Locke, Richard, and Kathleen Thelen. 1993. "The Shifting Boundaries of Labor Politics: New Directions for Comparative Research and Theory." Paper presented at the American Political Science Association Annual Meeting, Washington, DC, September 2–5.

Love, Joseph L. 1993. "Federalismo y Regionalismo en Brasil, 1889–1937." In *Federalismos Latinoamericanos: México/Brasil/Argentina,* ed. Marcello Carmagnani. Mexico, DF: Fondo de Cultura Económica.

Lowi, Theodore. 1964. "American Business, Public Policy, Case-Studies, and Political Science." *World Politics* 16 (July): 677–715.

Mainwaring, Scott. 1993. "Brazilian Party Underdevelopment in Comparative Perspective." *Political Science Quarterly* 107 (4): 677–708.

————. 1999. *Rethinking Party Systems in the Third Wave of Democratization: The Case of Brazil.* Stanford: Stanford University Press.

Mainwaring, Scott, and Aníbal Pérez-Liñán. 1997. "Party Discipline in the Brazilian Constitutional Congress." *Legislative Studies Quarterly* 22 (2): 453–83.

Mainwaring, Scott, and Timothy R. Scully. 1992. "Party Systems in Latin America." Paper presented at the Latin American Studies Association Meeting, Los Angeles, September 24–27.

————, eds. 1995. *Building Democratic Institutions: Party Systems in Latin America.* Stanford: Stanford University Press.

March, James G., and Johan P. Olsen. 1989. *Rediscovering Institutions: The Organizational Basis of Politics.* New York: Free Press.

Martínez-Lara, Javier. 1996. *Building Democracy in Brazil: The Politics of Constitutional Change, 1985–1995.* New York: St. Martin's.

Martz, John. 1990. "Ecuador." In *Latin American Politics and Development,* ed. Howard Wiarda and Harvey Kline. Boulder, CO: Westview.

Mayer, Kenneth R. 1995. "Closing Military Bases (Finally)—Solving Collective Dilemmas Through Delegation." *Legislative Studies Quarterly* 20 (3): 393–413.

Mayhew, David. 1974. *Congress: The Electoral Connection.* New Haven: Yale University Press.

Mayhew, David. 1991. *Divided We Govern: Party Control, Lawmaking, and Investigations, 1946–1990.* New Haven: Yale University Press.

McKelvey, Richard D. 1976. "Intransitivities in Multidimensional Voting Models and Some Implications for Agenda Control." *Journal of Economic Theory* 12:472–82.

Meneguello, Rachel. 1994. "Partidos e Tendencias de Comportamento: O Cenário Político em 1994." In *Anos 90: Política e Sociedade no Brasil,* ed. Evelina Dagnino. São Paulo: Brasiliense.

————. 1998. *Partidos e Governos no Brasil Contemporâneo: 1985–1997.* São Paulo: Paz e Terra.

Menes, Rebecca. 1997. *Public Goods and Private Favors: Patronage Politics and Amer-*

ican Cities During the Progressive Era, 1900–1920. Ph.D. diss. Harvard University.

Montinola, Gabriella, Yingyi Qian, and Barry R. Weingast. 1995. "Federalism Chinese Style: The Political Basis for Economic Success in China." *World Politics* 48:50–81.

Moraes Filho, José Filomeno de. 1997. "Ceará: O Subsistema Partidário e o Retorno ao Multipartidarismo." In *O Sistema Partidário Brasileiro,* ed. Olavo Brasil de Lima Junior. Rio de Janeiro: Fundação Getúlio Vargas Editora.

Morlino, Leonardo. 1996. "Crisis of Parties and Change of Party Systems in Italy." *Party Politics* 2 (1): 5–31.

Nacif, Benito. 2001. "The System of Governance in the Mexican Chamber of Deputies: Changing Partisan Balance and Persistent Patterns of Behavior." In *Legislative Politics in Latin America,* ed., Scott Morgenstern and Benito Nacif. Cambridge University Press.

Nicolau, Jairo César Marconi. 1992. "A Representação Política e a Questão da Desproporcionalidade no Brasil." *Novos Estudos Cebrap* 33 (July): 222–36.

Niemi, Richard G. 1983. "Why So Much Stability? Another Opinion," *Public Choice* 41:261–83.

North, Douglass. 1981. *Structure and Change in Economic History.* New York: Norton.

———. 1990. *Institutions, Institutional Change, and Economic Performance.* Cambridge: Cambridge University Press.

Novaes, Carlos Alberto Marques. 1994. "Dinâmica Institucional da Representação: Individualismo e Partidos na Câmara dos Deputados." *Novos Estudos Cebrap* 38 (March): 99–147.

Oliveira, Gesner. 1996. *Brasil Real.* São Paulo: Mandarim.

Olsen, David M., and Michael L. Mezey. 1991. *Legislatures in the Policy Process: The Dilemmas of Economic Policy.* Cambridge: Cambridge University Press.

Ordeshook, Peter C., and Olga Shvetsova. 1994. "Ethnic Heterogeneity, District Magnitude, and the Number of Parties." *American Journal of Political Science* 38 (1): 100–123.

"Parties Ignore Itamar's Ultimatum . . ." 1992. *Folha de São Paulo,* December 10, 2.

Peterson, Mark. 1990a. "Developing the President's Program: The President as a Strategic Player." Paper presented at the Midwest Political Science Association Annual Meeting, Chicago.

———. 1990b. *Legislating Together: The White House and Capitol Hill from Eisenhower to Reagan.* Cambridge: Harvard University Press.

Pierson, Paul. 1996. "The Path to European Integration: A Historical Institutionalist Analysis." *Comparative Political Studies* 29 (2): 123–61.

Pinheiro, Daniela. 1997. "Obras, Verbas, e Votos." *Veja,* November 12, 32.

Polsby, Nelson. 1968. "The Institutionalization of the U.S. House of Representatives." *American Political Science Review* 62 (1): 144–68.

Power, Timothy. 1993. "The Political Right and Democratization in Brazil." Ph.D. diss., University of Notre Dame.

———. 1997a. "Neoliberal Orientations among Brazilian Politicians: A Research Note." Paper presented at the Southern Political Science Association Annual Meeting, Norfolk, Virginia, November 5–8.

————. 1997b. "Parties, Puppets, and Paradoxes: Changing Attitudes toward Party In-stitutionalization in Post-Authoritarian Brazil." *Party Politics* 3 (2): 189–219.

Power, Timothy, and J. Timmons Roberts. 1995. "Compulsory Voting, Invalid Ballots and Abstention in Brazil." *Political Research Quarterly* 48 (3): 795–826.

Putnam, Robert. 1993. *Making Democracy Work: Civic Traditions in Modern Italy.* Princeton: Princeton University Press.

Resende-Santos, João. 1997. "Fernando Henrique Cardoso: Social and Institutional Re-building in Brazil." In *Technopols: Freeing Politics and Markets in Latin America in the 1990s,* ed. Jorge I. Domínguez. University Park: Pennsylvania State Univer-sity Press.

Rezende, Fernando. 1990. "Descentralização e Eficiéncia: A Tomada de Decisões para o Desenvolvimento sob a Constituição de 1988." In *Políticas de Desenvolvimento para a Década de Noventa.* Brasília: PNUD.

Riker, William H. 1964. *Federalism: Origin, Operation, Significance.* Boston: Little, Brown.

Rocha, Leonel e Expedito Filho. 1997. "A Caça aos Votos." *Veja,* February 2, 32–34.

Rodden, Jonathan, and Susan Rose-Ackerman. 1997. "Does Federalism Preserve Mar-kets?" *Virginia Law Review* 83 (7): 1521–72.

Roett, Riordan. 1978. *Brazil: Politics in a Patrimonial Society.* New York: Praeger.

Rolim, Francisco Sales Cartaxo. 1979. *Política nos Currais.* João Pessoa: Acauã.

Roniger, Luis. 1990. *Hierarchy and Trust in Modern Mexico and Brazil.* New York: Praeger.

Rua, Maria das Graças. 1995. *Brazilian Congressional Guide, 1995–1999.* Working Pa-per 95–3. Washington, DC: Institute of Brazilian Business and Public Management Issues, George Washington University.

Sabino, Mario. 1999. "Ele Está Radiante." *Veja,* January 20, 44–47.

Salisbury, Robert, and John Heinz. 1970. "A Theory of Policy Analysis and Some Pre-liminary Applications." In *Policy Analysis in Political Science,* comp. Ira Sharkan-sky. Chicago: Markham.

Samuels, David. 1998. "Careerism and its Consequences: Federalism, Elections, and Policy-Making in Brazil." Ph.D. Diss., University of California, San Diego.

Samuels, David. 2001. "Political Ambition and Pork-Barrel Politics in Brazil." In *Leg-islative Politics in Latin America,* ed. Scott Morgenstern and Benito Nacif. New York: Cambridge University Press.

Santos, Fabiano Guilherme M. 1995. "Microfundamentos do Clientelismo Político no Brasil: 1959–1963." *Dados* 30 (3): 459–96.

Schmitter, Philippe. 1971. *Interest Conflict and Political Change in Brazil.* Stanford: Stanford University Press.

Schneider, Ben Ross. 1991. *Politics within the State: Elite Bureaucrats and Industrial Policy in Authoritarian Brazil.* Pittsburgh: University of Pittsburgh Press.

Seabra, Catia. 1999. "A Hora da Reforma Política." *O Globo,* March 15, internet.

Secretaria da Educação e Cultura do Estado da Bahia. 1992. "Sistema de Avaliação do Ensino Básico do Primeiro Grau." Unpublished manuscript.

Seligman, Albert L. 1997. "Japan's New Electoral System: Has Anything Changed?" *Asian Survey* 37:409–28.

Shepsle, Kenneth A. 1978. *The Giant Jigsaw Puzzle.* Chicago: University of Chicago Press.

———. 1988. "Representation and Governance: The Great Legislative Tradeoff." *Political Science Quarterly* 103, no. 3 (autumn): 461–84.

Shepsle, Kenneth A., and Barry R. Weingast. 1987. "The Institutional Foundations of Committee Power." *American Political Science Review* 81:85–104.

Shepsle, Kenneth A., and Barry R. Weingast. 1984. "Legislative Politics and Budget Outcomes." In *Federal Budget Policy in the 1980s,* ed. Gregory B. Mills and John C. Palmer. Washington, DC: Urban Institute.

Shugart, Matthew Soberg, and John M. Carey. 1992. *Presidents and Assemblies: Constitutional Design and Electoral Dynamics.* New York: Cambridge University Press.

Skocpol, Theda, Peter B. Evans, and Dietrich Rueschemeyer, eds. 1985. *Bringing the State Back In.* New York: Cambridge University Press.

Smyth, Regina. 1998. "Candidate Responses to Mixed Electoral Systems." Paper presented at the American Political Science Association Annual Meeting, Boston, September 3–7.

Soares, Gláucio A. D. 1973. *Sociedade e Política no Brasil.* São Paulo: DIFEL.

Sola, Lourdes. 1992. "Heterodox Shock in Brazil: Técnicos, Politicians, and Democracy." *Journal of Latin American Studies* 23 (February): 163–98.

"Soltando as Amarras." 1997. *Jornal do Brasil,* July 3.

Souza, Celina. 1991. *Políticas Públicas Baianas: Análises e Perspectivas.* Salvador, BA: Editora Universitária Americana.

———. 1997. *Constitutional Engineering in Brazil: The Politics of Federalism and Decentralization.* New York: St. Martin's.

———. 1998. "Intermediação de Interesses Regionais no Brasil: O Impacto do Federalismo e da Descentralização." *Dados* 41 (3): 569–92.

———. 1999. "Decentralisation, Local Autonomy, and Metropolitan Influence: The Case of Salvador, Bahia." In *The Challenge of Environmental Management in Urban Areas,* ed. Adrian Atkinson, Julio Dávila, Edésio Fernandes, and Michael Mattingly. Aldershot, Eng.: Ashgate.

Souza, Maria do Carmo Campello de. 1976. *Estado e Partidos Políticos no Brasil (1930 á 1964).* São Paulo: Editôra Alfa-Omega.

Stallings, Barbara. 1978. *Class Conflict and Economic Development in Chile, 1958–1973.* Stanford: Stanford University Press.

Stein, Robert M., and Kenneth N. Bickers. 1995. *Perpetuating the Pork Barrel: Policy Subsystems and American Democracy.* Cambridge: Cambridge University Press.

Steinmo, Sven, Kathleen Thelen, and Frank Longstreth, eds. 1992. *Structuring Politics.* Cambridge: Cambridge University Press.

Stepan, Alfred. 1999. "Toward a New Comparative Analysis of Democracy and Federalism: Demos Constraining and Demos Enabling Federations." Paper presented at the Conference on Federalism, Democracy, and Public Policy, Centro de Investigación y Docencia Económicas, Mexico City, June 14–15.

Straubhaar, Joseph, Organ Olsen, and Maria Cavaliari Nunes. 1993. "The Brazilian Case: Influencing the Voter." In *Television, Politics, and the Transition to Democ-*

racy in Latin America, ed. Thomas E. Skidmore. Washington, DC: Woodrow Wilson Center Press.

Sullivan, Terry. 1987. "Headcounts, Expectation, and Presidential Coalitions in Congress." *American Journal of Political Science* 87:567–89.

Tendler, Judith. 1997. *Good Government in the Tropics.* Baltimore: Johns Hopkins University Press.

Thelen, Kathleen. 1993. "West European Labor in Transition: Sweden and Germany Compared." *World Politics* 46:23–49.

Thibaut, Bernhard. 1996. *Präsidentialismus und Demokratie in Lateinamerika: Argentinien, Brasilien, Chile und Uruguay im Historischen Vergleich.* Opladen: Leske und Budrich.

———. 1998. "El Gobierno de la Democracia Presidencial: Argentina, Brasil, Chile y Uruguay en una Perspectiva Comparada." In *El Presidencialismo Renovado: Instituciones y Cambio Político en América Latina,* ed. Dieter Nohlen and Mario Fernández B. Caracas: Nueva Sociedad.

Tiebout, Charles M. 1956. "A Pure Theory of Local Expenditures." *Journal of Political Economy* 64:416–24.

Tobin, James. 1958. "Estimation of Relationships for Limited Dependent Variables." *Econometrica* 26:24–36.

Treisman, Daniel. 1998. "Decentralization and Inflation in Developed and Developing Countries." Unpublished manuscript, University of California, Los Angeles.

———. 1999. "Political Decentralization and Economic Reform: A Game-Theoretic Analysis." *American Journal of Political Science* 43 (2): 488–517.

Tsebelis, George. 1990. *Nested Games: Rational Choice in Comparative Politics.* Berkeley: University of California Press.

———. 1994. "The Power of the European Parliament as a Conditional Agenda Setter." *American Political Science Review* 88, no. 1 (March): 128–42.

———. 1995. "Decision Making in Political Systems: Veto Players in Presidentialism, Parliamentarism, Multicameralism, and Multipartyism." *British Journal of Political Science* 25:289–325.

———. 1999. "Veto Players and Law Production in Parliamentary Democracies: An Empirical Analysis." *American Political Science Review* 93, no. 3 (Sept.): 591–608.

———. 2000. "Veto Players in Institutional Analysis." *Governance* 13, no. 4 (October).

Tullock, Gordon. 1981. "Why So Much Stability?" *Public Choice* 37:189–202.

Valenzuela, Arturo. 1977. *Political Brokers in Chile: Local Government in a Centralized Polity.* Durham, NC: Duke University Press.

Valladares, Licia, and Magda Prates Coelho, eds. 1995. *Governabilidade e Pobreza no Brasil.* Rio de Janeiro: Civilização Brasileira.

VanDoren, Peter M. 1990. "Can We Learn the Causes of Congressional Decisions from Roll-Call Data." *Legislative Studies Quarterly* 15 (3): 311–40.

———. 1991. *Politics, Markets, and Congressional Policy Choices.* Ann Arbor: University of Michigan Press.

Viola, Eduardo. 1986. "As Eleições de 1985 e a Dinâmica do Sistema Partidário de Santa Catarina." *Cadernos de Ciências Sociais* 6 (1): 1–32.

Weaver, R. Kent, and Bert A. Rockman. 1993. "When and How Do Institutions Matter?"

In *Do Institutions Matter? Government Capabilities in the United States and Abroad,* ed. R. Kent Weaver and Bert A. Rockman. Washington, DC: Brookings Institution Press.

Weingast, Barry R., and William Marshall. 1988. "The Industrial Organization of Congress." *Journal of Political Economy* 96:132–63.

Weyland, Kurt. 1996a. *Democracy without Equity: Failures of Reform in Brazil.* Pittsburgh: University of Pittsburgh Press.

———. 1996b. "Neopopulism and Neoliberalism in Latin America: Unexpected Affinities." *Studies in Comparative International Development* 35 (3): 3–31.

Williamson, Oliver. 1983. *Markets and Hierarchies.* New York: Free Press.

Willis, Eliza, Christopher Da C. B. Garman, and Stephan Haggard. 1999. "The Politics of Decentralization in Latin America." *Latin American Research Review* 34 (1): 7–56.

Wilson, Bruce, and Roger Handberg. 1998. "Opening Pandora's Box: The Unanticipated Political Consequences of Costa Rican Legal Reform." Paper presented at the Midwest Political Science Association Annual Meeting, Chicago, April 23–25.

Index